3 0400 00315866 0

S0-AWB-921

Did God Have a Wife?

Did God Have a Wife?

ARCHAEOLOGY AND FOLK RELIGION
IN ANCIENT ISRAEL

William G. Dever

WILLIAM B. EERDMANS PUBLISHING COMPANY
GRAND RAPIDS, MICHIGAN / CAMBRIDGE, U.K.

For my Lady, P.

© 2005 Wm. B. Eerdmans Publishing Co.
All rights reserved

Wm. B. Eerdmans Publishing Co.
255 Jefferson Ave. S.E., Grand Rapids, Michigan 49503 /
P.O. Box 163, Cambridge CB3 9PU U.K.

Printed in the United States of America

09 08 07 06 05   7 6 5 4 3 2 1

Library of Congress Cataloging-in-Publication Data

Did God have a wife? archaeology and folk religion in ancient Israel /
William G. Dever.
p.   cm.
Includes bibliographical references and index.
ISBN 0-8028-2852-3
1. Israel — Religion.   2. Asherah (Semitic deity)   3. Jews — Folklore.
4. Israel — Antiquities.   5. Excavation (Archaeology) — Israel.   I. Title.

BL1650.D48   2005
299'.2 — dc22

2005040503

www.eerdmans.com

MARIGOLD LIBRARY SYSTEM

Contents

CONTENTS

Contents

Introduction

This is a book about ordinary people in ancient Israel and their everyday religious lives, not about the extraordinary few who wrote and edited the Hebrew Bible. It is also a book for ordinary people today who know instinctively that "religion" is about experience, not about the doctrines of scholars, theologians, and clerics who study religion dispassionately and claim authority. My concern in this book is popular religion, or, better, "folk religion" in all its variety and vitality.

This is a book that, although it hopes to be true to the facts we know, does not attempt objectivity; for that is impossible and perhaps even undesirable. One can understand religion only from within, or at least from a sympathetic viewpoint. As an archaeologist, I shall try to describe the religions of ancient Israel — not theoretically, from the top down, as it were, but practically, "from the bottom up," from the evidence on the ground.

This is a book mostly about the *practice* of religion, not about belief, much less theology. It is concerned with what religion actually does, not with what religionists past or present think that it should do. Beliefs matter, for they are the wellspring of action; and theological formulations may be helpful or even necessary for some. But archaeologists are more at home with the *things* that past peoples made, used, and discarded or re-used, and what these artifacts reveal about their behavior, than they are with speculations about what these people *thought* that they were doing. As Lewis Binford reminds us, "archaeologists are poorly equipped to be paleo-psychologists."

This is a book that attempts what is admittedly impossible, to draw a clear picture of a religious life that, as many have observed, is like a puzzle with many missing pieces. Even at best, it is not a "reconstruction," as though we could or should bring ancient religious beliefs and practices back to life. Like the peoples of ancient Israel themselves, the folk religions of ancient Israel are extinct. They have no practitioners today, however much Jews, Christians, and even secular humanists in the West may think that they are the heirs of the biblical traditions. I do not wish to replicate the religions of ancient Israel, even if that were possible. I hope only to offer a reasonable portrait, based largely on archaeological evidence, but incorporating information from the Hebrew Bible where I think it may be illuminating. A portrait may present a believable likeness; but it is not flesh and blood, it does not breathe. It will seem lifelike only to those who know the original and recognize it.

This is a book that does not presume to judge what was or should be regarded as religiously "normative." I can only try to describe what religious life was "really like" for most people in ancient Israel, in most places, most of the time. I do not know if this was "right" belief or practice (nor does anyone else, it seems). And I cannot prescribe any of these beliefs and practices for anyone else, since I can evaluate them only in light of my own rather parochial experience. The Hebrew Bible may indeed be revealing, but I shall not regard it here as Revelation.

From the experiences of many in ancient Israel — priests, prophets, kings, even scoundrels — we may distill some moral truths and lay down some ethical guidelines for a vastly different world. But each of us must decide for ourselves what the reported experiences of people in ancient Israel "mean," whether we learn of these experiences from stories preserved in the biblical texts or long-lost artifacts dug up from the soil of the Holy Land.

Finally, a word about my own biases (although they will be clear enough in time). I have been involved in religion one way or another throughout a long and adventuresome life. I was reared in a deeply religious family in small towns in the South and Midwest. My father was a fire-breathing fundamentalist preacher, sometime tent evangelist, for a while a missionary in Jamaica, from whom I inherited a lifelong love of the Bible. In time I went to a small, unaccredited church college in the hills of East Tennessee. Then it was on to a liberal Protestant seminary, where I did an M.A. thesis in the 1950s on the then-current "revival of biblical theology." Finally I went to Harvard to study Old Testament theology with the legendary George Ernest Wright, only to discover that while I had the necessary dogmatic temperament, I really had no talent for that discipline, and little patience. Indeed, theology by now seemed to me a dead end. What more could be learned from endless reinterpretation of the same texts? So I turned to the archaeology of the World of the Bible (as I thought of it then). Fortunately, Ernest Wright was not only a noted biblical scholar, but also a leading archaeologist. He became my mentor. Throughout my years in seminary and graduate school I had served as a parish minister, but in the mid-1960s I began a forty-year career in archaeological fieldwork in Israel and Jordan, in research and teaching and publication. The Hebrew Bible finally became real for me, indeed more "credible," because I dealt constantly with the tangible evidence. But the question remained: "What do these things *mean?*"

In late mid-life, after having lived in Israel for many years, dealing every day "hands-on" with the world of the Hebrew Bible and the remains of ancient Israel, I became a nominal Jew. Today I am somewhat active in the Reform community, but I am not observant, in fact not a theist. Like many Jews, I am essentially a secular humanist, but one who finds value in the Jewish tradition — especially Reform Judaism's emphasis on *praxis,* on a living community, rather than on systematic theology. I feel at home in this tradition, and it fits well with the interest in "folk religion" that prompted this work.

In the end, I have become more a student of religion than a practitioner — sometimes filled with nostalgia for what I suspect is "a biblical world that never was," but often a skeptic. I view the religions of ancient Israel as an ethnographer would — as cultural phenomena whose importance I try to appreciate, but finally as elements of a "lost world" in which I can participate only partially. If archaeology really is the "ethnology of the dead," what we need are what anthropologists call "informants," and we have none who are totally trustworthy. As I shall argue, the Hebrew Bible itself is not always reliable, because it is "revisionist history." And the archaeological artifacts, although not subject to editing in the same way as the texts, do not easily reveal their meaning. Nevertheless, I shall take a modest, optimistic, "functionalist" approach here, assuming that both texts and artifacts can be made to speak if we are persistent, if we are willing to try to "think and feel ourselves" empathetically into the past. Our knowledge of actual ancient religious beliefs and practices will still be incomplete, but such an approach is better than theory alone (and certainly better than theology alone).

A word about the scope of our inquiry. Except for drawing on "Canaanite" traditions, it will be limited to the biblical "period of the Judges" (12th-10th cents. B.C.) and the Israelite monarchy (10th-early 6th cents. B.C.). That is because "Israel" as a distinctive people and soon-to-be nation appear in the full light of history only here, in the Iron Age of ancient Palestine (see Dever 2003 for a full discussion). And my major topic here is "Israelite" religion, neither its precursors in the Bronze Age, nor its transformation into Judaism in the Persian-Hellenistic or "Second Temple" period (something quite different and requiring a separate discussion).

Finally, some practical matters, such as defining terms. I shall use the general term "folk religion" throughout, as defined in Chapter I, but in a generic sense, aware that it embraces a wide variety of beliefs and practices. For that reason, the term "religions" often and deliberately appears in the plural. "Palestine" here has no reference to modern conflicts in the Middle East and denotes the ancient land of Canaan, later biblical Israel. Similarly, I use the conventional "B.C." rather than "B.C.E." (before the Common Era), but I attach to it neither religious nor political connotations (this is the way it is used, for instance, in the *Israel Exploration Journal*). I use "Hebrew Bible" throughout, in keeping with mainstream biblical scholarship, because I wish to view this literature on its own terms, not as the Christian "Old Testament" that it became long after the period I am surveying here. Needless to say, "Bible" here always means the Hebrew Bible.

In order to make this book more accessible to nonspecialists I have eliminated the footnotes so beloved by scholars. In doing so, I make many statements that I cannot document, especially when summarizing an extensive and often controversial body of literature. Some of the basic literature will be found in the Bibliography for readers who wish to pursue certain topics further. The quotations I use in the text (for example, Jones 2000:13) can easily be found there under the various headings and authors' names. My rationale for the format here is that this is intended as a popular work. My scholarly colleagues can quarrel with me elsewhere for what they may see as oversimplifications. For more on individual sites, see further the encyclopedias listed under "Archaeological Sites," and also bibliographies in Nakhai 2001 and Zevit 2001. Translations of biblical texts follow the Revised Standard Version, except where noted.

I am indebted to too many people even to begin acknowledging them. To my parents, long gone, I am grateful for inculcating in me a deep respect for the Bible and an awareness of the awesome power of religion (even though they would be horrified to see how I have turned out). I have been fortunate in my teachers, and even more fortunate in my many graduate students over the years, who have been among my best teachers. I thank several colleagues who have made suggestions, though the final statement is my own.

I must mention several colleagues in particular who have made detailed and very helpful suggestions: Beth Nakhai, Susan Ackerman, Carol Meyers, James Sanders, and Ziony Zevit. I want to mention also several anonymous men and women friends who are not specialists but are sensitive readers. I own an incalculable debt to Susan and Carol, whose amazingly close reading of my manuscript revealed to me not only some egregious errors in biblical studies, but both conceptual and structural problems with some of my characterization of women's cults. I have followed their astute criticisms wherever possible, but I remained unpersuaded on a few methodological points. Let me clarify these at the outset.

Categorizing scholarly works by "schools" may be helpful or even necessary for purposes of comparison, but it can pose problems. This is especially so with "feminism," so let me define how I shall use the term. First, it may help to distinguish, as women colleagues often do, between (1) *scholarly* feminism, which is research and publication that focuses largely on particular women's issues, such as gender bias in scholarship; (2) and *political* feminism, which actively pursues an agenda that would give women full equality, access, and recognition in all areas of life. A woman might be committed to only one of these feminist movements, or to both; in what sense is she then a "feminist"? In theory at least, a man might also embrace one or both of these aspects of feminism. Thus I would insist that I am, politically speaking, a feminist. Nevertheless, I would not want to be described as either a "feminist" or a "masculinist" *scholar,* since both perspectives focus the inquiry too narrowly for me.

A second qualification has more to do with degree than kind: how far does one go in feminist enterprises? I distinguish here between (1) "mainstream" feminists — competent, honest scholars who happen to be women, and who focus on women's issues among *other* scholarly interests; and (2) "doctrinaire" feminists, whose extremist ideology trumps any scholarly credentials they might have, and who as a result become as chauvinist as the men whose agenda they reject.

Even the more sensible of the doctrinaire feminists are often characterized by what Susan Ackerman describes to me as "wishful thinking." They hope to reconstruct a past in which women's full equality (or even superiority) was actually realized, but which in their view has been obscured by male scholars. Thus they tend to ignore the realities of ancient patriarchal worldviews, such as the Bible's — hardly the way to combat patriarchy, it seems to me. Furthermore, positing such a "matriarchal Garden of Eden" is bad historical scholarship (more on this in Chapter IX).

Even alluding to possible differences in men's and women's approaches to the study of ancient Israelite religion raises another issue: Do such gender differences actually exist; and if so, do they shape the way the portrait of religion is drawn? To phrase the question more pointedly, who is better suited to write about women's religious beliefs and practices (that is, their experience of religion), as I am attempting here: a man or a woman?

In theory, I would like to say that it doesn't matter: good scholarship is simply good scholarship. In practice, however, women may be more likely to take up the topic, and they are probably also better suited to empathize personally with the plight of ancient Israelite women who have been so invisible in biblical scholarship until recently. That being said, my approach here may differ significantly from that of some women colleagues, but I undertake my own statement for what it is worth, and I alone must be held accountable. I encourage more women colleagues to do the same.

Whatever the results, I remain convinced that there are significant differences in men's and women's fundamental approach to religion and to the study of religion, men generally being perhaps more analytical (i.e., inclined to theology), and women by and large more attuned to the emotional aspects of religion (experiential). Neither approach is necessarily "better" than the other; but ironically here I side as a man more with the latter. I can only hope that I will not be thought presumptuous.

One other issue raised by reviewers should be addressed up front. That is the apparent contradiction between "folk" religion, with its veneration of Asherah (and perhaps other deities), and the fact that these elements of "pagan" religion found their way into the Temple in Jerusalem and thus became part of "official" or "state religion." There they were tolerated until the Deuteronomistic reforms (see below) in the late 7th century B.C., when "Book religion" began to prevail. But the apparent contradiction is easily resolved. Although originally part of the predominant folk religion in the countryside, always centered in the family, these "foreign" elements eventually penetrated into the urban cult in Jerusalem, where they finally came to be regarded as intrusive — if the biblical writers (the "Deuteronomists") are to be believed.

Some reviewers have suggested that my "Book religion" (following van der Toorn; below), which I have set up as a counterfoil to the more pervasive "folk religion," is late in the Monarchy, emerging only with the 7th-6th century B.C. Deuteronomistic reform movements. Thus they argue that for the earlier period in the Monarchy, not to mention the "Period of the Judges" (12th-11th cents. B.C.), I can reconstruct nothing *but* "folk religion." This overlooks, however, the consensus of mainstream biblical scholars that behind the admittedly late written tradition there is a long oral tradition. The major theological motifs of canonical Scripture, although I have downplayed their popular appeal, did not appear suddenly overnight. These themes (see Chapter VIII) had a long tradition among the literati who later wrote and edited the Hebrew Bible; so "Book religion" merely represents their final crystallization.

Finally, regarding the emergence of "Book religion," some reviewers have wondered whether I have made the dichotomy between that expression of belief and "folk religion" too strong. That would seem to depreciate *biblical* (i.e. canonical) religion, which after all was the only version that survived, and which for all its shortcomings eventually laid the major foundations for the Western cultural tradition. Now that that tradition is under sustained attack, both symbolically and physically, some may fear that my book will undermine the foundations. That is a concern of mine as well; but then all truly critical scholarship may appear subversive. I think that is a risk that we must take. I can only say that elsewhere I have mounted a sustained defense of the Western cultural tradition and its biblical roots (see, for example, Dever 2001).

Finally, what I know about "family," which shapes religion so fundamentally, I have learned in 50 eventful years with my own wives and children. Norma, a loyal companion in many years of exploration and travel, contributed much to life's long journey. Pamela, born a feminist and now a religious educator, has listened patiently to many trial formulations of ideas presented here and has sharpened my focus at many points. In particular, she has embodied many aspects of the Great Mother, to whom I hope I do justice here.

WILLIAM G. DEVER
Bedford Hills, New York
August 2003

1400-1200 B.C.	1200-1000 B.C.	1000-900 B.C.	900-600 B.C.
Canaanite culture	Biblical "Period of the Judges"	"United Monarchy"	"Divided Monarchy"
Ugaritic mythological texts	Oral traditions	Functional literacy; some written records	Pentateuch ("J," "E"), historical works ("Dtr."), some prophetic works now in written form (by *ca.* 7th cent. B.C.)
Late Bronze I-II	Iron I	Iron IIA	Iron IIB

Chronological and Historical Correlations
For explanation of the terms for the biblical tradition
in the righthand column, see Chapter III.

CHAPTER I

Defining and Contextualizing Religion

Our first task in approaching the religions of ancient Israel is obviously to specify what we *mean* by "religion." Surprisingly, virtually none of the dozens of works in the field, many of which we will survey in Chapter II below, attempts even a simple working definition. An exception is Ziony Zevit's *The Religions of Ancient Israel: A Synthesis of Parallactic Approaches* (2001), whose openness to the archaeological evidence, like mine here, may have prompted him to be more "realistic" than most commentators.

The Phenomenon of Religion

If religion reflects as universal and timeless a dimension of human experience as I maintain, there will have been millions upon millions of notions of what religion is and does. Among modern, more explicit formulations are those found in the classic works of anthropologists and folklorists such as E. B. Tylor (1871); W. Robertson Smith (1894); James G. Frazer (1925); Emile Durkheim (1915); E. E. Evans-Pritchard (1951); Mary Douglas (1969; 1975); and Clifford Geertz (1966). Other definitions are offered by philosophers and philosophers of religion such as William James (1985) and Karl Marx and Friedrich Engels (1967). Still other definitions come from more modern "religionists," such as Mircea Eliade (1969; 1979); R. R. Cavanagh (1978); Jonathan Z. Smith (1987; 1990); Hans H. Penner (1989); and Wilfrid Cantwell Smith (1997).

Some of these writers' views of religion are summarized by Zevit

(2001:11-22), whose own working definition of religion as it concerns us here is:

> religions are the varied, symbolic expressions of, and appropriate responses to the deities and powers that groups or communities deliberately affirmed as being of unrestricted value to them within their world view (2001:15).

The key terms here are "world view," "community," "value," "deity," "response," and "symbolic." These terms figure prominently in virtually all other definitions of religion. But the most important focus is, of course, on the divine, or "supernatural," and the driving force is something that we may call "ultimate concern." A recent definition summing up these ideas, yet quite simple, is that of Hans H. Penner: "Religion is a 'verbal and nonverbal structure of interaction with superhuman being(s)'" (1989:7, 8). Penner says that he is not completely happy with this definition, but he "cannot think of anything better." Neither can I, so I will employ it here. But "concern" for *what?* What *is* it that is thought to be something other than ephemeral, that is, "ultimate"? And of "ultimate concern" to *whom?*

Religion as "Ultimate Concern"

In order to organize the following inquiry into a framework for discussing "folk religion," let me try to specify some of the dimensions of the concerns that ordinary folk in ancient Israel had. Some of these may seem rather pedestrian to us, because, of course, we are presumably more sophisticated. But they were the stuff of real life for the ancients.

(1) *The concern for survival.* This was no doubt the overall concern, and it could scarcely be more fundamental or more urgent. By "survival" I do not mean simply the animal instinct to live, although that is assumed. I give the ancients enough credit to suppose that they could be more "philosophical" than that, even if they could not always analyze or articulate their feelings as we might. Existing under extraordinarily difficult conditions, in a marginal economy, they knew existentially that they lived in a mysterious, unpredictable, perilous world (which we would call Nature). In the midst of all their uncertainty and anxiety, they faced the ultimate threat: extinction. This would not be merely death by famine, dis-

ease, or natural and manmade disasters, but the possible obliteration of one's self, one's family, one's heritage and posterity. Today we might call this the threat of non-being, Søren Kierkegaard's "abyss" into which any individual might fall at any time. I suggest that for the ancients the threat derived from the perception that the universe was not "friendly." It was disordered, chaotic, fundamentally dangerous, if not evil. Even the gods could kill you, often for no apparent reason. Israelites could not comfort themselves with the much later (and non-Semitic) notion of the "immortality of the soul." When the body died, that was the end. Religion thus had first of all to deal with the problem of *survival,* in the most brutal, elementary sense.

(2) *Aligning one's self with the universe.* If personal survival was at stake, literally every moment, then it was essential to "personalize" the numinous powers that ultimately ruled the universe and to "get on their side." And these powers were perceived as the "other," the *sacred.* This was what Rudolf Otto may have had in mind when he coined the phrase the "idea of the Holy." Yet we must remember that the distinction between "sacred" and "secular" (or profane) is a modern one. It is a concept that would have been totally foreign and indeed incomprehensible in the ancient world generally. Religion was so taken for granted that biblical Hebrew, for instance, has no specific word for "religion." Human life was filled with ideas and experiences that were, of course, "religious," and there are many terms in the Bible for these. But religion could not be abstracted and analyzed; nor could it have been an option, as we moderns suppose. Living in antiquity was *being* "religious," as I shall stress throughout this work. That meant identifying, however difficult, with the gods who alone could confer on human life order, wisdom, power over evil, dignity, and in the end meaning and purpose. That *larger* sense of well-being was what fleshed out mere survival, made the concern "ultimate."

(3) *How to placate the deities and secure their favor.* If the gods really were in control, how could individuals act practically so as to avoid their wrath and secure the specific blessings that would enhance survival? Although the ancients would not have rationalized matters thus (how could you "rationalize" the supra-rational?), I suggest that the practical strategy involved the "care and feeding of the gods." That meant (a) accepting the myths about them as true, thus acknowledging not only their existence but their reality as all-powerful forces; (b) inquiring diligently as to what the gods by reason of their transcendence required of humans; (c) obeying the

gods, fearing them, and paying them homage in the form of gifts, offerings, sacrifices, rituals, services at sanctuaries, prayers, and vows; and (d) in some cases augmenting the life of piety with what was considered ethical behavior (more on this later). On a higher theoretical and moral plane, all this and other religious activity could be construed in ancient Israel as "fearing God and loving him," that is, obeying him gladly and thus achieving harmony with the divine order, or what we might call "salvation." But at the more mundane, everyday level, most of ancient religion in Israel and elsewhere was directed at placating the gods (and evil spirits), averting the evil that they might bring, and securing their specific blessings.

"The Care and Feeding of the Gods"

Blessings, of course, would be understood in terms of the practical benefits alluded to above, relating to survival and well-being: the health of oneself and one's progeny; material prosperity; escape from disaster; the continuing heritage of the family, clan, and people; and, I would argue, above all that sense of identity and pride that still dominates the thinking of people in the Middle East today. The gods could grant all this and more; but they could also take it away. It made *sense* to placate them, not by coming up with abstract theological formulae, or promising the devotion of the "pure in heart." Much more practical and efficacious was to give back to the gods a token portion of what they had graciously given. That was what sacrifice was: gifts of food and substance and even life. And it worked — or so it appeared when things were going well. (See further Chapter IV.)

Such a pragmatic definition of religion may seem to us primitive, even debased, as though religion were simply "magic." But that's precisely what religion *is*, or at least was, however much that may offend modern sensibilities. We want religion to be "nice": beautiful, aesthetically appealing, uplifting, ennobling, "spiritual," and above all tidy. But ancient religion was, as the anthropologist Eilberg-Schwartz (1990) puts it, rather messy. It was in fact "savage" — a brutal, often bloody, life-and-death struggle, the outcome of which was by no means certain. The modern, idealistic, romantic portrait of ancient Israelite religion is a comfortable delusion, but one that obscures the reality. Here I shall try instead to look at the religions of the *real* Israel, "warts and all."

4

On "Folk Religion"

The portrait that I have just painted may seem to some readers just another modern caricature — the bias of an archaeologist who is preoccupied with the material aspects of religious life and therefore minimizes its spiritual aspects. That raises the question of whether there were, in fact, *two* religions of ancient Israel. More than two? And if so, how am I justified in focusing so exclusively on one? At the outset I stated that this will be primarily a study of "folk religion," implying that this was the polar opposite of something else that we might call "official religion" or "state religion," or, better, "Book religion." In Chapters II and III, I will show how many scholars have assumed such a distinction, and how it has affected their understanding and presentation.

Here let me anticipate this discussion by setting forth my understanding of "religion in two dimensions." These categories are not rigid, of course. And they are somewhat artificial, since the ancients would not have recognized such distinctions. Nevertheless, they may be useful as theoretical antitheses, out of which might develop a synthesis. Here are some characteristics and focal points that I suggested provisionally years ago (1995), in chart-form.

"State Religion"	"Folk Religion"
Literate	Popular
Texts	Artifacts
Canon	Improvisation
Belief	Practice
Mythology	Magic
Verbal	Symbolic
Theology	Cult
Ideology	Action
Intellectual	Emotive
Dogma	Praxis
Rational	Mystical
Ceremonial	Ritual
Public	Private
Social	Individual
National	Local

State	Family
Ethics	Piety
Political order	Right relations
"Sacred"	"Profane"
Orthodoxy	Customary practice

Is there some validity to juxtaposing such polar opposites? Does each column represent a separate version of Israel's religions; and if so, which was normative? Did they overlap along a continuum? Virtually all scholars do recognize some such dichotomy, although there is great confusion about terminology, apart from the general state or official religion on the one hand, and "folk" religion on the other. (Below I shall adopt "Book religion" for the former.)

Before further defending my preference for a term to designate the phenomena in the right-hand column — my focus here — let me note briefly the terminology of other scholars, with some critical comments that may make a choice easier. John S. Holladay's seminal and widely quoted article in 1987 distinguished on the one hand "established, conformist, State" religion, and on the other hand "distributed, nonconformist, local" religion. Susan Ackerman's pioneering book (1992) used the term "popular religion" throughout, but she defined it mainly as "an alternate vision, a non-priestly, non-Deuteronomistic, non-prophetic view of what Yahwism was" (1992:216). That is accurate, but it sees this form of Israelite religion mostly in terms of what it was not, rather than in terms of what it was (although in all fairness Ackerman's treatment overall is more positive; see Chapters II, VI, VII).

Rainer Albertz's monumental history of Israelite religion contrasts "official religion" or "official syncretism" with "family religion," "personal piety," "internal religious pluralism," and "poly-Yahwism" (1994:19; 83).

Karel van der Toorn's initial work dealt with the "popular religious groups" (1994), but later he developed a term that I find one of the most helpful, "Book religion," or the canonical religion of the *literary* tradition as preserved in the Hebrew Bible (1997).

Jacques Berlinerblau (1996) has provided the most extensive and cogent analysis yet, complaining of the lack of terminological precision heretofore. Yet in the end, he too accepts the dichotomy of "official" versus "popular" religion, although he stresses the variety, as well as the legitimacy, of the latter (his "groups"; 1996:22).

Othmar Keel's and Christoph Uehlinger's monumental work on Israelite iconography is absolutely fundamental to a study of folk religion. But curiously, they do not define their focus except to call for going beyond the "state cult" to a consideration of levels of "family," "local," and "national" religion (1998:406).

Patrick Miller's landmark study *The Religion of Ancient Israel* (2000) contrasts "State religion" — orthodox, heterodox, and syncretistic Yahwism — with "family religion" and "local and regional cults." Mark Smith's survey of various deities (2002a) speaks of "popular religion" throughout. Ziony Zevit's *tour de force* simply stresses pluralism, speaking throughout of the many "religions" of ancient Israel.

None of these choices is without problems, as many of the authors admit. On the one hand, to refer to "State" or "official" religion presupposes that the religious establishment and the Israelite state were in agreement, if not in league with each other, and that the state had the power to enforce religious conformity. I very much doubt that. And the implication until all too recently that this biblically sanctioned, monolithic form of Israelite religion was "normative" must be rejected altogether. On the other hand, speaking of "popular" religion implies that it constituted a form of religious life that was not represented in the priestly and court circles in Jerusalem but was widespread only in the countryside. And that cannot be the case either.

The truth of the matter is that the various expressions of "native" Israelite religious beliefs and practices (not "syncretism"; below), under the rubric of "Yahwism," overlapped. And they were all tolerated in various combinations at one time or another. That is why we can never write a satisfactory history of any one "Israelite religion." And it is also why Zevit ends his 690-page discussion with a one-page "Reductio," stating that

> The multiplicity of Israelite religions attested in the different types of data considered in this study can all be explained reductively as biopsychological expressions of citizenship in a cosmos perceived as disharmonious (2001:690).

Given the problems enumerated here, as well as my deliberately narrow focus, I shall speak somewhat arbitrarily of "folk religion" throughout what follows.

7

Folk Religion: Toward a Methodology

I shall advance in Chapter III the proposition that in history-writing of any kind, the choice of method is fundamental, because to a large degree it determines the outcome of the inquiry. Where you arrive depends not only upon where you think you're going, but also upon how you decide to get there. Having announced as my goal the elucidation of folk religion, how do I propose to *do* that? In particular, is there a specific method that might differ from that suitable for an inquiry into religion in general?

In Chapter II I explore the approaches of various traditional "schools," such as the "history of religions," which is diachronic and comparative, and "biblical theology," which tends to be topical and normative. Then I argue that neither is satisfactory, the first because it is too broad, and the second because it is too narrow. Neither focuses on the *reality* of the religions of ancient Israel — especially theology, which even in its most innocent guise remains essentially an enterprise of apologetics, and moreover seems to conceive of religion merely in terms of ideas rather than of practice.

"Religionists" (if we may use that term) have entered the discussion more recently, raising the question: Is a phenomenology of religions possible? Or, to phrase it another way: Is it possible to develop a general "social science" theory of religion without resorting to philosophy of religion or theology? (See, for example, Jensen 1993.) I am doubtful about either a true "science" of religion, or some overarching theory that is capable of comprehending religion universally. But I shall adopt the notion of "phenomenon" here, because I regard ancient Israelite religion as a particular, concrete example of *religion as a cultural phenomenon.*

As an archaeologist and an anthropologist, and thus a historian, I shall argue that philosophy and theology are distractions. These disciplines may well be legitimate and interesting in their own right; but they get us nowhere in the inquiry into *ancient* folk religion. Indeed, they are barriers to understanding, because they are later, modern constructs forced back upon ancient Israel's thought-world and the behavior of most folk who were part of it. Therefore, in order to comprehend Israelite folk religion *on its own terms,* I shall take an approach that may be called "descriptive" rather than "prescriptive." I am well aware that postmodernists and other skeptics who prevail in many disciplines today think this naïve. For them, there *are* no "facts," only social constructs; ancient texts do not refer to any reality but have to do only with other texts and ideologies, theirs and ours. But I shall ignore what I regard as postmodern piffle (Dever 2001) and get on with the task as I see it, which is historical and descriptive of realities that did exist after all.

The real problems with a phenomenology of religion are not with skepticism, much less with religion *per se*. The problems lie in the challenge that all the social sciences face today: how to "represent" or portray the realities with which they purportedly deal, Durkheim's "social facts." Our knowledge about such facts is, of course, always a social "construct," if knowledge does not drop down from heaven but must be created by us on the basis of subjective human perceptions. My point of departure from what is commonly called revisionism, however, is simply the insistence that our constructs must be founded on *facts* wherever possible, not on ideological fancies. And I shall employ archaeological data to provide an empirical, factual basis for understanding the practices (if not the beliefs) of Israelite folk religion.

"Phenomenology of Religion"

A phenomenological approach is sometimes called "functionalism," because it focuses more on what societies actually *do* than upon larger social theories.

Let me specify further what I mean by a "phenomenological" or "functionalist" approach. Such an approach operates as follows:

(1) It relies upon observing society directly, in action rather than in theory.
(2) It does not necessarily "reconstruct" but uses typical case studies.
(3) It seeks to understand society "from within" — what folk say about themselves — whether through words or symbolic actions.
(4) It emphasizes individual creativity, rather than trying to develop large-scale "typologies."
(5) Its objective is Geertz's (1973) "thick description," not necessarily explanation.
(6) It makes use of "organic models," assuming that social systems operate in some ways like biological systems (notions of interacting "subsystems," seeking and maintaining equilibrium).

(7) Its methods are basically inductive, that is, working from the particular to the general, rather than deductive, or seeking "law-like generalizations."

(8) It does not eschew ideology, but it assumes that the exact content of belief systems is irretrievable, although their observation is possible through inference.

Phenomenology and functionalism have a long history in anthropology and ethnography, from Durkheim through Malinowski, to Radcliff-Brown (Layton 1997:18-39). Yet for all my confidence in these approaches, I do acknowledge two problems at the outset. First, there is the tendency (some would say inevitable) to fall into the trap of what is called "reductionism," or the assumption that a thing *is* only what it *does*. That is obviously an oversimplification, even a caricature of human activity. This is particularly true in the case of religion, because it would reduce the transcendental dimension of religion — the "spiritual" — to a set of trivial, meaningless activities (much as behaviorism did in psychology).

The basic fallacy of all reductionist schemes that attempt to explain (or even to describe) human behavior can be illustrated by giving some examples. One might say of eating, for instance, that it is "only the human animal's masticating the dead remains of other animals or plants and imbibing liquids." Would that do justice to the enormous aesthetic pleasures of food and drink, not to mention the larger role that cuisine plays in various cultures? Similarly, reductionist schemes obscure, downplay, or debase the *symbolic* significance of religion, essential to religion, as we shall see.

Closely related to the problem of reductionism in purely descriptive explanations of human behavior is "determinism." By this I mean the notion that the "causes" of individual behavior and socio-cultural change are essentially mechanical rather than the result of ideology, that is, of human choice and intent. Determinism can take many forms, such as environmental determinism, which holds that culture is shaped and constrained only by the impersonal, immutable "forces of Nature." In this case, religion would be seen merely as a predictable, universal human response to the challenge of survival, largely through technological innovation. Or, in the Marxist paradigm, religion is only "the opiate of the masses," the illusion that must be sustained by oppressors in order to manipulate and exploit the proletariat. Religion at its most banal may in fact function that way; but surely it can be and has been something nobler than that. And above all, religion is not static, not predictable, but rather a *dynamic* force. It is that open-ended, surprising, exciting aspect of religion that I shall explore here, even if we cannot "explain" it all. Again, religion in terms of what it actually does, but not overlooking its transcendental dimension.

One other critique of phenomenology of religion must be mentioned here. That has to do with the question of whether, in abandoning a strictly "scientific" method, it does not abandon *real* method. Much of the phenomenological approach in past has taken for granted the necessity for "empathy," or sympathetic participation somehow in the *experience* of religion, not simply developing theories about religion. The assumption is (1) that one can "get into the minds" of the practitioners of a given religion; and (2) that such "idealism," based on intuitive and impressionistic approaches, does not rule out defensible judgments and genuine scientific discourse.

The preference of most critics might be for a "*science* of religion" or as I would put it, "a secular understanding of the Sacred." I seriously doubt that that is possible, or even desirable. Religion is not about science: empirical evidence; the testing of laws; and predictions. Religion is about the mysterious, contingent dimensions of human life and experience; not about the physical, but about the metaphysical. Thus, while religion is not necessarily "irrational," it is more concerned with the supra-rational. A rational explanation of myriad religious experiences, even if possible, would miss the point. I concur with the distinguished religionist Mircea Eliade, who states:

> Thus, the historian of religion is in a position to grasp the permanence of what has been called man's specific existential situation of 'being in the world,' for the experience of the sacred is its correlate (1969:9).

In other words, the observer must become a participant in order to understand, if not directly then at least by putting oneself within "understanding distance." It is impossible to grasp *any* religious tradition by approaching it with contempt, or hostility or an air of superiority (in that case, why bother?). But while observers must not condemn out of hand, neither can they simply adopt the truth-claims of any particular religion at face value, for that would also result in a loss of perspective. And a *balanced perspective* is what is required — a balance of disinterested critical judgment, but also of positive appreciation. To give up either is to become an ideologue

11

on the one hand, or a cynic on the other. We cannot be truly "scientific"; but we can and must be *systematic* if ours is to be a disciplined inquiry. (Of the related issue of "objectivity" I shall have more to say in Chapter III.)

I shall try to strike the needed balance. Again, my approach will be to describe as far as possible the *actual religious experiences* of the majority of folk in ancient Israel, especially those left out by the Hebrew Bible. But I shall not try to "relive" those experiences, much less to force them upon others as an example of what religion ought to be. I ask readers to with-hold judgment, perhaps even to forgo it indefinitely.

My first goal is simply a factual description of a lost reality — folk re-ligion in ancient Israel — using surviving artifacts, the "material remains of the cult," as our best clues. Where I can, I shall resort to the biblical texts for at least theoretical evidence of *beliefs*; but these texts will be considered secondary sources (see Chapter III). What I hope will emerge is a vital, convincing portrait of a "people without a history" (at least a written his-tory) — of those whom the book of Daniel has in mind in speaking of "all those who sleep in the dust" (12:2). It is archaeology, and archaeology *alone*, that can bring back those anonymous, forgotten folk of antiquity and give them their long-lost voice, allowing them to speak to us of *their* ultimate concerns. We must listen, especially to women, whom patriarchy has rendered largely mute.

The "Context" of Folk Religion

In archaeology, everything depends ultimately upon *context*. An individual object, no matter how interesting in itself, is largely meaningless, "lifeless," if it has been ripped out of context — that is, out of the larger behavioral and cultural system within which it once functioned, and which gave it significance. That is why archaeologists are so apparently obsessed with ex-cavating and recording carefully, why archaeology is not "treasure hunt-ing" but is an attempt at piecing together an *entire* extinct social system or lifestyle. Popular religion in ancient Israel was once part of a functioning cultural system, and it is lifeless when removed from that system and stud-ied abstractly, as in so many works reviewed here. Only *archaeology*, with its focus on ordinary folk and everyday life, can reconstruct a "real life" context, one in which religion actually functioned and did not serve sim-ply to fire the literary imagination of a few idealists. Thus we need to ask:

"What was daily life really *like* in ancient Israel?" And in particular, how did the reality of everyday life affect the way in which Israelite religions were conceived and practiced?

(1) *The natural world.* First, we need to look at Israel's (ancient Palestine's) unique geographical and geo-political setting. We must remember that we are dealing with an area west of the Jordan River that is about the size of the state of New Jersey. It is only 250 miles long, the southern half barren desert, and varies from about 30 to 70 miles wide. Israel looms "larger than life" in our Western imagination because of its spiritual significance, but it was a tiny country. The entire population in the Iron Age never exceeded about 150,000 (today it is some ten million in a comparable area). The few large cities cannot have contained more than about 3,000 people; and an average town would have had a population of only some 500-1,000; and most areas were rural, with a very low population density. Jerusalem in the time of Solomon had perhaps 2,000 people, and at its height in the 8th century B.C. it probably had no more than 5,000 people.

Not only was Israel insignificant in size, it was also vulnerable because of its geo-political situation. It was a small coastal strip along the bend of the Fertile Crescent, sandwiched in between the great empires of Egypt and Mesopotamia. It lagged far behind them in all the early advances of civilization. More significantly, because of its exposed position as a "land bridge" between Africa and Asia, Palestine and later Israel were frequently trampled over, subjugated, and occupied for long periods by foreign powers. Think of the long succession of peoples who have overrun this general area along the Levantine coast in historical times: Amorites, Hittites, Hurrians, Egyptians, Philistines, Assyrians, Babylonians, Persians, Greeks, Romans, Muslims, European Crusaders, Turks (not to mention the British and French). No single political entity ever ruled the area in antiquity for more than about 400 years, and that was ironically the rather feeble Israelite-Judean monarchy (*ca.* 1,000-600 B.C.). And never was the country truly united.

Added to the disadvantages of size and location, Israel suffered from a lack of any natural resources that could have brought it trade, financial independence, or prosperity. The land is a geologist's ideal field laboratory, fascinating in its diversity, but it is a mostly hostile environment for human habitation. The southern deserts were uninhabitable except for brief periods when complex technology made runoff irrigation possible, as in Roman-Nabataean times; or when the wilderness provided a desperate retreat, as for Byzantine monks. The central and northern part of the country is a land of great, almost insurmountable contrasts. This area extends from the barren shores of the Dead Sea nearly 1,300 feet below sea level, to the rugged forested mountains of upper Galilee some 4,000 feet above sea level. All along the north-south central "spine" of the country, these mountains constitute a barrier to movement, except for a few natural east-west ravines. The hill country was so formidable that it was not densely occupied until Israelite times, and then only thanks to widespread terracing and the construction of cisterns and reservoirs to supplement the few perennial springs. The coastal plain in antiquity was largely a malarial swamp. The rolling inland foothills (the biblical Shephelah) were fertile and well watered, but they were in the hands of the Philistines in Israelite times. The point here is that Israel's "fractured geography" meant that for most of the time its society and political structure were "fractured" as well.

In addition to poor, thin, rocky soils, even in the best of areas, there was the problem of water. There are no real rivers except the Jordan, and that ran in a channel so deep that the waters were largely inaccessible and emptied uselessly into the Dead Sea. Elsewhere there are few perennial springs, and primitive technology could not manage deep wells. Most of the area was devoted to dry farming. That depended upon rainfall that could vary from none in the deserts to some forty inches in upper Galilee. But it was always too little or too much; in the wrong times or places; never predictable. The long summers from May to October are hot and dry, the rains falling only in the winter months. But droughts occur every few years, and crops even in prime agricultural areas often fail. Finally, even in years of bountiful harvests, as much as a third of the grain crop could not be adequately stored and was lost to dampness, rot, and vermin.

If arable land and available water were scant, other natural resources were almost nonexistent. There was timber in the upland areas, but much of the land had already been deforested by Israelite times (the process began with the first villages in the Neolithic period, *ca.* 8,000 B.C.). Copper ore had been mined in the southern Negev desert and the Jordan Valley from the third millennium on; but the mines are isolated, in the blistering desert, far from sources for the charcoal needed for smelting. Tin, essential for alloying copper to make bronze, does not occur anywhere closer than Anatolia or Afghanistan. There are some iron deposits in Transjordan, but iron technology was primitive and inefficient, even in the "Iron Age." Nowhere are there deposits of gold, silver, precious stones, or even other useful minerals.

Ancient Palestine's poor natural environment, precarious geo-political situation, unreliable subsistence, fractured social structure, and political instability mean that we must keep constantly in mind one fact. Ancient Israel was a truly *marginal* economy and society. The country was always poor compared to its prosperous neighbors; always powerless compared to their might; always on the verge of extinction (as finally happened). It may be unsettling to some readers, but the fact is that ancient Israel was an obscure cultural and historical backwater of the ancient Near East. It would have been long forgotten except for its one memorable contribution to civilization: the Hebrew Bible, and the memory of Israel's faith and vision of human destiny that it enshrines.

(2) *The social and political world.* Turning now from the larger, "external" world of Nature, what was Israel's peculiar social and political *adaptation* to this world like? We have already noted the fractured landscape, broken up into many different environmental niches, or microcosms. This natural diversity resulted in a relatively wide diversity of lifestyles and cultural values for such a small country, making it extraordinarily difficult to achieve any kind of social or political unity.

Think by comparison of Mesopotamia, with its vast, homogenous landscape along the thousand-mile length of the Tigris and Euphrates valleys: it attained large-scale state-level integration as early as 3000 B.C., and true "empires" by the late 3rd millennium B.C. And Egypt was unified up and down the Nile for 600 miles or more under pharaohs of the First Dynasty well before 3000 B.C. But Palestine first achieved statehood only with the United Monarchy of Israel, *ca.* 1000 B.C. And many would regard even that as more a "chiefdom" than a true "state" as anthropologists define these political entities. Even so, within a century this nascent union had split into the northern kingdom of Israel and the smaller southern kingdom of Judah. The north was more prosperous, but it was riven by old tribal rivals and was unstable from the beginning. The south, often involved in civil war with the north, survived longer under the Davidic dynasty.

Political conditions were so deplorable that the writers of the biblical books of First and Second Kings approved of only two kings. They predicted the collapse of the state and were proven correct by the Babylonian destruction in 586 B.C. The political history of both Israel and Judah was "nasty, brutish, and short," as the saying goes, characterized by dissension, treachery, corruption, frequent bloody assassinations, and ultimately the failure to create a viable state. The institution of kingship itself was debated. Even the biblical writers, who speak hopefully of "all Israel," are often at odds with each other. As a result of all this, people at all levels of society were constantly aware of the political disorder and chaos that threatened the very foundation of their lives. How could *anyone* plan for the future?

Israelite society was also a victim of stress created by a harsh environment. The majority of ancient Israelites were essentially subsistence farmers eking out a miserable existence on small plots of land. Sometimes they were freeholders, other times not much better off than serfs or indentured servants, and from time to time even slaves (despite the biblical ideal). Others were merchants and artisans in the villages and towns, but these market towns were dependent upon the agricultural hinterland. The vast majority of Israelites were what Marx would have called the "proletarian" class. Only in a few larger cities could anyone have hoped to find a greater measure of prosperity and achieve an elite social status based on entrepreneurship and the creation of heritable wealth. The few true elites were probably found among a few large landholders and in Jerusalem, in court and priestly circles (those who wrote the Bible). In the north, aligned with the capital at Samaria, we know of a landed gentry from records found in the excavation of the palace archives.

From the evidence we have, both textual and archaeological, it appears that Israel was hardly a "middle class" society. It was bottom-heavy, with a preponderance of lower-class folk — theoretically "free men and women," but in reality at the mercy of the tiny but rapacious upper class in whose hands wealth and power were concentrated.

These social inequalities in ancient Israel help to explain the message of the great 8th-7th century B.C. prophets and their call for social justice. They extolled the virtues of the "poor of the land" (Hebrew *'ănîyîm ha-'ārets*) — the majority, who were often oppressed and disenfranchised. Amos is outraged and thunders:

> Hear this, you who trample upon the needy,
> And bring the poor of the land to an end,
> Saying, "When will the new moon be over,
> That we may sell grain?
> And the sabbath, that we may offer wheat for sale,
> That we may make the ephah small and the shekel great,

And deal deceitfully with false balances,
That we may buy the poor for silver and the needy
For a pair of sandals,
And sell the refuse of the wheat?"
The Lord has sworn by the pride of Jacob:
"Surely I will never forget any of their deeds."   (Amos 8:4-7)

And again, the voice of doom of Yahweh, Israel's God:

Woe to those who lie upon beds of ivory,
and stretch themselves upon their couches,
and eat lambs from the flock,
and calves from the midst of the stall;
who sing idle songs to the sound of the harp,
and like David invent for themselves
instruments of music;
who drink wine in bowls,
and anoint themselves with the finest oils,
but are not grieved over the ruin of Joseph!
Therefore they shall now be the first
Of those to go into exile.   (Amos 6:4-7)

Micah is equally passionate; Yahweh declares:

Woe to those who devise wickedness
And work evil upon their beds!
When the morning dawns, they perform it,
Because it is in the power of their hand.
They covet fields, and seize them;
And houses, and take them away;
They oppress a man and his house,
A man and his inheritance.
Therefore thus says the Lord:
Behold, against this family I am devising evil,
From which you cannot remove your necks;
And you shall not walk haughtily,
For it will be an evil time.   (Micah 2:1-3)

(3) *The world of the family.* Moving to the still lower (but fundamental) socio-economic scale of rural areas and everyday life, how did most people in ancient Israel actually live? First, they lived in hamlets, villages, and small towns of no more than a few hundred people. Based on the most recent and most sophisticated demographic estimates, that would be as much as 80-90 percent of the total population. (Here it may be helpful to remember that as recently as a century ago, 80 percent of Americans lived on farms; today it is less than 2 percent.) Some of these villages had been established early in Israel's history, when the society was almost exclusively rural and non-urban. But others had grown up during the monarchy as satellites of the few urban centers, in a pattern that anthropologists call a "three-tier" hierarchical system. Like a triangle, the configuration here is one of a great many small sites on the bottom; far fewer medium-sized sites in the middle; and a very few large sites (true cities) on top.

This pattern of what we call "site type and distribution" — always fundamental to archaeological investigation — means that the bulk of the Israelite population lived in *relatively isolated, traditional areas.* Furthermore, the basically conservative culture of rural areas was intensified by the fact that society was kin-based, and thus in a sense inbred. Young people were constrained to marry within the clan, even the larger family. Marriage to first cousins was often preferred. As in an Arab village of 100-300 today, everyone was related by blood to everyone else. Only in the cities was personal status entrepreneurial, rather than kin-based.

Most people were thus removed from the centers of political power, religious authority, and international tensions, insulated from the decision-making processes that shaped national culture. They would have known somehow that they were "Israelites," but they didn't carry passports. And the orthodox religious ideals enshrined in the Hebrew Bible would have been foreign to them throughout most of Israel's history, at least until the Deuteronomistic reforms toward the very end. And even that did not reach the masses (more on that below).

Furthermore, most people's daily lives revolved even more provincially around what we would call the "extended family." This would be a two- or three-generation family group of up to fifteen to twenty people, consisting perhaps of a surviving older parent; an aunt or uncle; and the primary couple and their children. Other groups might consist of an aging couple with several married sons and their wives and children. This is what anthropologists call a "patrilocal" form of social organization, in which married sons bring their new wives to their own home, that is, their father's house, to reside and raise children there. The ancestral house is simply added to as the extended family grows, eventually becoming a family compound with several dwelling units grouped around a central courtyard and sharing many common facilities for food storage and preparation and the like.

Most families in the Middle East have traditionally lived this way until recently (known as "stem families"), and many still do in small towns and villages. In the villages, several such extended families and household clusters, all sheltering blood relatives, would make up the entire population of a few hundred people. Within walking distance, there would be other such villages, also kin-based and claiming descent from the same tribal ancestor, real or imagined. This pattern produces an extremely *close-knit society,* based on family ties, commonly shared traditional values, and loyalty to the clan and to tribal sheiks rather than to any external authority such as the State.

I lived in primitive Arab villages in the Hebron hills for many months in the years following the 1967 war and have experienced firsthand the reality of such traditional family life. It has all changed now, but forty years ago it felt like stepping back into biblical times — into another world. It is hard not to romanticize it, because the simpler life, the close associations of people, the daily rhythms all had their appeal. But what I remember is how *hard* life was for almost everyone in the village.

The ethnographic data alone are compelling, but they are confirmed by a study of the biblical texts. In 1985 Lawrence Stager, a colleague at Harvard, published a brilliant article entitled "The Archaeology of the Family in Early Israel," in which he used both ethnography and the then-new archaeological data on the Israelite settlement in Canaan to elucidate the description of the "house of the father" in the pre-Monarchical stories in Joshua, Judges, and Samuel. A modified version of Stager's scenario would reveal the following ascending "levels" of social structure, which remained much the same even during the more urbanized period of the monarchy.

(1) Individuals who lived in and identified with the "house of the father" (*gever*).
(2) The "father" himself, or *paterfamilias* (*'āv*) of the nuclear family and compound, the "house of the father" (*bêt-'āv*)
(3) The extended family or clan (*mishpāḥāh*).

(4) The larger lineage or "tribe" (shēvet; maṭṭeh).

(5) The whole "people of Israel" (běnê-yiśrā'ēl).

Dozens of biblical stories about everyday life in ancient Israel reflect this family-based social structure. For instance, look at the story in Joshua 7. In assembling the people of Israel to punish Achan for his disloyalty at the battle of 'Ai, Joshua calls up the whole "tribe of Judah" (shēvet-yěhūdāh). He then summons the "family of Judah" i.e., the "clan" (mishpāḥāh-yěhūdāh). Finally he brings out the "household" (bêt) of Achan, "man by man" (ligvārîm), that is, the whole family of Achan, "his sons and daughters." And as dramatic (and horrifying) evidence of family solidarity, when Achan is sentenced to death, his whole family was executed with him, and even his property was destroyed. "Collective punishment" may be morally repugnant to us; but in ancient Israel it was deemed necessary to preserve the integrity of the larger "family," the "běnê-Israel," the people as a whole. The family — not the individual — is the core of society.

(4) *The world of the household.* What about the more immediate context in which ordinary people lived and carried out the various tasks of everyday life, the family household? What did a typical town or village house look like, and what went on there? Can we tell anything from the physical remains about people's notion of identity, about their sense of meaning and purpose in life?

We now have enough archaeological data to reconstruct a typical Iron Age house and its furnishings in considerable detail. Nearly all the houses, even those in urban areas, are based on the "four-room" or "pillar-courtyard" house plan of the early settlement period. This type of house was first developed in an agricultural society and economy, so it was self-contained and could easily accommodate the large families that we have just discussed. Such a house featured an open central courtyard, around which there were arranged in a u-shaped layout three banks of rooms, separated by partitions and stone columns that supported the second story. The courtyard had a hearth or oven, food-processing installations, and work areas. The two or three rooms on each side were stables, usually with cobbled floors for mucking them out, and often with stone mangers. The back room or rooms were typically storage areas for foodstuffs, provisions, and tools. The second story would have had anywhere from five to eight small rooms, which were the living quarters and sleeping chambers for the

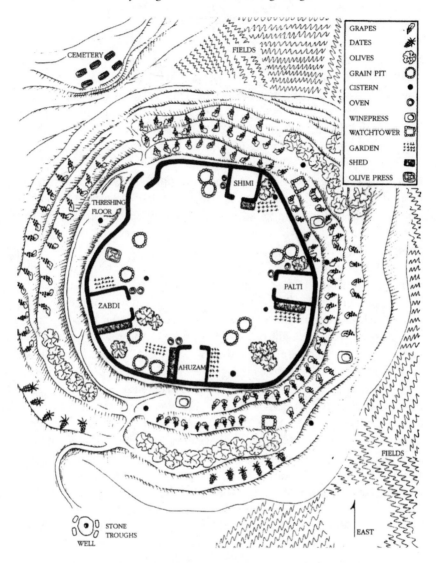

Hamlet with four family compounds around open courtyard;
population *ca.* 50-60
Borowski 2003, Fig. 7.1

21

large family. The flat, tamped mud roof was used for drying and processing food in good weather.

These houses were simply constructed of stone foundations with
mudbrick walls. But they were easy to build, naturally well insulated, and
practical for large families in both rural and urban areas. The average
house could be as large as 16 by 16 meters, or to translate into feet, 850
square feet of living and storage space for one story, 1,700 for both. That
may sound a bit small for a big family. But ethnographic estimates figure
about ten sq. meters of total living space per person, so the 850 square feet
of the upper living quarters could accommodate seven to nine people,
more than the average family size of five or six. And the other one or two
houses in the family compound would add another dozen or so to the
"house of the father," yielding a total of 15 to 20 persons, as estimated
above.

We must also remember that while a woman might bear many children, mortality rates were so high for infants and small children that probably no more than three or four would have survived to adolescence. That
would yield a number of only five or six people for the nuclear family
(much lower than the eight of earlier estimates). Add the surviving older
generation, plus married sons and their wives (see above), and you get our
total of 15 to 20.

While many houses recently excavated are well preserved (ironically
best so when they had been suddenly and violently destroyed) and can
thus be reconstructed in plan, their furnishings are more difficult to describe. In fact, there probably would have been little of what we would call
furniture, that is, fixed items such as tables, chairs, beds, cupboards, etc.
People ate on the ground outdoors in good weather, or otherwise they
gathered around low tables or on the floor indoors.

There were no chairs; people sat on portable benches, and mostly on
the floor. Bedding was stored in the daytime in stacks along the walls, as
was the meager clothing most people had. They slept huddled together on
the floor upstairs, warmed by what covers they had, augmented somewhat
by the warmth generated by the animals stabled below. This was efficient
in another way. The dung from these animals — collected, mixed with
straw, and sun-dried in patties — served as the principal fuel for cooking
in the courtyard hearths and ovens.

There were also very few tools or utensils. In the typical house there
were only simple cooking pots and a few common serving bowls or plat-

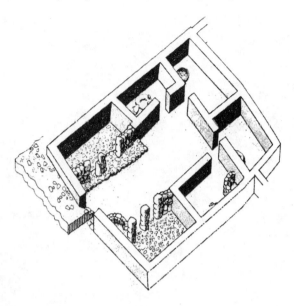

Ground plan of "four-room" or "pillar-courtyard" house
James Hardin

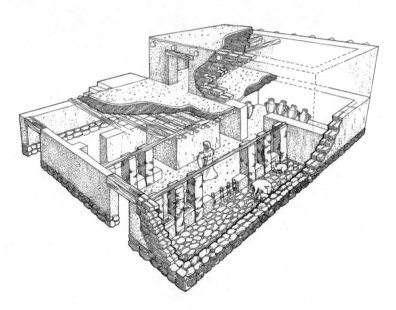

Artist's reconstruction of the Israelite "four-room house"
Giselle S. Hasel

An "extended family" compound; cf. p. 21
King and Stager 2001, p. 18

ters out of which people ate mostly by hand. Jars and jugs were used for storing and pouring water, milk, or wine. Larger storejars served to store liquids or dry foodstuffs. The ceramic repertoire that is now archaeologically well attested for the 8th-7th centuries B.C., for instance, is simple and illustrates this utilitarian lifestyle. We have bronze or iron knives, but no "tableware." Other than these few utensils, a typical house would have had stone grinding implements for milling flour; mortars, pestles, and pounding stones; a few flint blades; some bone tools for sewing, weaving, and leather work; and a few crude iron farming tools. If the household produced its own wine, olive oil, and pottery, as some did in the rural areas, these installations would have been on the ground floor or outdoors, and they would have had their own simple implements. There were no sanitary

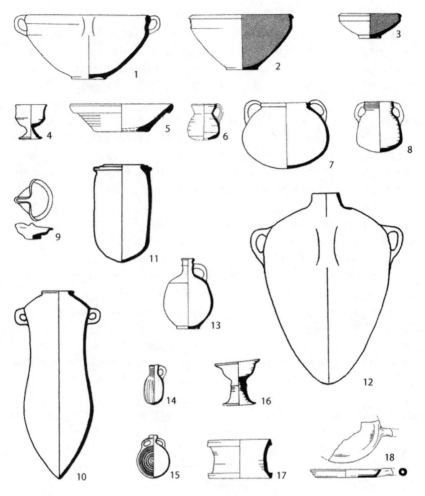

Typical 7th cent. B.C. Judean pottery
Dever 2001, p. 232

facilities at all, not even "outhouses." And there was, of course, no running water. There was also no heat, except for human and animal warmth and a bit from cooking. In the cold and rainy winter months these houses would have been very damp and drafty, and people were probably sick much of the time. And in summer the houses could be stifling hot, so people often slept on the roof.

The multitude of daily tasks that were necessary to keep a large family functioning, whether in the village or in town, would have been mostly gender-specific, and they would have consumed all the waking hours for both sexes, adults and children. The daily schedule can be reconstructed reasonably well. People lit their houses, if at all, only with single-wick saucer-lamps burning smoky olive oil, so they rose at first light and went to bed shortly after dusk. Breakfast would have been a piece of bread, perhaps some olives, egg, and yogurt or cheese. Lunch was piecemeal, especially for the men in the fields. The evening meal would have been much like breakfast, but more a family-style meal, perhaps with a couscous-like dish, a seasonal vegetable or fruit, and even a bit of chicken or meat now and then (a real luxury).

It was difficult to process food of any kind, except for making hard cheese or drying meat and preserving olives, dates, and the like. So the menu depended mainly on what was in season, or what the crops had happened to yield in a good year. Wheat, barley, and oats were harvested in April-May; grapes ripened over the late summer; and figs, pomegranates, and olives came in August-September. It has been estimated that the typical Israelite farm family had a plot of a few acres; owned up to a dozen sheep and goats, a donkey, a cow or two, and a few chickens. In a good year, a family could expect to feed themselves, and perhaps even store or trade a bit of the surplus. One lean year, however, was a severe hardship; and more than one was a disaster. Malnutrition was not uncommon, and there were many diseases and aliments caused by an inadequate diet (but no diabetes).

Arthritis was prevalent, even in teenagers, due to the hardship of stoop labor in the fields. Women developed what we know today as carpal tunnel syndrome from long hours squatting and grinding grain. Or they had calcium deficiencies from prolonging nursing, possibly in the hope of avoiding conceiving too many children. Everyone had bad teeth from grit in the stone-ground flour. Overall life expectancy was only about 30 years, probably less for women. If a woman managed to survive her childbearing years, however, she might live to 40 or more. A man of 50 was an "elder," respected for his remarkable longevity and for his (supposed) wisdom having attained those years.

In the predominantly rural areas, men's tasks were principally the heavy work in the fields — terracing, plowing, planting, weeding and pruning, harvesting, ferrying tools to and from the fields and harvested crops back to the village. Fields could be as far away as a mile or two, so the day was long. It was hot and dusty in the summer months. The labor was back-breaking, even when plowing with a donkey or an ox.

Women's work was mainly although not exclusively at home: harvesting some things; preserving, preparing, and cooking food (a constant task); spinning, weaving, and making all the family's clothes, bedding, and floor coverings; making baskets and pottery; caring for both the elders and a house full of children; and, as I shall show, tending to the family shrine and all of the religious rituals, rites of passage, and so forth. This was demanding enough when a woman was young and well, but the family responsibilities went on in any circumstance. And men did not usually share the burdens, even though they had some leisure time during the off-seasons of the agricultural year. (They were probably in the village common-house, talking religion and politics, as they can still be found in the mosque or coffeehouse today.)

Children were expected to put in long hours as well, girls helping their mothers, especially hauling water, and boys in the field alongside their fathers, or in the more distant pastures herding the flocks (sometimes for days at a time). There was little time for play, and children (if they survived) grew up fast, their sexual awareness quickened by living so closely with adults and observing their behavior. Girls were usually betrothed at 13 or so, and married shortly thereafter. They had little or no education, and no real options: they were expected to be wives and mothers (and God help them if they were not). Boys may have had some tutoring at home (there was no "schooling" except possibly tutoring in a few larger towns), but they, too, were expected to follow their father's vocation. In particular, they were to be responsible for keeping the family together; maintaining family respect and pride; marrying their daughters well; and preserving the family heritage. In practice, however, women played a much larger role in all this family "maintenance" than usually thought, even though they were less visible (see below).

The above sketch applies to rural and village life; but life was not much different in small market towns, especially for women and children. In the period of the divided monarchy, there were only a half-dozen or so real "cities," and none of these except perhaps Jerusalem had a population of more than 2,000-3,000. Beersheba, the southern border fortress and town, may have had 500 people. Lachish, the biggest fortress in Judah, could scarcely have had more than 1,000 people. The important market town and administrative center of Beth-shemesh was about the same size.

In these towns a small middle class did flourish, however — merchants of various kinds; artisans and craftspeople; builders; people in a variety of professions such as teachers, physicians, civil servants, military personnel; and perhaps even some religious officials.

The existence of such a middle class, attested in biblical texts but largely invisible in the archaeological record, raises the question of literacy. Would such a class, however small, have been literate enough to produce a "Bible," or even to read one? In the ancient world generally, the populace was almost totally illiterate. Even priests and kings could not read and depended on a small cadre of professional scribes to communicate and to carry on their affairs. In ancient Israel, our earliest Hebrew inscriptions come from the settlement horizon, the 12th-11th centuries B.C. There are only a few, but they do include an abecedary (the letters of the alphabet) and a schoolboy's chalk exercise tablet reciting a mnemonic poem that gives the planting and harvesting seasons (like "Thirty days hath September"). Then there are a handful of fragmentary 10th-9th-century inscribed materials. But writing does not become widespread before the 8th century B.C., and then the *corpus* indicates only what I would call "functional literacy." That is, a number of people could write their names, numbers, and the names of a few commodities. But that is a far cry from being truly *literate*, able to read literary material such as we have in the books of the Hebrew Bible. It has been estimated that even in the Roman period, no more than 5 percent of the population was literate by the above definition. In ancient Israel the figure was certainly lower. That has important implications for the question I have raised here concerning how early the Hebrew Bible could in fact have been written, and whether ordinary people could have read it if they had had it.

(5) *The "larger" world.* Beyond one's own village and district where family lived, beyond Jerusalem the capital of which people had at least heard, what did ordinary folk know of the larger world? What of Israel's neighbors mentioned in the Hebrew Bible — Aramaeans to the north; Phoenicians and Philistines along the coast; and in Transjordan Ammonites, Moabites, and Edomites? Then there were Assyrians and later Babylonians on the distant horizon, who overran Israel in the late 8th century B.C. and then Judah in the early 6th century B.C. The first peoples mentioned above were other West Semitic peoples — Israel's "first cousins" — with a similar material culture (even the Philistines had been acculturated by the 8th-7th cent. B.C.)

Yet it is clear that most ancient Israelites knew these peoples only by hearsay, and may even have regarded them as largely fictional. A few adventurers and traders may have ventured abroad, but no one else. Even the biblical authors, who deal with these various peoples in writing, had little direct contact with them (although what they did know was reasonably accurate). It was not only isolation and the resultant ignorance that insulated most Israelites, but probably also the xenophobia encouraged by the biblical (and popular?) notion that Yahweh had "chosen" Israel alone. The others didn't matter.

Religion and the "Good Life"

The above portrait of daily life in ancient Israel is brief and ought to be supplemented by reference to King and Stager's splendid recent book *Life in Biblical Israel* (2001; see also Bibliography below). Yet very few biblical scholars writing on Israelite religion (Chapter II) have paid any attention to the "real-life" context that we archaeologists consider the essential context. If the sketch of the lives of most people that I have attempted here is even close to the reality, it is evident that for most people it was not the orthodox, biblical theology promulgated by clerics and reformers that mattered, but the "good life" that they hoped to enjoy. And given their rural, agricultural, and marginal existence, what *was* the "good life" for which they longed?

The biblical ideal — at least that of the prophets, some of whom seem to reflect a view close to that of everyday Israelites — is clear. Micah's vision of the fulfillment of Israel's destiny in the Day of the Lord expresses the hope best:

> "Come, let us go up to the mountain of the Lord,
> to the house of the God of Jacob;
> that he may teach us his ways and we may walk in his paths."
> For out of Zion shall go forth the law,
> And the word of the Lord from Jerusalem.
> He shall judge between many peoples,
> And shall decide for strong nations afar off;
> And they shall beat their swords into plowshares,
> And their spears into pruning hooks;
> Nation shall not lift up sword against nation,

Neither shall they learn war anymore;
But they shall sit every man under his vine
And under his fig tree,
And none shall make them afraid;
For the mouth of the Lord of hosts has spoken.　　　　(Micah 4:2-4)

Amos's vision of the "good life" in the fullness of time is equally compelling. He is a villager from Tekoa, a "herdsman and dresser of sycamore trees" (7:14).

"Behold, the days are coming," says the Lord,
"when the plowman shall overtake the reaper
and the treader of grapes him who sows the seed;
the mountains shall drip sweet wine,
and all the hills shall flow with it.
I will restore the fortunes of my people Israel,
And they shall rebuild the ruined cities
And inhabit them;
They shall plant vineyards and drink their wine,
And they shall make gardens and eat their fruit.
I will plant them upon their land,
And they shall never again be plucked up
Out of the land which I have given them,"
Says the Lord your God.　　　　(Amos 9:13-15)

Here, then, is what might seem in our "materialist" approach to religion to be an altogether secular view. The "good life" is the simple, everyday joy of being alive, well, secure, surrounded by one's family, taking pleasure in good things. But the vision of Micah and Amos is also a deeply *religious* one, in which physical and spiritual realities are in harmony. That is why Norman Gottwald's profound observation is worth repeating:

Only as the full *materiality* of ancient Israel is more securely grasped will we be able to make proper sense of its *spirituality* (1979:xxv; italics Gottwald's).

But what does it *mean* for a people to live "on the edge," facing a never-ending struggle simply to survive? In particular, how does the physical environment shape the cultural and *religious* environment and thus provide the all-important "context" for actual religious practices noted above? If religion generally is "ultimate concern," as defined above, nothing in ancient Israel was of more fundamental and urgent concern than *survival.* And religious practices should be expected to reflect that reality above all else. The material remains of the cult that I shall survey (Chapter V) show that typical practices do.

CHAPTER II

The History of the History:
In Search of Ancient Israelite Religions

Throughout more than two thousand years of interpretation of the Hebrew Bible in synagogue and church, scholars, clerics, and laypeople alike have assumed that if the Bible is about history at all, its focus is principally on the history of ancient Israel's *religion*. It has seemed obvious that the Bible's stories — whatever actual events may have prompted them, whatever their literary value may be — are meant ultimately to inform us about Israel's journey to faith, and prompt us to ours. Thus it is commonplace to regard the Bible as a profoundly, almost exclusively, "religious" book. Yet I shall argue presently that the Hebrew Bible is not an adequate source *in itself* for reconstructing a reliable portrait of Israelite religions as they actually were.

The "History of Religions" School

For the sake of our story, however, let us pursue the assumption that the Hebrew Bible might indeed reveal all that we need to know about Israelite religion. Certainly most of the architects of modern critical biblical scholarship, and not only the ancients, thought so. When it began in the mid-late 19th century, modern "higher criticism" (i.e., literary and historical criticism of biblical texts, just like secular texts) was thought, of course, to be destructive, especially for the faith of modern believers. But it was the advent of modern higher criticism in late-19th-century Europe that ultimately provoked the bitter "Modernist-Fundamentalist" controversy. By the early 20th century, fundamentalism (named after the multi-volume *The Fundamentals,* published in 1909) had split most American Protestant denominations. Yet from the beginning the "modernist" critics did not pursue questions of philological analysis, composite authorship ("source criticism"), late date, and theological bias out of hostility (like modern "deconstructionists"). Rather they hoped that such objective analysis, freed from centuries-old dogma, would lead them to the *true* meaning of the biblical texts at last.

Most of the first critical studies sought to reconstruct Israelite religion on the basis of new understandings of the biblical texts, such as Rudolf Smend's *Lehrbuch der alttestamentlichen Religionsgeschichte* (1893; = *Textbook of Old Testament Religious History*); Hugo Gressmann's *Biblische Theologie des Alten Testament* (1905; = *Biblical Theology of the Old Testament*); and Ernst Sellin's *Alttestamentliche Religion im Rahmen der andern altorientalischen* (1908; = *Old Testament Religion in the Context of Other Ancient Near Eastern Religions*).

These and other early works, appearing first in German and later in French and English, gave rise to the "history of religions" approach, which was sometimes called simply "comparative religion." The latter was a misnomer, however, since little critical knowledge of other ancient Near Eastern religions was available at the time. Even the study of ancient Semitic languages and cultures was rudimentary, principally because archaeology was in its infancy and had recovered little comparable material. Thus what resulted from early studies based largely on the biblical texts themselves was what I would call "histories of the history of the *texts about* religions," rather than of religion itself.

The "Myth and Ritual" School

An outgrowth of the early textual and theological interest in Israelite religion soon came to focus more narrowly on religious rituals, or the "cult" (by which we shall mean hereafter nothing derogatory, but simply "practice," that is, worship in the broad sense). This approach was furthered not only by rapidly expanding archaeological discoveries of ancient culture, but also and particularly by the fascination of the late-19th- and 20th-century public with new field-studies in ethnography. "Folklore" studies around the world seemed to promise some universal insights into the phenomenon of religion, especially magical rites and the myth-making sur-rounding them.

Already in 1874 the work of the Dutch scholar Abraham Kuenen had appeared in English as *The Religion of Israel*. Then there appeared in 1884 a major work written in English by William Robertson Smith, *Lectures on the Religion of the Semites*. It was followed shortly by Sir James G. Frazer's exotic three-volume work *The Golden Bough: A Study in Magic and Reli-gion* (1890; 1900), as well as his *Folk-Lore in the Old Testament: Studies in Comparative Religion* (1918). British scholars, heavily influenced by what is still called "social anthropology" in England, often sought out what were called universal seasonal "patterns" in cultic activities supposedly con-nected with such events as annual "enthronement festivals," as well as more sporadic prophetic and magical rituals. Representative works of this genre included those of Sidney H. Hooke, *Myth and Ritual* (1933); *The Lab-yrinth* (1935); and the edited volume *Myth, Ritual and Kingship* (1958). Other British "patternists" were Aubrey R. Johnson, in his *The Cultic Prophet in Ancient Israel* (1944); and E. O. James, *Myth and Ritual in the Ancient Near East* (1958).

The Scandinavian branch of this school tended to be more ex-treme, positing not only celebrations of "divine kingship" in ancient Is-rael, but even of the *hieros gamos,* or "sacred marriage" of the gods. In these rites, priests and priestesses, the king and queen, or even "cult prostitutes" supposedly acted out the mysterious and magical union of divinity and humanity by performing ritual sexual intercourse in the sanctuary or even in public worship. Thus was born the pervasive notion of ancient Canaanite and Israelite "fertility cults," to which I shall turn presently.

There never was much actual evidence for the more titillating aspects of such cults. And today, of course, even the hint of sexual (and sexist) overtones in religious practice is politically incorrect. Yet one recalls that even circumspect scholars were once fascinated (and at the same time re-pelled) by the "licentiousness" of Canaanite religion. Thus my own teacher G. Ernest Wright, a proper Presbyterian clergyman as well as a leading ar-chaeologist, wrote in his *Biblical Archaeology:*

> The sexual emphasis of Canaanite religion was certainly extreme and at
> its worst could only have appealed to the baser aspects of man. Religion
> as commonly practiced in Canaan, then, must have been a rather sordid

and degrading business, when judged by our standards, and so, it seems, it appeared to religious circles of Israel (1957:13).

Of course, the key phrase here is "judged by our standards." But standards change and improve with better knowledge and insight into ancient customs.

Old Testament Theology

It should not be surprising that a major approach to the study of religion in the Hebrew Bible (or, more precisely, the Christian Old Testament) should be called "biblical theology." As we have seen, most people thought of the Bible all along as a fundamentally theological book. Indeed, the school that is still called "biblical theology" emerged as a distinct *discipline* with biblical studies as early as 1787 with a famous inaugural address at Altdorf by Johann Philipp Gabler. Since then, hundreds of Old Testament theologies have been written, ostensibly dealing with the *theological formulations* that were thought to constitute Israelite religion (how could "religion" *not* be theology?).

Works of this type up to the present are too numerous even to mention. But despite the continuity of effort, there have been frequent obituaries of the "biblical theology" movement — some mourning its passing, others rejoicing. A pivotal work would be Brevard Childs' *Biblical Theology in Crisis* (1970), which predicted the early demise of the movement. But note less than a decade later James D. Smart's *The Past, Present, and Future of Biblical Theology* (1979). One observation seems relevant, however. Much of the current concern to "revive" biblical theology comes from conservative or evangelical Christian circles, where the authority of Scripture is still thought to be at stake. Thus InterVarsity Press's *Biblical Theology: Retrospect and Prospect* (edited by S. J. Hafemann).

More liberal surveys, such as J. H. Hayes and F. Prussner's volume *Old Testament Theology: Its History and Development* (1985), tend to be retrospective and focus largely on the problems posed by such an approach. More sanguine, however, are the works of two of Old Testament scholarship's leading figures, now retired, Walter Brueggemann (1992) and James Barr (1999), as well as essays in the most recent handbook edited by Ollenburger, Martens, and Hasel (1992), *The Flowering of Old Testament*

Theology: A Reader in Twentieth-Century Old Testament Theology, 1930-1990. Nevertheless, important recent essays by both Christian and Jewish scholars, namely those of John Collins (1990) and Jon Levenson (1993), have rejected even the possibility of a historically grounded biblical theology. These are devastating critiques, because the dominant Protestant scholarship of the movement has always grounded faith in what is called *Heilsgeschichte* ("Salvation history"), that is, in inferences drawn from the "mighty acts of God" in *history.* But what if there *is* no reliable history, as much of contemporary "minimalist" biblical scholarship (below) asserts? Does that leave faith without a foundation? To that question I shall return. But let us look first at two recent works that seem less anchored in history and ought therefore to be less vulnerable to virulent attacks on biblical historicity.

The limitations, indeed the hazards, of theology for our inquiry into ancient Israelite religions may be seen most clearly by looking briefly at two recent Old Testament theologies. The first is the 1997 *magnum opus* of Walter Brueggemann, a leading Lutheran scholar and seminary professor. His 750-page *Theology of the Old Testament: Testimony, Dispute, Advocacy* (1997) is a work of immense erudition, based on a lifetime of productive scholarship. It has numerous merits, among them an unusual combination of the most rigorous critical scholarship, commitment to Christian faith, and a passionate, almost pastoral concern for the relevance of the Hebrew Bible. It is far from "confessional," however, and moves resolutely in the direction of moderate "revisionism." For instance, Brueggemann accepts a post-monarchical date for all the biblical materials. Thus he states frankly that "the Old Testament in its final form is a product of and a response to the Babylonian exile" (1997:74). He is also willing to live with religious pluralism, both in ancient Israel and today, with what he describes as constant "tension."

One of the strengths of Brueggemann's work is his separation of two strands of biblical faith: a "core testimony" more aligned with the creation/Zion themes; and a "counter testimony" drawing upon the Mosaic/prophetic/Job/lament/psalms motifs, with its call to social justice. Finally, there is Israel's "unsolicited testimony." Brueggemann even recognizes intuitively that archaeology might produce data to illuminate one of his polar tensions (especially his "unsolicited testimony" — our "folk" circles), but with only one passing reference (to me: 1997:xvii).

Brueggemann's acutely modern sensibilities and his desire to make faith relevant beyond intellectual circles might have made use of current archaeology, because it could have bolstered his case. But he, like nearly all his predecessors in this discipline, is oblivious. And the reasons seem clear to me. (1) First, his is an unabashedly Christian apologetic, even to a defense of the term "Old Testament" rather than the more neutral "Hebrew Bible." (2) Second, it may be an intellectual triumph, but for all the author's pleading for "faith in action" in the contemporary situation, this seems to me another "disembodied" treatment of religion. Brueggemann almost never deals with the *practice* of religions, ancient or modern, at least that of most peoples.

Thus despite his immense and sincere effort, I come away from reading Brueggemann's book with sadness. I cannot escape the conclusion that it entirely misses the point of our inquiry into ancient Israelite religion. Perhaps Brueggemann would respond that of course it does: ancient Israelite religion is the forerunner of Judaism. But most Christians have traditionally believed, rightly or wrongly, that it all began back there for them as well. Perhaps the real problem here is defining "biblical religion" largely *theoretically,* in terms of its ideas rather than of the typical practices of its adherents. This is, after all, an academic book like most, written for other academics. I can only protest "but that's not the way it *was* in ancient Israel."

A brief look at another work may also be instructive, Erhard S. Gerstenberger's *Theologies in the Old Testament* (2002). Gerstenberger, a German Lutheran and Marburg University professor emeritus, exhibits an even warmer pastoral concern than Brueggemann. He identifies himself specifically with the causes of women, minorities everywhere, Third World Christians, and other disenfranchised groups. The title in the plural is deliberate, for as Gerstenberger declares, "The Old Testament, a collection of many testimonies of faith from around a thousand years of the history of ancient Israel, has no theology, nor can it" (2002). But he regards the frank acknowledgment of the pluralism of the Hebrew Bible (my term) not as a disaster, but rather as a liberating force: "It frees us for the honest, relaxed assessment of the theological achievements of spiritual forebears that they deserve" (2001:1).

Much of Gerstenberger's survey focuses admirably on family, clan, tribe; on villages and small towns; and on common social structure. All this is the context of our Israelite folk religion. But under "sources" for the monarchy, for instance, Gerstenberger cites me and another archaeologist or two only in a footnote, then simply moves on. He makes only minimum use of the actual archaeological data. He does note somewhat wistfully that scholars have found it "difficult to take seriously the lesser literature which in fact comes 'from ordinary people'" (2001:67). By lesser literature he means non-biblical texts. But it is *archaeology* that provides the *real* "minority readings" of ordinary people, in material culture remains, as I argued at the close of Chapter I. It is a pity that Gerstenberger did not grasp the potential there, for he himself writes powerfully for many ordinary, confused people today. This is not just another academic (meaning all too often "unreal, irrelevant") study of religion. It, too, is a work of Christian apologetics and uses Israel's popular beliefs largely as grist for a Christian mill.

In any case, even before the currently fashionable skepticism, "biblical archaeology" had been plagued by problems endemic to *all* theological approaches to Israelite religion. Although once an advocate of the revival of "biblical theology" (I wrote an M.A. thesis on the subject in the 1950s), I would argue that from the very beginning the movement has been characterized by *inherent* weaknesses. It has been:

Clerically dominated

Androcentric

Establishment-oriented

Focused on unrealistic concepts of "the unity of the Bible" and "normative religion"

Static, denying evolutionary developments

Didactic and governed by Christian apologetics

Lacking sound historical foundations

Obsessed with verbal formulations, and largely insensitive to symbolic representations

Oblivious to revolutionary archaeological data

Increasingly irrelevant in the modern "secular" world

So what do I *really* think of "biblical theology"? I have concluded, albeit somewhat reluctantly, that it is useless in the attempt to reconstruct a reliable portrait of ancient Israelite religion. Indeed, it is a barrier to understanding, because it imposes medieval and modern constructs of synagogue and church, often arbitrary, upon ancient Israel. Thus it obscures the variety and vitality of Israel's religious experience, at least the experience of most people. In my opinion, theology may be a legitimate task of the modern exegete, but it must be kept strictly separate from the task of the historian. It is not the historian's job to produce data to justify *any* particular theological system.

In short, as an archaeologist, I am asking: "What *happened* in history?" And as a historian, I may speculate on the question: "What did these events mean *then?*" But to theologians and philosophers of religion, I leave the question: "What do these supposed events mean *now*"? (Here I follow Krister Stendahl's classic 1962 essay on "Biblical Theology.") On matters of faith I do have a personal opinion, as will be seen. But my judgment on such matters lies outside my area of professional expertise and carries no weight beyond my own peculiar experience (some would say very peculiar).

Sociological Approaches

I have already discussed several early schools of biblical studies that were influenced to some degree by what we would now call anthropology — particularly folklore and comparative analyses, which focused on "societies." Implicit in this approach was the notion that Israelite religion is best understood in the larger context of Israelite society as a whole, not simply the small, elite groups — the literati — that eventually produced the Hebrew Bible as we have it. This approach had already shown promise, because it began to deal with religion not just as a theological ideal, but as a functioning *reality,* with a "real-life" context (of which I shall say much more later).

There were some notable early works reflecting what came to be called simply the "sociological school," such as Max Weber's classic *The Protestant Ethic and the Spirit of Capitalism* (1930; translated from the German original of 1904-1905), and *Ancient Judaism* (1952), which sought to derive modern religious and socio-cultural norms from the worldview of ancient Israel. Later, the distinguished Jewish historian Salo Baron produced a three-volume work entitled *A Social and Religious History of the Jews* (1937), which began with the biblical period, and in which the coupling of the two key terms is significant. But mainstream biblical scholars, conservative as always, were not much influenced by these broader sociological treatments until the 1960s. Since then, however, a self-conscious "sociological school" has burgeoned. It has become perhaps the single most significant influence in contemporary biblical studies, and even in archaeology.

A recent convenient introduction to the sociological school will be found in a collection of essays edited by Charles Carter and Carol Meyers, entitled *Community, Identity, and Ideology: Social Science Approaches to the Hebrew Bible* (1996). For their part, Syro-Palestinian and biblical archaeologists have not yet produced an explicit theoretical statement advocating a social science approach. One of the most recent handbooks, however, is entitled, significantly, *The Archaeology of Society in the Holy Land* (Levy 1995).

The point of departure for the study of Israelite religion sociologically came in 1979 with the publication of a Berkeley professor, Norman K. Gottwald, entitled *The Tribes of Yahweh: A Sociology of the Religion of Liberated Israel, ca. 1250-1050 B.C.E.* Note the key terms: "religion"; "liberated"; "sociology." I cannot possibly do justice here to Gottwald's bold, controversial programmatic statement, which many now regard as one of the most seminal works of 20th-century American biblical scholarship. The irony is that it was first hailed as revolutionary; then subjected to withering criticism (partly because of its anthropological jargon and Marxist orientation); and before long overlooked. The fact is that had Gottwald had the advantage of the archaeological data that we now possess, his prescient model of "indigenous origins" for early Israel could easily have been documented, as I have shown in my *Who Were the Early Israelites and Where Did They Come From?* (2003). And his stress on ideology (including religion) as a "prime mover" in cultural change is in keeping with the latest and best trends in anthropology and archaeology today, which are moving away from excessively materialistic and determinist explanations (as we discussed them above).

A Revival of Interest in Israelite Religion

Despite the works cited above, it is true, as I have observed several times since the mid-1990s, that the *specific* topic of Israelite religion, especially cultic practice and folk religion, has been relatively neglected until recently (Dever 1995; 2002). *Theology* has been central throughout the history of modern biblical scholarship, but "religion" in the wider sense that I define it here has been curiously neglected. The reasons for that neglect, however, are not as inexplicable as they may seem, as I shall show (Chapter III). Meanwhile, a perusal of the literature, both in English and in other languages, indicates that fewer than ten general, full-scale works on Israelite religion or its major aspects were published in the 1980s; some 30 in the 1990s; and already in this century more than a dozen (five in 2001 alone).

Obviously I cannot offer an adequate critique of the thirty or more books on our topic published in the last decade or so (but see Dever 1995 for the period up to that time; and also the Bibliography here). Nor could I even categorize them in terms of any specific "school," new or old. These works represent, in fact, an eclectic approach, although one that is commendably less confessional (i.e., less clerically and theologically oriented), less narrowly philological, than works of a previous generation. My critique here will confine itself largely to the use of *archaeology* in recent works, a source of information that I regard as crucial, yet still largely unappreciated. I characterize each work briefly only here, since I go into considerable detail on points of disagreement in Chapter V, in the course of presenting the archaeological evidence that is missing.

(1) *General works on Israelite religion.* The most important, and most typical, recent books are those of Rainer Albertz (1994); Susan Niditch (1997); John Day (2000); Judith M. Hadley (2000); Patrick D. Miller (2000); Beth Alpert Nakhai (2001); Mark S. Smith (2001; 2002a); and Ziony Zevit (2001).

Albertz, a Protestant scholar, churchman, and Professor of Biblical Exegesis and Biblical Theology at the University of Siegen in Germany, had written a two-volume work on Israelite religion in 1992, now translated into English (1994). I reviewed the first volume enthusiastically because it was one of the first to make considerable, and generally competent, use of the pertinent archaeological data. Albertz also gave attention to folk religion (his "family religion"), heretofore neglected, especially by scholars of Albertz's basically theological orientation. (He had addressed this topic even earlier, in 1978 in a German work on "religious pluralism" and "personal piety.") Finally, Albertz recognizes the debt owed by Israelite religion to Canaanite religion. He states that "to describe 'Canaanite religion' sweepingly as a 'fertility religion' when we know so little of its details is largely a caricature created by Protestant prudery" (1994:87; more on "fertility cults" in Chapters VI, VII). At the time, his work on Israelite religion was unique in beginning to take the archaeological data seriously. The neglect of others would be eventually remedied, but not immediately.

The next synthesis to appear was *Ancient Israelite Religion* (1997) by Susan Niditch of Amherst College. While of interest because this was, astonishingly, the first book-length work on the subject by a woman scholar (in 2,500 years), Niditch's book is a disappointment. It is brief (123 pages); reads mostly like an undergraduate syllabus; and despite noting some archaeological discoveries and extra-biblical texts and giving a few references (1997:14-25; Bibliography) seems oblivious to the potentially revolutionary nature of the current archaeological data. One of the strengths of Niditch's work, however, is that it pays attention to the larger social setting, including the role of women, in the religious beliefs and practices of ancient Israel. Here she was already able to use preliminary works of the few other women scholars writing then, such as Phyllis Bird (1987) and Carol Meyers (1988). I have also cited these pioneering scholars approvingly (1995), later adding subsequent works by them (Bird 1991; Meyers 1991a; 1991b). And I shall devote more space below to the issues of gender and the "religion of hearth and home" that these women scholars have rightly raised (Chapters VII, IX).

John Day of Oxford University, who wrote a seminal article on the female deity Asherah in 1986, produced a full-scale work in 2000 entitled *Yahweh and the Gods and Goddesses of Canaan*. This went well beyond a study of various deities; and "Canaan" referred more to the world of ancient Israel than that of Canaan in the Bronze Age. Among the strengths of Day's book are his exhaustive discussion of various "Israelite" deities and his frank recognition that "absolute monotheism was first given explicit expression by the prophet Deutero-Isaiah in the exile and became fully operative in the post-exilic period" (2000:228). Yet Day does not even cite any of the major archaeological handbooks available to him: Weippert (1988); Mazar (1990); Ben-Tor (1992); and Levy (1995). He discusses briefly Mazar's "Bull Site"; the Ta'anach cult stand; a few of the Kuntillet 'Ajrûd drawings on storejars; and the Judean terra cotta female figurines (all treated extensively in Chapter V below). But this is only the tip of the iceberg archaeologically. Furthermore, throughout this work Day declines to define religion in terms of practice, and especially the practices that I shall treat under the rubric of folk religion — surely the most common expression of Yahwism in ancient Israel, if numbers mean anything. In short, while an excellent discussion of the "theology of the pantheon" as it may have operated in elite intellectual circles, this book scarcely seems concerned with the actual realities of religious life and experience for most folk in ancient Israel. I shall contend that only *archaeology*, not canonical texts, can reveal that reality.

Judith Hadley, an American student of John Emerton at Cambridge, published her 1989 doctoral dissertation in 2000 as *The Cult of Asherah in Ancient Israel and Judah: Evidence for a Hebrew Goddess*. I hope I will be forgiven for observing that although Hadley does not cite me under "previous research," I anticipated her conclusion that the old Canaanite goddess Asherah functioned in the cult of ancient Israel, possibly as Yahweh's consort, as early as 1983 (see Dever 1983; 1984; 1987; 1990; 1999). My identification of an actual "cult of Asherah" in the early 1980s was based on my discovery in 1968 of the Kh. el-Qôm tomb inscription mentioning "Asherah," to which Hadley devotes an entire chapter (on Asherah, see Chapters VI, VII). The other archaeological data that Hadley deals with — cult stands, figurines, and the like — had all been discussed by me and others previously. Thus, while Hadley's collection of archaeological material is well documented and certainly useful, I find very little that is original here. In particular, she fails to show how any of the archaeological artifacts (or texts) illuminate "folk religion" — the actual religious practices — or address the ultimate concern of most ancient Israelites. Again, despite a welcome lack of a theological agenda and an awareness of the potential of material culture remains for illuminating the cult and a number of illustrations, this is another "disembodied" portrait of Israelite religion.

Patrick D. Miller, a student of Frank M. Cross at Harvard, Presbyterian churchman, and long-time seminary professor, devoted a distinguished career to studying Israelite religion. His *magnum opus* published in 2000 is entitled simply *The Religion of Ancient Israel*. It is perhaps the most expert, sophisticated, and balanced discussion yet of the biblical texts in the context of their ancient Near Eastern environment. Yet it is little more than a study of these texts. Of the basic archaeological handbooks noted above, only Weippert (1988) is listed in the Bibliography. The Kh. el Qôm and Kuntillet ʿAjrûd inscriptions (Chapter V) are discussed in some detail, and even illustrated, as are the Taʿanach stand and the female figurines. But scarcely any other archaeological data are adduced. Throughout, the almost exclusive focus is on *ideas* — the characteristic theological propositions of the Hebrew Bible — even though Miller acknowledges that the texts are mostly late and highly formulaic. Only in his discussion of local and family cults, and especially of the long-neglected role of women (2000:29-40; 201-206), does Miller "come down to earth." And even here, he is reluctant to acknowledge any role of Asherah as a deity, "patroness of mothers," despite the overwhelming archaeological evidence (below). He can only conclude:

> The goddess was not present. . . . Either the feminine deity was implicitly absorbed in Yahweh from the beginning along with all other divine powers and so had no independent existence or character, or the radical integration of divine powers in the male deity effectively excluded the goddess(es) (2000:30).

For Miller, as for so many others, the Hebrew term "asherah" denotes simply a tree-like *symbol,* a "mediating entity" associated in some vague way with Yahweh, not the well-known Canaanite goddess Asherah (see further Chapters VI, VII). Consequently, I find Miller's comprehensive and exhaustively documented study — probably the best of the text-based works — disappointing, in the end quite conventional. It would be good if it were the last work of its kind, because it seems to me that it says all that *can* be said as far as the biblical texts are concerned. (But that is, of course, high praise.)

Mark S. Smith of New York University published one of the first systematic discussions of Israelite deities in his book with the intriguing title *The Early History of God: Yahweh and the Other Deities in Ancient Israel* (1990). Especially in the revised edition (2002a), this book is a masterly, thoroughly documented study of the various deities of Israelite theology and cult — literally all you ever wanted to know about the subject. The Preface to the second edition is the best update summary of the subject available, and it also sets forth what ought to be henceforth some of the main lines of research. Finally, compared to the first edition (1990), there is now much more use of archaeological material. Nevertheless, despite his critique of the inadequacies of many other scholars and his acknowledgment that "synthetic archaeological research has reached a new level of sophistication" (2002a:xvii), I regret to say that I find Smith's work is not informed by any archaeological data that would change his almost exclusively text-based approach in any *essential* way. Thus he says of the crucial question of understanding the term "A/asherah" that despite the new evidence since 1990 he is still not inclined to accept the likelihood that it names a goddess. He rejects the observation of some critics that his interpretation is "psychologically unprepared to deal with the opposite outlook," countering tentatively with the claim that the "*Zeitgeist* (world view) of our age psychologically preconditions advocates to desire a goddess in ancient Israel" (2002a:xxiv). He states:

> In conclusion, I am not opposed in theory to the possibility that Asherah was an Israelite goddess during the monarchy. My chief objection to this view is that it has not been demonstrated, given the plausibility of alternative views (2002a:xxvi).

It is precisely my intent here to demonstrate that a cult of Asherah *did* flourish in ancient Israel.

My critique is even more à propos of Smith's related work *The Origins of Biblical Monotheism: Israel's Polytheistic Background and the Ugaritic Texts* (2001). Here Smith does make a definitive case for the prevalence of polytheism until very late in the development of Israelite religion, based on his expert command of the preceding Ugaritic ("Canaanite") mythological and other Late Bronze Age texts. But once again, the vast archaeological data and literature are largely invisible. Thus we have an idealistic rather than a realistic portrait of ancient Israelite religion, although one that is closer to the real-life situation than previous ones (see further Chapter VIII).

Another synthetic work published on our topic is Beth Alpert Nakhai's *Archaeology and the Religions of Canaan and Israel* (2001). Here I find it difficult to be objective, since this is a revised version of her 1994 Arizona doctoral dissertation done under my supervision. Readers will not be surprised to find that this work accords to archaeology primacy of place. Much of the archaeological data that I shall treat here is cited and summarized by Nakhai. She also begins, as I do, with a summary and critique of previous research, as well as an effort at a theoretical working definition of "religion." However, this is largely a compilation of pertinent data and their possible correlation with many biblical texts, rather than a full-scale reconstruction of Israelite popular beliefs and practices, as I shall undertake here. Nevertheless, one hopes that Nakhai's book will draw attention to the rich but overlooked data that are now available.

The last work to be considered in this genre is Ziony Zevit's magisterial 821-page work *The Religions of Ancient Israel: A Synthesis of Parallactic Approaches* (2001). Zevit, a professor at the Reconstructionist University of Judaism in Los Angeles, had worked on this massive project for 15 years (as

I know from collaborating with him from time to time). In a dust jacket review, I described Zevit's work as "the most ambitious, the most sophisticated, the most important study of ancient Israelite religion ever undertaken." Such high praise is due, of course, to Zevit's extensive use of archaeological evidence, often based on first-hand re-examination and treated with an expertise that I have not seen in any other non-specialist. Certainly no other current biblicist can match Zevit's command of a broad range of archaeological data, which he, like me, takes as a "primary source" along with texts (thus the term "parallactic," as well as "religions" in the plural). In addition, where other commentators virtually ignore the vast literature on the "philosophy of religion" and the most appropriate investigative methods, Zevit devotes the first 80 pages of his book to these topics. That alone makes this work unique; and one can only hope that such an approach will "mainstream" the study of Israelite religion (for the first time in its long history).

Zevit's own method rejects the skeptical and minimalist approaches of many European "revisionist" biblical scholars, whose "deconstruction" of the texts — their only accessible data — leaves them historians without any history (as shown in Dever 2001). While freely acknowledging that no historian can be entirely objective, Zevit is nevertheless something of a "positivist." He prefers "an ill-defined modernism" to the postmodern paradigm now in vogue in many circles, somewhat akin to my "functionalist" approach here. As he puts it:

> Israelite religion is most approachable through its manifestations in physical evidence discovered in archaeological excavations that have uncovered cultic artifacts and structure (2001:79).

That is so similar to my approach that readers may suspect collusion. Yet Zevit is an observant Jew, and I am a former Christian now turned secular humanist. (See further below in Chapter III why "ideology" is *not* everything, as postmodernists claim.) For all his optimism, however, Zevit concedes that weaving together the various strands of the texts and artifacts may produce a tapestry that contains only "a fuzzy portrait of Israelite religions that differs from the clear portraits usually presupposed" (2001:80). "Fuzzy"? Perhaps; but somewhat more in focus than previously, I shall argue.

(2) *Works on Israelite "Folk Religion."* In Chapter I, I sought to distinguish folk religion — the beliefs and practices of ordinary people, clearly

the majority in ancient Israel — from what has been called "official" religion, but it is now better termed "Book religion" (van der Toorn 1997; see further Chapter IV). It would seem obvious that biblical scholars would have paid attention to this expression of religion, widespread as it was. But such religion is best revealed by the archaeological evidence, and as we have seen, biblical scholars by and large have ignored such data. Nevertheless, a few works in the past decade have emphasized folk religion, so let us review them briefly.

The first explicit work on folk religion is that of Susan Ackerman of Dartmouth College, another student of Frank Cross, entitled *Under Every Green Tree: Popular Religion in Sixth-Century Judah* (1992). Ackerman begins by noting that the elitist biblical establishment has typically dismissed "popular religion" as the religion of the ignorant, superstitious masses, and thus unworthy of serious consideration. It is not the religion of the canonical texts. She goes on to say:

> Popular religion is in this sense about losers. But ironically, perhaps these losers probably held the majority and represented the mainstream in their day. A description of Israelite popular religion is thus an essential component in any treatment of Israelite religion as a whole. Indeed, broadly speaking the program that is called for here is a rewriting of the history of the religion of Israel so as to take popular religion fairly into account (1992:2).

As for defining popular religion, Ackerman says that, in effect, it is everything that those who wrote the Bible *condemned*.

> It is not the religion of the Deuteronomistic school, the priests, or the prophets, the three groups from whom the majority of our biblical texts have come and the three groups who are the most influential in defining what biblical religion is (1992:1).

I couldn't have said it better myself. And the program that Ackerman called for in 1992 is precisely what I shall undertake here, because the crucial data are archaeological, and no other archaeologist has attempted the task. Indeed, most archaeologists have studiously avoided the subject, for reasons that we may explore later. I shall return to the specifics of Ackerman's treatment of both the textual and the archaeological evidence for a "Mother Goddess" later in discussing Asherah in Chapters VI and VII.

Shortly after Ackerman's highlighting of folk religion came the Dutch scholar Karel van der Toorn's *From Her Cradle to Her Grave: The Role of Religion in the Life of the Israelite and Babylonian Woman* (1994). This slender volume is a remarkably sensitive portrayal of the unique concerns of women in religious life. It is, in fact, a work that pioneers feminist scholarship in a sound way, based on a "disinterested" consideration of the facts that we now know. Van der Toorn states his objective as treating the subject of "the average woman . . . the ordinary, the common" (1994:14). He intends to "inquire after folk piety — because that is where we must locate the religious experience of the average woman [even if] we run up against many lacunae" (1994:15). Such religion, which he believes much more conservative, van der Toorn opposes to "state religion" that may be characterized by more intellectual evolution. Throughout his inquiry, in fact, van der Toorn eschews a *theological* approach, especially modern constructs forced back upon the ancient texts. As he says, "the experienced reality must be the deciding factor" (1994:17). He is concerned, precisely as I am here, with "what happened in the past, not with what perhaps *should* have happened" (1994:16). As for defining "religion" in practice, he is willing to concede that "much of it was not purely religious but magical" (1994:16).

One of van der Toorn's most perceptive observations about the religious lives of women in antiquity is as follows:

> The most commonplace things get lost most easily. Moreover, it is possible that certain religious activities were carried out without words following an unwritten ritual. They have left behind no traces in our texts (i.e., biblical texts; 1994:144).

As I would put it, women were, in the words of the distinguished ethnographer Clifford Geertz, "the people without a history" — that is, without a *written* account that survives. Women have not left us their Bible. They, together with other disenfranchised and marginalized groups in ancient Israel, have become "invisible" — *except* in the archaeological record, where there has been no one to edit them out. The *artifacts* are van der Toorn's "things that get lost." But I shall show that they have been found again. And they help to allow ordinary folk to speak to us of what it was *really* like in ages gone by. Unfortunately, despite this precocious work on folk religion, van der Toorn adduces almost none of the rich archaeological data that we now possess, not even the ubiquitous Asherah or "Mother Goddess" figurines that must have spoken powerfully to women and their concerns as guardians of hearth and home (see Chapters V, VI).

In 1997, however, van der Toorn edited a splendid volume entitled *The Image and the Book: Iconic Cults, Aniconism, and the Rise of Book Religion in Israel and the Near East.* Here there are several provocative chapters on Israelite iconism, or the use of images to represent the deity, which most previous scholars argued never existed because the Second Commandment strictly forbade them (Ex. 20:4; the Bible must be right, mustn't it?). The chapters on iconism — the major theme of the symbolism that produced the volume — are virtually the first studies ever to take seriously the possibility that despite the biblical injunction, many Israelites did make images, not only of Yahweh but of other deities. The biblical *maṣṣēbôt* or standing-stones can even be considered "images," although they do not actually model anthropomorphic features. But the difficulty of assessing the ambiguous evidence led most commentators to suggest something like "*de facto* aniconism," the theoretical prohibition of images, or "empty-space aniconism," the very absence of images as a kind of symbolic-only representation. Uehlinger, however, of the "Freibourg school" discussed below, saw real iconism in ancient Israel throughout the monarchy and adduced considerable archaeological evidence of figurines in particular. (I have responded to these authors in a forthcoming paper entitled "Did God Have a Face?" and I will return to the subject below.)

Several chapters also explore aspects of Israelite polytheism, by now tacitly acknowledged by many biblical scholars. The most stimulating chapter is by van der Toorn himself, "The Iconic Book: Analogies between the Babylonian Cult of Images and the Veneration of the Torah." Van der Toorn posits a contrast between "book religion" and "ritual religion" or folk religion. He argues that "many things can assume the functions of an icon" (1997:229). Therefore, he suggests that the Torah, or Pentateuch, became *itself* an "icon" — the Book of "the religion of the book." He then shows that just as in ancient Babylonia, in Israel "the cult of images had long been the rule" (1997:239). Only during the Josianic reforms in the late 7th century B.C. and the exile in the 6th century B.C. did images pose a problem. By then the Book — the canonical Hebrew Bible now taking shape — had become the effective "image." A *Book* had been substituted for traditional symbols of Yahweh; the Deuteronomistic historians exchanged the "Statue for the Scroll" (1997:247). Van der Toorn's analysis is brilliant and breathtaking. But why did it take biblical scholars so long to see the reality of cult images? I think it was because they were blinded by the propaganda of the biblical texts, and also did not consider seriously the tangible remains of archaeology that might have supplied a corrective lens.

At about the same time that van der Toorn was drawing attention to folk religion, a young American scholar, Jacques Berlinerblau, trained both in biblical studies and in sociology, was also turning to the subject. An early article in 1993 was soon followed up by *The Vow and the "Popular Religious Groups" of Ancient Israel: A Philological and Sociological Inquiry* (1996). Here again "folk" religion — especially as enshrined in women's pious activities in vows and prayers — is contrasted with the "official" religion portrayed in the texts. Berlinerblau begins appropriately with a quote from the social historian E. J. Hobsbawm in *History from Below: Some Reflections* (1988) about "grassroots history" and how the historian finds out about this only by asking the appropriate questions. And Berlinerblau, like me, believes that we have been asking the wrong questions about Israelite religions, or at least unproductive ones. He attributes the neglect of the essential component of folk religion to the contempt in which so many scholars (elitists, of course) have held it. Berlinerblau notes some all-too-typical epithets in the scant previous literature. Popular religion has been dismissed as "vulgar"; "hopelessly irrational"; "naïve"; "primitive"; "prelogical"; "infantile"; "socially retrograde"; and even "idiotic" (1996:18). No wonder that the importance of this phenomenon has escaped us; understanding requires *empathy*, as I argued in Chapter I.

Berlinerblau proposes to redress the balance by defining a focus on "popular religion." But he, like previous scholars, finds that very difficult. Part of the lack of consensus he attributes to the fact that "the chrysalis of 'popular religion' studies coincides with the emergence of the postmodern movement in research universities" (1996:19, 20). That movement, however, as I have argued in detail elsewhere (Dever 2001), has been largely detrimental to properly historical studies because of its extreme skepticism toward all "metanarratives," including of course the great metanarrative of the Western cultural tradition, the Bible. Thus I am unpersuaded by Berlinerblau's linking of the two generally. Yet if he means only to draw attention to postmodernism's insistence on "the neglected, the forgotten, the repressed, the marginal, the excluded, the silenced, the dispersed" (following Rosenau's *Post-Modernism and the Social Sciences,* 1992:8) then, although an old-fashioned modernist, I am in enthusiastic agreement.

Finally, Berlinerblau's "new methodology" focuses not on the direct or "explicit" approach through texts, because these almost always deliberately or inadvertently distort the reality. Berlinerblau's preferred "implicit" method uses the biblical and other texts, but mostly by reading between the lines so as to discern *hidden* realities, of which the biblical writers were consciously aware (a typical postmodern and "deconstructionist" way of reading texts). I myself had suggested something similar (1994b). The *real* popular religions of ancient Israel consisted precisely of what the biblical writers *condemned,* that is, of what they were aware of and disapproved of, but could not try to prohibit without mentioning (as also Ackerman). Thus they tacitly acknowledged not only the existence of "pagan practices," but their popularity. This was, as Berlinerblau puts it, "information the literati never meant to tell us, but inadvertently told us anyway" (1996:44).

Nevertheless, despite his welcome redirection of the inquiry on non-traditional sources, Berlinerblau never mentions *archaeology* as a source. One of the reasons is that his investigation focuses narrowly on "vows," which are admittedly difficult to recognize in material culture remains alone, apart from "votives" (the interpretation of which Berlinerblau is very skeptical). In any case, he misses a great opportunity by almost totally ignoring the rich archaeological evidence that I shall present here in Chapters IV, VI.

The most recent work, although it does not deal so explicitly with folk religion, is a series of essays by Dutch scholars on the faculty of theology at Utrecht University, edited by Bob Becking and others, entitled *Only One God? Monotheism in Ancient Israel and the Veneration of the Goddess Asherah* (2001). I shall treat some of the individual essays in this volume below in presenting my own reconstruction of the cult of Asherah (Chapter VI). But here I do want to applaud this belated recognition by mainstream biblical scholars that there *was* such a cult, and in particular to commend Karel J. H. Vriezen's illustrated chapter summarizing a good deal of the archaeological evidence.

(3) *Art historical and symbolic approaches.* I have mentioned Vriezen's use of illustrations above largely because they are conspicuously absent in many other studies of Israelite religion (many major works do

not have a single illustration). To an archaeologist, that is incomprehensible. But it reflects once again the preoccupation of philologically trained biblical scholars with *words* rather than *things* — with theological formulations rather than the symbols that for most people represented the reality of religious beliefs and practices. A picture really *is* "worth a thousand words."

A refreshing exception to the myopia of most biblical scholars is seen particularly in several works of Othmar Keel and his colleagues of the "Freibourg" school in Switzerland since the 1970s. This school has used art history to document ancient Near Eastern iconography — how the gods and their veneration are depicted in representative art — in order to place ancient Israelite religion in its larger context. The fundamental concept here is that of "symbol."

A symbol is simply something chosen to represent and typify a larger reality; usually it is an object or a pictorial image. A symbol may also be, of course, verbal (as with van der Toorn's "Book" above). But in the sense I shall use the word here, it denotes a tangible object or image that is thought to give access to some invisible, abstract reality — a deity or deities — and enable the individual to appropriate its meaning and power. Focusing on the outer symbol, as an archaeologist working with material culture or physical remains is accustomed to do, does not deny the primacy of what the symbol "points to," for without that reality the symbol would be meaningless. Likewise, biblical scholars who typically dismiss objects like figurines as "mere symbols" miss the point. Theologians, if they presume to contribute anything to liturgy, should be more sensitive to the need for symbols. Yet in my experience, those who deal with ancient Israelite religion are often not even *aware* of the power of symbols. This is especially true of Protestants, who characteristically emphasize the "word" over the "sacraments." And, not coincidentally, most of the writers on our subject have been Protestants.

The Freibourg school's employment of art history has drawn the interest of very few biblical scholars until very recently. This is probably because of the rather narrow philological and theological training of most biblicists (as well as possibly the biases mentioned above). For archaeologists, however, art history has been a congenial and indeed necessary subdiscipline from the beginning, and I have chided biblicists for their neglect (1995). The artifacts we archaeologists deal with are obviously *things*, things that have "meaning" or they are not worth studying. I would even define archaeology as "the science (or the art) of material culture," of things. For us, an artifact is an "encoded message" about the past, just as a text is for those who study the Hebrew Bible. And as many archaeologists insist today, if we master the vocabulary, grammar, and syntax of material objects, we can then read them *as* "texts" — parallel and often complementary ways of viewing the past.

In a recent piece entitled "On Listening to the Texts — and the Artifacts" (1977a) I attempted to outline the similarities between texts and artifacts in another one of my charts, as follows.

Texts	Artifacts
Writing system	"Language of material culture"
Vocabulary	Artifacts of all types
Grammar	Formation processes
Syntax	Ecological socio- cultural context
Author, composition, date	Date, technology
Cultural context *(Sitz im Leben)*	Overall historical setting
Intent	"Mental template" of makers
Later transmission, interpretation	Natural-cultural transformations
What the text "symbolizes"	What the artifact "symbolizes"
How its "meaning" is relevant today	How its "meaning" is relevant today

If the notion is apt, then a more specific comparison can be suggested.

Biblical Texts	Archaeological Artifacts
(as preserved)	(as preserved)
1. Concretize thought and behavior	Concretize thought and behavior
2. Symbolic, "encoded" messages of past	Symbolic, "encoded" messages of past
3. Express deliberate intent, imagination	Express deliberate intent, imagination

53

4. Selective, elitist by nature	Broadly representative, "populist"
5. Heavily edited in transmission	Constitute random sample
6. Reflect principally ideology	Reflect common practice
7. Closed corpus	Dynamic, expanding source of data
8. Continuous tradition	"Broken" tradition
9. Only a residue of past	Only a residue of past
10. "Curated artifact"	Curated artifacts"
11. Refract the past	Refract the past
12. Literature	"Real" life

In this treatment, I shall obviously focus on the right-hand column, on the assumption that it illustrates "folk religion" better, while the lefthand column typifies van der Toorn's "Book religion" better.

The first large-scale synthesis of the approach of the Freibourg school appeared in a magisterial 1992 German work by Othmar Keel and Christoph Uehlinger, translated into English as *Gods, Goddesses, and Images of God in Ancient Israel* (1998; I had already hailed the original in 1995). This was one of the earliest works of biblical scholars to regard archaeology and the artifactual record as *primary* sources for understanding ancient Israelite religion, as the authors make explicit from the very first page in addressing the issue of monotheism/polytheism. Their bibliography is exhaustive; and the book has nearly 400 illustrations, many of them of obscure seals, seal impressions, and figurines unfamiliar to most biblicists. (Elsewhere, this school has published several volumes of such seals, thousands of them.)

Paralleling what I said above, Keel and Uehlinger argue that pictures, i.e., "symbols," are if anything *more* evocative of the past than are texts, because the so-called "precise and unequivocal meaning" of texts is an illusion. They are convinced, as I am, that pictures provide a deeper understanding of the religio-historical evolution of Israel than does a purely text-oriented approach. If, as others have observed (Smith 2002a:16), we are "working with a puzzle that is missing many or most of its pieces," then it behooves us to search where the missing pieces are most likely to be found: in the *tangible* remains unearthed by archaeology. It seems to me that nearly all the pieces that might be found in the texts have been found, after 150 years of the most determined and ingenious modern critical scholarship. Perhaps we are reaching the point of diminishing returns from this source (Chapter III).

I shall return many times to Keel and Uehinger's provocative insights. For now, let me simply note a few other pertinent works of the Freibourg school (see Bibliography), especially those of Keel himself more specifically on the symbolism of Israel's principal devotional literature, Psalms (1997). I would also mention the German works of Urs Winter on iconographic images of the Mother Goddess in Israel and the ancient Near East (1983); and of Sylvia Schroer on the Israelite "art" that many biblicists declare non-existent (1997). Of particular interest is Keel's recent work now in English (1998) on what turns out to be a crucial factor, the association of Asherah with tree-imagery (to which I shall return in Chapters VI, VII).

(4) *"Feminist" approaches to Israelite religions.* I have noted above two recent books on Israelite religion by women, rare examples, those of Ackerman (1992) and Niditch (1997). Neither is what I would call a self-conscious "feminist" scholar, that is, focusing primarily on gender issues, and neither book particularly highlights women's concerns in the religious life of ancient Israel. In fact, either book could just as easily have been written by a man (and I have noted van der Toorn's "feminist" reading; 1994). In any case, is an "engendered" approach necessary? Preferable? If religious *activities* in the ancient world were gender-specific, as I believe many were, then women's varying experiences may be thought best addressed by a modern woman observer. But that is not necessarily so. (I have addressed these issues in the Foreword.)

In addition to the two book-length works noted above, I would cite several recent seminal articles and chapters in books by excellent women scholars. The "invisibility" of women in the principal record we have of ancient Israel, the Hebrew Bible, has been noted and lamented by several female scholars who have attempted to deal with Israelite religion recently. Carol Meyers, both a biblical scholar and an archaeologist, in *Discovering Eve: Ancient Israelite Women in Context* (1988), as well as in several other treatments (Chapter VII), has pointed out the biases not only of biblical scholarship, but also of archaeology. She argues that because this discipline, too, has been dominated until recently by males, archaeological research design has concentrated almost exclusively on reconstructing "political history." Syro-Palestinian archaeologists have excavated fortifications, temples, palaces, industrial and public installations, etc., obviously at the expense of investigating domestic areas where private and family life might be illuminated.

The interest of such scholars typically has been focused on "great men and public events." Does that sound familiar? This is precisely the focus of the patriarchal writers and editors of the Hebrew Bible. And it is surely no coincidence that most biblical archaeologists until recently were originally (and primarily) biblical scholars — and coincidentally white, male, Protestant, clerics or ex-clerics. I think that Meyers is right on target. In particular, her plea is well taken that if archaeologists and biblical scholars pay closer attention to "her *mother's* house" they will produce an alternate and better window through which to view Israelite religion. That is because most of religious practice was not centered in the vast public rituals that the biblical writers envision, much less in the formulation of orthodox theology with which they were preoccupied. The center was rather in observances of the fundamental unit of Israelite society, the *family* — where all individuals were originally nurtured. The home was largely the province of women, whose principal concerns were not necessarily those of either the Establishment or of the men who wrote the Bible. Theirs was the "religion of hearth and home."

As I have argued elsewhere, there may be fundamental differences, socio-cultural if not biological, in the way men and women view religion. Neither view is necessarily more sophisticated or more normative; but being a document produced by males, the Bible reflects one view to the virtual exclusion of the other. Only archaeology, with its emphasis on the unedited material, not the textual remains of the cult, can give back to Israelite women their lost history. Carol Meyers grasps this point intuitively; and her attempt to reconstruct the overall domestic roles of women in ancient Israel is laudable, particularly as it uses the model of the "domestic mode of production." But in earlier works she does not deal specifically with religion, except in passing.

In a later, very provocative article entitled "'To Her Mother's House': Considering a Counterpart to the Israelite *Bêt 'āb*" (1991b: i.e., the "House of the Father"), Meyers looks specifically at the "family household" in ancient Israel, arguing that it was the primary focus of religious life for most folk. This is, however, largely a textual study of women's roles in family life that had religious connotations. Surprisingly, it does not cite any of the archaeological data that Meyers knows very well. A much more detailed examination of the subject, well illuminated by pertinent archaeological data, is Meyers' chapter on "The Family in Early Israel" in the edited volume *Families in Ancient Israel* (Perdue, Blenkinsopp, Collins, and Meyers 1997).

Finally, another article of Meyers focuses on public roles of women in the cult, "Of Drums and Damsels: Women's Performance in Ancient Israel" (1991b).

A similar feminist approach is taken by Phyllis A. Bird, who has addressed the question of religion, at least obliquely, in several discussions of gender differences in ancient Israel (Bird 1991). Bird complains, however — quite rightly — that "We lack direct access to women's perceptual world through written sources, and our limited artifactual evidence, which is of undetermined 'authorship,' is mute" (1991:311). The notion that archaeology is "mute," borrowed unthinkingly from other biblical scholars, is one that I have refuted elsewhere. Yet it explains why Bird is able to say so little that is substantive, rather than merely speculative.

I think that Bird is very perceptive, however, in setting up a contrast between male and female concepts of religion, although this must perforce be based more on psychological insights and on modern ethnographic parallels than on textual or artifactual evidence. She argues that men, including, of course, those in ancient Israel, are more concerned with public prayer and other ceremonial rituals of a social nature, but that this "represents a narrow definition of religion identified with a set of formal practices or symbols" — the biblical text itself, I would add, being the most striking such "symbol."

Bird continues:

> There is, however, a wider area of practice, feeling, and cognition characterized by understandings of social obligation and welfare, of duty to family, community, nation, or people, of 'right' action or conduct pleasing to God, that might be subsumed under a broader definition of religion (1991:104).

Bird thinks that this realm of religion was more the concern of women in ancient Israel. She goes on to illustrate how several aspects of "popular religion" hinted at in the Hebrew Bible found concrete expression in women's cults, such as individual prayers, veneration of local shrines, feasts, ancestral and funeral cults, magic rituals, and the like. She argues that these religious practices related to particular needs "were favored by women and better suited to the general rhythms and the exigencies of their lives than were the major communal rites and celebrations" (1991:103). I could not agree more. The tendency of the male writers of the

57

Bible — and, not coincidentally, the vast majority of modern commentators, who have been male — to dismiss the popular cults as "superstition" rather than "true religion," that of the literary tradition, is instructive. But as Bird asks, what is religion? Who decides, and how? She hints at a dichotomy that I develop further, namely religion as "dogma" or "praxis" (below).

In my opinion Bird comes closer than any other female scholar, feminist or otherwise, to grasping the importance of women's cults in ancient Israel, not as "superstition," much less heterodox "goddess worship," but, as she puts it, as a "vital aspect of religious pluralism *within* a national Yahweh cult (that) is just beginning to be explored" (1991:107). Yet because the biblical texts are largely silent on this, and archaeology is "mute," Bird can scarcely get further. For instance, she notes the terra cotta female figurines but remarks rather wistfully,

> We are uncertain of their function or name, and we cannot connect them with certainty to anything in the biblical text. They challenge the conventional boundaries between sacred and secular, domestic and foreign cult, orthodox (Yahwistic) and idolatrous practice (1991:103).

Bird is particularly perplexed by the "anomalous distribution" of the figurines, i.e., found in so many kinds of contexts. I would simply observe in passing that (1) these figurines clearly represent "Asherah" (not "Astarte"), the principal Israelite female deity and patroness of mothers; (2) such "images" of Asherah are hinted at in many biblical passages, always condemnatory however; (3) they obviously functioned as talismans to aid in conception, childbirth, and lactation — "prayers in clay," as Ziony Zevit has aptly termed them (2001:274); and (4) their distribution is anything but "anomalous." The fact that they occur in all kinds of contexts is proof of their widespread popularity and evidence further that the distinction between "sacred" and "secular" is a modern construct and would have been inconceivable in ancient Israel. Unable to grasp the significance of the figurines, as well as much other archaeological evidence of sympathetic magic (Bes and Eye-of-Horus amulets; miniature furniture; astragali, etc.), Bird does not carry to conclusion her perceptive observations on women's highly significant role in popular religion in ancient Israel (see further Chapter VII).

The neglected role of women in the ancient Israelite cult is so crucial that I shall devote a major part of Chapter V below to the archaeological evidence, still far from being adequately understood and exploited. And in Chapter VII, I shall explore the nature and role of women's cults, returning to the works of Bird, Meyers, and other women scholars (see also feminism in Chapter IX).

An Overall Critique of Previous Scholarship

In discussing each of the many works above on Israelite religions, I have offered a brief critique, implying that their deficiencies justify yet another approach such as mine here. It is time now to summarize the general inadequacies that virtually all share, for these will be my point of departure.

(1) Nearly all of the conventional works, and even some of the few exceptions that I have noted, seem to be preoccupied with religious *ideas*. These ideas derive, of course, almost exclusively from the Hebrew Bible, conceived as though it were a "theological textbook" in which one can look up any topic essential to an understanding of Israelite religion. In Chapter III on "sources" I shall show why this assumption is flawed. Here let me simply observe that such a myopic focus on religion in terms of intellectual concepts results in what I have called a "disembodied" picture. It is a sort of still-life portrait, distant and frozen in time, lacking warmth and vitality, one that ultimately leaves many of us cold. There may be theological convictions, especially in older, conservative works. But there is no *passion;* and that is what religion is all about. It is as though most writers on "religion" have little experience of the real thing (or possibly have tried it and didn't like it). Some works by professors of religion are even overtly hostile, especially those of biblical "revisionists," who like all postmodernists declare at the outset that "all history is fiction," and all claims to truth are merely "social constructs." If the Hebrew Bible is all a pious hoax, I do not see how it can be morally edifying (Dever 2001).

More recent, less conventional syntheses such as those of Niditch (1997) and Miller (2000) are more realistic, more willing to see diversity in belief and practice (as also Brueggemann 1997 and Gerstenberger 2002). But even these fail to define "religion" essentially as the practice of the *majority.* They still assume that theology — that is, the orthodox beliefs of the few who wrote the Bible — was prior and gave rise to practice. The reverse is the case, as far as I can see. Religion (certainly "folk religion") arises out of the exigencies of real-life experience (Chapter I). Theological formulations and even the "official" cult come later, largely as a reaction against practices already widespread (as I show in charting the evolution of the literary traditions of the Hebrew Bible in Chapter VIII). As for abstract theological concepts, these are always products of the clerical establishment, of the literati, of the elites of the day — in this case, the right-wing, ultra-nationalist religious parties who wrote the Bible. This is why some wags dismiss theology as "God-talk," in effect "talk about talk."

The above is precisely what van der Toorn aptly calls "Book religion" (1997). But I argue that for most people in ancient Israel — who didn't yet have the Book, and couldn't have read it anyway — such religion was unknown and in any case would have seemed irrelevant. They may have possessed some of the older oral traditions that ultimately came to be enshrined in the written Bible (such as the "Mosaic" traditions; below). The religious practices of common folk, however, were informed not by the canonical literary tradition and its late, "orthodox" ideals, but rather by centuries-old religious myths and rituals, many of them going back to Canaanite Bronze Age traditions (Chapter VIII).

To be sure, my view of the pervasiveness of folk religion is unconventional, and it will be disturbing for those who believe that the Bible "tells it like it was" (and should have been). But I shall defend it, because for archaeologists most portraits of Israelite religions simply do not have the "ring of truth" about them. This is not the Israel *we* know. (Zevit 2001 is a refreshing exception, because the "facts on the ground" are taken seriously here.)

(2) The theological orientation that I have deplored generally requires some further comments. "Theology" by definition has traditionally been understood to be a "systematic" and "dogmatic" discipline. That is, it seeks to find the central, unifying "themes" of the Bible; to set these forth in terms of a coherent and comprehensive set of propositions about God and his will; and to defend these as the authoritative teaching of the Bible, the essence of religion. But the search for the "unity" of the Bible, so essential to theology, is a relatively recent quest, one that arbitrarily imposes modern concepts upon the ancient world of the Bible. Not only does this quest misunderstand and misrepresent that reality, but it obscures the variety and vitality of Israelite religion as it actually functioned in its own society. The theological enterprise in general has thus been obscurantist. But the overwhelmingly Protestant "biblical theology" movement in particular

has been so scholastic — obsessed with the Word — that it has often been blind to the power of *symbol, ritual* and *myth.*

Catholic biblical theologians, the minority, have been much more sensitive to the symbolic dimensions of religious experience and piety, that is, to liturgy. And Jewish scholarship, with its emphasis on religious practice, has typically opposed "biblical theology" altogether (Levenson 1993). Obviously the approach of the latter two communities is more congenial to me here, since in folk religion symbol, ritual and myth, not orthodox theology, are the essence of religious life. My "functionalist" approach (Chapter I) assumes that religion is essentially what most people *do,* not what theologians and clerics say they *should* do.

(3) A further weakness of the theological orientation is that it, like the canonical biblical literature with which so many theologians resonate, is overwhelmingly androcentric. Despite Harold Bloom's *The Story of J,* there are no women among the writers and editors of the books of the Hebrew Bible (and relatively few in its stories). And there are no women writers at all in the long history of "biblical theology." A few very recent feminist scholars like Phyllis Trible, Rosemary Radford Ruether, Elisabeth Schüssler Fiorenza, Athalya Brenner, and others (below) have protested the biases of the dominantly patriarchal "biblical theology" movement. But I do not understand them as intent upon producing full-scale alternate "theologies" of their own (perhaps just as well; see Adela Yarbro Collins 1985).

The male chauvinist approach of the whole history of theology, indeed of the Hebrew Bible itself, raises the intriguing question of whether women would have produced a different, and in some way better, version of Israel's history, faith, and religious practice. I firmly believe that they could have done so, and may still do so. And by "better," I mean truer to the *reality,* not necessarily more "normative" theologically. Because of my own sympathies, I shall devote a major portion of the discussion below to women's cults and the veneration of the goddess Asherah (Chapters VI, VII).

(4) My greatest misgiving about most works on Israelite religion, as I have repeatedly said above, is that they tend to ignore the rich archaeological data that I consider indispensable. There may be many reasons for this: elitist disdain for the mundane; contempt for popular religion as superstition and "magic"; hegemonic concerns; fear of losing the "privileged readings" that control of the canonical texts is thought to confer; or simply ignorance, whether innocent or willful. And I readily confess that until recently archaeologists have been partly at fault, for they have been negli-

gent in publishing their results — especially in accessible and non-technical works and in convenient handbooks. Nevertheless for ten years now there have been several excellent dictionaries and encyclopedias (Freedman 1992; Sasson 1995; Meyers 1997; Stern 1993; Weippert 1988; Mazar 1990; Ben-Tor 1992; Levy 1995). In addition, I and other archaeologists have been calling for, *pleading* for, a dialogue with biblical scholars for 20 years and more (Dever 1983; 1994b; 1995; 1997a; 1997c; 2000; and references there). Thus there is no excuse for continuing the unproductive "two monologues" that Halpern (1997) has aptly characterized.

There is, I fear, a deeper reason for many biblical scholars' neglect of archaeology. They simply do not grasp its revolutionary potential — another aspect of ignorance, however, and no more forgivable. For more than a generation now, nearly every history of ancient Israel, every Old Testament theology, has mindlessly repeated the assertion that archaeological data can only be "subjectively" interpreted, or worse still that in the end archaeology is "mute." (Examples are too numerous to cite; but see Dever 1997d.) But as a colleague in biblical studies has observed (Knauf 1991), the Hebrew Bible is "mute" for you if you do not know Hebrew. Or, as I like to put it, "archaeology is *not* mute, but some historians are deaf." Artifacts are, of course, subject to interpretation no less than texts. But they are less biased and have been less deliberately "edited" than texts, especially tendentious texts such as those of the Hebrew Bible. (More of that on "sources" and "objectivity" in Chapter III.) The fact is that we are about to experience an archaeological "revolution" in the study of ancient Israelite religion, one that will render *all* previous histories obsolete (Zevit 2001 is a harbinger). If they are not more alert to current trends in broad scholarship, beyond their own disciplines, many biblical scholars will soon discover that the revolution has bypassed them.

CHAPTER III

Sources and Methods for the Study
of Ancient Israel's Religions

The quality of any history, including the history of Israelite religion, is determined to a large extent by the nature and limitations of the available sources. We can speculate, but we can actually know no more than the sources are able to tell us. In the case of ancient Israelite religions, there are obviously two sources: written and non-written remains, or, broadly speaking, texts and artifacts.

One could argue that both sources are essential, since the former deal with *beliefs*, while the latter reveal *practice.* That distinction may provide a good working hypothesis, and I have contended elsewhere that it does (1994b); but the separation of the two aspects is somewhat arbitrary. Belief informs practice, and practice reflects belief. A pragmatic distinction between the two may be useful, however, and even necessary for purposes of analysis. But the ancients would have found such a distinction incomprehensible, because they would not have been analytical in the first place. Religion was simply "in the air," so they could scarcely have considered it abstractly, as we moderns do. Religion was what those in ancient Israel *did.* That is why the Hebrew Bible, for all its apparent obsession with the subject, has no generic term for "religion," as we have seen; it was not necessary.

Both written and artifactual sources are basic, and therefore we cannot dispense with either. Here I shall proceed, however, as an archaeologist, more concerned with practice (cult) rather than with theory (theology). Therefore, I will consider the archaeological data as a "primary" source. Textual scholars, even those who are usually open to new approaches, will no doubt protest that I have downgraded the Hebrew Bible to a "secondary" source. But as I shall show, it is — if one chooses to focus as I do on folk religion, or for that matter primarily on religious practices. That does not omit the questions many will have — how and why the Hebrew Bible came to be written and may still be valid — but it does postpone these questions until we have surveyed the other, alternate sources for Israelite religion (Chapters IV, VIII).

The Biblical Texts and Their Limitations

For more than a century now, critical scholars have known that the so-called Pentateuch (or "Five Books of Moses") and the historical works in the great national epic sweeping from Joshua through Kings are problematic as "sources." These texts cannot simply be picked up and read in a straightforward manner as though they constitute objective factual history in the modern sense, based on contemporary eyewitness reports. The former books (at least Genesis through Numbers) are by late, anonymous, composite "authors" and editors, produced at least five hundred years after a "Moses" would have lived. And the Book of Deuteronomy, all about Moses, is almost certainly a late monarchic theological homily put into the mouth of a Moses and then attached to both the Pentateuch (making it five books) and the other "historical" works.

It is true that the original 19th-century theory of composite authorship widely known as the "documentary hypothesis," or "source criticism," has come under fire recently for splitting the texts into too many independent sources, sometimes arbitrarily and overconfidently. Thus the original theory has been much revised. Nevertheless, the composite authorship and late date of the textual sources relevant to our inquiry here, in their present form, are beyond dispute, as are their theological biases. Let us look at the "schools" that the documentary hypothesis generally recognizes (see further Bibliography).

(1) *The "J" document.* This source, designated "J" for the divine name "Yahweh" that it prefers (*Jahweh* in German), runs mostly through Genesis, Exodus, and Numbers. It was originally thought to be the earliest prehistory and "theological" reworking of tradition in the Hebrew Bible, dating to southern circles as early as the 10th century B.C., perhaps from the court of David and Solomon. Today many biblical scholars (and the few archaeologists who deal with the question) would lower the date of J's

composition, if it is indeed an individual work, to the 9th if not the 8th century B.C. "J" is "salvation history" on a grand scale, beginning with the creation and the flood, continuing with the promise of redemption and prosperity to the Patriarchs and Matriarchs, and moving on to the Exodus and the foreshadowing of the conquest of the Promised Land. Even the current, somewhat radical reworking of the "J" hypothesis would not challenge the basic *theological* character that I have outlined here. I shall return later to its themes, since one has to question how relevant they would have been to actual religious practices during the monarchy. But if the date of J were indeed post-exilic (6th-5th century B.C.), as "revisionists" and some others now claim, this source would tell us nothing whatsoever about supposed "ancestral religion," and of course nothing about the monarchy since the story would end before then. "J" would constitute only late Jewish propaganda, an "origin myth."

(2) *The "E" document.* This material, termed "E" because it uses the alternate name for God, "Elohim," is thought to stem from a northern source. It was originally dated to the 9th century B.C., but now it is more commonly dated to the 8th century B.C. because of its "prophetic" interests. "E" parallels "J" in some senses, with alternate versions of some of the same stories (beginning with Abraham). Eventually it was interlaced with "P" by later editors (perhaps as "J/E"). "E" often conceives of God's revelation in the form of dreams, reflecting especially on sin and guilt, and emphasizing "the fear of God." It also elaborates the central themes of the Sinai Covenant and God's working out of his demands for loyalty in the history of his people. Probably an independent source originally, it is strongly didactic in character, somewhat akin to the Deuteronomist history (below).

(3) *The "P" document.* This material, from anonymous "Priestly" sources, appears especially in Leviticus. To some, "P" seems late and somewhat artificial, with its heavy emphasis on exclusive monotheism, on holiness as ritual purity, and on the sacrificial cult. Its "priestly" view of salvation is set, however, in Israel's prehistory in Canaan, especially in the wandering in the wilderness. Later the "P" editors reworked J and E, incorporating its materials into theirs to produce the books of Genesis through Numbers as we now have them. Many scholars date P late in the Judean monarchy, while others prefer a postexilic date, at least for the final reworking and editing. Whatever the date, I shall argue here that "P's" preoccupation with the Wilderness tradition and its concern with affairs was

largely irrelevant for folk religion during the monarchy. I shall defend this notion in dealing below with the Temple and Temple theology.

(4) *The "Deuteronomistic history."* The most important source for us, because it is more overtly historical and covers the whole period of the monarchy, is the "Deuteronomistic history," often designated "Dtr." It runs from the book of Deuteronomy (added to Genesis, Exodus, Leviticus, and Numbers to form the "Pentateuch") through Kings. Mainstream scholarship has long held that the core "Dtr's" content may have been the scroll that the editors of Kings claim was found by Hilkiah the High Priest hidden in the archives of the Temple in the story in II Kings 22 (below). According to this plausible explanation, the scroll — not "hidden," but probably planted there by Yahwistic enthusiasts — became the basis for Josiah's sweeping attempts at reform in the late 7th century B.C. (II Kings 23). This school of reformers shaped the book of Deuteronomy ("Second Law") itself in the form of three long sermonic discourses put into the mouth of Moses in the Wilderness. Purporting to be the very words of Moses, the "founder of Israelite religion," this *corpus,* however artificial its literary setting, would have been the ideal constitution for reforms late in Judah's history. This was a time when writers had learned the bitter lesson of Israel's fall, when it was near extinction itself at the hands of the Babylonians. After all, Deuteronomy is a call to *repentance* — a demand for the wayward people of Israel to restore the pure, monotheistic ideals of its original "pure" religion.

This historical retrojection and the apparent deceit involved do not mean that Deuteronomy and the Deuteronomistic history in Joshua-Kings were all "pious fiction," as the "revisionists" claim. There were likely older oral "Mosaic traditions" available to the editors, as well as written sources. And their intentions in using these sources were honorable, even perhaps justified theologically. Furthermore, it was common throughout antiquity for later historians or religious reformers to lend weight to their reworking of tradition by assigning their own writings to revered earlier figures. (Later Jewish literature abounds with such "pseudepigraphical" works, such as *The Testaments of the Twelve Patriarchs; Testament of Moses; Odes of Solomon,* and so forth.)

What may be more important for our study of Israelite religions here is the fact that the Book of Deuteronomy is a potential source for Israelite religion, at least late in the monarchy (although it was reworked and edited finally in the post-exilic period). Still more importantly, the Deuteronomistic school has provided us all the *earlier* textual material that we shall ever have.

66

These editors took up the themes of Deuteronomy and combined them with various annalistic traditions both oral and written to produce the great national epic history of Israel from beginning to end in the books of Joshua, Judges, Samuel, and Kings as we now have them, a sort of "theocratic history." This history is thus governed by the central Deuteronomistic theological themes: loyalty and obedience to Yahweh alone; the demands of the Covenant; the Jerusalem Temple as the exclusive dwelling of Yahweh; prophetic calls for repentance; and the inevitability of divine retribution.

The significance of what scholars call the Deuteronomistic history can scarcely be exaggerated, for it comprises *the* canonical history of ancient Israel, complete with warnings not to add or delete anything (Deut. 4:2; 12:32). Despite the obvious theological biases of its authors and editors, this history of early Israel and the monarchy is virtually the only "history" that we have in the Hebrew Bible. Thus wherever we can provide some archaeological *commentary* and *control,* we shall come back to these Deuteronomistic texts. But unlike that of so many other observers, our account of Israelite religion will not be a literalistic and simplistic "paraphrase of the Bible." It will be an independent, secular history (as far as that is possible; above).

(5) *The prophetic literature.* While not properly historical in basic character, the earlier prophetic works do provide authentic sources for our inquiry into Israel's religions. These works are pertinent first of all because they deal overwhelmingly with religious beliefs *and* practices. In addition, the prophetic oracles and public pronouncements are placed in the context of "real life" settings and thus describe in some detail the behavior of ordinary folk, much more so than does the book of Kings with its "royalist" ideology. In fact, as suggested above, it would not be misleading to say that the *real* religions of ancient Israel consisted precisely of all the things that the prophets *condemned,* all of them incidentally illustrated by archaeological discoveries, as we shall see.

The major observers on whom I shall rely are the 8th-century prophets Amos, Hosea, Isaiah, and Micah; and the 7th/6th-century prophets Jeremiah and Ezekiel (see Chapter VII). Needless to say, this assumes rejecting the absurd "revisionist" contention that all these great biblical personalities are not historical at all, but are much later, fictional "literary constructs." I regard the prophets, along with mainstream biblical scholars, as contemporaries of the 8th-6th-century kings of Israel, of reforming priests and prophets, and of those who produced the first written versions of the Tetrateuch/Pentateuch and the Deuteronomistic history. They therefore provide at least some valuable eyewitness accounts. These reports are especially significant when a prophetic discourse differs from the official party line and reflects real-life conditions that we readily recognize in the archaeology of the Iron Age.

(6) A final textual source may be found in the lyrical or so-called "devotional literature," principally Psalms; and to a limited extent in some of the "wisdom" literature, such as Proverbs, Ecclesiastes, and Job. These works, however, while they do reflect folk piety and beliefs, are difficult to use for several reasons, even though they are routinely cited uncritically by standard histories of Israelite religion. Most of this literature is nearly impossible to date or place in proper historical and cultural context. For example, the composition of the various poems now contained in the book of Psalms may extend over six centuries or more. (The frequent attribution to "David" or "Solomon" is fictional.) They were obviously used in worship; but when, under what circumstances, and by whom? Are they purely literary creations, as they appear to be in their present form? Or do some reflect a long tradition of vernacular oral poetry and song well known to ordinary folk, as suggested by close parallels with the 14th/13th-century Canaanite mythological texts from Ugarit in Syria (below)?

Job is even more problematic, not only historically but theologically. It is a strange, unorthodox work by any criteria, hard to reconcile with any other biblical literature. And Ecclesiastes is more Greek than "Hebrew." Nevertheless, the very exotic character of some of the devotional and wisdom literature attests to the *variety* of religious expressions that were once accepted and embraced in ancient Israel, even though they are sometimes forgotten by modern scholarship. The "Freibourg school" (discussed in Chapter II above) has certainly seen the potential of this literature. Keel has a whole lavishly illustrated book on Psalms (1997; first published in German in 1972).

Some Caveats

Whatever potential value the various biblical texts may have for illuminating Israelite religions, in practice they must be sifted through critically. This is necessary in order to separate out a "core" of any reliable historical information that there may be, keeping in mind the general character of the various literary strands outlined above. However, even at *best* the textual sources in the Hebrew Bible are limited for our purposes, and I would argue often severely so. There are many reasons for this.

(1) First, all the biblical texts in their *present written form* were produced relatively late in Israel's history. Most were composed no earlier than the 8th century B.C. ("J" and "E") or the 7th century B.C. ("Dtr," possibly "P"; above). And then these underwent extensive editing and reworking in the exilic and postexilic period, that is, after "Israel's" history was over. Considering that the "Period of the Judges" and the Monarchy extended from *ca.* 1200 to 500 B.C., our texts cover only about 200 years or one-third of that, and only the last one-half or so of the Monarchy. The formative period, *ca.* 1200-1000 B.C., is not directly illuminated by contemporary texts at all, except possibly for some archaic Hebrew poems like the "Song of Deborah" (Judges 5), which some scholars would regard as an original composition of the 12th-11th century B.C. (see also Exod. 15; Deut. 32, 33).

The late date of composition and editing assumed here is not in debate among mainstream scholars. There remains only the question of whether *behind* the admittedly complex literary process there would have been older oral traditions, as well as a few eyewitness written accounts (such as court archives), that would have preserved and handed down some reliable historical information. This possibility cannot be dismissed, and even rather radical scholars acknowledge it; but it cannot be proven. In defense of the idea of older sources, however, we should note that the biblical writers even mention specific sources, unknown to us, such as the *Book of Jashar* (Joshua 10:13) and the *Book of the Chronicles of the Kings of Judah* (repeatedly in Kings). And for several generations biblical scholars have posited that "folk memories" — sagas, legends, and myths of various kinds in poetic form — were probably transmitted in popular culture for centuries before being incorporated into the written literature. The ethnographic evidence of oral tradition from many cultures, ancient and modern, is certainly persuasive.

Despite the evidence, the current biblical "revisionists" reject out of hand an early date for *any* of the biblical literature. They place the composition (not merely the editing) of all the biblical texts in the Persian period (6th-4th century B.C.), or increasingly in the Hellenistic era (3rd-1st century B.C.). For the minimalist "revisionists," none of the biblical texts is a source of information for *anything* in the Iron Age. Indeed, "biblical Israel" and its religion are only late literary constructs — fictions of Jewish groups in Hellenistic Palestine desperately seeking a self-identity in an age of assimilation. The Hebrew Bible is thus a pious hoax, its "Israel" simply invented. My approach here is neither "maximalist" nor "minimalist." It attempts to steer a middle ground, recognizing that the use of any biblical text requires trying to find a plausible real-life context for that text. Where datable archaeological artifacts and textual references seem to *converge*, we may be on safe historical ground. My recent book *What Did the Biblical Writers Know and When Did They Know It?* (2001) is based on many dozens of such "convergences." The biblical writers know a lot, and they knew it early. They *could* be good historians, by the standards of the day — when they wanted to be.

(2) That leads me to the second limitation of the biblical texts. Its writers and editors were historians of a sort, but they were highly selective in what they chose to include. It is often overlooked that they were mostly elites, literati attached to court and priestly circles in Jerusalem. Taken together, they can hardly have constituted more than a fraction of one percent of the population. They were certainly not representative of the masses that we are considering here. There are some exceptions, to be sure, such as the prophet Amos, who styles himself "a shepherd" (1:1). He rails against the privileged classes of his day "who oppress the poor, who crush the needy" (4:1). And in many biblical passages, mostly prophetic as well, the writers extol the "poor of the Land" as being closer to Yahweh's favor.

Nevertheless, the prophets overall are hardly country bumpkins, to judge from the lofty literary style of the writings attributed to them. I have long thought that if the oracles of prophets like Isaiah had originally been "sermons" delivered in public, people in the countryside would scarcely have understood them. Think of the elegant Hebrew, the complex syntax, the sophisticated literary allusions, the subtle play on words. All this would have been lost on at least 90 percent of the population of ancient Israel and Judah, most of whom were uneducated villagers and farmers. That Isaiah was a patrician is also indicated by his status as an aristocratic advisor, almost a Prime Minister, under kings like Ahaz and Hezekiah. And Jeremiah was born into a priestly family (1:1).

The other biblical writers, principally those who produced the Deuteronomistic history, were doubtlessly elitists as well, as seen in both their chosen subject matter and their literary style. They really did constitute a "school," even a sort of Academy, which at least during their heyday under the long rule of Josiah (640-609 B.C.) was under royal patronage. And why not? One of the dominant motifs in shaping their epic history in the Book of Kings was the centrality of the Royal Temple in Jerusalem as the *exclusive* dwelling place of Yahweh. What could be more elitist? Many people in ancient Israel, however, had probably never been to Jerusalem in their whole lives, and they had never seen the Temple. Had they not known Yahweh?

A striking example of the chauvinist nationalism of the Deuteronomistic school, their obliviousness to the rest of the country, is seen in their coverage of the famous siege of Sennacherib in 701 B.C. The fall of the fortress of Lachish, just 80 miles southwest of Jerusalem, was considered so significant by the Assyrian king that he commissioned artists to execute huge stone reliefs showing the siege and destruction of Lachish. He displayed them back home around the walls of one of the principal rooms of his palace for all to see. (They are now in the British Museum.) Yet the editors of Kings mention Lachish only twice (II Kings 18:14, 17), noting merely that Sennacherib was there. Then they give almost two chapters to an extraordinarily detailed account of the siege of Jerusalem (II Kings 18:13–19:37). Why? Because the siege of Jerusalem was miraculously lifted, and the Temple of Yahweh was spared. But Lachish, which was totally destroyed and its population slaughtered (as the excavations make horrifyingly clear), was of no concern to the biblical writers. Their cavalier attitude in this case is but one example of their selectivity, the result of their political and theological biases. Theirs is obviously *not* a "disinterested," fair, and balanced history of Israel and its religions.

(3) The perspective of all the biblical writers is a factor that limits their usefulness in another regard. It is no exaggeration to say that all the biblical literature — especially the historical and prophetic works — constitutes what is essentially "propaganda." The writers make no pretense to objectivity. They are openly partisan, championing the cause of extreme nationalism and orthodox Yahwism, that is, the Truth as *they* see it. They have no tolerance for divergent views, not even when they are held by kings, all of whom they despise except for the "good" reformist kings Hezekiah and Josiah. These extremists were, of course, minority parties given the historical reality in 8th-7th century Israel. But it is *they* who wrote the Hebrew Bible. The Hebrew Bible, as one of my theological friends (I have a few) likes to say, is a "minority report." As we would put it today, the writers were "spin doctors." Thus the Bible is ancient "revisionist history," on a grand scale.

(4) That observation leads me to a final point, of critical importance in looking to the Hebrew Bible for a picture of Israelite religions. The Bible's portrait throughout is an "idealistic" one — not a picture of Israelite religion as it was at all, but a picture of what it *should* have been, and would have been if these zealots had actually been in charge. Ironically, the very condemnation of "folk religion" by the editors is what reveals many of the very characteristics that I shall document here. In trying to suppress popular cults, they inadvertently confirm their existence.

In sum, the degree to which the biblical texts can be taken as reliable historical evidence is crucial to our inquiry. The "historicity" of the Bible is perhaps the most hotly debated topic in biblical studies today, with "minimalists" and "maximalists" battling it out in the literature. Since I have dealt with this controversy at length in a recent book (Dever 2001), here I shall only state my own position briefly.

I reject absolutely the assertion of some "revisionists" that the Bible is not about history at all, and only *recently* has anyone ever wanted it to be. The first statement is mindless: it all depends upon what one *means* by "history." And the second is simply not true. Until the recent fad of creeping skepticism, most people, even more liberal biblical scholars, assumed that the Bible *was* history in some sense. On the other hand, the Hebrew Bible is obviously not history in the modern sense, that is, "disinterested," objective, balanced, academic history. In keeping with most mainstream biblical scholarship today, I shall often (although not always) regard the Hebrew Bible as "historicized fiction" — stories that are based on some genuine historical events, but always told in such a way as to advance the ideological agenda of the writers and editors. In the end, this is not "history," but "his story." The story is all about God — about religion in that sense — but embodying the writers' idiosyncratic *version* of Israelite religion. We have already seen, and will see again, why nearly all ancient and even modern commentators have bought into the Bible's propaganda. But, of course, we must remember that "propaganda" has its positive uses, too, and the best of it is based at least on some facts.

(5) That brings me to a final consideration of the Hebrew Bible as literature rather than history. Today the preoccupation of many biblical scholars is with the Bible as "literature," to the extent that *history* no longer matters much. It is not a question of whether the stories tell us anything about actual events in the past, but only about how these stories "function"; not what the stories say, but "how they are able to say what they say."

Since the stories are all myths anyway (i.e., fiction), their ancient and modern use must be to give them theological legitimacy. In approach to the Hebrew Bible, there are no privileged experts, no right interpretations, only whatever will "sell" to a particular community. Thus the emphasis of New Literary Criticism and the New Historicism advertises itself to the "margins," any anti-establishment constituency — the radical left; the world of grievance politics; doctrinaire feminism; psychological criticism; extreme third-world liberation theology; the Green movement; and, more recently, queer theory (see further Exum and Clines 1993; Hens-Piazza 2002). I regard much of this as "radical chic." Of *course,* the Bible is "literature" (what else?), especially didactic literature, and therefore it is more about the literary imagination of a few creative minds than it is about "real life." But I shall try to show that what makes this literature believable at all is that it does reflect *some* actual events. That's why the stories "work."

Non-biblical Texts

Until archaeology began to bring to light the long-lost world of the Bible in the mid-19th century, the Hebrew Bible was the only surviving body of literature from ancient Israel (that is, Israel of the Iron Age). It stood alone like a silent sentinel, witnessing to a fascinating but enigmatic past, with no comparative literature that would enable us to evaluate it in context. With the beginning and still continuing discovery of hundreds and hundreds of other documents, all that has changed. Today the non-biblical literature bulks larger than that of the canonical literature. And even though much of it is "secular," some of it sheds comparable light on ancient Israelite religions.

The available literary sources that are pertinent here include: (1) Egyptian texts; (2) the Canaanite texts from Ugarit on the Syrian coast; (3) the extensive Neo-Assyrian and Neo-Babylonian records; (4) a number of Aramaic and Moabite royal inscriptions; (5) a few fragments of Hebrew monumental inscriptions; (6) hundreds and hundreds of 8th-6th-century B.C. Hebrew ostraca (inscribed potsherds), inscribed objects, graffiti, and even a few intact tomb inscriptions; and (7) thousands of inscribed seals and seal impressions (see Davies 1991; McCarter 1996; Sass and Uehlinger 1993). When any of this vast written material reflects Israelite beliefs and practices, I shall bring it into the picture below. It may be especially revealing because it constitutes an *independent* witness, free of the biases we have noted above in the biblical texts (although it may contain other biases).

Archaeology as a "Primary Source"
for History and Religion

Apart from textual remains, material culture remains or non-epigraphic evidence brought to light by archaeology constitutes another major source for illuminating the history and religions of ancient Israel. That should be obvious, but it is not, for reasons that I shall explore presently.

Elsewhere I have published numerous studies of the nature, methods, objectives, and history of Syro-Palestinian or "biblical" archaeology (Bibliography). Here a few general statements must suffice. Archaeology has as many definitions as practitioners, but it could be regarded simply as what good archaeologists *do*. Or, as I prefer, "archaeology is the science of material culture" — a way of writing history from things. If that is true, then archaeology is obviously a *parallel* way of viewing the past, alongside texts. And its goal is the same: understanding the past on its own terms, as far as possible. That is precisely what I argue here — indeed, that archaeology can provide a *corrective* to texts and thus may constitute an equal or even superior source of information.

That is a bold claim, and it challenges the long-held assumption of biblical scholars that their *texts* are the "primary sources" (practically speaking, the only source). Let me therefore defend my view of archaeological data as primary sources, often indeed superior.

(1) Archaeological data are already more extensive than all the biblical texts put together, and they will be much more so in future. The canonical biblical text is static, a "closed book," frozen in time, to which there will be no more additions. But archaeology is dynamic, making revolutionary new discoveries daily, open-ended, theoretically almost limitless in its potential. I would argue that archaeology is our only source of genuine *new* information about ancient Israel. Endless reinterpretation of the same relatively few texts, however ingenious, tends to produce only more interpretations, not new facts. Of course, archaeological facts require interpretation, just as texts do; but the facts do multiply.

(2) Second, archaeological data are more varied in type than the kinds of data typically included in the biblical texts. Despite the many gen-

res of biblical literature, all the textual sources suffer from the deliberate selectivity noted above. But archaeological data are incredibly diverse, not "selected" by anybody or anything except the human and natural factors that govern their preservation ("formation processes of the archaeological record"). And the artifacts come not only from the sacred ideas and institutions that the Hebrew Bible focuses on almost exclusively and approves of, but from the whole range of "secular" activities of ordinary people in every conceivable everyday-life situation. The biblical texts were heavily edited right from the beginning, and they have undergone continual reinterpretation by Synagogue and Church for 2,000 years and more. But what we call "the archaeological record" has not been edited by anyone. The artifacts are, therefore, more "objective" than texts, at least until the modern interpretive process begins. Surely such an unbiased source provides a more comprehensive picture of what life was *really* like in ancient Israel than do the biblical texts. For several generations now, biblical scholars have sought what they call the *Sitz im Leben,* or "real-life setting" of texts. But in practice, this means only what I would call a *Sitz im Literature* — the literary context of the *texts.* Archaeology's goals in "reconstruction" are much more broadly cultural and truly historical.

(3) I have already discussed the relatively late date of the biblical texts in their present form, restricted to about the latter one-third of Israel's history and constituting contemporary "eye-witness" accounts only for that period. But archaeological artifacts, most short-lived, are by nature contemporary with all the periods that we are seeking to reconstruct. That holds true except for a few "curated items." Yet even these are found in contexts where they are reused, so whatever their original use they now reflect the secondary period of use. Biblicists are sometimes skeptical of archaeologists' relatively confident dating of artifacts, whole assemblages, and strata, which we usually date to a margin of error of no more than ±50 years. (Strata are layers in which archaeological materials are found in an excavation.) But mainstream archaeological scholarship rarely disagrees even that much, thanks to modern means of dating, including increasingly scientific methods such as Carbon 14 dating. Meanwhile, biblical scholars disagree over the dating of the major biblical texts by *centuries.* The "revisionists" go further; they opt for a Persian-Hellenistic date and thus dismiss all the texts as after-the-fact. We archaeologists can certainly fix the chronology and thus the context of our archaeological data much better than that.

(4) I have argued that the biblical texts, produced by a small circle of literati, are elitist. Yet the archaeological data, as suggested above, are "populist" by nature. They are very broadly representative of every class of society, every profession, and in particular women, who are marginalized in the texts. The texts reflect special interest groups; the artifacts reflect vernacular culture.

(5) The theological biases of the biblical texts and their "idealist" perspectives means that they reflect ancient editorial decisions, and they are therefore vulnerable to modern interpretative decisions. The "facts" in biblical studies always seem to be in dispute. But as Albright pointed out long ago, at the beginning of the "archaeological revolution," our finds constitute *realia*. They constitute tangible remains, facts on the ground that often produce an interpretive consensus. I could list hundreds and hundreds of such indisputable facts, unlike "the assured results of biblical scholarship" that change every generation. Artifacts do require interpretation, of course; pots don't come with a label attached. But it is possible to identify with certainty that a particular vessel *is* a cooking pot — a parallel "text to be read," as I shall show below in speaking of "objectivity."

(6) Finally, the Hebrew Bible, as we have seen, is largely "theocratic history," with all the problems that poses. Archaeology, on the other hand, produces a "secular history" of ancient Israel that I would argue is often more realistic, more comprehensive, better balanced, and ultimately more satisfying. It is certainly so for the understanding of folk religion.

Depreciating Archaeology: Who and Why

If archaeological data are so potentially powerful for illuminating the Israelite cult, why the neglect among biblical scholars that I have mentioned (Chapter II) in my critique of mainstream works? Much of the failure to take archaeological data seriously stems simply, I regret to say, from a lack of understanding about what archaeology is and does. Biblical scholars typically acknowledge that archaeology may provide some raw data. But they argue that the "subjectivity" of all interpretation prohibits us from gaining any useful information. It is claimed that excavations "rarely confirm or discredit discrete events" (Knoppers 1999:211). More specifically, Niditch's *Ancient Israelite Religion* asserts of archaeological information that it is "fragmentary and presents no real set of beliefs or world views, no real answers to complex questions about Israel's religious tradition" (1997:25). Smith's recent major work does not even mention archaeology (only some archaeologists) in surveying trends since 1990. He states of our difficulty in really understanding Israelite religion that archaeology requires interpretation and "can alleviate only some of the difficulty" (2002a:xxiii). Even conservative scholars, who have typically applauded archaeology for "proving the Bible," are often skeptical nowadays. Thus K. Lawson Younger declares that "Syro-Palestinian archaeology itself is infused with many subjective assumptions derived from various, and sometimes contradictory, philosophical perspectives (including in many instances assumptions based on the Bible itself)" (1999:201).

More significantly, a recent handbook, *Can a "History of Israel" Be Written?* (Grabbe 1997), contains essays by "revisionists" that are uniformly negative about archaeology as a source. Grabbe opines that "a great deal of interpretation of artifactual and other evidence has directly depended on information found in the biblical text" (1998:24). This is simply not true. Carroll caustically dismisses "the current obsession that archaeology can make good the defects of the Bible": "archaeology produces only a 'bogus history'" (1997:90, 93). Niehr declares of archaeological data that "compared to the written primary sources this evidence is a mute one so that deciphering these sources is still more open to misunderstanding than is the case with written sources" (1997:159).

The two best recent works on Israelite religion overall, those of Albertz (1994) and Miller (2000), do cite a commendable amount of archaeological data (above). But both are reluctant to make direct connections with religious belief and practices. That is, they do not see how to *make inferences about behavior,* which is just what archaeologists do all the time. Miller, for instance, repeats the canard of many others when he says of archaeology that "the interpretive task is as large or larger than it is for written remains." Again, "our judgment about the artifactual comes from what we know of the literature, both biblical and extrabiblical" (2000:xvi).

The biblical "revisionists," skeptical of anything and everything to the point of being nihilists, have an unusual take here. As "historians" who have rejected the Hebrew Bible altogether as a source, they would appear to fall back necessarily on archaeology as their only other possible source. Some, like Thompson, do invoke archaeology; but then they caricature it so that it is indeed useless, as in his *The Mythic Past: Biblical Archaeology and the Myth of Israel* (1999). Whitelam's *The Invention of Israel: The Si-*

lencing of Palestinian History (1996) goes even further in maligning archaeology and archaeologists. Lemche is less negative, but he, too, regards archaeological data as largely "mute" without written remains (1998:30). Davies' *In Search of "Ancient Israel"* (1992) simply ignores archaeology altogether as irrelevant. At least that is more honest.

Not surprisingly, recent works of the "Freibourg" art-historical school (above) utilize archaeology much more seriously, and expertly. An example is the iconographic treatment of Keel and Uehlinger, who have no hesitation in identifying archaeology as a "primary source," as supplying the "missing pieces of the puzzle" (1998:2, 5). That is precisely my position here as an archaeologist. Several of the essays in *Only One God?* (Becking and others 2001), although they are by biblicists and theologians, are just as explicit, especially the detailed survey by Vriezen, "Archaeological Traces of Cult in Ancient Israel" (2001:45-80). Hadley's work on Asherah likewise is dependent upon the archaeological as well as the textual data (although she, too, is primarily a biblical scholar). In addition, the sensitivity of the authors in *Only One God?* and of Hadley to the archaeological evidence for a cult of Asherah was anticipated at least implicitly in the writings of feminist scholars like Phyllis Bird and Carol Meyers (Chapter II), as well as in the work of other women scholars.

Finally, several other scholars who have dealt increasingly with folk religion have seen the potential of archaeology. One of the pioneers, van der Toorn, made only minimal use of such data in his first work (1994). But later he was much more positive about such data in emphasizing the limitations of "book religion" (1997; Chapter II above). On the other hand, Berlinerblau, one of the first scholars to address the topic of folk religion explicitly (although criticizing the terminology; above), looks hopefully to archaeological discoveries but thinks that they "will not be immediately, or abundantly, forthcoming" (1996:170). He advocates, rather, a "new approach" now. I agree with that, at least.

I have suggested that the obliviousness of most biblical scholars to archaeological data is due to their being uninformed. Yet that is hardly an excuse for "scholars." Some archaeologists read in *their* field. As for dialogue, I and other archaeologists have been drawing attention to the rich archaeological data for at least a generation now. In addition to several extensive recent handbooks (routinely ignored by the works criticized in Chapter II), there have been several periodic "state-of-the-art" surveys in recent years. For instance, I myself have written nearly a dozen of these in the last 20 years (especially 1985; 1992; 2000), plus many more articles specifically on the relation of archaeology to the study of Israelite religion. In fact, I was the first to argue for a "cult of Asherah" in ancient Israel (1984), based on the newer *archaeological* evidence. That was heresy 20 years ago, but now it is so taken for granted that most biblical scholars have forgotten where the idea originated.

Yet despite our publications in mainstream journals, symposia volumes, and standard biblical dictionaries and encyclopedias, biblical scholars rarely even cite *any* of this material. Most of the publications I discuss here cite only the publication of my Kh. el-Qôm inscription (below), none of my many theoretical, methodological, and programmatic essays. As for my repeated call for a *dialogue* between archaeology and biblical scholars (since 1973), virtually no biblical scholar has even mentioned such a desideratum. Halpern (1997) and Keel and Uehlinger (1998:4, 5) are rare exceptions.

Is the neglect of archaeology by biblicists as naïve, as innocent, as all this suggests? Perhaps not. First, in some instances, as among the "revisionists," we meet not merely with neglect, but with thinly-disguised hostility. Here I can only surmise that these ideologically-driven scholars know intuitively that it is *their* Israel that has been "invented," not ours. Perhaps a real, archaeological Israel and its witness to the vitality of religion would be inconvenient for their theories. As for a few textually oriented scholars, mainstream biblicists, I have the sense, fair or not, that they are on the defensive, defending a "turf" that they control against an unwelcome intruder. (What if archaeology really *were* a "primary source"?) Finally, for some of the hardcore theologians discussed above, their assumption is that religion is all about elegant intellectual formulations; don't bother them with the rather messy reality.

Setting the (Archaeological) Record Straight

To give the skeptics and hold-outs discussed here the benefit of the doubt, is there any validity to their "minimalist" view of archaeology? There is none whatsoever, for anyone who knows the *first* thing about archaeology today.

(1) In the first place, the portraits of archaeology by some biblicists are caricatures, especially those of the "revisionists." This is largely because

their target is an old-fashioned kind of prove-the-Bible "biblical archaeology" that was long ago discredited in *archaeological* circles. More than 30 years ago, for instance, I observed the death of traditional "biblical archaeology" and wrote its obituary (Dever 2000 and references there back to 1973, 1985). It is true that there followed a period of controversy, with fundamentalists and even a few mainstream biblical scholars protesting what they thought was the loss of the biblical connection. But professional archaeologists by and large agreed; and in the end, few mourned the passing of an amateur enterprise that had really been a branch of biblical studies, not of archaeology. For at least 20 years, "Syro-Palestinian" archaeology, as it is now commonly called, has been a separate, professional, secular discipline — freed at last to conduct a dialogue with biblical studies, no longer one of two monologues. The term "biblical archaeology" now designates only the dialogue *between* archaeology and biblical studies, documenting the "coming of age" of archaeology, and biblical scholars cannot be excused for being unaware of the evolution of what is still a related discipline.

It is this sort of ignorance that leads to diatribes like Thompson's in *The Mythic Past: Biblical Archaeology and the Myth of Israel* (1999). This book has nothing whatsoever to do with archaeology, at least as practiced by any archaeologist today. And Whitelam's *The Invention of Ancient Israel* (1996) is even more outrageous — a slanderous attack on Israeli archaeologists and their American colleagues as "Zionists." (Whitelam's ideological agenda is transparent, as shown in Dever 2001.) Fortunately, these two scholars who think themselves provocateurs are marginal figures.

(2) A common denominator of critics of archaeology is that artifacts, like texts, "require interpretation." That is obvious, and hardly news to any archaeologist I know. But critics overlook the fact that the "hermeneutical (or interpretive) process" for both classes of data is very similar, since as I have shown elsewhere both are "texts" to be read, with closely comparable methods (Chapter II and Dever 1997a).

(3) As for archaeology's being "mute," I have dealt with that ill-informed and absurd notion above. The silence of the archaeological record is deafening. Artifacts are at least as eloquent as the biblical texts; and their message is more varied, more reflective of "real life." The real issue is not what information is conveyed for history-writing, but what *kind* of history one wants. The Hebrew Bible writes mostly theocratic history, and biblical scholars resonating with that write mostly the history of *theology,*

or "political history," or occasionally narrative history. Yet there are many *other* kinds of history upon which one might focus. Here are only some of the above and other kinds of history:

(1) "Political history": largely the account of "Great Men" and their public deeds; it is usually chauvinistic, episodic, propagandistic. (2) "Narrative history": a running history of events, largely descriptive; presumed to be factual, but selective, and rarely explanatory. (3) "Socio-economic history": a history of society and social institutions, including their economic foundations; focuses on family, clan, social classes, "mode of production" (sometimes Marxist), the State. (4) "Intellectual history": the history of ideas, their context, their evolution, especially ideological and religious conceptions; this is primarily the history of texts, of the growth of literary traditions. (5) "Cultural history": a larger, contextual, all-embracing evolutionary social history; it focuses on settlement type and distribution, demography, subsistence, socio-economic structure; political organization, and finally on "ethnicity." (6) "Technological history": a history of human manipulation of and adaptation to the environment and the transformation of Nature through technological innovations; deals with the long-term "conditions of civilization." (7) "Natural history": a geographical history of the physical world, of the environment, of culture as ecological "adaptation"; Pliny's *Historia naturalis*. (8) "Material history": the study of artifacts as "correlates of behavior": a "history written from things."

It is clear that archaeologists *are* historians, simply students of human culture over long time spans, basing themselves mostly on material culture remains (although not excluding texts when they find them, since these are also artifacts). And while they cannot presume to write all the types of histories as outlined above, archaeologists are well suited to category 2; and they are uniquely equipped for categories 3, 5, 6, 7, and 8. Only in categories 1 and 4 — political and intellectual history — are archaeologists at a disadvantage vis-à-vis textual historians. If all these "kinds" of history-writing are essential, and they are, then biblical scholars *must* engage in dialogue with archaeologists in the future.

What Archaeology Can and Cannot Do

I have taken some pains here to point out the limitations of the biblical texts for writing the history of ancient Israel or illuminating its religions.

And I have presented a "positivist" portrait of archaeology and its potential that some (including many biblicists) will find unpersuasive. One critic has already characterized my view as "over-confidence" in the discipline of archaeology, a sort of "hard objectivism" (Younger 1999:201). But I have never argued that archaeology is "objective," only that the interpretation of its data is no more subjective than the interpretation of texts, or indeed than is characteristic of any other social science discipline. It has often been observed that archaeology is not a science but is more like an art-form. Still, I would argue that archaeology can be systematic, disciplined, explicit in its hypotheses and methods for testing them, and reasonably confident in judgments about "the balance of probability" — which is all that any other form of history-writing can claim.

The issue of "objectivity" is indeed pertinent to all our related historical disciplines, now more so than ever, largely because of the "revisionist" challenge. As with other postmodernists, the fundamental stance of biblical scholars of this school is "incredulity toward all metanarratives." Obviously the Hebrew Bible is the *great* metanarrative of the Western cultural tradition, the overarching "story" that gives that tradition its presumable superiority and universal meaning. That is precisely what the biblical "revisionists" reject. As with all claims to knowledge, any propositions about the history and religion of ancient Israel are merely "social constructs," that is, *fiction*. As many of their publications declare, ancient Israel is a myth; it has been "invented" by Jews and Christians as a tortuous exercise in self-identity.

The fundamental point here is the "revisionists'" assertion that in viewing the past no objectivity is *possible*. We, the subjects, are the ones who are doing the observing. So it is not the ancient facts (there are none) that determine our reconstructions, but our modern self-consciousness, our needs today, and particularly our *ideology*. Indeed, for the "revisionists," *all* readings of texts are about ideology — issues of race, gender, class, power, and ultimately politics. There is no "objective," real world out there to be known, no Truth, so we have only our perceptions, always flawed. We can never know "how it really was in the past," as former generations of scholars are said to have assumed (some actually did so).

I have reviewed the fallacies of postmodernist theories of knowledge and the fad of biblical "revisionism" elsewhere at length, with particular references to their misuse of archaeology (Dever 2001). A few remarks will suffice here. (1) First, "ideology" has become *the* issue in a frenetically skeptical age, almost to the exclusion of everything else. But why this should be so, and how the denial of traditional values and beliefs will usher in the utopia that postmodernists seem to envision, we are not told. It seems that there are no "facts" — except theirs.

(2) Contrary to the "revisionists," biblical criticism, of any school that I know, has never claimed to be "objective." The distinguished Oxford professor emeritus James Barr has pointed out that that is a caricature (2000:50-53). And not since the death of 19th-century "positivism" have *any* respectable historians been naïve enough to think that they could be entirely objective. All that good historians claim is that we must *attempt* to be objective overall, and that, as Barr says, some degree of objectivity is better than none at all.

(3) The term "ideology" is always used by the "revisionists" in a negative way — inevitable, but bad, ideally to be eliminated. That is because they typically define ideology in Marx's sense of "false consciousness," that is, people's perceptions of the world that are not based on reality, but on the *illusions* that they require to sustain themselves and to order and control society. But what *is* the "real world," if there are no facts to be known? And if everything is ideology, why is the ideology of the "revisionists" any better than ours or anybody else's?

(4) In any case, ideology is neither inevitable in its extreme manifestations — that is, "fanaticism" — nor is it always false. First, I concede that we all have an ideology, in the sense of a set of ideas with which we approach any phenomenon or experience; but that does not make most of us ideologues. The noted anthropologist Clifford Geertz has caricatured this view as saying in effect: "I have a social philosophy; you have a political opinion; he has an ideology" (quoted in Brettler 1995:194). Second, an ideology, if it is essentially a set of beliefs, is not necessarily false. Some beliefs are truer than others, that is, based on better facts. Others reflect, if not social realities, then at least the realities of the believer's own world. It all depends upon what one thinks the "real world" *is*.

The specific issue here is whether *archaeology*, as a historical discipline, can or should be objective, whether modern ideologies do not inevitably compromise its inquiries into the past. Unless we can answer this question, our look here at the ideology of ancient Israelites — their view of the world, their religious beliefs and practices — will be as illusory as theirs. (It is no coincidence that in rewriting the history of ancient Israel the "revisionists" rarely treat religion: they cannot.)

Whether or not archaeology can write history all depends upon what one *means* by "history," as I have argued above. One widespread definition is that of the Dutch historian Johan Huizinga: "History is the intellectual form in which a civilization renders account to itself of its past" (quoted in Brettler 1995:11). But this may imply, as above, that history is not about objective facts, only about our own subjective needs. I assume rather that history is about *both*, in proper balance Therefore, I do not deny the role of ideology, but I will regard it positively, in the sense of the French historian George Duby as

> A system (possessing its own logic and structure) of representations (images, myths, ideas or concepts) existing or playing a historical role within a given society (quoted in Brettler 1995:13).

If religion, even in its practical expression as cultic activity, is about ideology, then that is what we shall seek to understand here. Whether that ideology is "true," I leave to the reader, since mine is a descriptive task.

But ours is also a *historical* task, if the description of ancient religions is not to be mere fancy, what we may want it to be. That raises the question of method, as well as the sources which I have been outlining here, and the motivation (or ideology) of individual writers (below). The outcome of any history will be governed, and even determined in large part, by these variables, not just by the available "facts." The historiographical model that I as an archaeologist have long used is what might be called the "jurisprudence" model, influenced to some degree by the idealist British philosopher of history R. G. Collingwood (see his classic work *The Idea of History*, 1946). The essential working assumptions of this model for history-writing are these:

(1) The historian is best understood as first a detective, then a juror rendering a judgment.

(2) The basic task is that of evaluating all the evidence, direct and indirect.

(3) The jury consists of oneself and one's peers, that is, readers, who must be convinced.

(4) The trial entails interrogating the witnesses, texts and artifacts, the historian acting both as prosecuting and defending attorney.

(5) The judge is history itself, that is, posterity.

(6) The judgment cannot claim absolute truth, since that is known only to the one on trial, the "past."

(7) Justice therefore, a "right reading," consists of a judgment based largely on the "preponderance of the evidence," the result being a verdict sustainable "beyond a reasonable doubt."

Using the jurisprudence model, I think that even though we cannot re-create the past, we can arrive at an understanding of the past that is rational, and not ideologically driven; defensible, yet open to criticism (see further Brettler 1995:142-44).

I am insisting here that archaeology in particular deals with a *tangible, real world*. Yet readers may not be convinced by my arguments that the interpretation of archaeological artifacts is more "objective," and therefore often more trustworthy, than the interpretation of biblical and other texts. So let me propose a practical test for evaluating the "factuality" of our two sources for reconstructing the realities of everyday life in ancient Israel.

Let us reconstruct an imaginary text about an ancient Israelite cooking pot and its uses in the 8th century B.C. The owner or "author" might describe, for instance, (1) the cooking pot itself, what it looked like and how it was made; (2) how he or she had acquired it; (3) the food that was cooked in the pot and how it was prepared: (4) what the hearth was like and the time of cooking; (5) the way the meal was served and received. But would such a text really be a trustworthy, "objective" account? One might observe that the "author" may not have actually witnessed any of these purported events, but was simply producing an imaginative *literary* account. Or, even if basically factual, this story might not give us any indication of the writer's biases. Did he or she like this cuisine at all? Finally, this narrative may not be about "food" at all, but may be a metaphor for something else (like the biblical parables), such as "the nourishment of the soul." In short, this text, like many others, may not reflect an "objective reality," but rather a subjective perception. And the reading of this text may not be about facts as much as it is about *perceptions* and *interpretations* — ancient and modern. Thus, despite the confidence of many textual scholars in their hermeneutical principles, as opposed to the supposedly "subjective" interpretative principles acknowledged by archaeologists, there is no assurance that we have arrived at the objective "truth" of the matter.

Now for purposes of comparison, let us look at something real, something tangible rather than theoretical: an *actual* 8th-century B.C. cooking pot, another witness to "meaning." Questions of "subjective interpretation" aside, what if anything can we actually learn from this alternate witness to ancient cooking and eating? I would argue that in this case we can know with *near-scientific certainty* the following: This vessel is a "cooking pot"; it imitates an older prototype, one that we can easily illustrate; the clay is from local clay beds; the pot is wheel-made; it was fired at a certain temperature in the kiln; it was probably made by a woman in a village workshop (to judge from ethnography); it was used for certain specific foods; it comes either from Israel or Judah; and it dates to a very narrow time period. It is even possible to show what the cooking pot "means" within the context of its own economy and society, since it is what archaeologists call a "type-fossil." Such knowledge is not altogether scientific, but it *is* empirically based, not merely speculative. It conforms to the "jurisprudence" model of history-writing discussed above.

Above all, this case study shows that whatever role ideology may play in the production and interpretation of texts, it does not always play any significant role with artifacts and their analysis. Our cooking pot does not *have* any "ideology." The maker no doubt did have in mind what archaeologists call a "mental template," a commonly shared idea of what an 8th-century cooking pot ought to look like. But such a notion of cultural norms is hardly an idiosyncratic, oppressive "ideology." And this notion is in fact a *reality,* in that it depends not simply on "social constructs" but on actual earlier vessels or prototypes that we can prove were slavishly copied over long periods of time. That is called comparative ceramic typology — a major tool of modern archaeology — and it is much more "scientific" than the "typologies of ideas" typically employed by textual scholars. It deals with *realia,* the interpretation of which sometimes can be objective.

Here is another cautious observation on the interpretation of texts and artifacts. It is important to remember that a biblical text itself is a "story," already an *interpretation,* as virtually all scholars today agree. It is not an objective factual report of things exactly as they happened (if they happened at all). Therefore, any later interpretation — ancient or modern; Jewish, Christian or other — is an interpretation of an interpretation. The result suffers from a *double* subjective interpretative process. But our cooking pot is pristine when dug up, not a theoretical "interpretation" of anything, only the embodiment of a common conception of what really did exist after all: a standard repertoire of 8th-century B.C. cooking pots. Our understanding, once we dig up the cooking pot and begin to study it, does rest upon an interpretation. But this is first-hand, subject to *modern,* more quantifiable rules. We are not simply at the mercy of ancient interpretations, unable to penetrate behind them to some original reality that the writers presumably knew but disguised in their deliberate or unintentional ideological agenda.

Why Another History?

Dealing with the issues of ideology and objectivity raises another, related question, perhaps even more fundamental: that of motivation. Given all the pitfalls of investigating ancient Israelite religions, *why* would anyone bother? In other words, who writes such histories, and why? Few seem to have raised these questions, but I think that they are both interesting and instructive in our case.

The basic facts are clear and beyond dispute. (1) All "Old Testament theologies" over the past two centuries have by definition been written by male Christian Old Testament scholars, many of them ordained clergymen, and most of them seminary professors or members of university theology and religion faculties. There have been only a handful of Roman Catholic writers, all marginal, and, of course, no Jewish scholars at all. In fact, several prominent Jewish scholars have specifically disavowed *any* "biblical theology" and have sharply criticized the whole movement, such as Harvard's Jon Levenson in his article "Why Jews Are Not Interested in Biblical Theology" (1993). His points are the same as mine here: (1) this has been from the beginning a Christian apologetic enterprise; and (2) such approaches to the Hebrew Bible *(sic)* can be either "theological" or "historical," but they cannot be both, that is, *truly* historical. That position is typically Jewish, the lone dissenting voice being that of the Israeli scholar Moshe Goshen-Gottestein, who has suggested that a Jewish "Tanakh theology" might be possible ("Tanakh" is a common Jewish term for the Hebrew Bible).

(2) In the "history of religions" and sociological approaches, again most scholars have been at least nominally Christian; a few have been secularists. No full-scale Jewish history can be cited except the 1935-55 multivolume work in modern Hebrew by Yehezkel Kaufmann, abridged by Moshe Greenberg in a one-volume English version in 1960 as *The Religion*

of Israel. While "conservative," this is not an Orthodox treatment as many suppose. Kaufmann was not religious, avoided theological discussions, and accepted modern critical scholarship. He did, however, argue that ancient Israel was monotheistic from earliest times (below). Women are represented only by Susan Ackerman (1992) and Susan Niditch (1997; but see also the *Jewish Study Bible*, 2000-2005).

(3) In more recent writing on folk religion, I can find no Jewish scholars except Berlinerblau (1996), who is a secularist. But Raphael Patai's *The Hebrew Goddess* (1967/1990) was an astonishing early work (below).

(4) No archaeologist — Israeli, European, or American — has ever written on ancient Israelite religion. At best a few Israelis have published descriptive presentations of some of the discoveries that I shall treat in Chapter V. Israeli archaeologists, in particular, have an aversion to the subject of religion. They are virtually all secularists, who have had to fight the attempt of the Orthodox religious establishment in Israel to halt all archaeological activities. Raz Kletter's synthetic work on the female figurines (1996) is a notable exception. Women Israeli archaeologists are scarcely represented even at this elementary level (but see Ruth Hestrin 1987; 1991; below, Chapter VII). Only a few American Conservative and Reform Jewish archaeologists have shown any interest in our subject (among them Carol Meyers).

Are there any revealing "patterns" here? Any clue to ideological biases that could affect the outcome? I can only suggest a few possibilities. (1) One is that the overwhelmingly Christian and conservative interest in the history of such studies is likely due to the conviction that revelation and "biblical faith" — God's mighty acts in history, and their consequences — originate in ancient Israel's religious life, institutions, and Scriptures. Jews outside the Orthodox tradition are not bound by such assumptions. And secularists either don't care, or reject these assumptions completely.

(2) The striking lack of interest among archaeologists, who now control much of the basic data, as I argue, is harder to explain. I have noted reasons for the Israeli indifference above. But my generation of American Syro-Palestinian archaeologists nearly all came out of the "biblical archaeology" movement, that is, from biblical and even clerical backgrounds. I can only theorize that most archaeologists are still principally *technicians* — increasingly good at the basic tasks of excavating, recording, and publishing the raw data. But they are not trained as historians, much less as

philosophers of history; and they are rarely disposed to ask the "Big Questions." That is a pity.

So why am I attempting what will have to presume to be a pioneering work, however modest and preliminary? Because it is time. And because perhaps I seem to have a unique background and experience (Introduction). I can wear a clerical miter; a yarmulke; or no hat at all. So let us proceed to what I hope can be a relatively unbiased look at the evidence for folk religion.

CHAPTER IV

The Hebrew Bible: Religious Reality or Theological Ideal?

I have already stressed that there is a rather sharp dichotomy between what most of the writers and editors of the Hebrew Bible prescribe as the "religion of Israel" and what we can now describe as the reality of religious practices in many other circles. This is the crux of the contrast that I have posed between "Book religion" and "folk religion," the latter being what I shall try to characterize here largely on the basis of the archaeological remains. Thus in my view, the Hebrew Bible's portrait of the religions of Israel is problematic because it is so "idealistic" — that is, so narrowly *theological* in intent (even if not in the sense of modern, systematic "biblical theology"; Chapter II).

Yet in insisting upon the theoretical, largely impractical nature of the religious ideals in the Hebrew Bible, produced by urban elites, we must not dismiss the theological ideals altogether. After all, people, even uneducated and unsophisticated people in the countryside, *did* have religious ideas and beliefs. However vague and inarticulate these beliefs may have been, they informed their religious practices. And even if not derived from the biblical literature (mostly late), these popular, "unorthodox" beliefs were probably related in some way to the textual *tradition*. That would apply particularly to the long, older oral traditions that lay behind the literary tradition and indeed may go all the way back to Israel's origins at the beginning of the Iron Age (*ca.* 1200 B.C.). What, then, are the essentials of Israelite "Book religion," and also the fundamental building blocks upon which all later "biblical theologies" are constructed?

The literary process that formed the Hebrew Bible as we now have it stretches over many centuries, is exceedingly complex, and includes many diverse traditions (Chapter III). Yet there is a scholarly consensus that biblical literature includes the following motifs or theological propositions.

(1) The revelation of God ("El") to Abraham in Mesopotamia, his call for the ancestors to journey to Canaan in faith, and his promise to make their descendants a great multitude.

(2) The promise of the Land repeated to Patriarchs and Matriarchs by God (now named "Yahweh"), who has chosen Israel as his own exclusive people.

(3) Liberation from Egyptian bondage as a sign of Yahweh's power and grace.

(4) The giving of the Torah at Sinai and the peoples' covenant with Yahweh; obedience as "holiness" (ritual purity) and sacrifice.

(5) The conquest and inheritance of the Land of Canaan as the fulfillment of promise and the symbol of Israel's destiny among the nations.

(6) Jerusalem ("Zion") as the eternal abode of Yahweh, the seat of the Davidic line of kings on the throne, and the locus of the Levitical priestly authority.

(7) The primacy of faith in and loyalty to Yahweh alone, enshrined in the keeping of the "Torah" and the teachings of the prophets.

At the very least there is some reason for moderns, critical scholars or not, to regard these biblical propositions with some hesitancy. Several of them are unlikely to be grounded in actual historical facts (the conquest of all Canaan; exclusive monotheism from the beginning). Others are actually debatable on moral grounds (the annihilation of the Canaanite civilian population; God's "election" of Israel alone). And still other theological assertions rest entirely upon the ancients' assumption of direct, divine revelation (now known as the doctrine of "verbal inspiration") about which many people today have intellectual reservations (the call of Abraham; Yahweh's speaking in person to Moses; the miracles of the Exodus). Nevertheless, these themes do represent the biblical ideal of religion, so we must take them seriously (if perhaps not necessarily literally). Above all, we must deal *critically* with the biblical texts as a possible witness to religious realities, because not all of these texts are necessarily contemporary, nor are they of equal historical value. Let us look first at the overall biblical language.

PART I.
CULTIC TERMINOLOGY IN THE HEBREW BIBLE

The Hebrew Bible, not surprisingly, has hundreds of words that describe various aspects of the religious thought that pervades its discourse. Some of these terms may seem obscure to us, reflecting as they do the realities of ancient experiences, which are not ours and with which we find it hard to sympathize. Nevertheless, in view of the "phenomenological" and "functional" approaches outlined in Chapter I, let us look first at some biblical language and its apparent psychology (Part I); and then at the religious activities that are apparently being described (Part II).

Bāmôt, or "High Places"

The Hebrew Bible mentions "high places" used in cultic rites dozens of times, usually condemning them as reminiscent of pagan "Canaanite" practices and therefore forbidden. The usages of the Hebrew term *bāmāh* (pl. *bāmôt*), however, are far from uniform, and it is not even clear in some cases what the term actually means. The etymology of the Hebrew word is uncertain, but it can refer to "heights" *generally.* The word has few cognates elsewhere. But the evidence from some West Semitic dialects, presumably related to earlier Canaanite, suggests the meaning "back," as the back of an animal. The ancient biblical versions are vague, showing early confusion. The Greek translation of the Hebrew Bible, called the Septuagint, simply rendered the Hebrew term *bāmāh* as *bama;* and the Latin Vulgate has *excelsa,* "height." I suggest that further etymological analysis will not get us very far.

It is usage — particularly the effort to connect this term with actual archaeological examples — that will prove more illuminating. There have indeed been several such efforts at correlating the textual and artifactual evidence, but these are very technical and in most cases reach no solution (below). The fact that few *archaeologists* have been involved in these efforts suggests to me the need for another attempt.

A recent investigation, based on a Harvard dissertation, lays the proper foundations, Elizabeth LaRocca Pitts' *"Of Wood and Stone": The Significance of Israelite Cultic Items in the Bible and Its Early Interpreters* (2001). LaRocca-Pitts' main points concern (1) the differing use of the term *bāmāh* in the various strands of biblical literature discussed above (Chapter III: "J," "E," "Dtr," and the prophetic literature); (2) the fact that high places were not always connected with the use of cultic statuary such as "standing stones" (below); (3) that there is no simple evolution from "pagan Canaanite" to "orthodox Yahwist" high places; and (4) that in general the high places were acceptable, at least tolerated, before the construction of the Solomonic Temple, after which time their use in Israelite religion gradually declined (2001:127-159).

Despite the ambiguities of the translation of *bāmāh* as "high place," I shall use the term here for convenience, pointing out, however, that it is something of a misnomer. It does not always refer to a hilltop sanctuary, as in the biblical condemnation of illicit worship "on every high hill and under every green tree" (I Kings 14:23; cf. Isaiah 57:5; Hosea 4:13, etc.). I shall regard a high place here simply as a specific type of public cult-place, usually open-air, and typically prominently located.

Several biblical references support this general description. I Samuel 9:5-14 describes how Saul and his retainers approached a town looking for a "seer" and were directed toward a high place just inside the gate where sacrifices were being made, to which they "went up." II Kings 23:8 is more specific in describing how Josiah "broke down the high places of the gates that were at the entrance" of the city of Jerusalem. These appear to have been open-air shrines in large public plazas. But elsewhere high places may have been roofed, to judge from the report of Jeroboam's construction of "houses on high places" (I Kings 12:31). Hebrew *bêt bāmôt* here could conceivably mean "temple-high places," that is, high places *functioning* as a shrine or "temple." Elsewhere, many passages speak not of natural hilltops themselves serving as shrines, but rather of high places being "constructed" and "torn down," indicating that they were constructed.

Let me turn now to the use of the term *bāmāh/bāmôt* in larger cultural and religious context to see how they are "phenomena." First, *bāmôt* are connected in many texts with non-Yahwistic practices that are viewed as a continuation of earlier, "pagan" influence from Canaanite deities and rituals. In these passages the *bāmôt* are uniformly condemned, of course. Jeroboam, the northern kingdom's first king, is castigated for setting up "golden calves" at high places at Bethel in the south (an old cult center) and at Dan in the north, where incense was burned (I Kings 12:28-31; II Chronicles 11:15). Hoshea, the last king of the northern kingdom in Israel before its fall in 722/721 B.C., is blamed for the catastrophe because he "set up pillars and Asherahs on every high hill and under every green tree, and there burned incense on all the high places" (*bāmôt;* II Kings 17:10, 11). Associated with the abominable high places in this text are also idol-worship; Ba'al worship; the veneration of "all the host of heaven"; "divination and sorcery"; and even child sacrifice (II Kings 17:16-18).

The prophet Ezekiel in the early 6th century B.C. (6:3, 6) repeats the condemnation of high places and their altars (here specifically for incense) "upon every high hill, on all the mountain tops, under every green tree, and under every leafy oak" (cf. also Ezek. 16:16-22). One particularly famous high place is singled out, actually named "Bamah" (Ezek. 20:29-31). Ezekiel's contemporary Jeremiah also rails against the high places. He, too, specifies that the veneration of Canaanite deities there included child sacrifice. This was especially true of the high place called "Tophet" below the Temple Mount in Jerusalem, where they "burned their sons and daughters in the fire" (Jer. 7:31; cf. 19:5 ["the high places of Ba'al"]; 32:35).

In the late Judean monarchy (8th-7th century B.C.), the only two kings that the Deuteronomistic historians approved of were Hezekiah in the 8th century B.C. and Josiah in the late 7th century B.C. Both attempted to purge Israelite religion of "Canaanite" practices, partly under the influence of the prophetic "Yahweh-alone" movement (below). Among their specific targets were the high places and the "asherahs," the incense altars, and the other associated cult paraphernalia in the Temple (II Kings 18:3, 4; II Kings 23:4ff). I shall return to the detailed treatment the biblical writers give to the much-disputed "Josianic reform," because apart from its propagandistic nature and agenda, their very condemnation of "folk religion" inadvertently provides us with its best definition. Folk religion was, in fact, everything that Josiah and his reformist colleagues wanted to put a stop to.

Curiously, polemics against the high places among the idealistic reformers of the late monarchy are conspicuously absent in descriptions of religious life in the United Monarchy in the 10th century B.C. Saul visits a high place in a town in Judah to look for a "seer" at the local high place near the gate (above). The biblical writers relate this with no hint that such things were considered unorthodox then, despite their own opposition (I Samuel 9:5-14). Later Saul visits another apparently authorized high place at Bethel, on his way to being crowned king. There he is met by a band of prophets who differ in this case from the later, "classical" prophets by being ecstatics, put into a trance by musical instruments and dancing wildly (I Samuel 10:1-5). Again, there is no hint that any of this is irregular, or "non-Yahwistic."

Saul's successor David — a "man after God's own heart" — leaves Zadok the priest and his own men to visit the high place at Gibeon. There he offers animal sacrifices on the altar and appoints musicians for "sacred song." The writers even comment specifically that this was "according to all that is written in the law of the Lord which he commanded Israel" (I Chronicles 16:37-42). Even Solomon — builder of the Temple in Jerusalem — is described as going to the high place at Gibeon, along with the "whole assembly" of military and religious leaders of Israel, where the Ark of the Covenant was said to have been enshrined (as formerly at Shiloh; I Kings 3:3-15).

The acceptance of local high places and their legitimacy by the Deuteronomistic writers and editors of Joshua–Kings — the source of all the above texts (except Chronicles, which is dependent) — may seem surprising, given their single-minded agenda of centralizing *all* worship around the Temple in Jerusalem. But the explanation may be found in a rationalization that is tucked away in a parenthetical comment in I Kings 3:3. Here the writers observe realistically that "the people were sacrificing at the high places, however, because no house (Temple) had yet been built for the name of the Lord" (I Kings 3:2). This is an interesting little "footnote," because it shows that the writers and editors of the Hebrew Bible *did* possess earlier information, contrary to the assertion of the "revisionists." And rather than suppressing this information, they could incorporate it with some sophistication.

Family and Household Shrines

In ancient Israel there must also have existed household or private shrines, indeed in far greater numbers, especially before the building of the Jerusalem Temple. In combing the best sources for the period of the Judges (12th-11th centuries B.C.), I find many references to family cultic activities even though the texts are later. There are only a few actual *descriptions* of the expected locations, however — for instance, in houses or courtyards. Yet there are several passages that do refer to household shrines (the Hebrew would be *miqdāsh*, from a verb meaning to "set apart," "make holy," and thus "to consecrate").

We have in Judges 17:4-6 references to "graven and molten images" and "teraphim" (images) in a "shrine" (the Hebrew reads "a house of gods") in the house of one Micah, along with an "ephod" or priestly garment for one of his sons whom he has installed as a family priest.

The story of Gideon's call by Yahweh to deliver his people contains an even more detailed description of a family cult (6:11-33). While plowing in the field, Gideon meets and speaks with an angel of Yahweh sitting under "the Oak at Ophrah," probably an "*asherah*-tree" (below). As a token of his obedient response, he brings to the oak offerings of a roasted lamb and unleavened cakes, placing them on a rock or altar-like platform, where they are miraculously consumed by fire. Gideon then builds a large altar to consecrate this as a holy place, which is said still to stand at Ophrah "to this day" (that is, the writer's time). While this part of the story takes place in an open area, not in private, it nevertheless has to do clearly with the local family customs of a rural, agricultural community. Gideon is a farm boy — his humble origins are the point of the story. The rest of the account, however, concerns a house-cult. Gideon goes from the field to his father's house, where he dwells with his family. And later that night, he is instructed by Yahweh to "pull down the altar of Baʻal which your father has, and cut down the 'asherah' (or 'Asherah') that is beside it" (6:25). He is then to build a new altar and sacrifice a bull on it. Note here elements of the same combination of items that we have previously seen — a *miqdāsh* (although the term is not used here); an altar; and an "asherah," together with animal sacrifices.

Elsewhere in the book of Judges various religious activities are mentioned that almost certainly took place in rural areas and were largely observances typical of family cults. These include yearly festivals with feasting, dancing, and betrothals at Shiloh (21:16-24); animal and grain offerings presented upon an altar ("the rock to the Lord") by Manoah and his family (13:15-21), as well as vows made by Manoah (13:2-7); gifts of silver consecrated to Yahweh (17:1-4); and laments for the dead, as in the infamous case of Jephthah's daughter (11:34-40; or, on an alternate reading, the "death" of pre-pubescence).

Temples

I have noted the Deuteronomistic "school" above (Chapter III). For the writers and editors of the orthodox history of Israel in Joshua through

Kings (all the textual evidence we have), there was only *one* temple, that constructed by Solomon under divine edict in Jerusalem. That was the inflexible *ideal*, the way it was supposed to be. But was it the *reality*? And if so, what can we actually say about such a temple, the biblical descriptions of which sound so fantastic?

I have treated the Solomonic Temple elsewhere in depth (Dever 2001:144-157 and references there; add now Bloch-Smith 2002). Here let us look briefly at the biblical texts, mostly the detailed description of construction in I Kings 5–8. The main points concern the longitudinal shape and tripartite (three-room) plan of the building, with an inner sanctum at the rear; the construction of finely hewn masonry combined with carved and gilded wooden panels; and furnishings consisting of gold-overlaid wooden cherubs (or winged creatures) and bronze basins and brazier. The inner walls and the furniture featured several iconographic motifs: cherubs; palm trees; "open flowers" (lilies?); "chain work"; pomegranates; gourds; lions; and oxen.

The plan of the building, the chisel-dressed masonry, and the various decorative motifs are all clearly of Phoenician inspiration, as we now know. They confirm the biblical account that "Hiram, King of Tyre" supplied Solomon with materials, craftsmen, and artisans (I Kings 5:1-12; 7:13, 14). A number of 9th-8th century B.C. Phoenician-style temples are now known from modern-day Syria. Of particular significance is the well-preserved Aramaic temple of ʿAin Derʿa in northwestern Syria, which exhibits more than 50 almost exact parallels with the Jerusalem Temple as described in Kings.

The biblical "revisionists" (above) insist that this "fantastic" Temple never existed and that the description was made up by the biblical writers living in the Persian or Hellenistic era centuries later. But the rich comparative archaeological data we now have from near-contemporary sources make it absurd to suggest that Solomon's Temple was "invented." It still stood in the 7th century B.C. when the Deuteronomistic writers described it. And the elaborate details of their description could have come *only* from eyewitness sources. To be sure, some of the Hebrew words used in the biblical descriptions are rare, and textual scholars have had some difficulties in understanding them precisely. But to me as an archaeologist, these terms are all quite clear in the light of the many Iron Age parallels that we now have. This language is difficult only because these are *technical* terms for architecture and furniture, with which the biblical writers (and modern commentators) were largely unfamiliar (Dever 2001:145-153). But they were amazingly accurate in their description — even if they did paint the Temple, like Solomon, "larger than life." Once again, behind the obvious biblical propaganda (royalist here), we can discover some essential facts, especially with the help of archaeology.

Yet two aspects of the biblical propaganda and the ideal must be questioned. (1) *Was* the Jerusalem Temple the only such temple during the monarchy, as the Deuteronomistic writers imply? (Presently I shall describe at least one other full-fledged temple from the 8th-7th century B.C., at Arad.) (2) In addition, was the Jerusalem Temple — impressive as it was, and under royal patronage and priestly supervision — *really* the focus of national religious life? According to the biblical requirements, all males in Judah were to make three annual "pilgrimages" to Jerusalem to worship there. But it would be unrealistic to suppose that such a regulation ever was, or could be, entirely enforced. Many people in ancient Israel had probably never been to Jerusalem in their whole lives. And even if they did get there, they would not have been admitted to the Temple, the "house of the deity," largely a royal chapel.

It appears that *whatever* actually went on in the Jerusalem Temple and its precincts, the activities were conducted by and for a small priestly class, not even the majority of the small population resident in Jerusalem. For most people in ancient Israel, the Temple liturgy and the official Temple theology of the orthodox parties who wrote the Bible were unknown, and they would have been irrelevant in any case. Despite the fact that many today still resonate with "Book religion," it was not the *real* religion of ancient Israel, at least for the majority.

Cult Paraphernalia in the Hebrew Bible

In surveying sanctuaries, shrines, and temples generally, we have encountered a number of technical terms for the furnishings, or "paraphernalia," that are commonly found associated with them, singly or more frequently in combination with each other. Apart from the general observations on the nature of the structures themselves, these specific items should offer us vital clues to the religious functions that were carried on at each place, which is our larger concern here. So let us look at some of the things found in the "holy places."

(1) "Standing stones." The Hebrew term *maṣṣēbāh* (from a verb meaning "to take a stand") refers to a standing stone that was erected to serve various functions. It could be used as a boundary marker; as a victory stela; or, as we shall use the term here, as an item of cultic furnishing. As with the term *bāmāh*, etymology is not definitive, so I shall concentrate on textual usage, particularly on identifying possible archaeological examples (Chapter V).

The biblical references to *māṣṣēbôt* (the plural) in cultic usage nearly all suggest that the basic reference is to a stone erected to commemorate the appearance or presence of a deity (Genesis 28:18; a "theophany"). It is often connected with rites for making a covenant with the revealed deity. The covenants established with Yahweh by Jacob (Genesis 31:45), Moses (Exodus 24:4), and Joshua (Joshua 24:26, 27) are all illustrative. In addition, *māṣṣēbôt* usually appear as part of the furnishings of a typical high place (I Kings 14:23; II Kings 18:4; 23:13, 14), or even of a temple (as in Jerusalem: I Kings 16:32; II Kings 3:2), sometimes near an "idol" (Leviticus 26:1; Deuteronomy 7:5; 12:3; Micah 5:12).

Despite ambiguities once again, the term *māṣṣēbāh* does not denote an "idol" (there are other Hebrew terms for that), but rather a stone "stand-in" for a deity. It is perhaps not even a sort of aniconic or "non-anthropomorphic" symbol of the god himself (although it is a symbol). I shall use the term *māṣṣēbāh* here to refer to any sort of deliberately erected stone — large or small, occurring singly or in multiples — that symbolizes the *presence of a deity,* thought to be particularly visible and efficacious in this particular place.

(2) *Altars.* The generic Hebrew term for altar, *mizbēaḥ,* comes from a verb meaning to "slaughter," that is, to make an animal sacrifice. (There are, however, other types of sacrifices; more on them below). Thus the basic meaning of the biblical term is much less confusing than those discussed above, and the connection with actual artifacts is somewhat easier. But in order to make any such connections, we need to distinguish several different types of altars, first in the textual usage.

There are references to large outdoor altars constructed for general sacrifices, often burnt animals. These would include that built by Noah for offerings after the flood (Genesis 8:20); Abraham's altar erected upon his arrival at Shechem (Genesis 12:7), as well as others he set up at Bethel (Genesis 13:4) and Hebron (Genesis 13:18); and Moses' altar in the Sinai (Exodus 17:15). It seems significant that these simple "Canaanite"-style altars are associated principally with the early stories of the Patriarchs, and they were probably made simply of earth and unhewn stone, erected outdoors.

There are other large altars mentioned later in the monarchy that seem to be more structural and stylized, with four "horns" at the corners. These altars were no doubt fixed in place, either at outdoor shrines or in temples. Such altars were of stone, and some were large and heavy enough to have served as anchors in the Levitical "cities of refuge" and in the Jerusalem Temple. There people seeking sanctuary could throw themselves onto the horns of the altar and plead for mercy (Exodus 21:14; I Kings 2:29-34). There are also wooden horned altars mentioned in connection with the Tabernacle in the Wilderness (Exodus 30:1, 2; 37:25-28), apparently both for animal sacrifice and for burning incense.

Small portable four-horned altars are also attested archaeologically. These are now shown almost certainly to be for burning incense, as proven by both the biblical and the archaeological evidence (below). The Hebrew term *ḥammānîm* denoting them is rare and occurs principally in very late literature, such as P and Chronicles. And it is significant that all the references *condemn* incense burning as "foreign" (such as Leviticus 26:30; II Chronicles 14:4; 34:4, 7; cf., earlier, Ezekiel 6:4-6 and Isaiah 17:8, 27:9).

Finally, the existence of small portable altars can be inferred, also for burning incense. In II Kings 23:12 there is a reference to the use of a small altar on the roof of King Ahaz's palace. Confirmation of such usage has been found in a collapsed roof with an altar on it in the excavations at Ashkelon. From the postexilic period we have several such small limestone altars, often decorated with incised geometric patterns, one of which is inscribed showing that it was used for incense.

A clue to understanding the biblical altars, especially the larger ones, may lie in the fact that the biblical texts often locate them at the high places, as well as associating them with other cult paraphernalia such as the standing stones (above), the mysterious "asherah" (below); and sometimes with cult statuary (which I shall discuss below under figurines). Such a consistent *pattern* of related artifacts constitutes what archaeologists call an "assemblage," and this is much more culturally significant than an artifact occurring alone or at random. Thus I shall return to ask what these things "mean."

(3) *"Asherahs."* The Hebrew word *'ăshērāh*, occurring over forty times in the Hebrew Bible, has long suggested to scholars some connection

with the well-known Canaanite Mother Goddess Asherah. The etymology of the Hebrew word is unclear, but it may derive from a verb meaning "to tread, go straight." The 14th-13th-century B.C. Canaanite mythological texts from Ugarit on the coast of Syria portray Asherah there as "Lady Asherah of the Sea," her name meaning (according to come scholars) "She Who Treads/Subdues Sea." Her role in the cult is as the consort of El, the principal male deity of the pantheon, as "Mother of the Gods." Later I shall take up the vexed problem of identifying Asherah as a specific deity in the Hebrew Bible directly (Chapter VI), but first let us look more closely at the biblical usage of the term *'ăshērāh*.

Much of the time the term *'ăshērāh* apparently refers to a wooden pole, or even a living tree. According to the several verbs used, this object should be cut down, chopped into pieces, and destroyed, probably by being burned. Thus it is clear that the *'ăshērîm* were prohibited cult symbols associated with "Canaanite" religious practices. But symbols of *what,* or *whom?* The biblical writers do not specify in any passage. It is simply assumed (1) that readers know what these things are; and (2) that they are obviously non-Yahwistic and therefore to be condemned. But the point here is that in *all* cases, the original consonantal text can be read either "the asherah" (the symbol) or as "Asherah" (the proper name of the Goddess herself).

No one disputes the latter. It is *context,* or syntax, that governs the meaning. It is noteworthy that in at least a handful of cases, the term *'ăshērāh must* refer to the Goddess Asherah herself, not merely to a "symbol." Thus I Kings 15:13 describes "an abominable image made for Asherah"; one cannot make an "image" *for* an image (cf. also II Kings 21:7; 23:4). I Kings 18:19 mentions "the four hundred and fifty prophets of Baʿal and the four hundred prophets of Asherah." If "Baʿal" is a deity — as he certainly is, and well known in the Hebrew Bible — then so is "Asherah" (cf. II Kings 23:4). Judges 3:7 uses the plural form, *'ăshērôt,* but so does it for Baʿal — "the Baʿals." And again if "Baʿal" is a (pluriform) deity, so is "Asherah." Some scholars, puzzled by the plural here, have sought to emend (or change) the Hebrew text from *'ăshērôt* to *ʿashtarôt* (making the name related to the word for "shame"; cf. also Judges 2:13; 10:6; I Samuel 7:3, 4; 12:10).

I would argue that the apparent ambiguity of the biblical texts here and there, *as we now have them,* is due to the authors' and editors' ambivalencies, as well as those of the medieval Masoretic scribes who added the vowel points. Originally the biblical writers were embarrassed by the notion of a "Hebrew Goddess," but they could not condemn her and her cult without tacitly, but covertly, acknowledging her existence. Still, the less said the better! By the time the literary process had produced the final canonical texts, the old Mother Goddess had been driven underground and all but forgotten. Thus the final redactors of the Hebrew Bible *did not know* who "Asherah" had been, or whether she had existed at all. But the consonantal text — now Scripture — could not be altered. So the text we have implies that we are confronting in *'ăshērāh* only a "symbol." But again, a symbol of *what? of whom?* Functioning in what *religious circles?* And how did a "mere symbol" actually *work?* I believe that only archaeology, not the rather confused biblical texts, with their theological "squeamishness," can answer these questions (below).

The above may seem largely speculation. Nevertheless, the way the ancient versions of the Bible rendered the Hebrew *'ăshērîm* is revealing. The Greek Septuagint translation (dating from roughly the 2nd century B.C.), as well as the Latin Vulgate, were obviously much closer to the original, unvocalized Hebrew text than either the medieval Masoretes or we. And both understand *'ăshērîm* as "groves," that is, connected with *trees*. The Septuagint regularly translates *'ăshērāh* with Greek *alsos,* "sacred grove; hallowed precinct." There are a few exceptions; two where *dendron,* "tree," is used; and one where we have the goddess Astarte. (And the Septuagint also translates *bāmāh,* "high place," with *'alsos,* so they saw both connected with trees.) The Latin Vulgate follows the Septuagint: *locus,* "sacred grove" (36 times); *nemus,* "forest" (3 times); and Ashtaroth (once). The ancient versions are followed by the King James Version, which usually translates *'ăshērîm* as "groves," keeping in mind the association of high places and asherahs with "every high hill and green tree." Other ancient Jewish versions, such as the Mishnah (5th-6th centuries A.D.), understood the *'ăshērîm* as connected with trees.

Thus it seems clear that originally in ancient Israel there was a Goddess named "Asherah," who was associated with living trees and hilltop forest sanctuaries, and who could sometimes be symbolized by a wooden pole or an image of a tree. This tradition concerning a goddess became anathema in time, however, and was perpetuated only in veiled references in the Hebrew Bible, in later Jewish tradition, amd in Jewish and Christian versions of the Hebrew Bible. I have called her "Asherah Abscondita." But she would come back to life in modern times, resuscitated by archaeology (Chapter VI).

PART II.
CULTIC ACTIVITIES IN THE HEBREW BIBLE

My stated focus in this work is on "the practice of religion," that is, on the cult, based on material culture remains. We have surveyed the theoretical religious beliefs (or "theology") in the Hebrew Bible. But let us look now at the biblical *ideal* of religious practices, before seeking that reality in archaeology.

The Sacrificial System

The major cultic or liturgical activities prescribed in the Hebrew Bible under the general rubric of "worship" include first of all sacrifice. The "psychology of sacrifice" may seem complex, and it is in the literary tradition. In essence, however, a sacrifice is simply a *gift* presented to the gods. This gift is presumed to be relatively costly, and thus a proper tribute; a symbol appropriate to the wish or intent implied; and, hopefully, efficacious. This deeply rooted, universal human instinct to present offerings to the gods long preceded the Israelites in Canaan and in the West Semitic world generally and is attested in some of our oldest written records. And, as we shall see, there was little that was innovative in the biblical sacrificial system, except, of course, its eventual focus on a single deity.

The Hebrew Bible recognizes several acceptable forms of sacrifice. Here I shall only summarize briefly, referring the reader to some standard work for details (such as Albertz 1994; Miller 2000; and especially deVaux 1962).

(1) The first is the "burnt offering" (from the Hebrew verb *ʿōlâ*, "to go up"), or "holocaust." In this offering, one of the "kosher" or permitted animals — sheep, goats, cattle, and birds — was slaughtered. Its blood was thrown around the altar, then the carcass was dismembered and all or parts of it burned on the altar, the rising smell said to be "a pleasing odor to the Lord." Priestly supervision of the entire ritual is usually presupposed (but probably was not always involved). The blood was not to be consumed, for the Levitical principle was that "the life is in the blood," and all life is God's.

(2) A second type of sanctioned offering was the "cereal" or grain offering *(minhâ)*. Here wheat or barley, as well as flour, was usually mixed

with olive oil, together with an aromatic substance such as frankincense, and burned upon the altar. But leaven or yeast was strictly forbidden, as well as honey; the latter could, however, be offered separately as gifts of "first fruits."

(3) Another type of sacrifice was the *shelem* offering. The translation of the term is much debated, but it seems to be related to *shālôm*, "wholeness, well-being" (eventually "peace"). It denotes in all likelihood an offering that, perhaps in combination with other types of sacrifices, was designed to enhance general health, prosperity, and good fortune. Both priests and ordinary folk could consume the meat from these offerings. They could be presented either publicly or privately, intermittently or at regular festivals and celebratory occasions.

(4) There were also "purification" offerings (*ḥaṭṭā't*) that were intended to atone for specific sins, especially sins that made one "impure" and thus unable to appear in the sanctuary or Temple. The subject of "ritual purity" is too complex to go into here (there is a vast literature). But the essential idea, so foreign to most of us, was that not only did sinful acts, deliberate or unintentional, constitute an "impurity," an offense to the deity, but so also did certain bodily conditions. Among these were menstruation, nocturnal emissions, and coming into contact with the discharges accompanying childbirth or with a corpse. Eventually, the rites of purification and forgiveness of sins became enshrined in the rituals of the Day of Atonement (below).

(5) "Reparation" offerings (*'āshām*) were sacrifices to make restitution to someone wronged by presenting a symbolic gift to God. The harmed individual could also be "compensated" with gifts of money or other items.

(6) Other miscellaneous offerings included tithes; "freewill" offerings; "first fruits" of the harvest; thanksgiving offerings; votive gifts; and the like. It is even possible that child sacrifice was practiced on occasion in ancient Israel (below).

Some Caveats Regarding Sacrifice

All these sacrifices are outlined in detail (more than one wishes to know), principally in the very programmatic scheme presented in Leviticus 1–17. These texts, however, are regarded by most scholars as exilic and postexilic, that is, dating from after the fall of Jerusalem in 586 B.C. If so, then they may have arisen largely out of what I call "nostalgia for a biblical past that never was." That is, they would be not only highly artificial for *any* situation during the settlement horizon and the monarchy, but little more than priestly propaganda. On the other hand, some scholars hold that although the literary form and the rigid legislation are late (Leviticus stems from the "P" or priestly school; Chapter III), the *contents* may be earlier and may reflect customs dating from Israel's origins in the Sinai (if those are historical).

We shall see presently whether archaeology can help to resolve the question of how "real" the sacrificial system was, and how early it may have been in operation, if at all. Meanwhile, it should be recalled that despite the presumed legitimacy and centrality of the Levitical and Deuteronomistic sacrificial system during the monarchy, the prophetic movement could vigorously oppose sacrifice. Thus Amos, speaking for Yahweh, thunders:

> I hate, I despise your feasts,
>> and I take no delight in your
>> solemn assemblies.
> Even though you offer me your burnt
>> Offerings and cereal offerings,
> I will not accept them,
>> And the peace offerings of your fatted beasts I will not look upon.
> Take away from me the noise of your songs:
>> To the melody of your harps I will not listen.   (Amos 5:21-23)

Yet the prophetic protest may be best understood in context as *hyperbole* — a rejection not so much of the sacrificial system *per se* as of the self-righteousness and hypocrisy that dependence upon it could produce. Above all, sacrifice — the ritual appeasement of Yahweh — was no substitute for genuine piety, which entailed charity toward others. As the passage in Amos declares in the very next sentence:

> But let justice roll down like waters,
>> And righteousness like an everflowing stream.   (Amos 5:24)

Prayers and Vows

Another basic aspect of worship and piety in ancient Israelite religions would have been prayers, vows, and other ways of addressing and responding to Yahweh, less "symbolic" and more directly verbal. Yet the two would certainly have overlapped, since it was inevitable that words — various liturgical formulae — would have accompanied acts of sacrifice in the cult. The Hebrew Bible, in fact, contains many such explicit formulaic prayers, such as blessings and curses; sayings for the offering of "first fruits"; and so forth. These and other prayers could be offered publicly or privately; individually or collectively; spoken or sung. The classical collection of Israelite prayers is, of course, the Book of Psalms. But there must have been hundreds of other popular prayers and songs of praise that have not survived. Certainly the collection that we happen to have is rich, varied, deeply moving, and rightly beloved as a testament to religious faith by the ancients and moderns alike. There are, however, several limitations to the use of this literature here.

First, although many of the Psalms are attributed to early figures like David or Solomon, that attribution is almost certainly fictional. The fact is that many of the Psalms in their present form are relatively late and may reflect mostly the religion of the late monarchy. That does not deny the many, sometimes astonishingly close comparisons of vocabulary, style, and thematic material between the biblical Psalms and the 14th-13th-century Canaanite mythological poems from Ugarit in north Syria (Coogan 1978). The tradition of prayers and songs is obviously as old as religion itself. But the *literary* tradition tends to be elitist.

Second, the Psalms are literary works of the highest order, and it is hard to believe that many of them were even known to ordinary folk, much less regularly recited by them. These may have been largely prayers for the Jerusalem Temple and festivals connected with it. The pious impulses of the Psalms, however, were probably widespread even quite early, and they could go back to very old oral traditions of public and private worship. But we cannot be more specific than that about the "real life" settings or usage of the Psalms.

Finally, however great a role prayer may have played in liturgical rites, it is invisible in the archaeological record with rare exceptions (but see Chapter VI on figurines as "prayers in clay"). As for vows, those have been treated by Berlinerblau, whose work I have discussed above. If vows entailed carrying out extreme acts, the impact of these, too, would be difficult to detect in material culture remains (but see below).

Festivals

The calendar in ancient Israel was, in effect, a liturgical calendar. It was based, however, on the annual cycle of nature, the principal agriculture seasons of which were already fixed in Canaanite culture. But they were borrowed and by now identified with specific events in Israel's own peculiar history. The seasonal feasts thus became celebrations not of Nature's cycles, but of "God's mighty acts in history," *Israel's* history.

The scheme of major festivals in the Hebrew Bible (apart from the Sabbath) is as follows, although some are late historically. (For the Canaanite background, see Chapter VIII.)

(1) *Rosh ha-shanah* ("head of the year"). This feast should come in early fall to coincide with the onset of the annual rainy season and the early planting of winter wheat. Since Israel had adopted a lunar calendar, New Year's could fall as early as September or as late as October. The fact is, however, that while such feasts were common everywhere in the ancient Near East, "New Year's" is not specifically mentioned by this name anywhere in the biblical texts. *Rosh ha-shanah* thus may have been introduced only in postexilic times, becoming popular in later Judaism. Nevertheless, farmers would always have marked this season in some ritual way.

(2) *Sukkôt*. Almost contemporary with the New Year in the fall, whether specifically celebrated or not in ancient Israel, was *Sukkôt* ("booths," or "Tabernacles" in later Latin translations). It coincided with the fall harvest season, when grapes, melons, many fruits, and freshly-pressed olive oil made for a bountiful and joyous feast indeed. Thus it was sometimes called simply "Ingathering." (Our modern American equivalent, of course, would be Thanksgiving.) During this harvest season whole families (or even clans) of farmers and villagers would camp out in tents or huts in the fields, in order to guard and harvest the crops more efficiently. The formal celebration lasted for seven days and included music, dancing, and apparently a bit of good-natured drunkenness (cf. Eli's suspicion that Hannah was tipsy in I Samuel 1:14, 15). It was also a time when large families and clans got together, and young people were encouraged to wander off by themselves and perhaps indulge passions that might lead to

betrothal (Judges 21:19-21). The feast may originally have been the most important of all — "the Feast of Yahweh" — and it was supposed to be one of the two or three times when pilgrimages were made to the central sanctuary in Jerusalem. Yet its very nature as a universal harvest festival suggests that *Sukkôt* would have been widely observed in the rural areas, accompanied by rites typical of folk religion — perhaps with less formal theological justification, but with considerable spirit (or spirits). In the literary tradition, however, *Sukkôt,* originally an old Canaanite fall harvest festival, became associated with the dwelling of the Israelites in Sinai in temporary "huts." Thus it was construed as a celebration of the giving of the Law. In later Jewish tradition, *Simḥat Torah,* "Joy of the Torah," was coupled with *Sukkôt* and celebrated at its end.

(3) *Pesach.* This feast probably originated in the old Canaanite spring pastoral feast that featured the sacrifice of young lambs. In Israel, *Pesach* (etymology possibly "protect") was combined with an old "feast of unleavened bread," then "historicized" by connecting it with traditions of the Passover in Egypt, when the angel of death spared Israel's firstborn because of the lamb's blood smeared on the doorways. It was to be celebrated at the full moon on the tenth day of the first month in spring (Abib). The principal rituals involved feasting on the symbol-laden lamb; remembering Israel's hardships in the wilderness by eating unleavened bread and bitter herbs; and renewing family and covenantal obligations. Passover was (and still is) primarily a family event, in which the whole extended familial group gathers around the Seder table, and even children participate. Some such festival must surely have been a vital part of folk religion in the rural areas. The Deuteronomistic histories late in the monarchy made Passover an annual pilgrimage festival, for which all males were supposed to come to the central sanctuary in Jerusalem, in keeping with their Temple theology (above). But as I have said, this was the ideal, not the reality for most people.

(4) *Shāvuʿôt. Shāvʿuôt* ("sevens") follows Passover after seven weeks of seven days, plus one. It was a late spring–early summer festival, falling at the time of the all-important wheat and barley harvest. Like several other Israelite festivals, it had its origins in the old Canaanite agricultural calendar. This festival did not have an obvious connection to "salvation-history," as Passover had. But, like that festival it, too, came to be associated with renewal of the covenant because of the "renewal" of the grain harvest. *Shāvuʿôt* may be of secondary importance in the literary tradition, al-

though it became one of the three "pilgrimage feasts." But in a predominantly agricultural economy and society, it would have played a much larger role, and a spring harvest festival would likely have been accompanied by the typical rites of folk religion.

(5) *Yom Kippur.* The "Day of Atonement" (from a verb meaning "to cover") may have originated relatively late in the monarchy, or even in the exile. But in Jewish traditions it came to rank with Passover as one of the preeminent festivals (not really a "feast," since it mandated fasting). It was finally fixed in the fall, shortly before the New Year and came to be a time of reflection and repentance — of "New Year's resolutions," as it were. Whether this festival, more "theological" than "practical," played any role in ancient Israel is doubtful.

(6) *Other feasts and festivals.* There are references in the Hebrew Bible to celebrations of the New Moon. This is not surprising, given ancient Israel's lunar calendar, as well as the importance of the cycle of the moon for farmers. But these celebrations do not seem to have been formalized or historicized, much less connected with the Temple. Some scholars, especially those of the "myth and ritual school" (Chapter II), have sought to reconstruct an annual "enthronement festival" in which Yahweh was enthroned in his Temple, and the king as his divine representative was once again legitimated. There may be hints of this in some of the Psalms (Psalms 47, 68, 93, 96–99, etc.), but all this is very speculative. "Divine kingship," common elsewhere in the ancient Near East, was a notion foreign to most of Israel's thinking. *Yahweh* was "king," and perhaps he was re-enthroned. Finally, there are several Jewish feasts that began only much later, such as Hanukkah, the "Festival of Lights," connected with the purification of the Second Temple during the Maccabean wars in the second century B.C.; and Purim, to commemorate the supposed victory of Esther and Haman over the Persian king Ahasuerus. These festivals, however, have nothing to do with ancient Israel, and they are in fact based mostly on legends.

CHAPTER V

Archaeological Evidence for
Folk Religions in Ancient Israel

For reasons that I have discussed thus far, it is difficult even for theology to "systematize" religion, particularly folk religion. This form of religious life was based not on the organization of theoretical principles, but rather on that most unorganized of all phenomena: human experience. Nevertheless, in order to present in a systematic way the archaeological evidence that we now have for folk religion, I shall try to group various types of data according to aspects of religious belief and practice that most analysts would recognize.

At the outset, I stress that these categories are certainly not arranged in an order from greater to lesser importance (perhaps on the contrary), but proceed more from public to private observances. Also, since I am going to organize the evidence topically, I shall sometimes lump together things all the way from early to late in Israelite history (12th-7th century B.C.). That is defensible largely because folk religion is fundamentally conservative and changes only slowly over time. In Chapter VIII, however, I will come back to chronology, which after all is basic to archaeology. There I will try to re-arrange the data so as to show something of the evolution of both "Book religion" and folk religion.

The locus of religious life is any place deemed "holy" because it is thought to be where the gods dwell in a uniquely accessible way, and therefore it is set apart or "consecrated." For purposes of analysis, one might distinguish between small, local shrines; open-air "cult places"; larger communal sanctuaries; and monumental temples (above). But such distinctions are somewhat artificial. What matters is the sense of the *divine presence* in any of these places. And in any case, we do not happen to have equivalent archaeological data for all these types of sacred installations.

Local Shrines and Family Religion

By a "shrine" I mean a local holy place that served either a nuclear family, or at most a small group of related families. We now have archaeological evidence of at least a dozen of these places, ranging in date from the 12th to the 7th centuries B.C. I will survey a few of these in order to give some idea of their common features, then proceed to speculate what went on at such places. Finally, we shall see if the biblical texts treated in Chapter IV, although mostly later, reflect any of the beliefs and practices of such shrines and folk religion. Here chronology may be significant.

Major cultic sites in ancient Israel, *ca.* 12th-6th centuries B.C.

Cult "Room 65" at
ʿAi; 12th cent. B.C.
Zevit 2001, Fig. 3.14

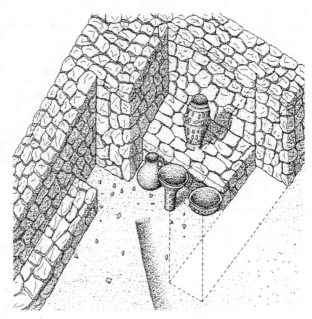

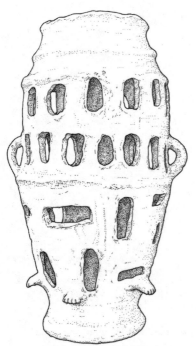

Fenestrated offering stand
from ʿAi cult room
adapted from Israel Antiquities Authority
by Valerie Woelfel

112

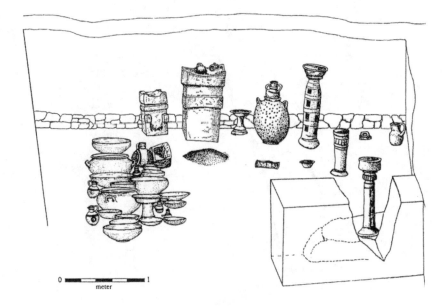

"Cult Corner 2081" of Str. VA/IVB at Megiddo; 10th cent. B.C.
Zevit 2001, Fig. 3.55

(1) The earliest household shrine known is a two-room installation in a 12th-century B.C. domestic complex at the tiny village of Tell el-Wawiyat in lower Galilee in the Netofah valley near Nazareth. Among the "exotic" contents that are usually taken to denote cultic activities, there were a low column base; an ornamental basalt stone tripod bowl; a mold for making jewelry and bits of gold; and a broken female figurine (Nakhai 2001:173). It may well be, however, that Wawiyat (identification unknown) was still a predominantly "Canaanite" village at the very beginning of the Iron Age, as many Galilean sites were (Dever 2003:208-211).

(2) In the 12th-11th century B.C., the small hilltop village of ʿAi northeast of Jerusalem was certainly Israelite. Here there was found a unique large room, "Room 65," with low benches around the walls. The contents included specialized ceramic vessels, some of which would fit on the top of a cult stand; a cylindrical stand with open "windows" around the column and an enigmatic row of human feet around the bottom; two animal figurines; and bits of jewelry.

113

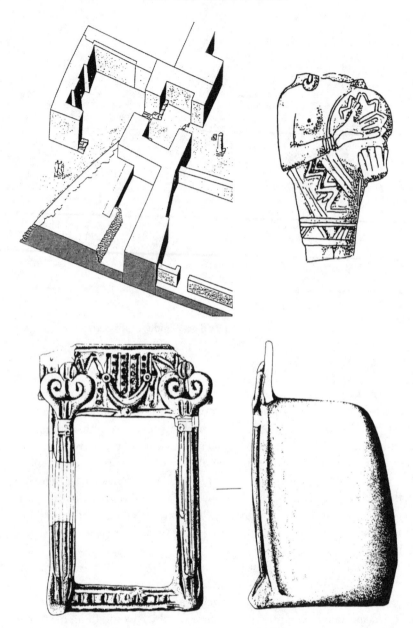

Above left, plan of gate shrine at Tell el-Farʻah; 10th cent. B.C.;
above right, terra-cotta female figurine; *below*, *Naos*, or model shrine
Chambon 1984, Pl. 66

114

(3) Nearby and contemporary, Kh. Raddana (possibly biblical "Beeroth") also had 12th-11th century B.C. household shrines in two building complexes. Noteworthy are low "altar"-like stone platforms, and especially a unique, large multi-handled bowl with bullhead spouts, probably for libation offerings.

(4) In the 10th century B.C., the age of the United Monarchy, these "Canaanite" style shrines continued in use, even though according to the later texts of the Hebrew Bible all worship was to have been centralized in Jerusalem under priestly authority. The "cult corners" of two Str. VA-IVB buildings at Megiddo, along the southern reaches of the Jezreel Valley, are especially well preserved. "Shrine 2048" was in the entrance hall of a large, well-constructed building. A doorway led into an adjoining chamber, flanked by two standing stones (*māṣṣēbôt;* above). A four-horned altar had once stood in this room. Objects from the main room included two other horned altars; a stone offering table, stand, tripod mortar and pestles; ceramic offering stands, juglets and other vessels; quantities of burned grain; and a bowl containing sheep and goat astragali (knucklebones). Another installation, "Shrine 228," contained an offering basin, table, and bench; several standing stones; stone mortars and pestles; horned altars; a terra cotta model; and a possible male figurine. This shrine appears to have been deliberately put out of use.

(5) Tel Reḥov in the northern Jordan Valley, biblical "Rehov," has an initial 10th-century B.C. Israelite level (Str. V). From this period comes a small shrine adjacent to a large courtyard in the lower city. Associated with the shrine were a stone altar on a mudbrick platform, flanked by four rough standing stones and a stone-supported "offering table." Near the platform there were found a square, fenestrated cult stand; several chalices; animal and female figurines; several seals, and the head of a bronze bull. The nearby courtyard produced evidence for the preparation of "sacred meals," including a large quantity of wild goat bones (Mazar 1999; Mazar and Camp 2000).

(6) To the west, in the Jezreel Valley, the small 10th-century B.C. Israelite village of Tel ʿAmal (Str. III) yielded evidence of another local shrine. A three-room building with a long history yielded votive vessels; a ceramic offering stand; stone stands; and a female figurine (Levy and Edelstein 1972).

(7) Tell el-Farʿah north, probably biblical Tirzah, in the northern Samaria hills, probably had another 10th-century B.C. level shrine (Str. VIIb),

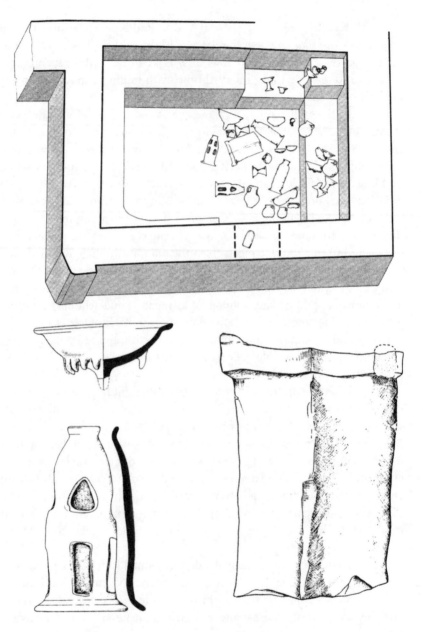

Top, "Cult Room 49" at Lachish, 10th cent. B.C.;
below left, fenestrated offering stands; *below right*, four-horned altar
Aharoni 1975, Fig. 6; Pl. 43

although the evidence was found scattered. The finds included a *naos*, or terra-cotta model temple, and several female figurines.

(8) The northern Israelite capital of Samaria has mostly royal constructions, all on the acropolis. But "Locus E 207," a rubble-filled trench, produced quantities of cultic objects and pottery similar to those from Cave I in Jerusalem (below), indicating that nearby there had been a small 8th-century B.C. cult center at one time. Some scholars have suggested that this may have been where "feasts for the dead" (the *marzēaḥ*; below) were held; but if so we do not know whether these were private or public rituals, since the material was not found *in situ*.

(9) At the Judean fortress of Lachish, excavators found "Cult Room 49" in Str. V of the 10th century B.C. This was a small room with low benches around the walls. In the room were small, stylized four-horned altars; several terra cotta offering stands; and various types of cultic vessels.

(10) Tell Beit Mirsim, possibly biblical "Kiriath-sepher," exhibits a cave similar to that of Samaria (above), and this may also have been used for cultic meals (Holladay 1987:274, 275).

To judge from these small shrines and their cultic paraphernalia, what kinds of "holy places" were they? What rituals were being carried out there, and what sorts of religious beliefs are reflected? Few commentators are even willing to speculate (but see Holladay 1987). First, I suggest that all the above are *family shrines*, serving either a single nuclear family, or, more likely, a larger extended family compound (Chapter I). These shrines were for private worship, in which there were no regular fixed services, no priestly supervision, no prescribed theology, no need to conform. Various members of the family probably stopped briefly at these convenient shrines daily, singly or in groups, on an *ad hoc* basis as they felt the need. And here women played a significant role.

What did people do there, and why? The consistent pattern of artifacts at these shrines (above) is certainly suggestive. The repertoire includes various combinations of the following items, some shrines having a few, others many or all.

(1) Standing stones
(2) Altars, some "horned"
(3) Stone tables and basins
(4) Offering stands
(5) Benches

 (6) Jewelry
 (7) Ceramic vessels, many "exotic"
 (8) Animal bones and food remains
 (9) Astragali (knucklebones)
(10) Terra cotta female figurines

In the light of all that we have said thus far about folk religion, it requires no great feat of imagination to see what is going on here. And some of it even fits the ideal of the more "orthodox" biblical texts (as summarized in Chapter IV).

(1) Standing stones in the family shrines are obviously the biblical *māṣṣēbôt* discussed above. There I showed that the primary function of these stelae, according to the biblical texts, was to commemorate the appearance and the continuing presence of a deity. We might expect those stelae — often impressive monumental stones standing as much as ten feet high — to appear only in public shrines and temples, as indeed they do. But in family shrines and high places (below) we often encounter them as well. Here they are simply smaller versions, but no less potent for their diminutive size. The gods are not diminished in power; their symbols are only scaled down appropriately, perhaps now being more "intimate."

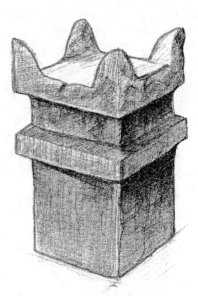

**Four-horned altar from
Megiddo; 10th cent. B.C.**
Vriezen 2001, Fig. 10

As I noted above, the standing stones, reminiscent of the old Canaanite cults, are finally prohibited by the 7th-century B.C. reform movements. But they had always been in use in folk religion, and they continued to be. For many, Yahweh (and perhaps other deities) did not live only in his house (*bēt*, "temple") in Jerusalem, but was present and cultically available everywhere. *Nothing* was more fundamental to family rites of worship than a visible, palpable symbol of the divine presence.

(2) The larger fixed-stone or mudbrick altars (biblical *mizbēḥôt*) must have been for animal sacrifices and other food-offerings — giving back to Yahweh or to other gods a token of what they had first graciously given. (Unfortunately, poor excavation techniques and faulty publications often preclude our saying what animals and food were offered, or how they were offered.) The animals would be those that villagers and farmers typically bred — sheep, goats, and cattle — and hoped to increase. And the other foodstuffs — principally grain, oil, and wine — would also have been appropriate agricultural products to offer if one hoped to enhance crop yields. The "theology" may not have been very profound, or spiritually uplifting; but it worked. The "horns" on some large altars may be bull or "fertility" motifs (see p. 116).

The 45 or so known smaller "horned altars" have been extensively studied, and they were clearly used for burning incense in these local family shrines, despite the later biblical writers' prohibition of such offerings outside the Jerusalem temple (Gitin 2002). Incense may have been used partly to mask the foul smell of bloody animal carcasses. But

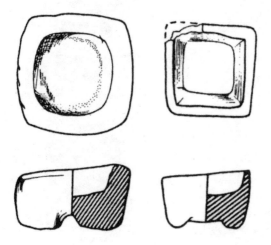

Small horned altars for incense, Beersheba, Str. II; 7th cent. B.C.
Aharoni 1973, Pl. 52:1-2

the further rationale was that the sweet, aromatic odor wafting skyward pleased the gods (as did the odor of roasting birds on the altar; Leviticus 1:17). These small horned altars, being portable, could also be taken up to the roof of the house (closer to heaven) for a ritual known not only from the Hebrew Bible but also from other ancient Near Eastern texts (Gitin 2002:100, 101).

What the "horns" may originally have signified is unclear. But it may be that, in addition to retaining some of the old cultic associations with "bull cults," these stylized horns later had become functional devices for supporting the bowls in which the incense was probably burned. There are also smaller, square limestone altars. A Persian period altar from Lachish is inscribed *lbnt*, "frankincense," by now cheaper than formerly, thanks to the growing spice trade with the Arabia peninsula. Nevertheless, even if rela-

Offering stand, with removable bowl;
Megiddo, 11th cent. B.C. (?)
Vriezen 2001, Fig. 11

tively costly, incense would have been deemed an appropriate gift to the gods. Anything that pleased and placated them was worth it (and after all, "sacrifice" by definition is costly).

(3) The stone offering tables and basins usually found in shrines are not ordinary kitchen utensils. These vessels are large, often made of expensive and difficult-to-work black basalt (volcanic stone), and come in a variety of elaborate shapes, such as fenestrated, tripod-footed bowls. The "tables" could serve as altars, like those described above, whose symbolism as "tables where the gods eat" is even clearer. Nor is this the only symbolism of feasts for the gods. The basins, bowls, mortars, and pestles are casually made of coarse, porous basalt, which is ideal for grinding grain to make flour for baking bread and cakes. Microscopic analysis of minute food particles preserved in the pores of the basalt vessels by one of my doctoral students (Jenny Ebeling) has revealed that they were actually used *in situ* for preparing food.

(4) Terra cotta "cult stands," or better simply "offering stands," are common at many small shrines, as well as in other cultic contexts (below). Many dozens of them are known from excavations, from the 12th to the 6th century B.C. But oddly enough (?), they are nowhere mentioned in the Hebrew Bible in connection with any of the sacrifices and offerings that are known. They are made of fired clay, with a flaring base, a round column from one to more than two feet high, and a top that may have either iconographic motifs or simply a socket for holding a separate offering bowl. Often the column is perforated with several rows of openings for incense-burning, suggesting windows, which leads some scholars to interpret these stands as multi-storied model temples (which do have a long earlier history).

Other stands, later in the Iron Age and now more specifically "Israelite," have a high slender column and drooping "fronds" around the top that are reminiscent of palm trees, often associated with the goddess Asherah (below). One of the strangest of all the stands is the one from the shrine at 'Ai discussed above (see p. 112), which has a row of human feet protruding around the base. I have suggested that while it was forbidden to portray the body or the face of Yahweh, these modest "feet" may suggest symbolically his presence in the sanctuary. (Or do we have a foot fetish?)

Whatever the psychology behind their form, given the notion of sacrifice, the stands functioned in a practical way. Incense could be burned in the column below, while offerings of food could be placed on the platform at the top with its retaining border or in a bowl set into the socket. No chemical analysis has been done on these stands, but it is reasonable to suppose that many of the acceptable offerings we have noted in the biblical texts could be presented, as it were, "small-scale." The failure of the biblical writers to mention these common offering stands may be because they disapproved of them, or more likely because they were for local home use, not for use in the Temple in Jerusalem.

(5) Benches around the walls in the household shrines were obviously not for worshippers seated for formal services, but served rather as places to put offerings that we have already discussed, various gifts to the gods (maybe even flowers). The small scale of these benches suits the modest size of the shrines.

The altars, tables, basins, stands, and benches described here all have to do with sacrifices and gifts for the gods. This is in keeping not only with the theological justification and theoretical ideal of the biblical conception, but it also accommodated the practical requirements of ordinary life. Worshipers implored the gods for life, health, prosperity, and progeny, offering what they had and hoping for the best.

The only thing "nonconformist" about such local family cults is that they were local, not connected with the Temple in Jerusalem. Here there were typically no official priests, only the *paterfamilias* — or, more often, the wife and mother of the household. There were probably few regular schedules of formal "services"; few prescribed liturgies; few theological creeds to affirm. As we have seen in Chapter IV in discussing high places, such local shrines were accepted matter-of-factly in the settlement period and early in the monarchy. They became anathema only under the late Deuteronomistic reforms, when attempts were made to suppress them and to centralize all worship in Jerusalem. Such attempts were, however, not only doctrinaire but also largely unsuccessful. In the countryside, people worshipped as they always had, and they almost certainly did not regard their practices as "non-Yahwistic." Theirs was simply an alternative approach, another way of expressing their beliefs and hopes.

(6) Molds for making jewelry and fragments of jewelry indicate that precious objects, as well as sacrifices, were presented to the gods in local shrines. The rationale is the same, of course: "giving back." Silver and gold were costly, but from time immemorial they had been brought to the gods in the hope of securing their favor — in other words, of securing increased

wealth (not to be too crass about the matter). It is rare, however, to find jewelry, gemstones, and the like *in situ,* because they would all have been looted long ago.

In any case, local shrines probably did not accumulate real wealth, nor was such an "endowment" necessary, since there were only local priests to subsidize. The Jerusalem Temple, on the other hand, became a wealthy treasury, which finally had to be stripped in order to pay tribute and buy off first the Assyrians and then the Babylonians. But "wealth" is relative; and a farmer's wife's gold earrings could be as worthy a gift as a king's ransom.

(7) Ceramic vessels were so common in households that they would be expected to appear in shrines, especially bowls and kraters (jars) for food offerings. Many of the vessels found in these shrines are, however, either more specialized, or are rather "exotic." Some, like pitchers and juglets, might have been used for libation offerings, for pouring out oil or wine (sanctioned in the Bible). Others, like footed chalices, would have been convenient for presenting food and drink offerings. Some ceramic vessels suggest that cooking and feasting were common activities at shrines — cooking pots, large and small serving bowls, and chalices for drinking (below). Small ceramic censers are also known, for burning incense. And small "trick-bowls" (Greek *kernoi*), with hollow rims and zoomorphic spouts for pouring out liquids, suggest libation offerings, which are of course mentioned in biblical texts (although no terms can actually be connected with these bowls). Also probably for libations are small ceramic zoomorphic figurines — usually quadrupeds — with hollow bodies and filling/pouring spouts.

We know of a ritual cultic banquet called the *marzēaḥ* from pre-Israelite Canaanite texts. This was supposed to be a communal meal in which one symbolically partook of food with the gods. It was sometimes connected with the idea of "feasting with the dead." And often it degenerated into a drunken feast. Evidence for the continuation of the *marzēaḥ* in the Israelite cult is scant and difficult to interpret. But some scholars reconstruct such a ritual from the only two texts we have, Amos 6:4-7 and Jeremiah 16:5-9. The first passage, which I cited above, describes a sumptuous banquet, but one of which the prophet was contemptuous for its excesses (including drunkenness). A religious connotation is implied, but not explicitly stated (in Amos' view, "false religion"). The passage in Jeremiah mentions a "house of mourning" (*bêt marzēaḥ,* connecting the feast

Chalices; Megiddo, Tomb 39 (10th cent.
B.C.); Megiddo, Str. VI
(10th cent. B.C.)
Amiran 1969, Pl. 68:12, 13

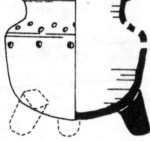

Incense burner;
Ta'anach, 10th cent. B.C.
Frick 2000, p. 101

Kernos; Kh. el-Qôm,
8th cent. B.C.
Photo: Theodore Rosen

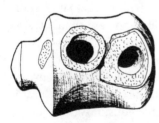

Libation vessel in form of a stylized quadruped;
Gezer, 11th cent. B.C.
Dever, Lance and Wright 1970, Pl. 37:9

124

without question to rites for the dead. Jeremiah is forbidden to participate; but that may have to do with his avoidance of all "normal" social intercourse. (See further Chapter VIII.)

These passages, while vague, do suggest that ritual banquets were sometimes held at local sanctuaries, although the biblical writers were suspicious of them because of their "pagan" associations. Nevertheless, feasting is said to have accompanied many of the approved annual festivals in ancient Israel (Chapter IV), and such rites are perfectly natural, found in almost all religions. What better way to celebrate the bounty of the gods and rejoice in their gifts? (One thinks, of course, of the Lord's Supper in the Christian church, although that is only a symbolic meal.)

(8) Burned bones and organic remains of food are found sometimes at the sanctuaries we have discussed. Such remains are too often overlooked or discarded by archaeologists ("garbage"), but re-examination suggests that here again we may have evidence of cultic meals (above).

(9) Astragali are sheep and goat knucklebones, usually found in hoards in bowls, polished or patinated from use. But used for what? The answer is clearly for "magic" — in particular, the practice of divination. The bones were shaken like dice, then thrown onto a table or onto the ground to see whether they formed a telling pattern and thus revealed something of divine intent. If they did, the gods had spoken, whether a good omen or a bad one.

An Excursis on "Magic"

Magic — that is, any form of fortune telling, sorcery, or witchcraft — seems to be strictly forbidden in the Hebrew Bible. The classic text is Deuteronomy 18:9-14, which is worth quoting in full:

> When you come into the land which the Lord your God gives you, you shall not learn to follow the abominable practices of those nations. There shall not be found among you any one who burns his son or his daughter as an offering, any one who practices divination, a soothsayer, or an augur, or a sorcerer, or a charmer, or a medium, or a wizard, or a necromancer. For whoever does these things is an abomination to the Lord; and because of these abominable practices the Lord your God is driving them out before you. You shall be blameless before the Lord

your God. For these nations, which you are about to dispossess, give heed to soothsayers and to diviners; but as for you, the Lord your God has not allowed you so to do.

It must be remembered that this passage is very late, part of the propaganda of the 7th-6th century B.C. Deuteronomistic reform movement (Chapter III). So all it really tells us is that by the end of the monarchy, in "official" Yahwistic circles, all forms of magic were regarded as foreign and ideally were to be purged from the Israelite cult. But there would be no *point* to condemning magic if it had not been widespread in folk religion. Why should it not have been, since it was popular everywhere else in the ancient Near East?

Works of Old Testament theology, not surprisingly (Chapter II), have downplayed or even denied the existence of magic in ancient Israel. Thus the leading scholar Gerhard von Rad stated that the historian of religion is struck by the dwindling role played by magic: "its absence already gives the Israel of the time an exceptional position within all the fairly comparable forms in the history of religion, especially the religion of the ancient East" (quoted in Jeffers 1996:7, 8). This, of course, is the standard *theological* conclusion, stemming from the notion that ancient Israel was (and had to be) "unique." Nothing could be farther from the truth, as the recent study of Ann Jeffers has shown, *Magic and Divination in Ancient Palestine and Syria* (1996).

More recent histories of Israelite religion are somewhat more realistic, but they still fail to convey the importance of magic. Albertz (1994) mentions some of the archaeological evidence (below) in dealing with "family piety," but only in terms of the general concern for health and well-being. He does not mention specifically any form of magic. Miller (2000) deals with demonology, divination, and oracular prophecy, but he speaks of other forms of magic only in a footnote or two, citing no actual archaeological data.

The types of magic attested in popular religion in the biblical texts *alone,* should have been a corrective. Deuteronomy 18 does not stand in isolation. More than a dozen types of magic are mentioned in the texts, and even though many are proscribed, not all are. And in any case, their existence is tacitly acknowledged. Without any attempt to be systematic ("magic" defies rationality, but not practical reason), we find evidence of at least the following in the "biblical world":

 (1) Demonology and exorcism (and angelology in some late texts)
 (2) Divination
 (3) Oracles (prophetic or other)
 (4) Soothsaying
 (5) Wise men and wise women
 (6) Magicians
 (7) Medicine men
 (8) Sorcerers, witchcraft
 (9) Interpreters of dreams
(10) Astrologers
(11) Priestly "blessings and curses"

In all cases, the biblical world is pervaded by *miracles* and the assumption that they are part of everyday experience, however foreign or repugnant that notion may be to us. Even the canonical prophets, no longer "seers" or ecstatics (I Samuel 9:9) but now statesmen, work miracles. And so do priests, who pronounce, and thus bring about, "blessings and curses."

All of these forms of magic grow out of *cosmology*, the view commonly held of the world, the universe, and "the powers that be." In ancient times in the Near East and in Israel as well, the worldview, the supposed "Semitic mentality," was characterized by what scholars have called "prelogical" or "mythopoeic" thinking. This is held to contrast, of course, with "empirico-logical" or modern scientific, *rational* thinking. In these definitions there is a not-so-veiled implication of superiority: "ours is religion; yours is superstition." Modern thought is rational, and therefore obviously better.

Here I would make two observations. (1) First, the ancient worldview, while not "rational" in the modern scientific sense, had a rationale of its own — a consistent view of the world *within* which it could be explained "how things work," how divine powers could be personally appropriated. (2) Second, "religion" *is* in effect "magic," unless one assumes that it is only about theological formulae. It is about the "metaphysical." In any case, the popular religions of ancient Israel throughout the monarchy (and even in later Judaism, where "the evil eye" is feared, below) were deeply rooted in the world of miracle and magic. Nevertheless, the *archaeological* data have never been systematically surveyed, so let us do so now.

(1) I have already mentioned astragali, found in family shrines at Megiddo and Ta'anach, used for divination. We also have some inscribed

pottery vessels that I would interpret as having to do with "sympathetic magic." One is a large 8th-century B.C. bowl from Beersheba reading *Qōdesh,* "holy." The other is an 8th-century B.C. bowl from my excavations at Kh. el-Qôm (biblical "Makkedah") reading *'ēl,* "God." While the first is speculative, I can see no reason for the latter inscription ("God" is not the possessor of the bowl) unless it is a magical way of securing divine favor. Perhaps it was even an offering bowl, of the sort used with the cult stands already discussed.

(2) Another inscribed vessel is a large 8th-century B.C. storejar from the fortress-shrine of Kuntillet 'Ajrûd, with a similar blessing written in paint: "May Yahweh bless you and keep you and be with you." This was probably placed in the shrine at the gate as a "votive," or sort of "stand-in" for the worshipper (of which more later).

(3) We have many inscribed bronze arrowheads from the period of the Judges (12th-11th century B.C.), some giving the (probable) mercenary's name as well as his patron deity. One reads: "Ben 'Anat (Son of the Goddess 'Anat), Servant of the Lion Lady" (an epithet of the Great Goddess, under her alternate name). It seems to me that these arrowheads were not inscribed with either the user's names or divine names simply as a

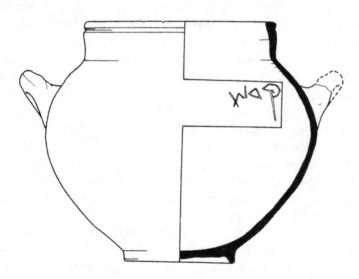

Large krater with incised inscription reading "Qōdesh," "Holy";
Beersheba Str. II, 7th cent. B.C.
Aharoni 1973, Pl. 69:2

novelty. Something *serious* is going on — warfare, the possibility of injury or death — and a devout wish is implied. There are only a few biblical texts that allude to divination with metals in seeking blessings. In the story in Joshua 8:18-26, Joshua is told by Yahweh to "stretch out his javelin" to insure a victory over the Canaanite city of ʿAi. More to the point is Ezekiel 21:21, which recounts how the Babylonian king Nebuchadnezzar stood at an intersection of two roads, one leading to Jerusalem, and "used divination" to decide the way by "shaking an arrow." The connection with "consulting the teraphim" and "looking at the liver" ("hepatoscopy") in this text makes it clear that we are dealing with magic (although not Israelite here, there is no suggestion by the biblical writers that it doesn't work).

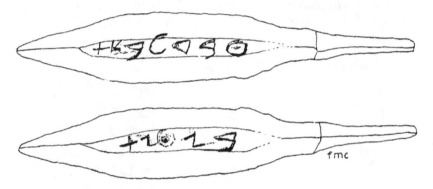

Bronze arrowhead, vicinity of Bethlehem, 11th cent. B.C.
Top: "Servant of the Lion Lady"; bottom: "Ben-ʿAnat."
Cross 1980, Fig. 5

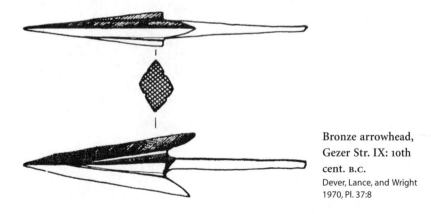

Bronze arrowhead, Gezer Str. IX: 10th cent. B.C.
Dever, Lance, and Wright 1970, Pl. 37:8

(4) An even clearer non-biblical textual witness is a 7th/6th-century B.C. inscribed silver amulet found in a tomb in Jerusalem, at Ketef Hinnom near the Kidron Valley. It was rolled up and meant to be worn on a thong around the neck, as a sort of "good luck charm." When carefully unrolled at the Israel Museum, the amulet was found to have an intact Hebrew inscription that was an alternate version of the famous "priestly blessing" of Moses in Numbers (still recited today):

Numbers 6:24-26	Ketef Hinnom
The Lord bless you and keep you.	May Yahweh bless you
The Lord make his face to shine	and watch over you.
upon you, and be gracious to you:	May Yahweh make his
The Lord lift up his countenance	face shine upon you
upon you, and give you peace.	And grant you peace.

Silver Amulet 2 from Ketef Hinnom,
Jerusalem; late 7th cent. B.C.
Barkay, Vaughn, Lundberg, & Zuckerman 2004, Fig. 30

Several things in this little-noticed discovery are significant for the study of popular religion. First, this inscription — our oldest surviving scrap of Scripture, antedating the oldest of the Dead Sea scrolls by nearly 400 years — preserves an alternate, "popular" version of our canonical biblical text. It differs in several ways. It combines the second and third benedictions; and it contains only 10 words in Hebrew as compared with the biblical 15. It is reminiscent of the probable "short version" of the same blessing in Psalm 67:1: "May Yahweh be gracious to us and bless us and make his face to shine upon us." The Ketef Hinnom blessing is thus highly significant for the practice of popular religion. In spite of the skepticism I have expressed above about "literary" formulae having much effect on popular religion, here we do have a "folk" version of what was obviously a widely used blessing, one that eventually found its way into the canonical texts in an "official" version.

Second, the person with whom the amulet was buried — a woman, to judge from the collection of fine jewelry — must have worn the amulet around her neck as a treasured personal belonging. The point is that using the text as an *amulet*, to ward off bad luck, is "magic." Yet I would argue that the amulet is really only an analogue for a form of the "phylactery." The phylactery was a small box containing slips inscribed with scriptural passages; it could be worn, or it could be affixed to the doorpost of houses (Deuteronomy 6:9; 11:20; the *"mezuzah"* that is still used today, containing these very words). Thus it appears that Scripture was already being used as "magic" — as an apotropaic device or "good luck charm" — in the period of the monarchy. (In later Judaism, leather phylacteries or "tefillin" were worn for prayer.)

Finally, the Ketef Hinnom amulet was not found out in the boondocks, where less sophisticated people may be forgiven for being "superstitious." It comes from the heart of Jerusalem, the religious capital, not much more than a thousand yards away from the Temple Mount. So much for "orthodoxy."

(5) There are other tombs and grave goods that also attest to popular religion. Evidence comes from a typical 8th-century B.C. Judean bench tomb that I excavated west of Hebron in 1968. The site of Kh. el-Qôm is probably to be identified with biblical Makkedah. One of the dozens of bench tombs in the Iron Age cemetery there produced a four-line Hebrew inscription, which I promptly published in 1969 but which was ignored by scholars for nearly a decade. Although there are linguistic difficulties, a consensus reading would run something like this:

For 'Uriyahu the governor (or the rich), his inscription.
Blessed is 'Uriyahu by Yahweh:
From his enemies he has been saved
By his a/Asherah.
(Written) by 'Oniyahu

I shall return to this inscription in Chapter VI, because I take the word *'ăshērāh* not as an "object of blessing" (a tree or pole), but as the proper name of the goddess Asherah. Here let me note simply something on this inscription that virtually no one has commented on: the clearly engraved *human hand*. It resembles almost exactly the much later Islamic *hamza*, or "Hand of Fatima," which is seen everywhere in the Muslim world. The hand-sign is a kind of "graffito" written on walls, over doorways, on amulets. One can even hold up the outstretched open right hand as a "good luck" sign. Its purpose is to ward off the "evil eye." It's *magic.* My el-Qôm hand is from an undisturbed 8th-century B.C. tomb, and it is clearly Israelite. But what does this sign *mean?* It is found with a "blessing formula," probably done by the same person. It can only have something to

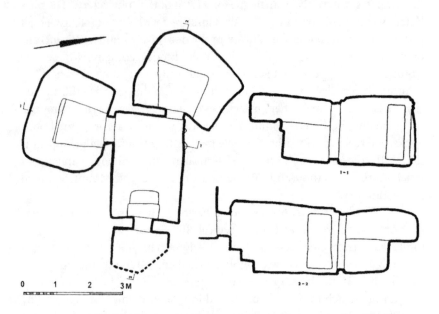

Plan and sections of a typical 8th-cent. B.C. Judean bench-tomb (Kh. Beit Lei)
Zevit 2001, Fig. 5.9

132

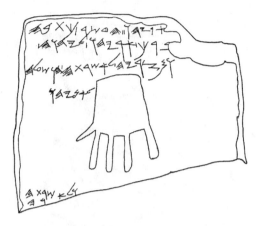

Inscription no. 3, from T. II at
Kh. el Qôm; *ca.* 750 B.C.
Lemaire 1977, p. 598

do with a wish for good fortune from "the hand of Yahweh." This expression, in the precise context of "blessing," occurs dozens of times in the Hebrew Bible. Its authors *wrote* about the "hand of blessing"; but in the countryside, people *drew* it without any hesitation. Perhaps you could not portray Yahweh himself, but picturing his hand was acceptable. One thinks of the famous Dura-Europa synagogue wall painting much later (3rd century A.D.), which shows Yahweh "appearing" to Moses from the heavens, but only his hand is visible. As for the much-feared "evil eye," that, too, is very Jewish, the *'ayin ha-ra'* which in later Judaism is warded off by eye-amulets, Aramaic formulae on "incantation bowls," and the like (below). It seems that the concept goes back to monarchic times, and why not?

(6) I have mentioned a few amulets above. We actually have hundreds of Iron Age amulets, mostly from Judean tombs, but again few biblical scholars have paid any attention to them. Amulets, by definition, are "magic symbols," used mostly to bring good luck (apotropaic, "turning away evil"). They would probably have been used by many people in ancient Israel, and, being among their most precious possessions, they were buried with the deceased. The most common ones found in tombs are Egyptian: "Eye-of-Horus" plaques; figurines of deities, especially Bes, guardian of the dead; and other faience (that is, glazed earthenware) items. It is possible that the model furniture found in some of the same tombs also had a magical significance. Mostly beds, couches, and chairs, these were perhaps to insure the dead "continuing in life," as it were, still using their domestic furniture in the "house of the dead" (on all this, see Bloch-Smith 1992:86-90, 94).

"Eye-of-Horus" faience amulets;
Lachish tombs, 8th-7th cent. B.C.
Adapted from Tufnell 1953, Pl. 34:8, 10

Faience figurines of the
Egyptian "good luck"
deity Bes; Lachish tomb,
7th cent. B.C.
Adapted from Tufnell 1953,
Pl. 34:14

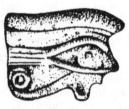

(7) Ancient engraved gemstones, set into signet rings, are exceptionally well known, and we have hundreds and hundreds of them from ancient Israel. Although they are overlooked by many biblical schools, Keel and Uehlinger have made a thorough study (see the "Freibourg school" in Chapter II), publishing hundreds of examples. I cannot survey the extensive evidence that they present, but it shows beyond doubt that many people in ancient Israel had seals, and that the rich iconography of the seals often has to do with the "astralization of the heavenly powers." This was

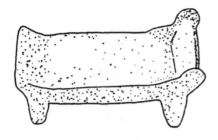

Model bed and chair, Lachish tombs 8th cent. B.C.
Adapted from Tufnell 1952, Pl. 29:21, 22

particularly prevalent in 7th-century B.C. Judah, under the influence of Assyrian and Babylonian astrological worship. It may be that ordinary folk who owned these "foreign"-style seals were not fully aware of their original symbolic meaning. But they certainly did not hesitate to use them, and they can hardly be considered simply "decorative." (See Chapter VII on the Queen of Heaven" and the figure on p. 233.)

Public Open-Air Sanctuaries

Moving up to the next level above family shrines and small private sanctuaries ("up" only in terms of complexity, not value), we come to the "high places" or *bāmôt*, the textual evidence for which I have already introduced (Chapter IV). Here again, the biblical references, however idealistic, are supplemented by archaeological examples.

(1) The earliest *bāmāh* we have is an open-air hilltop sanctuary of the 12th century B.C., discovered in 1981 by Mazar in the hill country of Ephraim and Manasseh near Dothan (Nakhai 2001:170, 171). It was named the "Bull Site" because of the principal find, a well-preserved bronze bull of Anatolian "zebu" type. The sanctuary itself is a rather typical high place, on an isolated hilltop. It consists of a partially preserved enclosure (or "temenos") wall; a stone-paved platform; and a large standing stone *(māṣṣēbāh)*. Among the few items found were some bits of 12th-century B.C. pottery; fragments of a terra cotta incense burner or offering stand; some pieces of bronze and silver jewelry; cooking pots and bowls; animal bones and flints; and, of course, the bronze bull (found on the surface).

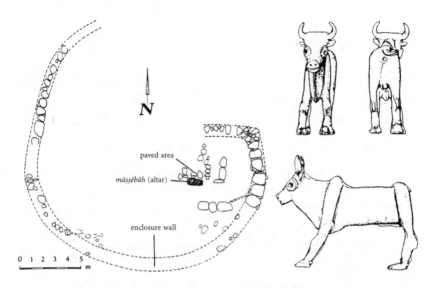

paved area

māṣṣēbāh (altar)

enclosure wall

0 1 2 3 4 5
m

N

Left, plan of "Bull Site"; *right,* the bronze bull figurine, 12th cent. B.C.
Adapted from Mazar 1982, Figs 2, 5

The "Bull Site" fits the biblical descriptions of high places quite well: non-domestic; in a public place; having an altar-like platform; featuring the *māṣṣēbāh;* showing evidence of sacrifices. Moreover, the bronze bull provides a *direct* connection with the biblical condemnation of *bāmôt* as "Canaanite." In fact, Mazar's Iron I bronze bull is almost identical to one found in the 1950s by Yadin at Hazor in a 14th-century B.C. "Canaanite" context. The principal epithet (or "title") of El — the high god of the Canaanite pantheon — in the 14th- and 13th-century B.C. texts from Ugarit in Syria is "Bull El," the bull being a symbol of ferocity and fertility in the ancient Mediterranean world generally. The "Bull Site" shows that the apprehension of the biblical writers concerning *bāmôt* was *real.* In the worship of early Israel, El was venerated alongside of, and sometimes in preference to, Yahweh, who theoretically was Israel's only national deity (although in many texts, "El" and "Yahweh" are both names of Israel's national god).

(2) At Hazor in upper Galilee, the excavations of Yigael Yadin in 1955-1958 brought to light a small outdoor *bāmāh* of the 11th century B.C. in an Israelite "squatter occupation" above the ruins of the destroyed Canaanite city (in Str. XI). This shrine consisted of a small rectangular structure in an

open area, with some benches around the walls, adjoining a stone pavement with four standing stones. The finds included two broken offering stands, and from under the floor a hoard of bronze implements in a jug. The group included a sword; two javelin heads and butts; an arrowhead; several adzes; a lugged ax; some miscellaneous pins and other items; and a sealed bronze figure of the deity El, almost exactly like hundreds of such

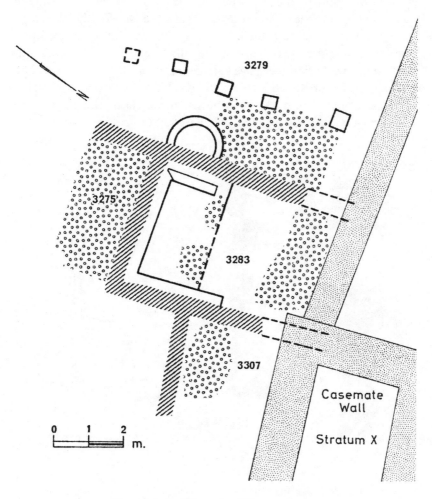

Plan of shrine, Hazor Str. XII; 12 cent. B.C.
Yadin 1972, Fig. 29

figurines known from Late Bronze Age Syria and Canaan. Yadin interpreted the *bāmāh* itself as "Israelite," but he noted that since this was a hoard, the objects could be either Canaanite (that is, holdovers from earlier periods) or Israelite. Other scholars, however, have naïvely assumed that the El figurine was Israelite, and thus evidence for "syncretism" (below). The fact is that *all* the similar El figurines known are Late Bronze Age, or pre-Israelite. The jug contained older bronze objects, no doubt dug up from the ruins by the "squatters," collected simply for their value in weight and set into the floor of the *bāmāh* as a "votive offering." There is a long Canaanite tradition of such hoards serving as votives in sacred precincts in Bronze Age Syria. This is especially true at Byblos, where thousands of bronze El figurines have been found in jar deposits. In any case, however, the Hazor *bāmāh* provides a strong link of early Israelite religion with that of old Canaan. I have considered the Hazor installation as a *bāmāh*, that is, a public shrine or sanctuary rather than a private one, be-

Bronze El figurine
from the jar hoard
Yadin 1975, p. 257

Seated bronze figurine of El;
Byblos, 14th-13th cent. B.C.
Negbi 1976, Fig. 55

cause it is located in an open area. In fact, in Yadin's "squatter occupation" of Str. XI, there are no houses, only huts and rubbish pits.

(3) At Tel Dan on the Syrian border, Israeli excavations since 1966 have brought to light what is no doubt a full-fledged *bāmāh* or high place, as well as related structures of the 9th-8th centuries B.C. In the following I shall not deal with the complex inner phasing, since it is only partially published and is unclear (see Biran 1994).

Situated on the uplifted northern end of the mound in a grove of trees above the copious perennial springs, the high place is comprised of many features. The principal installation is a raised square platform ten feet high and 60 by 60 feet, constructed of fine Phoenician style ("ashlar") masonry ("Bamah A-B"), approached by a monumental flight of steps. This is not a massive foundation for a now-missing temple structure, but rather what a *bāmāh* essentially was: a large outdoor altar. Two or three small "altar niches," however, seem to have been erected later (?) atop the platform at the rear. Other alterations were made to the *bāmāh* from time to time (below), but because it was so impressive, and also because of the well-known phenomenon of "continuity of sacred space" in the ancient Near East, the *bāmāh* continued in use into the Hellenistic period (a Greek inscription reads "to the god who is in Dan").

Fragments of a monumental horned altar found near the steps suggest that such an altar, about ten feet high, once stood in the forecourt at ground level, apparently with its own enclosure walls. Also in the court-

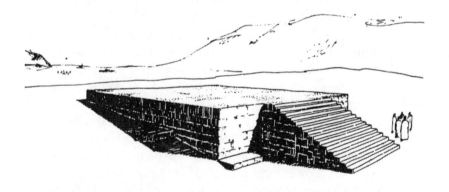

Artist's reconstruction of the Dan "High Place";
8th cent. B.C.
Biran 1975, p. 319

Plan of the Dan "High Place" area
Biran 1994, Fig. 163

yard was a rectangular pool with two steps leading down into it. A much smaller "horned altar" was also found in the vicinity.

In this area there was an installation that the excavator interpreted as for "water-libations," but it is almost certainly an olive press. Two large basalt slabs served as the pressing floor. A central sunken plastered basin and two flanking storejars set into the floor flush with the ground served for collecting the pressed oil. Twelve heavy stones, each with a hole in one end, had been used as weights on the end of the wooden beams that were stuck into sockets in the wall and bore down on baskets containing the olives. Such olive presses are very well known elsewhere in the Iron Age, especially at 7th-century B.C. Ekron. In the area of the olive press were found the faience head of a Phoenician-style male figurine; another male figurine in Egyptian style, seated and holding a lotus blossom (a king?); and two fragmentary painted offering stands.

To the west of the high place, separated by a courtyard or narrow

Horn of a large four-horned altar, Dan "High Place"
Photo: Hebrew Union College

Small portable horned altar, probably for burning incense
Photo: Hebrew Union College

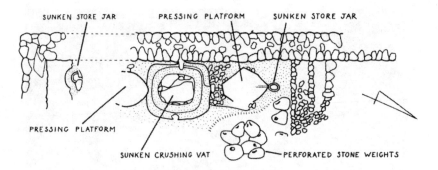

SUNKEN STORE JAR · PRESSING PLATFORM · SUNKEN STORE JAR · PRESSING PLATFORM · SUNKEN CRUSHING VAT · PERFORATED STONE WEIGHTS

Plan of the olive-pressing installation at Dan; 10th/9th cent. B.C.
Stager and Wolff 1981, Fig. 1

street, was a long tripartite (three-room) building ("Room 2746"). Added secondarily in the 7th century B.C., this may represent the biblical *lishkāh*, a "chamber" such as Jeremiah describes having been constructed near the Temple in Jerusalem (Jeremiah 35:4; see also II Chronicles 31:11, "chambers" built earlier near the Temple by Hezekiah). On the floor of the central room ("Room 2844") was a long stone altar with a flat stone top, covered with ashes and burned animal bones. Three well-preserved iron shovels for clearing off the ashes on the altar lay on the floor nearby; and a broken storejar set into the dirt floor was obviously the receptacle for the ashes. In the *lishkāh* itself ("Room 2746") were found a finely decorated bronze bowl; a socketed bronze scepter head; a Phoenician-style faience female figurine; a faience die (from a pair of dice?); two small portable stone altars; and a stamp seal impression reading "Immadi-Yo," "God is with me."

To the southwest of the *bāmāh* and *lishkāh* was "Building 9235," which the excavator speculated may have been the house of "Immadi-Yo" (above), possibly a priest. It was filled with domestic pottery; a basalt bowl; and an oxhead figurine.

The complex phasing of all the above areas cannot be worked out here, as I have noted. But a rough outline is possible. The much-altered structures designated "Bamah A" (9th-8th centuries B.C., Str. IV-III) and "B" (8th century B.C.; Str. II), together with the associated courtyard installations and "House 9235," were brought to an end by the Assyrian destructions in the north *ca.* 732 B.C. The *lishkāh* was then constructed sometime in the 7th century B.C. (Str. I) to continue some of the functions of the sacred area.

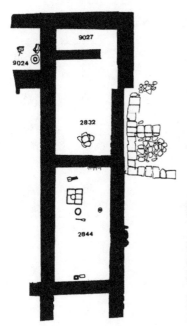

Plan of the *lishkāh* adjoining the Dan
"High Place," 7th cent. B.C.
Zevit 2000, Fig. 3:33

The altar of the *lishkāh* and the
iron shovels found nearby
Photo: Hebrew Union College

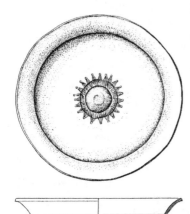

Bronze bowl found
near the altar of the *lishkāh*
Biran 1994, Fig. 154

143

Bronze scepter head
found near the altar
of the *lishkāh*
Biran 1994, Fig. 156

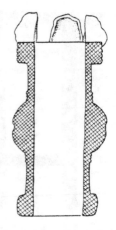

Faience female figurine in Phoenician
style; 8th/7th cent. B.C.
Biran 1994, Fig. 172. Photo: Hebrew Union
College

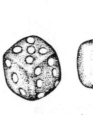

A faience die and its six sides; 9th cent. B.C.
Biran 1994, Fig. 157

Generalizing somewhat, and looking at the Dan high place as a whole, what can we say of the religious rites typically carried out there? (a) The large horned altar in the forecourt may have been used for animal sacrifices or other food offerings, as may have been as well the small portable altars in one room of the *lishkāh*. The low stone altar in the central room was used for animal sacrifice, to judge from the ashes, burnt bones, and shovels. The small horned altar found near the large one was certainly used for burning incense, as we now know (above). Much of this evidence for sacrifice is in keeping with the biblical ideal — even down to details like the iron shovels for clearing off the altar, which are mentioned as furnishing for the Temple in the Hebrew Bible (I Kings 7:40, 45; II Kings 25:14; Jeremiah 52:18). But the point is that according to the Deuteronomistic reformers, none of this should have been *here,* only in the Temple in Jerusalem (yet they do apparently mention the Dan installation; I Kings 12:30, 31).

(b) Other types of sacrifices are attested by the large cylindrical offering stands, which could have been used for both incense and food offerings (in bowls placed on top; and we do have a bronze bowl). The Dan stands are unusual in being painted; but that may reflect the Phoenician influence that we would expect (and indeed have in other objects) this far north. As noted above, these offering stands, while very common, are nowhere mentioned in the Hebrew Bible, another witness to "unorthodox" practices at Dan (and elsewhere).

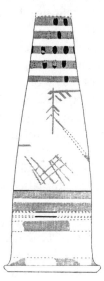

Painted offering stand;
10th/9th cent. B.C.
Biran 1994, Fig. 134

(c) The olive oil installation — obviously noncommercial and in a sacred precinct — is not a surprise, even though parallels are rare elsewhere. The biblical texts record the use of oil to anoint priests (Exodus 29:4-7; Leviticus 8:6-12) and kings (Saul: I Samuel 10:1). The oil used would likely have been produced under controlled supervision and consecrated as "holy" for this purpose. If there were local priests serving at the Dan sanctuary, an olive oil production facility on the premises would be quite practical.

(d) The "spring pool" in the outer courtyard, with a large tub nearby, is best explained by assuming that ritual lustrations, or rites of purifications, were part of the rites of worship. Dan is situated near powerful springs that feed the Jordan River, flowing below and above ground from melting snows on the slopes of Mt. Hermon in Syria. Sanctuaries in the ancient Near East were often located near springs. And the gods are often connected with either the depths of the sea or fresh water sources. El, the Canaanite high god, is said to be enthroned at the foot of Mt. Saphon at the "Source of the Floods," the headwaters of the "Two Deeps," where the salt and the sweet waters meet. Furthermore, "ritual purity" was fundamental to the idea of holiness in the Hebrew Bible (at least in late sources like "P"; above), and this condition could best be insured by washing with water. Some biblical prescriptions specify ablutions that should be made with fresh or even with running water. That is the case with individuals who come into contact with a corpse, who must wash themselves, their feet, and their belongings in "running water" (Numbers 19:16-19). Lepers must also cleanse themselves in running water (Leviticus 14:1-9).

Many other forms of "impurity" must be cleansed with water, such as that resulting from menstruation (Leviticus 15:19-32); from a bodily discharge (Leviticus 15:19-32); from touching an emission of semen (Leviticus 22:4-8); from the pollution of men returning from battle (Numbers 31:21-24). All these passages are from late, probably postexilic sources ("P"); but the customs of purification by lustrations of water are "sensible" and probably very ancient. And they still continue in Orthodox Judaism, as in the requirement that both men and women go to the *miqveh* or "ritual bath" monthly; and that all converts be immersed totally in water (the latter perpetuated in early Christian baptism).

(e) The faience die found in the south room of the *lishkāh* ("Room 2770") is especially significant, although other commentators seem to have missed it. It clearly has to do with "casting lots" — throwing the dice — to divine something, to produce an omen. It is one way of practicing divination, and it served the same purpose as throwing down the astragali (above; and also cf. Taʿanach). It is all about "magic," which as we have seen was a fundamental aspect of all ancient religions. Whether priests were consulted for these rites of divination as specialists, or whether ordinary people came to the sanctuary to perform the rites themselves, is uncertain (for the possibility of priestly functionaries, see below).

(f) The several figurines found in the Dan sanctuary area are also very significant — especially since four of the five are male. The faience female figurine, found in the north room ("9024") of the *lishkāh* under the floor, is clearly in the Phoenician style (p. 144). Whether imported or a local imitation, it is at home here in the north. Dan is only 25 miles due east of Tyre on the Phoenician coast. The biblical writers are accurate (if excessively judgmental) in denouncing the northern kingdom's religious practices as "pagan," that is, foreign to the Judean biblical ideal. Who the figurine represents is uncertain, but she is not likely to be a goddess and is probably a votive (more of that below in Chapter VI).

Three of the male faience figurines were found in or near a sunken storejar adjacent to one of the basalt slabs flanking the olive pressing installation. Two are headless, but the one holding a lotus blossom may represent a Phoenician deity (or king?). The third one consists of only a head, with what looks like the white crown of the Egyptian god Osiris. But since Phoenician art is known to be "Egyptianizing," this figurine, too, is best understood as Phoenician, perhaps representing a king. The fourth male figurine, also Phoenician and painted, was found in one of the "altar rooms" (or niches) atop "Bamah A" of the 10th/9th century B.C. The fragment of the head is so large — nearly four inches — that this "figurine" was probably part of a large incense stand. With it in the cult rooms were found some Cypro-Phoenician pottery and a fine bowl with a Phoenician-style trident engraved on the bottom.

The significance of the four male figurines in the sanctuary is considerable and may be underlined as follows: (1) Male figurines are so rare *anywhere* in ancient Israel in the 10th-6th centuries B.C. that out of some 3,000 Israelite figurines that we have, none but these four are demonstrably male (a few are uncertain because they are fragmentary or of unclear provenance). (2) The find spot near the olive-pressing installation is intriguing. But it may find an explanation at neo-Philistine Ekron, where nearly every one of the many 7th-century B.C. olive presses has a small horned altar in the same room, often conspicuously placed in a small niche. Since the

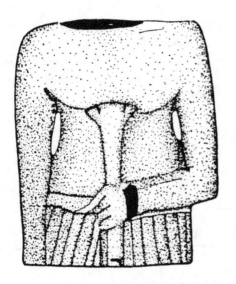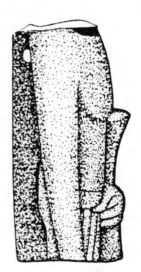

Faience figurine of a male deity
(or king?), holding a lotus stem; 10th/9th cent. B.C.
Biran 1994, Fig. 142

Ekron olive oil business was on an industrial level, it is obvious that "religion and commerce" went hand in hand. The ancient rationale should not be a mystery. Since the gods controlled everything, it made sense to invoke their blessing on *any* large-scale and risky enterprise. I suggest that at Dan, too, the blessing of "Phoenician" deities was sought when pressing olives — especially when the product was intended for liturgical use (above).

(g) At several points I have implied that at a full-fledged, public cult center like Dan, priests were probably involved. The best piece of evidence for this is the fine bronze scepter head already discussed (see p. 144). It is about four inches long, the cylindrical body decorated with what appear to be lotus blossoms, as columns sometimes are; with what may be eroded lion heads ringing the top and a hollow body to accept a wooden shaft. Phoenician ivory scepter heads of the 8th century B.C. are known from Dor on the coast, with pomegranate heads and attached ivory wands. The best parallel, however, is an 8th-century B.C. ivory scepter head in the form of a pomegranate, bought on the black market but likely a relic of the Temple in Jerusalem. The Hebrew inscription around the head reads: "Belonging to the Temple of (Yahwe)h. Sacred/holy for the priests." The carrying of a

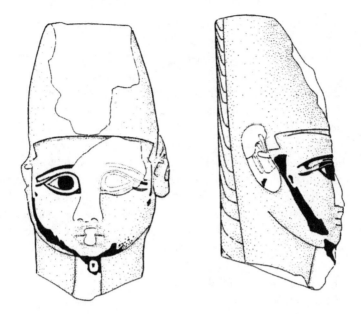

Head of a Phoenician-style male deity (or king?); 10th/9th cent. B.C.
Biran 1994, Fig. 139

raised scepter by priests (or by deities or kings) would clearly be a sign of authority. If that is so, then the presence of an exceptionally fine cast bronze scepter head at the Dan sanctuary would seem to indicate priestly authority being exercised there. Several of the public activities presumed

Inscription on head of the ivory scepter head; 8th cent. B.C.
Avigad 1990, p. 160

above — sacrifice, offerings, the production of olive oil, and divination — would be consistent with that presumption.

Given the exceptional archaeological data that we now have on the Dan cultic installations, it would be intriguing to see whether any of the evidence can be connected with the biblical texts. It turns out that it can, although few have pursued this. First, Dan figures rather prominently in the biblical tradition, particularly in connection with the cult. The shrine of Micah and his priestly sons, which we discussed above, is transferred to Dan when the city comes under Israelite control and is rebuilt in the period of the Judges (Judges 18). The texts mention specifically a "graven image" set up by the Danites and priests of the Mosaic line that served there "until the captivity of the Land" (that is, the fall of the northern kingdom in 722/721 B.C.; Judges 18:30, 31). In a fascinating reference, Amos 8:13, 14 predicts the latter, the utter destruction of those who swear by

> Ashimah of Samaria and say,
> "As thy god lives, O Dan," and
> "As the Way of Beer-sheba lives,"
> They shall fall, and never rise again.

The reference to "Ashimah," obviously a goddess, is puzzling, since such a deity is known only in ancient Arabia. But with a slight consonantal change in the biblical word 'āshîmāh (mem to resh) we could read 'ăshērāh, or "Asherah," the well-known goddess. The early Hebrew form of mem looks like this: ᛋ; the early Hebrew form of resh looks like this: ᛃ. A simple scribal error? Or a clever attempt to conceal the name of the hated goddess Asherah?

It is noteworthy that the Hebrew root of "Ashimah" seems to be 'āshām, "shame," making it more likely that the editors did not want to read "Asherah of Samaria" (the northern capital), but "shame of Samaria." To strengthen this suggestion, we now actually have the phrase "Asherah of Samaria" on an inscription from the 8th-century B.C. shrine at Kuntillet ʿAjrûd (below).

Still more significant is I Kings 12:25-33. This passage tells how Jeroboam I — one of the servants of Solomon, who seceded after his death and founded the breakaway northern kingdom in the late 10th century B.C. — made Dan his capital. There he set up a golden calf — reminiscent, of course, of the heresy of the Israelites at Mt. Sinai — an audacious declaration establishing his alternative to the Jerusalem Temple. He also "made a house on high places" (*bêt bāmôt;* I Kings 12:31). As I have pointed out above, *bêt* is the usual term for "temple"; and *bāmôt* is plural here, meaning "high places." The syntax is what is called a "construct relation," or a possessive relation, meaning that the phrase should be read either "house of high places," which makes little sense to me; or "a temple/sanctuary belonging to high places." The latter is precisely what we *have* at Dan: several sacred installations that are an integral part of the "high place" complex. I hasten to point out here that establishing this convergence between text and artifact is not old-fashioned "prove-the-Bible" biblical archaeology (which I have disavowed for 30 years). It is simply pointing out that an independent analysis of the two sources of information leads us to a "conclusion beyond a reasonable doubt," which I argued above is part of proper historical method.

A fair-minded person (neither an extreme skeptic nor a fundamentalist) can see the force of this argument that the Dan cultic installation is indeed an excellent example of what the biblical writers and editors had in mind in speaking of a *bāmāh* (although they condemned them, of course). Yet few of the works discussed above (Chapter II) even mention the Dan complex; and none connects it with the biblical texts as I have done here (nor do any other archaeologists). Zevit (2001:180-196 and elsewhere) is the sole, and predictable, exception, because *he takes archaeology seriously.* He concludes that there was "a major cult center at Tel Dan" (2001:181; but even Zevit does not make the direct biblical connection).

One other public cultic installation at Dan must be mentioned here, a small *bāmāh* built into the wall of the inner court of the city gate. It consists of five small undressed standing stones *(māṣṣēbôt)* some 12-18 inches high, arranged in a row. In front of them is a low stone altar, flanked by a wall to the right side and a dressed stone to the left. Nearby were found many vessels, including bowls, plates, cups, a censer, a footed chalice, and oil lamps. It is reasonable to see these as vessels that were used at the *bāmāh,* a "gate shrine" of the type we know elsewhere (below; and also mentioned in Jerusalem in II Kings 23:8).

(4) The 10th-century B.C. "Cultic Structure" at Taʿanach was probably a *bāmāh* rather than a simple household shrine. It produced a large olive-pressing installation (like Dan; above); a bowlful of astragali; iron knives; ceramic vessels; a mold for making female figurines; and two remarkable terra cotta stands with iconographic motifs, some of which I would connect with the Canaanite-Israelite goddess "Asherah, the Lion

The small *bāmāh* in the gate complex at Dan,
with stone bench and five *māṣṣēbôt;* 8th cent. B.C.
Photo: W. G. Dever

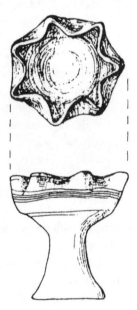

Seven-spouted chalice/lamp from
the "High Place" area
Biran 1994, Fig. 128

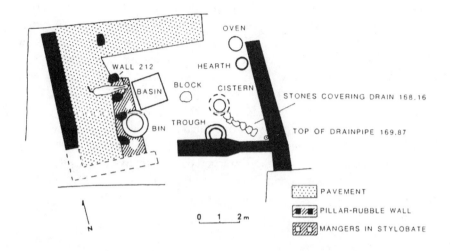

Plan of the Taʿanach "Cultic Structure"; 10th cent. B.C.
Adapted from Lapp 1964, Fig. 12

Olive press near "Cultic Structure"
Photo: W. G. Dever

Lady" (see Chapters VI, VII). The monumentality of the large offering stands, and especially the mold for mass-producing figurines, suggest that the Ta'anach "Cultic Structure" was a *bāmāh* serving the public, even though it lacks some expected features such as standing stones and altars.

(5) Tell el Far'ah (N.) exhibits two of the Dan *bāmāh* features at a shrine just inside the 10th-8th century B.C. city gate. These are a large standing stone *(māṣṣēbāh)* and a basin that served either for olive oil for anointing, or for water for lustrations. Such a "gate shrine" was obviously public. It made good sense as a place where everyone going and coming could seek blessings for a good journey or give thanks upon returning. These public gate shrines are known elsewhere (see above on Dan; below

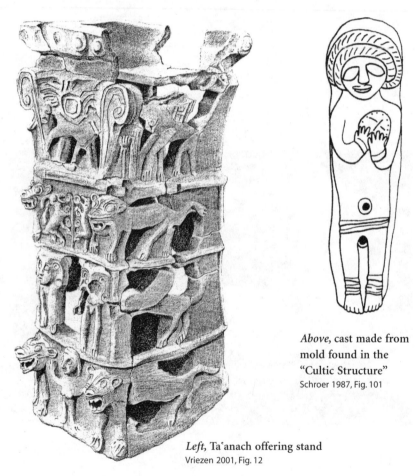

Above, cast made from mold found in the "Cultic Structure"
Schroer 1987, Fig. 101

Left, Ta'anach offering stand
Vriezen 2001, Fig. 12

on Kuntillet ʿAjrûd), and the biblical texts note them as well (the *bāmāh* visited by Saul; I Samuel 9:13).

(6) Two archaeological installations in Jerusalem or the vicinity may have been *bāmôt* (in addition to those condemned in II Kings 23:5-10, not directly archaeologically attested). The first is "Cave I" just south of the Temple Mount, excavated by Kenyon in the 1960s. This large cave produced dozens of late-7th-century B.C. zoomorphic and female figurines, most of them broken. Also in the cave were more than 1200 pottery vessels; twenty-one "horse and rider" figurines; one "rattle"; several model couches; two miniature stone incense altars; and one offering stand. Some of the intact bowls near the cave entrance had the remains of animal bones in them. Constructed or at least enlarged by humans, the rear was walled off to create a raised "domed" area. There were no human bones or anything else indicating that this was a burial cave (Holladay 1987:259, 260). It seems certainly to have served a cultic purpose (see below on some of the cult paraphernalia), and the large quantities of pottery and other objects make clear that it was more than a household shrine.

If Cave I was a *bāmāh* as I think it was (although not open-air), several references in II Kings 23:5 become intriguing: "high places round about Jerusalem"; "burning incense to Baʿal"; worshipping "all the host of heaven." The latter and the references to the "chariots of the sun" and the "horses dedicated to the sun" (v. 11) I have argued can be connected with

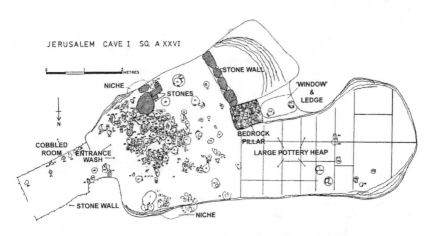

Plan of Cave I in Jerusalem; 7th cent. B.C.
Zevit 2001, Fig. 3:44

155

Top, "Tambourine" figurine; *center*, head of "pillar-base" figurine;
bottom, "pinched-face" figurine; Cave I, Jerusalem
Kenyon 1967, Fig. 10:2; 9:4; 10:1

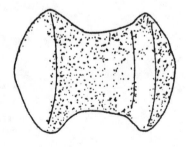

Terra-cotta "rattle," possibly
for ceremonial music;
tomb at Lachish, 7th cent. B.C.
Bloch-Smith 1992, Fig. 13D

the "horse and rider" figurines mentioned above. In the old Canaanite mythology, Baʿal was the "Cloud Rider," the weather god who rode across the
heavens daily in his chariot, governing wind and weather. In this view the
horse figurines, most without a rider, would have been symbols of Baʿal
and his heavenly horse-drawn chariot. Thus Josiah is said to have thrown
the "horses and chariots" out of the Temple. It might even be suggested, although hesitantly, that the figurines in Kenyon's cave deposit are actually
evidence of Josiah's purge of the Temple; the date is contemporary. The
overall evidence is better explained, however, if Cave I simply continued in
use as a favorite local *bāmāh*. (There are also other reasons to believe that
Josiah's reforms were not very effective; below.)

The other possible *bāmāh* in the Jerusalem area consists of some 20
large tumuli (stone-heaps) on hilltops on the western outskirts of Jerusalem. They were partially excavated in 1923, then reinvestigated in 1953. Associated with this complex are a perimeter wall, a large platform, a paved
area, some pits, and an enclosure full of burned animal bones. The few
tumuli that were excavated produced quantities of 8th-7th century B.C.
pottery, especially cooking pots and bowls. These tumuli may have had a
cultic function, probably associated with fasting of some sort, and possibly connected with funerary rites. If the latter were the case, the tumuli

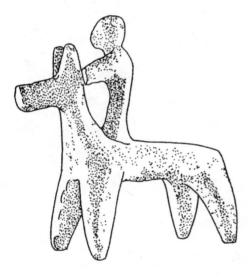

Horse-and-rider figurine;
7th cent. B.C.
Keel and Uehlinger 1998, Fig. 33b

may have been *symbolic* "burial cairns" or cenotaphs for noble or even royal families.

Gabriel Barkay (2003) has examined these tumuli and has suggested that they reflect the curious hints at the "burnings" that took place after the death of the kings of Judah (Jeremiah 34:5; II Chronicles 16:14). In Anatolia and Cyprus there is evidence for similar royal cenotaphs. (I return to the question of "cults of the dead" below.) To take another line of argument, we do have some evidence that *bāmôt* were connected with rites for the dead (above). And it is interesting that among Josiah's reforms were the destruction of the *"asherim"* in Jerusalem (or Asherahs?) and the defilement of their former places with human bones (II Kings 23:14). An irony? (Turnabout is fair play.)

(7) The biblical borders are said to have been "from Dan to Beersheba." We have discussed above the fragments of a monumental horned altar that once stood in the Dan cult complex (see p. 141). Oddly enough, the only other certain occurrence of a similar altar is at Beersheba, where Aharoni found an-

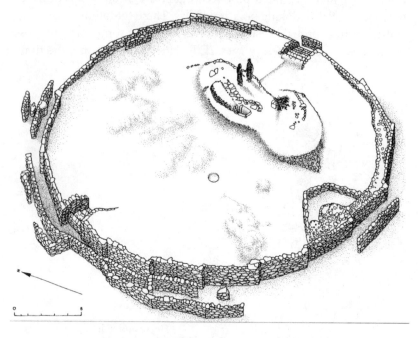

Plan of a large *tumulus* near Jerusalem; 8th cent. B.C. (?)
Zevit 2001, Fig. 4:4

other such altar, of almost identical proportions. However, it was not discovered *in situ,* but rather its dismantled blocks were found in *secondary* use, as building blocks incorporated into the walls of a later storehouse near the city gate. Aharoni speculated that the altar was once part of a now-missing temple-like complex that he thought had been located just below the Hellenistic cult complex in a prominent site on the mound. He called this the "basement building" because he argued that the superstructure had been destroyed down below the foundation level. Then the altar there was deliberately dismantled and the stones thrown out — later used as building blocks.

Aharoni dated this hypothetical "cultic reform" to Hezekiah in the 8th century B.C. But a reworking of Aharoni's generally "high chronology" shows that whatever happened took place more likely in the 7th century B.C. In this case, the reform of Josiah would provide a context, since it is reported that he "defiled the high places *(bāmôt)* where the priests had burned incense, from Geba to Beersheba" (II Kings 23:8).

Many scholars ridiculed Aharoni's speculation as typical of the worst abuses of "biblical archaeology" (among them Yadin). But as one who has no sympathy with that movement and its naïve attempt to "prove the Bible," I am willing to consider the notion. As I have argued in a recent book (Dever 2001), the biblical writers may have indulged in a good bit of "spin," but sometimes they knew a lot, and they knew it early. "Josiah's reforms" are often dismissed by biblical scholars, and they probably were not very effective. But the context of II Kings 23, with its polemics against "popular

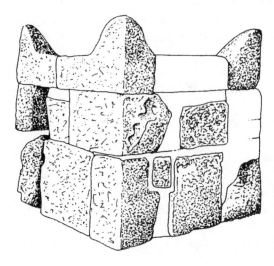

The large four-horned altar from Beersheba, as reassembled; 8th cent. B.C.
Adapted from photo: Israel Antiquities Authority

religion," can be well established by the archaeological evidence that we now actually have. There is nothing *intrinsically* fantastic about Josiah's having demolished a large *bāmāh* at Beersheba. (See also the case of the Arad temple, below; and see further Chapter VII on Josiah's reform.)

(8) Second in importance only to Dan is the 8th-century B.C. cult complex at Kuntillet 'Ajrûd in the eastern Sinai desert. It was excavated in 1975-1976 in a salvage operation carried out by Ze'ev Meshel, but the site is published only in preliminary reports (Meshel 1978). Nonetheless, it has attracted the attention of many scholars because of the spectacular material that it has produced. The site is a typical Middle Eastern "caravansary," or stopover station, on one of the desert routes crisscrossing the eastern Sinai between the Mediterranean and the Red Sea. It is on an isolated hilltop near small wells, still frequented by Bedouin.

Kuntillet 'Ajrûd is essentially a one-period site, occupied continually in the mid-9th to mid-8th century B.C. The pottery not only confirms that date but makes it clear that although remote this is an "Israelite" site, with both northern and southern (or Judean) contacts. The main structure atop the mesa is a rather typical Iron Age Judean desert fort, rectangular in plan with casemate (double) walls and square towers at the corner, and a partially open courtyard in the center. There are food storage and cooking facilities on the lower level, and steps indicate an upper level, no doubt with sleeping quarters. This complex was probably staffed and guarded by a small permanent force, but it would also have provided shelter and provisions for many desert travelers and traders.

Some scholars have questioned whether Kuntillet 'Ajrûd was a "fort," a "religious center," or even a "scribal school." I regard much of the debate as beside the point. The site is a fort; but it also serves quite sensibly as a sort of "inn"; and it has, as other sites do (above), an indisputable "gate shrine." The shrine consists of two rooms flanking the offset gateway as one comes into the courtyard from the plastered outer plaza. There are low benches around the walls of these rooms, and each is partially partitioned off across the back wall to form a *favissa*, or place to discard cultic items that must not be profaned by ordinary use. The walls and benches of the two side rooms are plastered, as are other portions of the larger complex. The "rationale" of the plan is clear; anyone coming or going must pass through the sacred area. There are two fragmentary outlying buildings at the far side of the plaza, but the gate shrine was the focal point of the entire complex.

The gate shrine was a center for several cultic activities. In the two

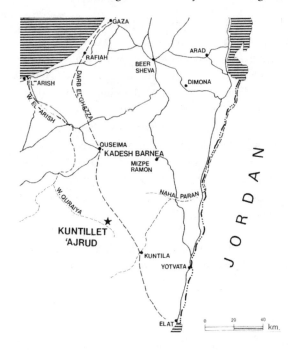

Map showing the location
of Kuntillet ʿAjrûd
Meshel 1978

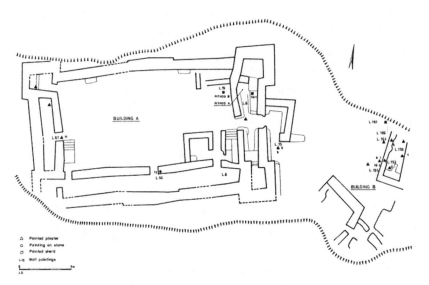

Plan of the Kuntillet ʿAjrûd fort
Meshel 1978

bench rooms, the *favissae,* and in the courtyard nearby were found several inscriptions painted in the plaster walls; two large storejars with painted scenes and inscriptions; and quantities of pottery. Elsewhere in the complex there are other painted plaster inscriptions and drawings, as well as a large, heavy stone bowl inscribed around the rim "Belonging to Obadiah, the son of Adnah; Blessed be he by Yahweh," no doubt a votive.

Many fragmentary Hebrew inscriptions were found at Kuntillet ʿAjrûd, but neither a catalog nor adequate photographs have yet been published. Zevit's translations, based on firsthand examination in the Israel Museum, are among the best (2001:372-404). Of particular interest here is that the corpus of Hebrew inscriptions contains clear references to at least four deities: Yahweh, El, Baʿal, and Asherah. Where the names of these well-known deities are *paired,* their occurrence is even more significant. Thus we find the names of male deities "in parallel" (a typical feature of Hebrew syntax), indicating that they are held in equal esteem, in texts like this one:

> To bless Baʿal on the day of w[ar,
> To the name of El on day of w[ar.

More revealing, however, are the names of "Yahweh" and "Asherah" paired on several inscriptions. A wall inscription in one of the bench rooms of the shrine reads

> To [Y]ahweh (of) Teiman (Yemen) and to his Ashera[h.

One large storejar ("Pithos A") has a long inscription that ends "I [b]lessed you by (or 'to') Yahweh of Samaria and by his Asherah." The second

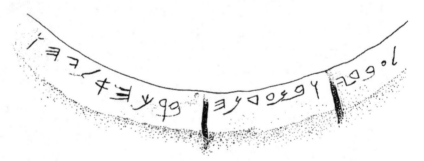

Stone votive bowl from Kuntillet ʿAjrûd
Ze'ev Meshel

storejar ("Pithos B") is similar but reads "Yahweh of Teiman and his Asherah." These "Yahweh and his Asherah" inscriptions at Kuntillet ʿAjrûd must be compared, of course, with the contemporary Kh. el-Qôm tomb inscription with the very same reading (Chapter VI). Both of these storejars also have elaborate, rather "exotic" painted scenes. "Pithos A" depicts the well-known Phoenician motif of a cow suckling her calf (identical to the motif on 9th-8th century B.C. carved ivory panels); a stylized palm tree (looking rather phallic) flanked by two rampant wild goats, a common motif in earlier Canaanite iconography; a large lion; what may be a bull; and, most importantly, a scene showing two standing male (?) figures with arms linked, and off to the right a seated female figure.

The Phoenician and Canaanite motifs are familiar, and they are not really unexpected if we are dealing with "syncretistic" folk religion, as is certainly the case here. But who are the three figures — so rare in Hebrew art that these are almost the only intact examples that we have (the others are on this same storejar; below)?

When I first saw these painted storejars with Meshel some 25 years ago, I was stunned, both by the scene and by the Hebrew inscription above it. I soon wrote two articles (1982, in Hebrew; 1984) arguing that the two figures to the left represented the Egyptian dwarf-god Bes (see p. 134), who is often portrayed bow-legged, with a leonine head and a crown, wearing a spotted leopard skin. The left-hand figure is apparently male, whether the

Painted scene on Pithos A
Meshel 1978

Processional scene on Pithos B
Meshel 1978

dangling thing between its legs is a phallus or the tail of a leopard skin. The right-hand figure, however, seems to be female, since it has breasts. Odd as that may appear, it does not pose a problem, since Bes is an androgynous deity and can appear as either male or female. In any case, Bes is an apotropaic deity, one who "turns away" bad luck, associated particularly with music, dancing, and celebrations in the cult. He was very popular, both in Egypt and throughout the Levant (even in Mesopotamia). Small faience Bes amulets are quite common in 8th-7th century B.C. Judean tombs, so his presence in cultic art at Kuntillet ʿAjrûd is not at all surprising. Some scholars, however, have gone further than I and would identify these two linked figures not as Bes representations, but rather as "Yahweh and his Asherah," as we read on some texts.

The seated female figure to the right is even more intriguing. Who *is* she, "Our Lady of ʿAjrûd"? I proposed in 1982 to identify her with the goddess Asherah, who is of course mentioned specifically in the Hebrew texts at the top of the scene. My reasoning first was that this semi-nude, bare-breasted female was not likely to be an ordinary Judean housewife or a worshipper, much less a priestess or a queen, that is, any human female. But the clincher for me was the "lion throne" on which the figure is seated. This is *not* a familiar side chair. Note the splayed, claw-like feet; the "pan-

**Hebrew inscription
and cultic scenes
on Pithos A**
Meshel 1978

eled" sides; the slightly tilted back; and the fact that the figure's feet are dangling in the air, suggesting a missing footstool.

Now it happens that "lion thrones" like these are very common in Ancient Near Eastern art and iconography, stretching back hundreds of years before Kuntillet ʿAjrûd. And as I discovered, "lion thrones" are *always* associated with deities or kings — never with ordinary human beings. The rationale is that the lions, symbols of ferocity, carried the throne on their backs. These "sacred" lions are often represented as cherubs — potent symbols of the divine presence and power — that is, with wings. And in nearly all cases, there is a low footstool in front of the throne.

Among the many parallel examples of lion thrones, I found one showing a Canaanite king on a carved ivory panel *ca.* 1200 B.C.; one on King Aḥiram's royal sarcophagus now in the Louvre (although this is not Solomon's contemporary "Hiram, King of Tyre"); and a nearly identical scene on an electrum pendant from Ugarit on the coast of Syria, dating to *ca.* 1300 B.C. The "folk art" at Kuntillet ʿAjrûd is primitive, of course, so the lion's feet are rather clubby; the feathers of the wings are very stylized on the side panels; the chair back (the tail) tilts only slightly; and, amusingly, the artist forgot the footstool. When one knows the long history of the "lion throne," however, it is clear that that is what the artist (if we can call him/her that) had in mind. And if this *is* a female deity, as seems most likely in a cult center, she can only be Asherah.

The evidence for that identification, which may seem speculative, lies first in the fact that the goddess is actually named on the associated in-

Electrum pendants; Syria, 14th-13th cent. B.C.
Negbi 1976, Fig. 134; 120

scription above. (Whether it is by the same hand, earlier or later, is irrelevant, since they are associated.) Second, we have a mass of inscriptional evidence from the Levantine Iron Age showing that a frequent epithet of the goddess Asherah was "the Lion Lady."

Finally, the only goddess whose name is well attested in the Hebrew Bible (or in ancient Israel generally) is Asherah (above). In earlier Canaan, the Great Goddess may be a cosmic deity who could be known by several names: Asherah; ʿAnat; Astarte; or Baʿalat or Elath (the feminine forms of "Baʿal" and "El"). Sometime she was associated with a particular cult and could thus appear in a local manifestation as "Baʿalat of Byblos" or the like. But by Israelite times, only the name Asherah survives in any clear sense. Astarte ("Ishtar") appears in the Hebrew Bible only rarely. And ʿAnat is attested only once in the personal name "Shamgar ben-ʿAnat" (Judges 3:31), and twice as a place name, "Beth-ʿAnat" (Joshua 19:38; Judges 1:33).

Thus if the Kuntillet ʿAjrûd female figure is a goddess, she must be identified with Asherah, the old Canaanite Mother Goddess. Not only that, but the Hebrew text specifies that she is *"Yahweh's Asherah."* I take that to mean that here she is Yahweh's Lady, his consort, just as Asherah was El's consort in Canaanite religion. Thus Asherah could be thought of in some circles as a divine consort, but to discredit her the biblical writers and editors couple her now with Ba'al. (In the older Canaanite pantheon, 'Anat is the younger god Ba'al's consort, while Asherah is El's consort, the "Mother of the gods.")

Not all scholars have been persuaded by my interpretation of the seated female and the accompanying inscription, especially since in 1982-1984 I was virtually alone in daring to speak of Yahweh's "consort." As for the inscription, there is admittedly a grammatical problem. In biblical Hebrew, a proper name like "Asherah" does not usually take a possessive suffix like "his." But there are some occurrences of such a construction in the parent Canaanite language, and also in late Hebrew and Aramaic. In any case, some scholars read the consonants *'a-sh-r* here not as "Asherah" but as "asherah," the tree-like *symbol* of the goddess. They read my Kh. el-Qôm inscription (below) the same way, thus "may X be blessed by Yahweh and his 'tree.'" I find that rather desperate, and I suspect that it reflects the reluctance of many biblical scholars even to consider the possibility that Yahweh may have had a female consort. Yet many scholars increasingly acknowledge that the Hebrew word *'ăshērāh* sometimes *must* be read "Asherah," and that this goddess *was* venerated throughout much of the monarchy. So why *not* as Yahweh's consort? All the other major deities in the ancient Near East were paired. How can we continue to insist that ancient Israel was "unique"? I will return to the issue of Asherah and her cult in Chapter VI in discussing women's roles in folk religion.

Monumental Temples

The most sacred tier of holy places discussed here would obviously be monumental temples, especially a temple like the Jerusalem Temple that served as a royal sanctuary and national cult center (at least in the Deuteronomistic ideal). Thus far, however, we have found very few actual examples from early Israel — but enough, however, to question the biblical notion that there were none except the Temple in Jerusalem, as the later writers maintained.

(1) The earliest Israelite monumental temple that we have is the Field V Migdal Temple at Shechem, the old tribal center in the heartland of Samaria, with traditions going even farther back into ancestral times (Gene-

sis 12:1-7). This impressive building was first excavated by the Germans in the 1930s and then re-excavated in the 1960s by G. Ernest Wright and an American team (my first fieldwork there in 1962; I later directed a campaign in 1973). The building has been called a *"migdal"* (Hebrew "fortress") temple because of its massive walls, up to fifteen feet thick; its two towers at the entrance; and its presumed second or even third stories. It was first constructed in the middle Bronze Age as a Canaanite temple, *ca.* 1650 B.C., and then reused with some alterations in the late Bronze Age, *ca.*

The Field V *migdal* temple at Shechem, with large *māṣṣēbāh* in forecourt
Photo: W. G. Dever

1400-1300 B.C. An alteration in the 12th century B.C. at the beginning of the Iron Age saw the addition of a large *māṣṣēbāh* or standing stone and an altar in the forecourt (Temple 1). Shortly after that, the building was destroyed, and it was used some time later (Temple 2) only as a granary (Stager 2003).

Wright connected the Field V temple with biblical traditions, beginning with those in Joshua 24. There it is said that at the close of the conquest of Canaan Joshua gathered all the tribes at Shechem, where he recited to them "all the mighty acts of God." He then instituted a covenant renewal ceremony in which the people solemnly bound themselves to obey all Yahweh's commandments. As a witness to this covenant, Joshua "took a great stone, and set it up there under the oak in the sanctuary *(miqdāsh)* of Yahweh" (Joshua 24:26). Wright took the Field V temple, with its newly erected *māṣṣēbāh*, to be this very "sanctuary." In his view, an old Canaanite temple of the patriarchal age (compare the "oak" here with Abraham's "oak" in Genesis 12:6) was *re-consecrated* as an Israelite sanctuary sometime around 1200 B.C. (Wright, *Shechem: Biography of a Biblical City*, 1965).

Wright then appealed to Judges 9, which relates how one of the later judges, Abimelech, went to Shechem to rally support for a bid to make himself king (his name means "My father was King"). As the account has it, "All the citizens of Shechem came together, and all Beth-millo, and they went and made Abimelech king, by the oak of the pillar" (*mūṣṣāb;* an alternate form of *māṣṣēbāh;* Judges 9:6). But one Jotham sows dissension: "Israel has no king but Yahweh." After three oppressive years, the Shechemites rebel, but they are put down by Abimelech, who shuts them up in the

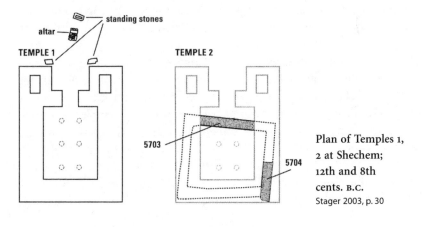

Plan of Temples 1, 2 at Shechem; 12th and 8th cents. B.C.
Stager 2003, p. 30

"Tower *(migdal)* of Shechem" and burns it down upon their heads. The text also calls this structure first "the temple of *Ba'al*-berith" and temple of *Ba'al* "of the covenant"; then, significantly, it is the "temple of *El*-berith," temple of *El* "of the covenant" (cf. Judges 9:4; 9:46). Wright saw here confirmation of the notion that the old Canaanite temple dedicated to *Ba'al* had been re-dedicated to *El,* one of the ancient names of Israelite Yahweh. He argued furthermore that it still served (presumably a few generations later in the period of the Judges) as the cult center for a covenant renewal ceremony.

Wright's views were met with suspicion in most circles, and with derision among European biblicists: here was "biblical archaeology" at its worst. Nevertheless, as one who has vigorously opposed old-fashioned "prove the Bible archaeology" for 30 years, and as an archaeologist who is familiar with Shechem firsthand, I have few objections. The Shechem "Migdal Temple" certainly could have served as an early Israelite public sanctuary — especially in the light of all that we have learned since the 1960s about continuities with Canaanite religion (Chapter VIII). There is such a thing as being too skeptical, dispensing with common sense too quickly. The biblical writers *remembered* this temple as genuinely "Israelite," and they tolerated its existence because it was pre-Solomonic and therefore not expected to conform to the Deuteronomistic ideal.

(2) The only known full-fledged Israelite temple of the monarchic period is the one excavated at Arad, east of Beersheba, by Yohanan Aharoni in the 1960s. This building was controversial from the moment of its discovery. Some scholars argued that it could not have been a "temple": there weren't supposed to *be* any. Others thought it simply a desert "tabernacle." Still others assumed that it might have been a temple of sorts, but surely not "Israelite." And estimates of the date ranged all the way from the 10th century B.C. to the 7th century B.C.

No final publication ever appeared, but several recent reexaminations of the excavated material have clarified matters considerably, especially the question of date (Herzog 2001). All now agree that it must be 8th century B.C., that is, post-Solomonic by some two centuries. The temple was thus in use not through four or five strata, but only in Str. 10-9. The revised chronology has major implications for relating the Arad temple to biblical history.

Iron Age Arad was a small fort east of Beersheba, on the Judean border with the Negev desert. The complex is roughly square, with thick offsets-insets walls. The temple occupies almost one-quarter of the inte-

General view of Arad temple
Photo: W. G. Dever

rior space, located in the northwest corner. It is the only well-preserved element within the fort. The use of the other spaces is uncertain, but they were probably the living and storage areas for the troops of the garrison, which must have been quite small. Some light is thrown on the size and function of the fort by the more than 100 ostraca found, documents written in ink on pieces of broken pottery. Most have to do with provisions, but some of them mention names that are known from priestly families in the Bible. One (no. 18) refers to the "temple of Yahweh," which I interpret not as the Jerusalem Temple, but as the local temple at Arad (contra Aharoni and some others).

The rectangular temple, like the one in Jerusalem, is basically tripartite in plan, with three rooms arranged along a central axis. The first room, with an off-center entrance, is an open courtyard with a large stone altar on one side wall and a corridor or storage area *(favissa?)* behind that. Near the altar in a walled-off compartment to one side were found an offering stand with a removable bowl and a large oil lamp. Nearby, there was a small bronze weight in the form of a crouching lion.

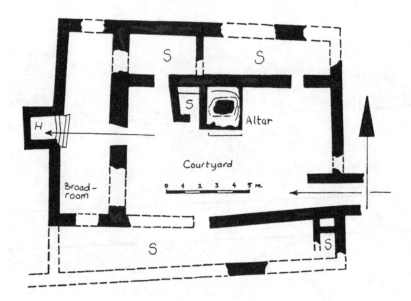

Plan of Arad temple
Keel 1997, Fig. 170

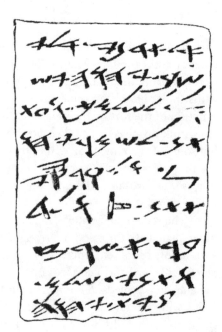

Arad ostracon no. 18
Aharoni 1981, p. 36

The next chamber was shallow but wide. There were probably low stone and mud benches around the walls, but these were poorly preserved. Beyond that, the third "room" was only a small niche (6 by 3½ feet), approached by a single step. The entrance was at one time flanked by two square, finely dressed stylized horned altars, which had some traces of burned "organic material" on the tops (unfortunately not analyzed). A curtain seems to have closed off this "inner sanctum" (Hebrew *děbîr*, "holy of holies" in the Jerusalem Temple). At the back wall there apparently stood two large undressed standing stones, one larger than the other, one with faint traces of red paint. But these *maṣṣēbôt*, as I take them to be, were not found there *in situ*. They were recovered (along with a third) from under a later plaster floor (Str. 8?), along with the two altars mentioned above (there is some confusion in preliminary reports; see Zevit 2001:166, 167). Some take these alterations as evidence of the attempted reforms of either Hezekiah or Josiah (as Aharoni himself did; see further Chapter VIII).

Due to poor excavation techniques all too common in the 1960s, as well as to inadequate publication, the Arad temple and its paraphernalia have rarely been taken seriously by scholars, even archaeologists. A recent treatment by Ze'ev Herzog (2001), an original staff member, acknowledges the faults of the project and salvages what information can be salvaged.

One of the small stylized
horned altars flanking the entrance
to the inner sanctum
of the Arad temple;
8th cent. B.C.
Vriezen 2001, Fig. 8

173

Inner sanctum of the Arad temple, with horned altars and *māṣṣēbôt*
Photo: W. G. Dever

Herzog agrees that the deliberate and careful dismantling of the cella (that is, the central cult room) of the temple, with the altars and *māṣṣēbôt* and their concealment beneath a Str. 8 plaster floor, is indeed to be connected with Hekeziah's reforms in the late 8th century B.C. II Kings 18:4 specifies that Hezekiah "removed the high places *(bāmôt)* and broke down the pillars *(māṣṣēbôt)* and cut down the Asherah (the *'ăshērāh)*."

Skeptics regard this passage, along with the account of Josiah's reforms (II Kings 23) a century later, as simply Deuteronomistic propaganda. These two "reformers" were the only Judean kings of whom these writers approved. Whether the idealistic reforms were successful or not, whether they in fact even took place, is irrelevant for our purposes here. The biblical writers' *knowledge* of folk religion, even though they disapproved of it, was accurate and realistic. There is no reason to think that they were unaware of an "illegitimate" temple and its incense altars and *māṣṣēbôt* at Arad, especially since this was a Judean royal fortress. It would have been an obvious target for an iconoclastic reform. And while this may be speculation, the deliberate dismantling of the temple and its replacement by another structure in the days of Hezekiah is an archaeological fact. I see no reason for skepticism here (see further Chapter VIII).

I would make several other observations about the Arad temple, regarding things that most scholars have missed. The bronze lion found near the altar, even though it is only a small weight, is significant. Shekel weights in the form of cast bronze animals are exceedingly rare, and their use as offerings is unknown as far as I know. The presentation of a lion here reminds me of the common epithet of Asherah, the "Lion Lady" (above). As though to underscore the plurality of deities, there is the fact that there are two *māṣṣēbôt* in the temple cella, one smaller than the other. If *māṣṣēbôt* symbolize the presence of deities, as the biblical witness unanimously testifies (above), then we have at least *two* deities venerated in the Arad temple.

Finally, I note the context of the Arad temple. It is a prominent, indeed disproportionately large, part of what is a Judean royal fortress (as the ostraca make clear). If I am correct in the interpretation of the finds, here we have evidence that the religion of barracks soldiers — ordinary folk — was often compatible with the "official" state cult. Not only do some ostraca seem to concern provisions for the temple and the casting of priestly lots, but others mention the "sons (descendants) of Korah," a well-known Levitical priestly family. Furthermore, two shallow platters (no. 102, 103) found at the foot of the large altar in the courtyard have an abbreviation *qôph-kāp*, probably for *qôdesh kōhănîm*, "holy object of priests."

All things considered, there is no reason to suppose that the Arad temple is unique or even exceptional. Rather it appears to be an example of what was probably a widespread phenomenon — local temples. Here is one even in a remote outpost, where supposedly "syncretistic" practices went on until they became unacceptable under the influence of the "Yahweh alone movement" of the mid-8th century B.C. (Chapter VIII). Yet few biblical scholars have seen the importance of the Arad temple (exceptions are Ahlström 1982; Albertz 1994; and the trenchant discussion of Zevit 2001:156-171).

Having established a sufficient archaeological database to illuminate folk religion, let me turn now to one of its most prominent aspects, the cult of Asherah. Here I shall try to show how far actual religious beliefs and practices differed from the ideal of biblical "book religion."

CHAPTER VI

The Goddess Asherah and Her Cult

We have already discussed the archaeological evidence for household shrines and most of the cultic paraphernalia typically associated with them in Chapters IV and V. Here the effort was to portray popular religion at the most fundamental level, that of the *family*. Now it is time, however, to focus even more closely on the role that women played in family religion and to explore further the question of whether many Israelite women had a patroness, the old Canaanite Mother Goddess "Asherah." That brings us to the one class of archaeological artifacts that we have introduced only briefly thus far, the terra cotta female figurines.

The Figurines: Who Is She?

From the 1920s onward, as excavations in Palestine mounted in number and broadened in scope, a series of small terra cotta female figurines that were unearthed came to be widely discussed and their meaning disputed. The discussion, in my opinion, has generated far more heat than light. There is no need to summarize the controversy here, especially since the recent exhaustive analysis of the Israeli archaeologist Raz Kletter has given the history in his *The Judean Pillar Figurines and the Archaeology of Asherah* (1996).

(1) First let us look at the basic types of these figurines; the numbers known; their date; and the contexts from which they come. (a) A few early figurines from the 10th-9th century B.C. depict a frontally nude female

176

with long hair, her arms at her side or her hands at the breasts. These would appear to continue a Late Bronze Age Canaanite tradition of plaque figures, either standing (votives?) or lying on a couch (mourners or deities). Most scholars identify the standing figurines with the well-known Late Bronze Age goddess Asherah, especially those with the distinctive bouffant wig worn by the Egyptian goddess Hathor, whom the texts clearly equate with Levantine Asherah as "Qudshu, the Holy One." An Egyptian New Kingdom plaque now in the Winchester Museum shows the goddess with her crossed chest-bands, astride a lion, and gives all three of her names: Qudshu (Asherah); Astarte; and ʿAnat. (b) Also mostly from the 10th-9th century B.C. in the north are a number of figurines that show a female holding at one breast a circular object that has been variously interpreted as a "frame drum" (tambourine), or possibly a molded bread cake. These may be nude or wearing a skirt. We have already noted them from Tell-el Farʿah (N.) and have pointed out a mold for mass-producing them found in the Taʿanach "Cultic Structure" (above). A few occur in Judah as late as the 7th century B.C.

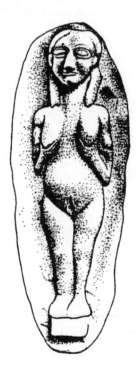

An early type of plaque figurine; 10th cent. B.C. (?).
Zevit 2001, Fig. 4.1.IIIa

Late Bronze Age plaque figurine,
possibly of a deceased female
lying on a couch or bier
Zevit 2001, Fig. 4.I.IIIb

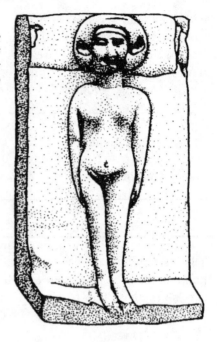

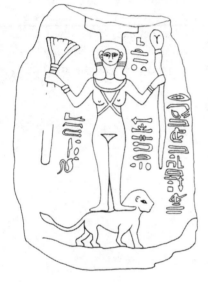

Egyptian New Kingdom plaque
in the Winchester Museum,
depicting the Goddess riding
on a lion and giving all three
of her names: (1) "Qudshu"
("Holy One," or Asherah-Hathor);
(2) 'Anat; (3) Astarte
Winter 1983, Fig. 37

Some of them may indeed be playing a frame-drum, since musical instruments are well documented in the cult, and often with women as performers (Meyers 1991a:16-27), but these seem more "Phoenician" in character. (Would *Israelite* women musicians have performed publicly half-nude?) Some of the circular objects on the Israelite/Judean examples, however, look to me more like the mold-made cakes with deeply incised patterns that are well known from the ancient Near East in connection with cultic feasts (cf. p. 154). We have molds from Mesopotamia; and Jewish women still bake "hamantashen," or three-cornered poppy-seed cakes said to represent Haman's hat in the book of Esther, for the festival of Purim, as do Eastern Orthodox women for their feasts. Several points seem relevant to me: (1) The *Phoenician* figurines hold the disc away from their chest, at an angle, as one naturally would with a frame drum. Furthermore, the disc here is undecorated, as a frame drum would be. (2) The *Israelite-Judean* figurines, on the other hand, clutch the disc (always decorated) tightly to their chest — no way to play a frame drum. (3) Finally, the Taʿanach mold (p. 154) — our best evidence for mass production, and from a well-dated context — features a very small disc, which can hardly be a frame drum and must be a molded or incised cake. I am reminded of Jeremiah's protest about folk religion in Judean villages of the 7th century B.C.:

> The children gather wood,
> the fathers kindle fire,
> and the women knead dough
> to make cakes for the Queen of Heaven.   (Jeremiah 7:18; cf. 44:17-19)

The "Queen of Heaven" is usually identified as Astarte (or Ishtar, another name for the Mother Goddess; Ackerman 1992), but that name is relatively rare in the biblical texts (above).

Far more common than all of these, however, are two types of later, specifically Judean "pillar-base" figurines, so-called because they do not model the lower body (which looks to some like a tree trunk). These proliferated after the fall of Samaria in the late 8th-7th century B.C., as Kletter has shown beyond doubt. Both types depict a nude female with prominent breasts. The first has a very stylized face, made by simply pinching the upper part with a thumb and the forefinger to form a crude nose and two impressions for eyes. The two hands lift up the breasts, as though to offer them to a nursing child. Sometimes they have side-locks or wear turbans. The second type of Judean pillar figurine has a finely modeled head with elaborate coiffure, separately mold-made and then attached to the body. These, too, feature prominent breasts, sometimes pendulous. The great American scholar Albright long ago dubbed both types *"dea nutrix"* figurines, emphasizing their representation of a goddess as a nursing mother (and only that, since the lower body is a featureless column with a simple flaring base).

Phoenician "pillar-base" figurine holding a
frame-drum, possibly a cult musician
Vriezen 2001, Fig. 15

(2) There is the matter of numbers of all these figurines, which is disputed. A catalogue published by Holland in 1977 counted 2711, and hundreds have been discovered since then, some 400 from Jerusalem alone. In the past, I have spoken of "about 3000" all told, but Kletter disagrees. Of the Judean pillar-base figurines, Kletter counts 854 examples (including 359 of Holland's *corpus* from Kenyon's excavations in Jerusalem; but not all of Shiloh's later excavations). It is specifically the late Judean pillar-base figurines that I shall consider here, because they are far more numerous, and they are also somewhat easier to interpret. Whatever the exact figure (many hundreds), it is agreed that they were exceedingly common in the 8th-7th century B.C.

(3) As I have said, in archaeology context is crucial. The pillar-base figurines may be common in general, but where *specifically* do they tend to occur? The answer is, in all sorts of contexts, nearly all domestic: in houses; in cisterns, pits, and rubbish heaps; and in debris of all kinds. But they are relatively rare in tomb deposits, as well as in clear cultic contexts (although the mold found in the Taʿanach "Cultic Structure" provides a very significant exception). As I have stressed above, context is fundamental to determining the meaning of archaeological artifacts, so we are led to conclude

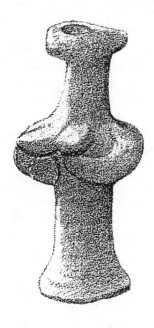

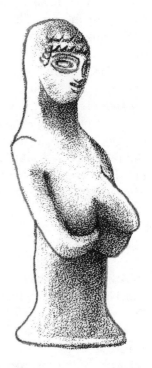

"Pinched-face" figurine; 7th cent. B.C.
Vriezen 2001, Fig. 14

"Pillar-base" figurine from Jerusalem; 7th cent. B.C.
Vriezen 2001, Fig. 13

that the female figurines have more to do with household than with community cults, more with ongoing life events than with death and funerary rituals. In any case, we are clearly dealing with *family religion*. But it is important to note that thus far there is no obvious "pattern" of distribution that would help to specify just what these figurines signified or exactly how they were used. They were certainly not "toys" (below).

(4) The "psychology" of the pillar figurines might be clarified if we could connect them with some terminology in the literature, in this case the biblical texts, the only witness that we have. There are several possible Hebrew terms for "figurine," but none are very persuasive.

(a) One possibility would be the term *tĕrāphîm*. The etymology is not known, but the word occurs fifteen times in the Hebrew Bible, where we have to determine its meaning by context. In Genesis 31:33-35 we have an intriguing story of how Rachel resisted Jacob's intent to break camp and move the tents. She did so by hiding the *tĕrāphîm* — the "household gods" (as the RSV correctly translates) — among the camel trappings, and then sitting atop the heap. She apologizes to her father Laban by saying that she is indisposed because she is having her period and cannot rise to meet him.

This passage implies several things about the images of the gods in the patriarchal stories. (1) They are plural, representing several deities. (2) They are associated with traditional nomadic lifestyles and were therefore portable. (3) They represent the ancestral deities (or deified ancestors?) of the clan — their continuing "presence" in the family group — and thus they were among the most valuable of the family's possessions. (4) They were small enough for a hoard of them to be concealed under a woman's lap. (5) Finally, they may have been principally in the custodianship of women.

Other passages may add to this picture. I Samuel 19:13-16 relates how Michal concealed her husband David's escape from Saul's wrath at the palace. She placed *tĕrāphîm* (in the plural, as always) in the bed where he had lain overnight and covered them with the bedclothes and a pillow of goat's hair. Here the *tĕrāphîm* (or one of them) appear to have been larger, that is, life-size.

Micah, whose family shrine we have discussed above, had *tĕrāphîm* in his house, used by his sons whom he had appointed as priests. The biblical texts (Judges 17:5; 18:17-20) mention the *tĕrāphîm* in connection with *pesĕlîm*, "graven or carved images," so the two types of images are not identical (below). Overall, the term *tĕrāphîm* seems to refer to relatively small, portable images of deities, although the terminology does not reveal the medium, except that it was probably not metal or wood (that is, they were not "graven, carved").

(b) Another possible biblical term for our figurines is *gillūlîm*. The verbal root means "to roll," but the noun derived from it means "(ball of) dung" and is sometimes used that way. In the plural, however, the word comes to mean "idol," but with the connotation that idols are as repugnant as excrement. Thus in Deuteronomy 29:17 *gillūlîm* are associated with *shiqûṣ*, "an abominable thing," presumably things "made of wood and stone." In Ezekiel, where the term occurs most often (late 7th–early 6th century B.C.), it is associated with high places (*bāmôt*), standing stones (*maṣṣēbôt*) altars, and other kinds of images (Ezekiel 6:4, 5). In Ezekiel the *gillūlîm* are images depicted on a wall; and Ezekiel 18:12 speaks of "lifting up one's eyes" to view them. Thus it may be that *gillūlîm* are painted images of deities. But if so, they do not survive (understandably so).

(c) I have already mentioned *pesel*, a "graven, carved image," the noun derived from a verb meaning "to hew into shape." Most of the biblical references suggest something carved from wood or engraved in metal (perhaps overlaid with silver or gold). Several references among the fierce polemics against idolatry in Isaiah and Jeremiah yield the clearest understanding of what a *pesel* is. Isaiah ridicules the idol *(pesel)*: "a workman casts it, and a goldsmith overlays it with gold" (40:19; cf. 30:22). Or again, he asks: "Who fashions a god or casts an image *(pesel)* that is profitable for nothing?" (44:10). And in the same passage there is a contemptuous description of a man who makes a "carved image" *(pesel)* of wood, then cuts it up to worship half of it and builds a cooking fire with the other half (44:14-20; cf. 45:20; also of wood; and Jeremiah 10:3, 4, of wood, overlaid with silver and gold). These *peselîm*, however sturdy and well made, will be "beaten to pieces" by Yahweh, declares the 8th-century B.C. prophet Micah (1:7). These are the very "images" that the Ten Commandments prohibits (Exodus 20:4; Deuteronomy 5:8), specifically because they represent deities. Those who make them "trust in graven images *(peselîm)* . . . say to molten images, 'You are our gods'" (Isaiah 42:17). And a passage in Kings denouncing Manasseh for his heresies describes the "graven image" *(pesel)* he made for Asherah and set up in the Temple in Jerusalem (II Kings 21:7).

(d) In some of the passages just cited, *pesel* is used in parallel with *massēkāh*. This term is usually translated "molten image" (from a verb meaning "to pour out"), and obviously it is also made of metal. How the two kinds of cast metal images are related is unclear.

(e) The rare word *semel* can refer to a forbidden idol or even an image of an animal (Deuteronomy 4:15-18), but it is unknown what these objects actually were. There are also a few other terms in the Hebrew Bible for "image," but these are usually more abstract, that is, they refer to God's or humanity's "image."

What have we learned from this excursus into terminology? Not much, I fear. We can only observe that some of these terms obviously refer to idols made of wood or stone, either portable or statuesque. The *gillūlîm* might be painted images, but painted on what we do not know. Only the *tĕrāphîm* could possibly refer to our small terra cotta figurines (less than 6-

7 inches high); and Michal's *těrāphîm* replacing David in the bed would seem to make that identification doubtful.

After long consideration of all the typical biblical language regarding "images," I have concluded that *none* of it fits what we actually have in the female figurines. How can one account for that?

I can think of only three possible explanations. (1) The first is that the biblical writers and editors simply didn't know about our figurines, so of course they do not mention them. I find that hard to believe, since the figurines were very common — and precisely in the late 8th–early 6th centuries B.C., when the literary tradition was beginning to take shape. I have argued, of course, that the biblical writers were "elitist," out of touch with ordinary people. But they were not oblivious to what was going on around them, because they do talk about many other aspects of folk religion in considerable detail. They must have been aware of the widespread use of our figurines.

(2) That leads to two other possible explanations for the silence of the Hebrew Bible. Perhaps the writers were just not interested in these figurines, so they ignored them. But there the same objection as above holds: they know a great deal about folk religion, and they are clearly interested in it (if only because they disapprove of it).

(3) I can offer only one other explanation, namely that the biblical writers and editors knew very well what the female figurines represented, and *therefore they deliberately suppressed any reference to them.* They did not wish to acknowledge the popularity and the powerful influence of these images, much less to enhance them by talking about them. ("Don't speak of the devil," as the saying goes.) Thus there is an attempt here to deceive readers, ancient and modern. Why? I think it must be because the images represented the goddess *Asherah,* whom the biblical writers abhorred (and probably also feared).

I have already shown how some of the biblical references to "asherah" are downplayed in the texts, reducing her as it were to only a "shadow of herself" — merely a *symbol* of the goddess, a pole or tree. And we have noted how later editors may have tinkered with the pronunciation of the related divine name "Astarte" to make it pronounced as "shame." There may be a further clue concerning what appears to be the obscurity of some biblical language, as in the word *mipleṣet.*

This word occurs only once in the Hebrew Bible, in I Kings 15:13 (= II Chronicles 15:16). This story describes how King Asa's mother Ma'acah made "an abominable image for Asherah," something of wood that Asa "cut down" and "burned." The verb from which this rare word comes means "to shudder," or to be horrified. But the modern translation of the noun as "abominable image" is only a *guess* at the exact meaning. Now if the biblical writers had *wanted* to be precise in mentioning this wooden image of or for the goddess Asherah, they had the more or less precise terms discussed above at hand. But they did not use any of these words. They chose what I would call a circumlocution, a way of "skirting the issue." They wanted to condemn Maʿacah for her veneration of Asherah, so they had to be specific about her most sinful act. But they call the Asherah image only an "abomination" — something too terrible to mention by name. We either have to conclude that this was a deliberate attempt to obscure a reference to Asherah and her images; or suppose that the writers didn't really know what a *mipleṣet* was, and were aware only that it was something very bad. I find the latter unlikely. I am confident that the biblical writers knew very well what a *mipleṣet* was; they just didn't want *you* to know. In my view, it is all part of the attempt of a hierarchical, male, orthodox Establishment to drive Asherah underground — an attempt that ultimately succeeded. And there she remained, until she was dug up recently by archaeologists. I can already hear the cries of protest that there was no such "conspiracy." But rather than raising theoretical objections, let us continue to look at the evidence — without theological presuppositions, if possible. As usual in the study of artifacts, it is *function* that offers the best clue as to what an object was. How did the figurines function, and what did that make them? Are they, as Zevit suggests, "Prayers in Clay"?

The first clue to function and thus to identity is found in the earlier Late Bronze Age version of these figurines, since they did not first emerge in Canaan in Israelite times. From about 1500-1200 B.C. we have a large series of metal or mold-made terra cotta plaque female figurines. Many are rather stylized, but all of them present a nude female figure frontally, with wide hips and full breasts. Sometimes the pubic triangle is exaggerated and graphically portrayed. The figure often wears a necklace, occasionally an arrow-quiver with crossed chest-bands. She may hold lotus blossoms, snakes, or even sacrificial animals in her outstretched hands. Very often she is riding on the back of a lion (or sometimes a war-horse).

There is no doubt whatsoever who this figure represents. She is the great Goddess of Canaan, under many guises. As we have seen, she goes by several, perhaps local, names: Asherah, ʿAnat, Astarte, Elath, or Baʿalat.

The hundreds of mythological texts from ancient Ugarit on the coast of Syria, known since the 1930s, introduce the first three names and tell us a great deal about the roles of the goddesses (Coogan 1978). Astarte is a deity associated with the stars and heavenly bodies (and can be androgynous). ʿAnat is simultaneously a fierce warrior goddess and the passionate lover of the storm god Baʿal — a goddess of love and death. And Asherah is the consort of the high god El, "Lady Asherah of the Sea" and the "Mother of the gods." (Some scholars see these as entirely separate deities, not as various manifestations of a cosmic female deity.)

The lore of the Canaanite gods and goddesses and the dramatic stories of their loves and wars and even their misadventures would have persisted throughout the Iron Age in Canaan. These oral traditions, preserved in poem and song, constituted a strong undercurrent in Israelite religious thought and practice (as we shall see in Chapter VIII). I have already noted how frequently El persists as one of Yahweh's names (see also Chapter VIII); how Baʿal and Asherah appear often in the biblical texts. Thus Israelites already knew of the centuries-old "Mother Goddess," and their por-

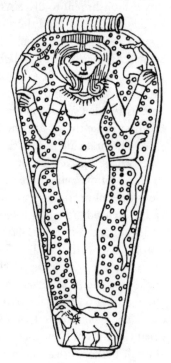

Gold pendant depicting Asherah on her lion,
with Hathor wig, holding ibexes and serpents;
Syria, 14th-13th cent. B.C.
Negbi 1976, Fig. 119

186

trait of her (if that's what the figurines were) would naturally have been similar to the Canaanite portrayals, especially since folk art is always traditional. Yet here the differences are more significant than the similarities.

The Iron Age Israelite figurines, at least the typical 8th-7th-century B.C. Judean pillar-base ones, never model the genitalia, or even the lower body at all. They emphasize the *breasts,* so much so that the eye is inevitably drawn there (there being nothing else to see). And here one must put entirely out of mind the modern fascination with female breasts as "sex objects." In the ancient world, breasts were associated with their most basic function: nursing an infant, whose very life depended upon the mother's having sufficient milk. Thus there is nothing "immodest" here (and also nothing to the charge of some feminists that sex-obsessed modern male scholars have invented the notion of "fertility goddesses"; below). Even today, one can see extremely modest Arab women in the villages nursing their babies in public. Albright's intuition in calling these figurines *dea nutrix* (the "Nursing Goddess") long ago was sound.

The point that I want to make here is that while the Canaanite figurines portray the goddess as a rather lascivious *courtesan* of the gods, the Israelite ones are much more "chaste" and portray her simply as a *nursing mother.* The Great Mother becomes a patroness of mothers everywhere (although still possibly a divine consort). In that sense, the more blatant sexuality of Canaanite religion is now restrained and redirected, without religion being, of course, any less "earthy," any less concerned with fecundity.

Although it is obvious that the female function of lactation is somehow part of the "psychology" of these figurines and their use, we are still left to speculate how they were actually employed, as well as who is represented (the two questions are intertwined). First, I have suggested elsewhere that the figurines were *talismans.* A talisman is a charm — a symbolic object (like Aladdin's lamp) that is supposed to work "magic," to bring some desired benefit. If we venture to ask what Israelite women (and men) would have wanted in using these figurines as talismans, one answer may seem obvious: babies — babies conceived and safely born and successfully reared through infancy. But since talismans were thought to work magic generally, they could also be used in the hope of securing any benefit that was desired. The figure of a woman with full breasts would have suggested the overall notion of "plenty," the gods' abilities to nourish the human family. And if we ask to whom such "prayers in clay" were addressed,

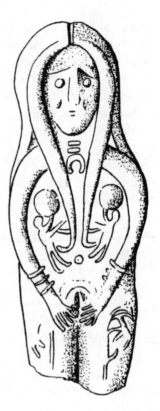

A terra cotta of the Great Mother,
displaying her vulva and nursing twins;
Revadim (Israel), Late Bronze Age
Keel and Uehlinger 1998, Fig. 82

the answer is equally obvious: to the local manifestation of Asherah, long venerated in Canaan as patroness of mothers.

One doesn't have to be a genius (or a woman) to figure all this out. Yet many scholars continue to wonder what these female figurines were, whom they represent, or how they functioned. Some have rejected outright the notion of "talismans." A few even go to the absurd extreme of declaring that the figurines are merely toys — which I call the "Barbie-doll syndrome" (but even "toys" are highly symbolic, of course). There are really only three reasonable possibilities. (1) The figurines represent a *goddess* (Asherah) to whom women (and men) prayed, and they were used as talismans generally. (2) They represent a *woman praying* to a deity (not necessarily female). (3) They are a sort of "stand-in" for the worshipper, a *votive offering* symbolizing the worshipper's prayers and vows. I prefer the first interpretation, which the majority of scholars today have finally come around to, and I have shown above why Asherah is the specific goddess who must be represented. But could a case be made for the figurines being votives? And could the figurines be both images of the Goddess *and* votives? I shall not deal here with the possibility that the figurines generally represent mortal women, since that seems out of the question to me (but cf. Carol Meyers 1988:162, 163 for this view, the Phoenician figurines especially as depicting dancers or musicians in the cult). Certainly the earlier Mesopotamian and Canaanite female "votives" are all images of the Goddess, not of humans.

A votive (from the Latin *voto*, "wish, vow") is an object presented, that is, "dedicated," to a deity, symbolizing and accompanied by a wish and a vow. (In another context, a votive could be something done in the performance of a vow.) Various vows are well known from biblical texts (the Hebrew term is *nādar*). There are several instructive examples. Leviticus 22:17ff. gives the "orthodox" rationale for making and performing vows, and it specifies that offerings and sacrifices are to be made, especially a "freewill offering" (22:18). This provides an important clue: vows are not mandated, they are *voluntary*. Psalm 56:12, 13 is a commentary, because it describes vows in general as an aspect of personal piety. Proverbs 7:13, 14 is even more instructive, because here we have the account of a housewife, dressed as a prostitute, who becomes enamored with a young man "without sense" and propositions him.

> She seizes him and kisses him,
> > And with impudent face she says to him:
> I had to offer sacrifices,
> > And today I have paid my vows. (Proverbs 7:13, 14)

The biblical writers may disapprove of this woman, but they inadvertently tell us that women in ancient Israel were accustomed to making vows (Berlinerblau 1996).

The story of another woman, Hannah, who used to go to the shrine at Shiloh to worship, is perhaps the most relevant for our inquiry here. Hannah was infertile and desperately wished for a child, but Yahweh had "closed her womb" (1 Sam. 1:5), as a result of which her husband Elkanah's other wife ridiculed her. So Hannah "wept and would not eat"; she was "deeply distressed and prayed to Yahweh." Then she "vowed a vow," saying that if Yahweh would give her a son, she would dedicate him to God all the days of his life as a "Nazirite" (1:7-11; the son was Samuel the judge and prophet). Here we see the essence of a vow. It is a "contract" with a deity: "if you do this, I will do that."

The biblical story of Hannah is marked by the propagandistic intent of the Deuteronomistic writers and editors, who are trying to explain why Samuel is "different." Nevertheless, it reveals some significant details about women and vows. (1) Hannah took the initiative in making this vow, virtually ignoring the priest Eli at the Shiloh shrine, and defying him when he berated her for being "drunk." (2) Hannah was "speaking in her heart; only her lips moved"; "pouring out her soul before Yahweh"; speaking "out of great anxiety and vexation." This was an intensely *personal* and *private* act of devotion. (3) Finally, the wish was granted. Hannah had the son she desired, and she fulfilled her vow by "lending" him to Yahweh (1:12-28).

The story of Hannah is set in the period of the Judges, as we now know, the 12th-11th century B.C. Jeremiah 44:15-23, however, describes folk religion in the early 6th century B.C. This passage contains some of our most candid and revealing witnesses to family and folk religion — especially to the role of women in the cult. We are told that women "offered incense to other gods"; "burned incense to the Queen of Heaven"; and "poured out libations" to her, as they had *always* done (that is, back in Judah). Significantly, all this was part of the performance of women's vows. The men are portrayed as being aware of these practices, but ambivalent; they stand around and let the women defend themselves to the prophet Jeremiah (surprise, surprise). What the women do is interesting. They are not docile. They go on the offensive. They say to Jeremiah: "We were doing just fine until you came along; our vows were *working*." And they declare that their husbands know all about this and even tacitly approve of it.

As I read this remarkable story, I am struck by several things relevant to folk religion. (1) The figure of Jeremiah represents the Jerusalem Establishment: orthodox priests; the prophetic guild (often close to the crown); the literati; politically correct theology. But when he appears to chide the exiled community off in Egypt, none of this matters much. The *women* have a major voice here. We are dealing not with "state" religion, for the state has disappeared. The family remains the center of religious life, as it always had been; and there women rule as well as men.

(2) Second, it is clear that while women were often shut out of public rituals and more formal observances of cult, they were accustomed to household and private forms of religious practice that were uniquely "real"

to them. These were more personal, more meaningful; and they found their expression chiefly in prayers and vows. Women could venerate female deities, if they seemed more accessible to them, more congenial, more likely to understand and fulfill *their* needs — not competing with, but different from those of men.

Jeremiah almost acquiesces. He does not thunder Yahweh's wrath, as the prophets usually did. He says in effect: "All right; you have said that you will surely perform your vows, so do it!" He does predict that it will end badly, but one senses that he accepts the reality. It is not orthodoxy that matters, but orthopraxy — *piety.* And the essence of piety in traditional daily religious life consists largely of prayers and vows, relating mostly to the practical concerns of the family, which often fall to women more than to men.

One can still see women's piety among traditional Roman Catholic families, especially in less-developed cultures. It is mostly the women who go to Mass and to the confessional; who invoke Mary's blessings; who perform vows and do penance; who tend the family shrine; who go on pilgrimages; and, of course, who rear the children in the tradition. And it is no accident that in traditional Roman Catholic piety, the most common epithet of Mary is "*Mother* of God." Popes and bishops may be somewhat uneasy about what some see as the dangers of "Mariolatry," but her popularity and veneration persist because for many she makes God more accessible. So women (mostly) pray the rosary again and again, because it helps them.

One of my women friends reminds me that in Russian and Greek Orthodox traditions there is an ancient service featuring the "Akathist Hymn," sung in praise and devotion to the "Theotokos," or "Holy Mother and Ever-Virgin Mary." Among the epithets of the Holy Mother are these (all direct quotes):

> Star revealing the Sun
> Seer of the ineffable will
> She of the fruitful womb, a fertile meadow
> Branch of the unwithering Vine
> Land yielding the untainted Fruit
> One from whom flow milk and honey
> Well-shaded Tree; tree of delectable Fruit
> Table full-laden
> Ever-flowing River
> Wine-bowl overfilled with joy

The "fertility themes" here are transparent (regardless of whether some doctrinaire feminists are repelled by them). And the "tree imagery" is particularly striking in the light of what we now know of Asherah as an ancient Israelite tree goddess (below). I shall also show later how the Mother/ Goddess persists even in Judaism, supposedly a rigidly monotheistic religion, in the figure of the Shekinah or "Matronit" (Chapter VIII).

(3) Prayers and vows are spoken, perhaps silently (as were Hannah's), but the promises made need to be "sealed" with something symbolic, yet tangible, if they are to be efficacious. As we have seen, the women in Jeremiah's story burn incense and make libation offerings to their patroness, the "Queen of Heaven," and in a similar passage in Jeremiah 7:1-18 they bake cakes for her. It is almost as though theology is "men's work," but piety and ritual are "women's work" (although it is not quite that simple). I do not imply any value judgment, but I suggest that in religion men are perhaps more analytical, women more emotional, yet more practical. And because women's instincts are to *do* something to symbolize their experiences, their prayers and vows, it is natural for them to present votives and votive offerings to the deity. Again, this is seen in traditional piety in many religious circles. Women light a candle and place it near the altar in the church; they may leave flowers in a chapel or a shrine; they may often pin a little prayer or a miniature replica of a body part on a saint's bier. (I have witnessed these rites of folk religion many times in the Spanish mission church of San Javier del Bac near Tucson; in Greek Orthodox chapels in the rural areas of Cyprus; in desert shrines in Jordan and Syria where Bedouin women come to pray; Chapter VII). These offerings are *votives,* which symbolize pious wishes and promises; visible signs that "tap into" the invisible divine powers. They are, in effect, "stand-ins" for the worshipper, who cannot always be physically present before the gods, but desires to petition them continuously.

Having digressed to consider vows and votives, let me return to the question above, of whether the female figurines really were votives. We can start with the advantage of already knowing what the related prayers here are for, and to whom they are being addressed. The prayers have to do directly or indirectly with "fertility." It may be fecundity, specifically conceiving, bearing, and rearing children safely. And if so, it is quite naturally Asherah the "Great Mother" who is being invoked (and perhaps also Yahweh through her). But "fertility" has to do with more than human reproduction, though that is fundamental. The animals must multiply and flourish, too, and the fields must yield a bountiful harvest, if the family and clan and people are to survive. And these matters, too, are in the hands of the gods, who fructify and bless every living thing.

The only question, then, is what a votive presented to the goddess of living things who is symbolized by the figurines would *look* like. That would seem easy, but it is not. We assume that a votive would probably be an image representing what is desired. If it is a child, a small doll-like figure might be presented as a votive offering, or a pregnant woman, and that is not what we have (below). Is it then an adequate milk supply that is desired? It is significant that the primary sexual organs are deliberately not depicted on the Israelite female figurines, only the breasts. So if the figurines were votives, the intent of the prayer would seem not to be conception or safe delivery, but lactation. Likewise, if the object is the fecundity of animals and the fields, then suitable votives would be animal sacrifice and food-drink offerings, for which we do have both textual and artifactual evidence. In short, either the female figurines are not votives *per se;* or we cannot tell what it is that they symbolized, beyond some general notion of "plenty."

When we encounter votives in folk religion today, the symbolic object that is chosen tends to "fit" the subject of the prayer and the vow. In Catholic churches like the one mentioned above in Tucson, a prayer for healing a hand, for instance, will be symbolized by pinning a miniature silver hand on the bier or costume of a saint. This object becomes, in effect, an "amulet" — a good luck charm that is worn not by the worshipper but rather by the effigy of the saint or the deity to whom the prayer and vow are addressed. If it is a leg that is afflicted, a leg amulet will be chosen. If there are sexual difficulties about which the worshipper is concerned, even the sex organs may be represented by an amulet. These amulets (*milagros* in Spanish), covering almost every conceivable illness or disaster, can be purchased cheaply in small shops near the churches. As I have already noted, the candle frequently left burning in a church has a similar symbolic meaning. The flame burning continually before God is the petitioner's constant prayer.

We can presume that small images of babies may have existed and might have been used as votives in household shrines, but admittedly we do not have any archaeological examples. It is possible, of course, that some of the incense and libation offerings in the passages in Jeremiah discussed above, which were presented by women to a female deity, had to do with prayers to conceive and bear and rear children (among other bless-

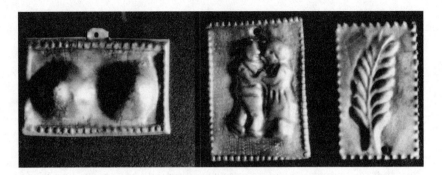

Milagros, or silver pendants used to bring good luck; Tucson, Arizona
Photo: W. G. Dever

ings). But we do not know that. The incense — "a pleasing odor to the Lord" (Leviticus 3:5) — was more likely a general, all-purpose offering. The libation offering, the pouring out of oil or wine, could well have accompanied prayers for a good harvest. We may note in passing that the story above of Hannah making prayers and vows to conceive a child does not mention her presenting a votive or votive offering at the time. But when the child is later born and weaned, she does "fulfill her vow" by making an offering at the shrine at Shiloh. It consists of a young bull to sacrifice, an ephah of flour, and a skin of wine (1 Samuel 1:21-28).

I am suggesting tentatively that the female figurines were connected principally though not exclusively with reproduction, but that they were not "votives" in the usual sense of that term. They are better understood as images representing the goddess Asherah, used as talismans to secure her favors. Indeed, after a long period of skepticism (not to mention ignorance of the archaeological data), most scholars have come around to this general position. The most exhaustive study is that of Raz Kletter, who himself first rejected this view (and dismissed me as a "devotee of the cult of Asherah"), but now supports it. After listing almost all of the scholarly opinions, he argues as I do that the figure represented can only be Asherah and that the figurines functioned largely in the realm of "magic." He also agrees that they had to do mostly with family religious life; that they are an aspect of folk religion, but with the proviso that they were not necessarily at odds with "official Yahwistic religion" (1996:202-205). I shall return to expand upon that observation shortly, in defining further the role of

Asherah in relation to Yahweh. Meanwhile, for speculation, since we have no biblical or non-biblical texts that we can connect with the figurines, we have archaeological artifacts that represent symbolic cultic activities, although no words explaining what the people doing these things thought or felt at the time. But even if the figurines were only votives, representing human women praying, they seem to be praying to a *female deity,* who could only be Asherah, whether as consort of Yahweh or as a hypostatization of his "feminine" aspects.

Votives, Vows, and Folk Religion

At this point, I want to return to two recent excellent studies of vows and their specific role in folk religion, which we have already mentioned (Chapter II). Karel van der Toorn's provocative study (1994) goes a long way toward reconstructing how important vows were, especially in women's cults, and what religious life revolving around the making and keeping of vows was "really like." Yet he thinks that although women probably went to public shrines to make their vows, "it is archaeologically difficult to prove the existence of such public shrines" (1994:96). I could not disagree more, on both counts.

On shrines, van der Toorn simply overlooks the detailed evidence that I have presented here. He notes the possibility of actually finding *bāmôt* in a single sentence, but he gives no examples. And while he has an eloquent account of "the fear of infertility" in the Hebrew Bible, nowhere does he speculate on how Israelite women actually *used* "magic" rituals to conceive, nor does he mention our figurines at all. This is another example of how "text-based" approaches to religion fall short. And this is ironic because in 1997 van der Toorn coined the very apt phrase "Book religion" to describe the deficiencies of this approach. Furthermore, he more than almost any other man has written about women's cults with great sensitivity.

Another innovative and very sophisticated study of vows and "popular religious groups" is that of Jacques Berlinerblau (1996). Yet Berlinerblau, too, is almost oblivious to the value of archaeological data. After noting some of the inadequacies of the biblical texts as a witness (as I have done here), he turns to archaeology only to conclude that "at present we do not possess a better source, be it textual or archaeological" (1996:42). He states categorically that "there is no archaeological evidence pertaining to the Israelite vow," and he specifically rejects my published statements regarding "votive" vessels or artifacts (1996:43; citing Dever 1990:132). His reasoning is simply that we have no non-biblical texts (sound familiar?) on any such objects, mentioning a vow (Hebrew *ndr*). He simply overlooks the fact that an object doesn't need to "say" that it is a votive to be one — especially in a largely illiterate society — because it is a *symbol*.

We actually have *many* objects that clearly are votives, some with Hebrew texts. To mention only one, there is the stone bowl found near the entrance to the shrine at Kuntillet 'Ajrûd (above, p. 162), which reads: "Belonging to Obadiah, son of Adnah. May he be blessed by Yahweh." This bowl weighs more than 400 pounds and could hardly have been a domestic vessel. Here it *must* be a votive, and it specifies in writing what the devotee's prayer is for. And there are two other inscribed votive bowls from Kuntillet 'Ajrûd, both bearing Hebrew personal names. Elsewhere we also have clear votive objects, discussed above — zoomorphic figurines; "miniature" couches; amulets of all kinds; the engraved hand in the Kh. el-Qôm tomb; and, of course, the several tomb inscriptions, which are in effect votive objects (below).

Overall, Berlinerblau's negative assessment of archaeological data is unwarranted. He says that we cannot "patiently wait for biblical archaeologists to unearth fresh evidence"; "archaeological harvest of this nature will not be immediately, nor abundantly, forthcoming" (1996:170). We don't have to wait. The relevant archaeological data are now at hand, for those willing to take a fresh and courageous look at popular religion (which to his credit Berlinerblau is generally willing to do).

Characterizing Asherah and Her Cult

I have introduced the goddess Asherah in several preliminary ways, so she is beginning to be known to readers. The evidence thus far has consisted of (1) the biblical texts that specifically mention her; (2) extra-biblical texts, like the inscriptions from Kh. el-Qôm and Kuntillet 'Ajrûd that speak of blessings granted by "Yahweh and his Asherah"; and (3) the female figurines that most scholars now acknowledge do represent her in some way.

There are, however, remaining questions that have to do with whether the existence of such a goddess in ancient Israel implies a "cult of

Asherah"; whether this aspect of popular religion was a "women's cult"; and how this cult might have been related to "official Yahwism." It is also interesting to speculate what happened to such a cult in later, more orthodox Israelite religion, as well as in later Judaism, but I shall defer that subject (Chapter IX).

The reluctance and the tardiness of mainstream biblical scholarship in recognizing that there was a "cult of Asherah" in ancient Israel are due, I think, to several factors. One is that virtually *all* previous works on Israelite religion have been written by men, usually representatives of the religious Establishment, often Protestant seminary professors and/or clerics. In addition, these scholars have been by definition intellectuals. They are literati, like those who wrote the Hebrew Bible, with whom they easily resonate, as though their interpretation were "the truth of the matter." Conspicuously absent among the observers of Israelite religion are women; minorities; writers who represent the Third World; non-specialists such as anthropologists and sociologists of religion; archaeologists (until very recently); and, of course, ordinary folk.

Postmodernists would dismiss typical commentators as "Europeanized white males" (or as some would say, "zero-signifiers"). The portrait we currently have of Israelite religion may not be quite that skewed, but it is definitely biased. What I am arguing here is that only *archaeology* can redress the balance. In fact, it is already beginning to do so. Recently I wrote to show that the almost 180-degree shift in the discussion of "Israelite monotheism" among biblical scholars in the past twenty years or so is largely the direct result of scholars gradually becoming more aware of the extra-biblical evidence. Unfortunately, that has been principally the textual data once again, especially the Kh. el-Qôm and Kuntillet 'Ajrûd inscriptions (Dever 1999).

I have already discussed these two pivotal inscriptions briefly (Chapter V), but a closer look at how various scholars have treated this evidence regarding the question of Asherah and her cult is instructive. My Kh. el-Qôm inscription was promptly published in 1969-1970, but in a somewhat obscure series. Not until the late 1970s and 1980s did other scholars take notice of it. (This despite the fact that in 1969 in Jerusalem I showed it to two of the world's leading experts in early Hebrew inscriptions: Frank Cross of Harvard, my teacher; and the legendary William Foxwell Albright, Cross's teacher.)

The Kuntillet 'Ajrûd inscriptions, discovered in 1977-1978 by Ze'ev

Meshel, were also promptly published in 1978 (although only in sketchy preliminary reports). Again, scholars slowly came to take these texts, also mentioning "Asherah," somewhat seriously. Yet almost *no* scholar saw (or was ready to admit) the truly revolutionary significance of these texts for our understanding of ancient Israelite religion. Here I shall be brief in reviewing some relevant works, since most all have been cited and discussed above (Chapter II). Also, a convenient tabulation of these and other scholars' views, with full bibliography, is found in Binger (1997:164-175).

Jeffrey H. Tigay. Tigay's study (1986) tried to establish the existence of monotheism throughout the monarchy by arguing that the majority of Israelite personal names were compounded with the name of "Yahweh" or "El," rather than that of some "pagan" deity. Thus the name of the deceased inscribed in my Kh. el-Qôm tomb is "'Uriyahu," or "Yahweh is my light." Tigay acknowledges, however, that his study was prompted by seeing the Kuntillet 'Ajrûd inscription with Meshel at the Israel Museum in 1978 (as my studies also were). And, while obviously on the defensive here, he admits that the 'Ajrûd and Kh. el-Qôm inscriptions provide "evidence which is certainly heterodox and may point in the direction of paganism" (1986:27).

In the end, however, Tigay understands "his 'a/Asherah" on both the inscriptions at issue here as referring not to the goddess herself, but only to some object, "his (Yahweh's) *'ashera.*" Thus the *'ăshērāh* is "a cultic symbol in the sanctuary" where devotees worship Yahweh (1986:27-30; as we saw above, this would be a tree or wooden pole). Tigay will admit only that "the references to YHWH and an *'ăshērāh* show at most the heterodoxy of one or more Yahwists at a distant site apparently frequented by others in addition to Israelites" (1986:29).

Tigay bases the latter assumption on the supposed "non-Hebrew" inscriptions of Kuntillet 'Ajrûd. But as Zevit points out (2001:376-378), these are *all Hebrew* inscriptions. Some may have been written by a scribe perhaps trained somewhere along the coast, where the Hebrew script could have been influenced by the very similar (almost identical) Phoenician letters of the alphabet. As for "distant sites," 'Ajrûd was a bit remote, but its material culture is standard 9th-8th-century B.C. "Israelite" and "Judean." And Kh. el-Qôm is in the *heartland* of Judah, less than 25 miles south of Jerusalem.

With all due respect, I cannot escape the conclusion that Tigay does try to confront the newer archaeological data, but he wants to have it both ways. He acknowledges the "sweeping Biblical indictments of popular religion," but he thinks that these "are based more on theological axioms than historical data." The texts may be "referring to the actions of small numbers of people" (1986:40). In ancient Israel there existed only "some superficial, fetishistic polytheism and a limited amount of more profound polytheism." This "ivory tower" view of Israelite religion is precisely what I am trying to counteract here, because it is oblivious to the *vast majority* of ancient Israelites and *their* religions.

Patrick D. Miller. Miller is perhaps the foremost American authority on ancient Israelite religion, with numerous publications to his credit. He is a clergyman and seminary professor, but also a critical and highly sophisticated scholar. Already in 1985 in an influential handbook Miller had commented on the Kh. el-Qôm and Kuntillet 'Ajrûd inscriptions and noted that they reflect "a religious component of some sort (cult object, sanctuary, or consort) that is universally condemned in the literature of the OT but seems to have existed alongside Yahwism" (1985:217). He also discussed family and "popular" religion, but his overall approach was still overwhelmingly text-oriented.

In 1987, as one of the editors of a major volume of essays, *Ancient Israelite Religion,* Miller discussed Canaanite religion. But he also dealt with the continuities into ancient Israel and raised the possibility of Asherah being Yahweh's consort more specifically (1987:59). Miller's *magnum opus* in 2000 has been discussed above (Chapter II), so here I simply point out that by now Miller is paying much more attention not only to folk and family religion, but also to the archaeological data. He does not think that the term '*ăshērāh* in our inscriptions necessarily refers to the goddess Asherah herself, but it is at least evidence of her presence in the cult. After considering the options, Miller adopts the more nuanced conclusion of Keel and Uehlinger (below) that the '*ăshērāh* is a tree-like symbol that serves as a "gender-neutral mediating entity" between worshipper and Yahweh, rather than an independent deity.

Miller concludes that if the goddess Asherah had been venerated in ancient Israel, it would only have been as a "hypostatization" of the supposed feminine dimensions of Yahweh. In this process, one aspect of the divine powers is personalized and elevated to the status of a quasi-independent deity. Thus in Proverbs 8 and elsewhere, Hebrew *hokmâ*, the "wisdom" of Yahweh, appears as "Lady Wisdom" (in Greek, "Sophia") and a participant with Yahweh in creation (2000:35, 36). I shall return to these notions presently, but at best they seem to me a reluctant compromise. And certainly Asherah and her iconography are *not* "gender-neutral."

Ancient Israelite Religion (Miller, Hanson, and McBride 1987). In the same 1987 survey, there are other articles that are relevant here (including mine on Canaanite religion; see Chapter VIII). Tigay's chapter does not go beyond his 1986 discussion (above). Kyle McCarter's discussion (1987:137-157) is characteristically up to date, lucid, well balanced, and thoroughly documented. Yet in the end McCarter, too, opts for the "hypostatization" explanation of the *ăshērāh* noted above. He does not think that we can read the term as "Asherah," or that Yahweh had any such consort. It is not the cult-object, the *ăshērāh* itself, that is hypostatized, but rather the *"trace"* of Yahweh's "effective presence." In effect, the *ăshērāh* is only a "symbol."

McCarter admits that this is a subtle distinction (1987:155). If so, it is too subtle for me. It seems to me that McCarter, like many other biblicists who reduce Asherah to a "mere symbol," misses the point. A symbol of *what?* Unless the goddess Asherah herself had been a living, potent deity and had been widely venerated, a "symbol" like a tree or wooden pole would have been meaningless, indeed a farce. And if it/she were powerless, why does it/she continue to appear alongside Yahweh? To speak of *ăshērāh* as "only" a symbol is like saying to a pious Roman Catholic woman that the crucifix she reveres is "only a pair of sticks." Or saying to a Jew who survived the Holocaust that the Star of David is "only a couple of triangles." This is reductionism with a vengeance, however well intentioned. McCarter seems to sense the contradictions of his "minimalist" position, however, because in his last footnote he says: "If she [Canaanite Asherah] was worshipped widely and prominently in the Iron Age under the name Asherah, it is difficult to imagine that the Israelite goddess *ăšērat yahweh* was not identified with her" (1987:155). I find this not only difficult to imagine, but impossible. My point here is precisely that Canaanite Asherah *was* Israelite Asherah, and that the phrase *ăšērat-yahweh* in our inscriptions refers to her as the *consort* of Yahweh.

Michael Coogan's chapter in *Ancient Israelite Religion* (1987:115-124) deals with Canaanite religion, but it stresses continuities with ancient Israel. As Coogan puts it, "It is essential to consider biblical religion as a subset of Israelite religion and Israelite religion as a subset of Canaanite religion" (1987:115). Note the implied priority and the hierarchy here: "biblical religion" derives from the *real* religions of Canaan in the Late Bronze and

Iron Ages. And of the Kh. el-Qôm and Kuntillet 'Ajrûd inscriptions, Coogan says that despite the grammatical difficulties (the possessive pronoun "his" with a personal name; above), the reading "Yahweh's Asherah," taking her as a consort, "is the most attractive of the possibilities" (1987:118). That is what I have said since 1982.

John S. Holladay's chapter in *Ancient Israelite Religion* (1987:249-299), widely quoted and discussed above, is still one of the best treatments of folk religion, or what Holladay calls "distributed" (rural) or "nonconformist" as opposed to "established" worship. Oddly enough, Holladay does not mention either Kh. el-Qôm or Kuntillet 'Ajrûd, except to argue that the latter "is better taken as an example of fortress gateway planning than religious architecture." He thinks that "no specifically 'religious' artifact (as opposed to inscribed artifacts) was found" (1987:259). I find this astonishing.

Saul M. Olyan. The slender volume *Asherah and the Cult of Yahweh in Israel* (1988) by Olyan, a Brown University professor, is an exceptionally valuable review of the textual evidence at the time. Like many other scholars then, Olyan takes the reading *'ăshērāh* on the Kh. el-Qôm and Kuntillet 'Ajrûd inscriptions to mean "Yahweh of Samaria and his cult symbol." The identification of Yahweh with Samaria recalls Ahab's erecting "an asherah" in the Temple of Baal in the capital of Samaria (I Kings 16:33). Despite his hesitancy to read "Asherah" on the two inscriptions, Olyan concludes that these inscriptions do imply a role for the goddess Asherah in both folk and "official" religion, and that her role was significant in both. As he puts it:

> (The goddess Asherah) was an acceptable and legitimate part of Yahweh's cult in non-deuteronomistic circles. The association of the asherah and the cult of Yahweh suggests in turn that Asherah was the consort of Yahweh in circles both in the north and the south (1988:33).

Olyan scarcely mentions the archaeological data, but he does fault Tigay (above) for minimizing the evidence from Kuntillet 'Ajrûd. And he concludes his work by saying: "We believe that in future more scholars will adopt the view that Asherah had some role in the cult of Yahweh" (1988:74). Olyan's prediction has now come true; and it is the archaeological evidence that has proven decisive.

Susan Ackerman. I have already noted above (Chapter II) Susan Ackerman's pioneering work *Under Every Green Tree: Popular Religion in*

Sixth-Century Judah (1992), the first extensive study of ancient Israelite religion by a woman. She concludes that choosing between the alternate readings "his asherah/his Asherah" on our two inscriptions is presently impossible. She goes on to declare, however:

> But for our purposes, it does not really matter. In the ancient Near East the idol was the god. *'šrth* at Kuntillet ʿAjrûd or Kh. el-Qôm could refer to Asherah's cult object, the stylized tree, or even to some hypostatized aspect of the female side of Yahweh. But what was the stylized tree or the hypostasis of the female side of Yahweh to the average worshipper? Nothing other than Asherah, the goddess (1992:65, 66).

In a later treatment, "At Home with the Goddess" (2003), Ackerman unhesitatingly identifies our female figurines with Asherah and shows how pervasive her cult was.

Rainer Albertz. Albertz is Professor of Biblical Exegesis and Biblical Theology at the University of Siegen in Germany. His monumental two-volume history of Israelite religion (1994) has been praised above for being one of the first works by a biblicist to try to come to grips with some of the archaeological data, a generally successful effort, as I have stated in reviews. Not only does Albertz deal with Dan and the "Bull Site" (above) as *bāmôt*, but he reads our two inscriptions as referring to "Yahweh of Samaria and his Asherah," Asherah being Yahweh's consort, at least in folk religion. He connects her cult with the female figurines and points out, as Olyan did, that the cult was adopted in "official," even royal, circles (cf. II Kings 23; and our discussion below). All of these phenomena Albertz interprets as aspects of family and personal piety, where *several* "Yahwisms" flourished until the very end of the monarchy.

Othmar Keel and Christoph Uehlinger. I have applauded the "art history" approach of the "Freibourg school" above, because its members have regarded archaeology as a primary source for history and religion, as I do here. The principal work of this school in English is entitled *Gods, Goddesses, and Images of God in Ancient Israel* (1998; translated from the German edition of 1992). Keel and Uehlinger begin their work by questioning my 1987 distinction between "belief systems" based on texts, and "cultic practices" best revealed by material culture remains. But that was chiefly a *practical* means of pursuing the investigation, not a denial of the importance of their essential relationship to each other. Their own approach to

the religion of ancient Israel is, in fact, very similar to mine in practice —
and potentially every bit as revolutionary (as some critics of both have recognized).

I cannot possibly do justice here to the richness of the iconographic
data that they present (see the review in Dever 1995). But on the specific
topic at hand, Keel and Uehlinger (1998:210-243) offer an important nu-
ance. They, as many others, read our two inscriptions as referring only to a
cultic object, not the goddess Asherah. In this case, the asherah was a "*mediating entity* that brings Yahweh's blessing and is thus conceived in the
mind in the shape of a stylized tree that was thus subordinate to Yahweh"
(1998:237). I agree with the centrality of the "tree" motif (which is not original with them), and I will explore it further below. But again, a "symbol"
of *what*? They imply a "cult of Asherah," but they are unable to specify
what that cult was or what it meant.

As for Kuntillet 'Ajrûd, Keel and Uehlinger claim that it was not "a
pilgrimage site or some kind of religious center"; that it was "set up using
Phoenician 'know-how'"; and that "it was probably in use no longer than
one generation" (1998:247). I can only express my disappointment at such
defensiveness from scholars who otherwise have shown great courage in
opposing the religious Establishment, not to mention making such positive use of archaeology. They seem to be mesmerized by the notion that
ancient Israelite religion was "largely monolatrous" (1998:248), that is,
practically speaking devoted to the worship of one deity, without denying
the theoretical existence of other deities. But it is clear, as most other scholars now acknowledge, that Asherah *was* a full-fledged deity, and that her
cult *did* flourish in ancient Israel alongside the cult of Yahweh, even as part
of it. In fact, elsewhere they imply as much themselves; they even identify
the figurines with Asherah (1998:331-336). They acknowledge that the
asherah as a cultic image was "present as a numinous symbol of power."
But the "numinous" *is* the deity or deities, nothing less (as Ackerman has
seen; above). It seems to me, with all due respect to Keel and Uehlinger's
enormous contributions to our inquiry, that they remain ambivalent; they
want to have it both ways. Oddly enough, they downplay Asherah, but
highlight the role of the "Queen of Heaven." (To that topic I shall return
presently.)

John Day. John Day, a Professor of Bible at Oxford, has written a
masterful work in *Yahweh and the Gods and Goddesses of Canaan* (2000).
The choice of "Canaan" in the title is significant, because it is under this

rubric that Day treats Yahweh and the other deities of Israel — more than a dozen of them. In his discussion of Yahweh and Asherah (2000:49-67) he begins by saying that it was the Kh. el-Qôm and Kuntillet 'Ajrûd inscriptions that prompted the revival of interest in Asherah (as I said in 1999). Like other scholars I have discussed, Day in reading the two inscriptions "Yahweh and his asherah" takes the latter as a cult symbol of the goddess. He acknowledges, however, that Asherah herself did play a major role in the cult alongside Yahweh, even though he does not regard her as Yahweh's consort. He thinks that the symbol of Asherah was the "source of blessing" (2000:52), as does Olyan (above). I considered that suggestion twenty years ago but rejected it, because it seems awkward to say something like "May Yahweh and his tree or pole bless you." Furthermore, if Yahweh himself is the ultimate source of blessing, as these scholars obviously believe, why does he *need* a tree-like symbol of Asherah to assist him? And if Yahweh does need her assistance in the cult, and she is then conceived as a "mediator" (Keel and Uehlinger; Miller), that would also seem to undermine his omnipotence.

While no one actually says as much, I think that several scholars in trying to acknowledge Asherah as a real "presence," but not equal with Yahweh, may be working with a model drawn from Roman Catholic piety, which I have discussed above. I applaud this model, and I suggest that it can be taken further. It may be that the little statues of Mary with her bleeding heart function in the same way that the female figurines did for women in ancient Israel. Pious women knew, as they still know, that these images are not "idols"; one does not worship the image, but rather uses it to approach God. These symbols are *potent aids* in prayer — in short, as I have argued above, talismans. The male clerics, being more sophisticated (?), may not need them — but they tolerate them, just as the husbands did in the story in Jeremiah 44 (above). So I do not disagree with the model that I think is implied here, as long as it does not deny that there *was* a widespread "cult of Asherah" in ancient Israel. Day does not do that, and in spite of seeing *asherah* as merely a cult symbol in our two inscriptions, he states after reviewing all the evidence concerning Asherah's relation to Yahweh: "The obvious conclusion that comes to mind is one of a god and his consort" (2000:60).

Judith M. Hadley. Hadley, a professor at Villanova University, in her more extensive review of the data in *The Cult of Asherah in Ancient Israel and Judah: Evidence for a Hebrew Goddess,* reaches much the same conclusions as above (2000:104, 105; 152-55). She also follows a number of other scholars in seeing the "tree" imagery as a clue to Asherah's character and role in the cult, a notion to which I shall return.

Mark S. Smith. The Early History of God: Yahweh and the Other Deities in Ancient Israel (2002a) by Mark Smith, a professor at New York University, covers much the same ground as Day, but with more extensive documentation and discussion of other scholars' views. In fact, it is a compendium of pertinent information. Smith's Preface (2002a:xii-xxxviii) is an especially thorough and welcome review of scholarship on our subject since 1990, with a section on "Asherah/asherah Revisited." Here and elsewhere, Smith's mastery of the Canaanite background in the Late Bronze Age texts from Ugarit in Syria is evident (although he questions the label "Canaanite").

Yet Smith is not willing to concede that Asherah was actually a goddess in monarchic Israel, much less Yahweh's consort (2002a:125-133). The evidence is "minimal at best." As Smith puts it: "It would appear that the Asherah continued with various functions in the cult of Yahweh *without connection* to the goddess who gave her name to the symbol" (2002a:133, italics mine). That is an astounding claim, and it reflects the same lack of understanding of what a "symbol" is that I noted above. Perhaps Smith, ordinarily a fine scholar, needs more of the "common sense" for which he castigates me (2002a:xix). He thinks that I am too "pragmatic." But religion is all *about* pragmatism — what actually *works*. Otherwise, it would have little appeal for the masses. Again, the view from the "ivory tower" is over their heads. A religion is what the majority of its adherents do, not what scholars think that they should do. And archaeology — whose arguments depend fundamentally on analogy ("common sense," based on the experience of common things) — can offer some of our best clues to the actual behavior of ordinary folk.

Only One God? Monotheism in Ancient Israel and the Veneration of the Goddess Asherah (2001). This volume, by a group of Dutch biblical scholars at Utrecht University, represents the cutting edge in scholarship — cutting through traditional views with a vengeance. It does so by focusing largely on the cult of Asherah, with special reference up front to the Kh. el-Qôm and Kuntillet ʿAjrûd inscriptions. The essays by Meindert Dijkstra and especially Karel J. H. Vriezen (the latter whom I know from Jerusalem in the 1970s) deal specifically with the cult of Asherah, with a thorough survey of some of the archaeological data. Bob Becking's essay looks at the

Assyrian evidence for what he terms "iconic polytheism" in Israel (see below here); and Marjo C. A. Korpel treats Asherah outside Israel. The most innovative chapters are the third essay by Dijkstra and the second by Becking, which are concerned with women's religions in the Hebrew Bible and the relevance of folk religion for theology today. All in all, this slender volume is like a breath of fresh air in the often fetid atmosphere of talk about Israelite religion.

Dijkstra's views are similar to those of the "minimalists" discussed above. But he does see that ancient Israelite religion was a "patchwork" and that the diversity "confirms the pluriform picture that lies in the Old Testament behind the layers of redaction and religious polemics" (2001:39). Vriezen's essay, already discussed above (Chapter II), is one of the best brief presentations of the archaeological evidence that we have. His discussions of both Asherah and the "Queen of Heaven" as goddesses, as well as the female figurines, are especially perceptive and judicious. (I shall return to these provocative essays again in Chapters VII and VIII in summing up.)

Ziony Zevit. I have lauded Zevit's work *The Religions of Ancient Israel: A Synthesis of Parallactic Approaches* (2001) at several points above. It is unique among works of biblicists in taking full advantage of the newer archaeological data ("tangible belief"), and it is truly revolutionary. Not surprisingly, Zevit goes as far as I do here in reconstructing a "cult of Asherah" in monarchic times. On my Kh. el-Qôm inscription (which he and I reexamined together in Jerusalem) and the subsequently discovered Kuntillet 'Ajrûd material, however, Zevit reads "Asherata." This is the *Phoenician* version of the goddess' name, without the final possessive suffix. Thus she is not necessarily Yahweh's consort (an independent deity?), but neither can she be a "mere cult symbol."

Tikva Frymer-Kensky. Frymer-Kensky's book *In the Wake of the Goddesses: Women, Culture, and the Biblical Transformation of Pagan Myth* (1992) deserves separate treatment. It deals in large part with ancient Mesopotamia, Frymer-Kensky's main area of expertise in her studies at Yale. It may appear from its title to be a feminist manifesto, but it is actually quite conservative, written partly from the perspective of Jewish Reconstructionism. Thus she offers by and large an apologia for Israelite monotheism, even though she acknowledges that it was a relatively late development as "myth was transformed." Not surprisingly, her view of "paganism" — a pejorative term that virtually no one else uses these days — is very negative. Where most other scholars today avoid value judgments, Frymer-Kensky does not hesitate to take a stand and defend it. This is an admirable work in its candor, but it is not representative of mainstream scholarship. Yet in speaking of Asherah, she acknowledges her existence as a goddess until the late reforms, although not as Yahweh's consort. And she connects the female figurines with the veneration of Asherah, a "visual metaphor . . . a kind of tangible prayer for fertility and nourishment" (1992:159). Finally, throughout her book, Frymer-Kensky speaks eloquently of women's special concerns in religion.

Conservative and Evangelical Scholarship. Most of the scholars whose works I am reviewing here represent the critical, liberal mainstream. That is not the result of any bias, but simply reflects the fact that almost everyone writing on Israelite religion in the past 15-20 years has been part of that consensus, and liberal scholars have naturally been more open to questioning monotheism. It is interesting to observe that some recent handbooks on biblical studies by more conservative scholars have often ignored the subject, and at best they have approached it quite defensively. An edited work entitled *Faith, Tradition, and History: Old Testament Historiography in Its Near Eastern Context* (Millard, Hoffmeier, and Baker 1994) has a chapter on "Old Testament Theology" (not surprisingly), but none on Israelite religion. A more recent book, however, does treat the topic, in Bill T. Arnold's chapter in *The Face of Old Testament Studies: A Survey of Contemporary Approaches* (Baker and Arnold 1999). Arnold reviews a number of the works I discuss here, so he cannot avoid the issues of polytheism and folk religion. But he is not really sympathetic with any of them. Of the Kh. el-Qôm and Kuntillet ʿAjrûd inscriptions, the most he will concede is that they "*may* indicate heterodox tendencies in pre-exilic Israelite religion" (1999:412; his italics). But such religious expressions represent "the fringes of Israelite culture"; they are not "normative" (1999:413). Yet the overwhelming consensus of mainstream scholarship today is that we can no longer *speak* of "normative," even if we assume that the Hebrew Bible encapsulates it.

A voice from the past, "crying in the wilderness." Over 30 years ago, I happened upon a curious book, Raphael Patai's *The Hebrew Goddess* (1967). When visiting Harvard later, I remember discussing his ideas with my teachers, who thought it heresy, but I never forgot it. Then in the 1980s and 1990s, Patai began to visit Tucson to see his physician daughter, a friend and colleague of mine, and I came to know him personally. Patai was a charming, cultured Old World Jewish intellectual, a polymath who worked in anthropology, sociology, Oriental studies, and Judaica. His book (one of more than 35), while rarely cited by biblical scholars, went through a second and a third edition (1978; 1990). Even the first edition turns out to have been brilliantly perceptive — 30 years ahead of anything else on our subject. The new archaeological data that I present here (some of which Patai was able to cite, along with my 1984 article on Asherah) only confirm what Patai knew all along about the existence of a "Hebrew" Goddess. How did he know it? Partly because he was alone among scholars writing then in having access to the rich lore of medieval Rabbinical scholars. (I shall take up Patai's views again in Chapters VIII, IX.)

CHAPTER VII

Asherah, Women's Cults, and "Official Yahwism"

Traditional biblical scholarship has only reluctantly admitted that there was a goddess Asherah who might have been known to some ancient Israelites and worshipped by them. Most of the more than 40 occurrences of the word *'ăshērāh* in the Hebrew Bible, as we have seen above, are taken to refer only to a wooden pole or tree-like object that was simply a "symbol" of some sort (often without asking, "A symbol of *what?*").

The assumption here was that from Mosaic times, before the conquest and settlement of Canaan, there had existed a "pure" (and, of course, divinely revealed) Yahwistic monotheism. All later reforms thus attempted to recall wayward Israel to its original religion, which was not simply an ideal, but the reality from the formative years onward. In adopting this view, modern commentators bought into the Deuteronomistic ideology and thus regarded Canaanite practices as intrusive, condemning them as "pagan." Folk religion, if it existed at all in ancient Israel, was seen as "syncretistic" — mixing orthodox and unorthodox beliefs and practices — and of course therefore false.

Asherah in Canaan

That naïveté should have been shattered with the discovery of the hundreds of Canaanite mythological texts from Ugarit on the coast of Syria, dating from *ca.* 1400-1300 B.C. Here the goddess Asherah, almost forgotten over the centuries, reemerged and could once again be seen as the principal female deity of the pantheon in Canaan in pre-Israelite times. She appears at Ugarit as the consort of the chief male deity El, the "Father of Years." But the texts imply that this is the older pair of reigning deities, and the two are no longer passionate lovers. El may even be impotent.

In one poem, El is pictured as seated drowsily upon his throne at the "headwaters of the two oceans," when he looks up and sees Asherah returning from a long journey.

> As soon as El espies her,
> He parts his jaws and laughs.
> His feet upon the footstool he puts
> And doth twiddle his fingers.

El then welcomes Asherah to his pavilion and offers her refreshments. He declares:

> See, El the King's love stirs thee,
> Bull's affection arouses thee.

But "Bull" El seems a bit cowed — twiddling his thumbs like an old man, boasting about a sexual prowess that he doesn't have any longer. In another poem, he actually is impotent, the text describing his *yad* (not "hand" here, but "penis") as "drooping." Younger female deities are brought in to "encourage" him, and all ends well. (One is reminded of the "young maiden" brought to David's bed in his old age to "warm" him, even though he was impotent; I Kings 1:1-4.)

Asherah's name, like most Northwest Semitic names, is a "sentence-name" compounded with a verb. Thus *Athiratu-yammi* means in all likelihood "She who treads/subdues Sea," the sea being seen in antiquity as the source of deep, mysterious, deadly powers. But whatever her name means, her usual titles are "Lady Asherah" and "Mother of the Gods." She is thus a sort of venerable matron, one who often intercedes with her husband El on behalf of the younger deities — especially Ba'al and his consort Anat (who are ferocious lovers and rivals of the older pair). In one well-known cycle of poems, Asherah pleads as a wife would with El to give Ba'al the "Storm God" a palace of his own. By contrast, Ba'al's lover Anat approaches El and threatens to "smash his head, make his gray beard flow with blood" if he does not comply. Canaanite Anat, the fierce warrior and courtesan, was largely forgotten by Israelite times. But Lady Asherah, the nurturing Mother Goddess, was remembered and venerated, at least in some circles.

Asherah in the Hebrew Bible

In truth, biblical scholars should have seen Asherah's presence all along, since it is transparent in the several passages in the Hebrew Bible where the word *'ăshērāh* must be read as a proper name (above) — and the name of whom, if not the well-known old Canaanite deity Asherah?

One passage to be considered is I Kings 16:32, 33, which recounts how Ahab took for a wife Jezebel, a Phoenician princess. At Samaria, his capital, he then built a temple for Baʿal, the chief Canaanite-Phoenician deity, and there he constructed an altar for Baʿal and "made an Asherah" (the RSV capitalizes the latter). These actions by the northern king enraged the Judean authors of the Book of Kings, but they duly report them; and it is precisely because of their reluctance that we should take their report seriously. Even if, as I have argued above, the *'ăshērāh* here was only a "cult image" of some kind, it nevertheless stood in a Canaanite-style temple in Israel's capital, and it represented the potent *cultic presence* of a female deity named Asherah. (Note that here Asherah is coupled with Baʿal, however, not Yahweh, in order to discredit her; see further Chapter VIII.)

The continuation of the story of Ahab's and Jezebel's heresies in I Kings 18:20-40 is the famous (if mythical) account of the contest on Mt. Carmel. Here Elijah and the prophets of Yahweh faced off against the 450 prophets of Baʿal and the "400 prophets of Asherah" to see which could miraculously strike fire upon a waterlogged altar. Since the Deuteronomists are telling the story, of course, Yahweh's prophets won and he was vindicated. Baʿal and Asherah were discredited, and the text describes how Elijah had the 450 prophets of Baʿal slaughtered. But several scholars have noticed the complete silence of the text about the "400 prophets of Asherah." It has been suggested by some that the text has later been tampered with so as to eliminate any reference to Asherah. But I would argue that had Asherah's prophets been executed, the biblical writers would have *exulted* in that fact and would gladly have included it in their story. So Asherah and her prophets were probably spared. Why — unless her cult was widely tolerated, despite the misgivings of some purists, and tolerated even in "official religion" in the north?

Asherah, Yahweh, and "Syncretism"

Further evidence of the cult of Asherah comes, not surprisingly, from Judah during the reigns of the only two kings of which the biblical writers approve: Hezekiah in the 8th century B.C.; and Josiah in the late 7th century B.C. In II Kings 18:4, Hezekiah is said to have "removed the high places *(bāmôt),* broken the pillars *(māṣṣēbôt),* and cut down the Asherah" (the latter presumably in the Temple). But his son Manasseh (the worst of the lot, remembered as one who "made Judah to sin") set up "a graven image of Asherah" in Solomon's Temple, where only Yahweh's name should have been established forever (II Kings 21:1-7). Thus Hezekiah's abortive "reform" was a failure. Why? Obviously because it lacked both popular support and subsequent royal approval. Asherah remained in the temple, at home alongside Yahweh, where many Israelites (perhaps most) thought she belonged.

II Kings 23 is the most revealing passage of all. This is the "set piece" of the Deuteronomistic historians and their revisionist history of ancient Israel: the story of the reforms of their hero (and no doubt patron), "good King Josiah." Among his iconoclastic deeds he, like Hezekiah before him, is said to have demolished all the high places and removed "the Asherah" from the Temple and burned it. In addition, however, he attacked other aspects of folk religion that had "infiltrated" the Jerusalem Temple, as the biblical writers saw it. And in describing these "pagan practices" they inadvertently give us valuable eyewitness details. In fact, what we have in II Kings 23 is nothing less than an "inventory" of the religious practices of *most* people in ancient Israel, not only toward the very end of the monarchy, but as they undoubtedly had been in place from the beginning (Asherah had been tolerated in the Temple until now).

Note the elements of folk religion here:

(1) "Idolatrous" priests
(2) High places *(bāmôt)* in all the cities of Judah and all around Jerusalem, even at the gates of the city
(3) Incense burned to Baʿal
(4) Standing stones *(māṣṣēbôt)*
(5) The worship of "the sun, the moon, and the constellations, and all the hosts of the heavens" in the Temple
(6) Horses and chariots dedicated to the sun at the entrance to the Temple

(7) Altars (for incense) on the roof of the Temple

(8) "Vessels made for Ba'al, for Asherah, and for all the host of Heaven" in the Temple

(9) Cult prostitution in the Temple (although this is in fact doubtful; below)

(10) Child sacrifice in the Kidron Valley below

Finally, one other heretical activity is noted: women "weaving hangings" for Asherah for the "houses of the male cult prostitutes" in the Temple (II Kings 23:7). The text is admittedly difficult, and biblical commentaries differ on the best interpretation of the terms translated "cult prostitutes" and "hangings" respectively. The second term in Hebrew is *bāttîm*, which in the plural usually means "houses" or "temples." The latter cannot be the meaning here, however, that is, "weaving temples"; nor does "houses" fit the context. It is clear that later editors, translators, and commentators were already puzzled by this reference. The Septuagint, a 3rd-2nd-century B.C. Greek translation, as well as other Greek texts, renders the term *bāttîm* as "garments, tunics." That may mean that their Hebrew text had *kotnôt*, "priestly garments," which is why some English translations read "vestments" (changing Hebrew *bāttîm* to *baddîm*, "white linen"). Some later Aramaic targums (expanded translations) have a word that means "curtains"; and at least one famous medieval Jewish commentator (Qimhi) reads "curtain enclosures."

Given all the textual difficulties, I suggest one of two possibilities. (1) The first is that the apparent "ambiguity" may be *intentional*, that is, the Deuteronomistic writers and editors were either confused (or perhaps embarrassed) by the term *bāttîm* and thus employed a circumlocution that we today do not understand. (2) The other possibility is that the Hebrew text as we have it is correct, and that the term *bāttîm* should be understood *periphrastically*, not as "houses" but as something like "tent-shrines" (as the earlier Tabernacle?). That cannot be proven, but it would make sense. Around both ancient and modern shrines in the Middle East one finds pavilions made of hanging fabrics. These "tents" are used for various purposes — sheltering visitors and pilgrims, selling souvenirs, and the like. Could it be that such tent-pavilions around the Temple housed the "cult prostitutes" (below?) and also the women who were "weaving" the fabrics? But whether the things that the women were making were "hangings" for tents near the Temple or "vestments" for an effigy of a deity in the Temple, they were *for Asherah*. She was present there with Yahweh in his house (Hebrew *bêt*, "house" or "temple"). Susan Ackerman has suggested that these women's cults in the Jerusalem Temple were not only tolerated, they were often under the sponsorship of the Queen Mother herself, as illustrated by the story of Ma'acah, who is said herself to have "made an abominable image for Asherah" in the Temple (I Kings 15:13; Ackerman 2003:459, 450).

Biblical scholars have generally been skeptical about "Josiah's reform" as narrated in II Kings 23. But I have written elsewhere to defend the account as realistic — if not theologically, at least in the light of what we actually know archaeologically about folk religion in late 7th century B.C. Judah (Dever 1994a). In the present context, it doesn't really matter whether the reformers were successful or not. The biblical text gives us a window through which to view folk religion, all the *more* valuable since it comes from its detractors and yet fits the archaeological context that we now have.

It is not only the historical texts that reveal how pervasive the cult of Asherah was, but also the 9th-7th-century B.C. prophetic texts. The striking "sexual imagery" in Hosea, often connected with *trees*, is especially telling. Hosea 4:12, 13 condemns those who "inquire of a thing of wood," who sacrifice "under oak, poplar, and terebinth, because their shade is good," and thus "play the harlot." What is wrong with al fresco rituals, with shade? And why does worshipping that way constitute "harlotry"? The answer lies, I think, in the fact that the goddess Asherah is closely *connected* with tree symbols, as we shall see below. And those who worship her "on every high hill and under every green tree" are forsaking Yahweh, the male deity, to prostitute themselves with a female deity. In folk religion, Asherah may have been his consort, and thus part of Yahwism, his lady; but to the orthodox Deuteronomist parties, she was the whore of pagan gods.

Hosea 14:8 has long intrigued scholars. Yahweh is speaking to his people Israel. The RSV translates this verse:

> O Ephraim, what have I to do with idols?
>> It is I who answer and look after you.
> I am like an evergreen cypress,
>> From me comes your fruit.   (Hosea 14:8)

The text seems to have suffered something in transmission. Some scholars emend (alter) line 2 slightly to read:

I am his Anat and his Asherah.

Whether that change is accepted or not, the context is about trees as life-giving "fertility symbols," as well as about Israel's apostasy in seeking life by departing from Yahweh, the only truly fruitful tree.

Another passage involving trees and idolatry is Jeremiah 2:27. Yahweh complains through the prophet's words that unruly Israelites "say to a tree, 'You are my father'; and to a stone, 'You gave me birth.'" It is tempting to suppose that the tree (literally "a wooden thing" in Hebrew) is a reference to Asherah, whose symbol is a wooden object, and that the stone (*maṣṣēbāh* here) is the familiar sacred standing stone often associated with the *'ăshērāh* and with high places (above).

Another corrupt passage that scholars have struggled to understand is Amos 8:14, which condemns those who "swear by Ashimah of Samaria." The suspicion here is that later editors have tampered with the text so as to obscure the original reference to their adversary Asherah (Chapter V). This is indeed plausible, in the light of references in I Kings 16:33 to an Asherah in the temple at Samaria (Chapter V), and also the Kuntillet 'Ajrûd inscriptions referring to "Yahweh of Samaria."

Now we are in a position to understand why Deuteronomy 16:21, 22 has Yahweh say to the Israelites as they are about to inherit the Land of Canaan:

> You shall not plant any tree as an Asherah beside the altar of Yahweh which you shall make. And you shall not set up a pillar *(maṣṣēbāh)* which Yahweh your God hates.

Asherah, her tree symbolism, and high places with altars in groves of trees were all held to be typical of Canaanite "fertility" cults and were thus anathema to the biblical writers. But why would later reforming priests and prophets condemn these things so vociferously *unless they remained popular* in Israelite religion? The reformers knew what they were talking about when they protested. Why haven't *we* caught on until recently? Theological biases? Archaeology removes the "rose-colored glasses," and the picture is now clearer (if disturbing to some).

Before leaving II Kings 23 with its candid, revealing portrait of folk religion, let me comment on a few of the ten points above where these may have to do specially with Asherah and women's concerns (by number).

(2) The high places *(bāmôt)* are associated with her symbol the *'ăshērāh* so often that it almost appears that these shrines were dedicated especially to the goddess. That would help to explain why they are the specific targets of much of the Deuteronomistic invective. Yet if so, it is obvious that men worshipped Asherah at these shrines as well. I suggest that the *bāmôt* were more conspicuous features of folk religion, and probably of the cult of Asherah, because they were *public* — more visible, more vulnerable to iconoclastic attacks.

(8) What were the "vessels made for Asherah"? The Hebrew word *(kēlîm)* does not provide any clue, since it is used for all kinds of things. But the fact that the things were "burned" implies that they were made of wood. They are not, however, the *asherah* poles of wood, since those are listed separately here. I can only speculate that these "wooden things" were pieces of furniture from within the temple, perhaps tables or benches, detestable because they pointed somehow to Ba'al and Asherah specifically. (On miniature furniture models, see Chapter V.)

(9) The reference to "male cult prostitutes" (II Kings 23:7; RSV) housed in (or around) the Temple is problematic and has been the subject of heated discussion. The Hebrew plural term here is *qĕdēshîm*, derived from a verbal root meaning "to set aside, consecrate." The nominal form can be either masculine or feminine. A "maximalist" reading was common among earlier scholars, who over-stressed the "fertility" motifs of Canaanite religion and regarded it as lascivious, given to sexual orgies. This bias resulted in part from the prudery of that generation of scholars (and its resultant fascination with sex), but it was fed as well by ancient biases.

Classical writers like Herodotus wrote describing how women in Babylon were compelled at least once in their lifetime to go sit in the Temple of Aphrodite and solicit a man to engage in sexual intercourse. Other ancient writers describe Phoenician religion as blatantly sexual. It is out of these prejudices, ancient and modern, that both the myth of the "sacred marriage" of the gods being acted out in cult celebrations and the myth of "cult prostitution" were created (see further Chapter VIII on "fertility cults").

There is neither etymological, cultural, nor historical evidence to support these notions. And among the excellent scholars who have helped to demolish such misreadings of the biblical texts are women who have written perceptively on ancient Israelite religions (such as Ackerman, Bird, and

Frymer-Kensky). All we can really say about the *qĕdēshîm* in II Kings 23:7 is that they were functionaries "dedicated" to temple service of some sort, but that the reformers disapproved of them and wanted them expelled.

Parallels to the females of this class of functionaries have been drawn with the *qadishtu* women in ancient Mesopotamia (the Hebrew word is cognate). But these women, although "dedicated" to temple service, were not prostitutes. Some attempts, however, to "salvage the reputation" of women cult personnel in the Jerusalem Temple may have gone too far in the other direction. Frymer-Kensky likens them to "vestal virgins" (1992:201).

One other aspect of the prostitution of women and cult performance should be mentioned here. Karel van der Toorn (1994) has made much of the slender evidence that women who made vows but were unable to fulfill them had to "buy" their way out of the obligation by paying with wages earned by prostituting themselves in the Temple. He appeals, for instance, to Deuteronomy 23:17, 18, where the usual word for harlot *(zônāh)* appears in parallel with both the masculine and feminine forms *qādēsh/qĕdēshâ*. The text there forbids paying for a broken vow with "the hire of a harlot." Few scholars would follow van der Toorn, however, especially when he sees prostitution as "payment of vows" being a part of the experience of the average Israelite woman. At most, it would have been a rare and distasteful experience.

(10) Finally, the problem of child sacrifice, which would have affected women extraordinarily, must be addressed here. Such sacrifices are judged harshly, and several texts say that they were expressly forbidden (Leviticus 18:21; Deuteronomy 18:10-12). This is what the "nations" *(gôîm)* do (Deuteronomy 12:31); what the pagans brought to Samaria by the Assyrians to replace deported Israelites do (II Kings 17:31); what the king of Moab, Israel's arch-enemy, did (II Kings 3:27).

Yet other texts in addition to II Kings 23:10 unhesitatingly describe child sacrifice among the Israelites, first already during the Wandering in the Wilderness (Psalm 106:37, 38; a late poetic text, however). One Hiel of Bethel "laid the foundations" of Jericho "at the cost of Abiram his firstborn, and set up its gates at the cost of his youngest son Segub" (I Kings 16:34). It is even noted by the writers that this "foundation sacrifice" was done "according to the word of the Lord" that Hiel had spoken, as though this was the result of a vow. Even kings of Judah such as Ahaz and Manasseh are said to have "burned their sons" as offerings, along with other proscribed cultic activities. Of course, the condemnation of the Deuterono-mistic reformers could be dismissed as extremist propaganda, since these two kings could do nothing but evil in their eyes.

Details in several texts, however, such as II Kings 23:10 and Jeremiah 32:35, ring true in the light of what we now know. In both passages, the sac-rifice of children in Jerusalem is said to have taken place at a site called "Topheth," in the Valley of Hinnom below the Temple mount. And the god to whom the children were sacrificed as a burnt offering is specified as "Molech." A god called Molech is known from some Canaanite and espe-cially from later Phoenician sources, the latter partly contemporary with monarchic Israel. Phoenician and later Punic votive inscriptions actually describe a sacrifice of children called a *mulk*. And ancient writers like Diodorus Siculus, Philo Byblius, and Kleitarchos give horrifying accounts of a great bronze statue of the god Kronos, in whose outstretched arms children were placed over a fire.

Finally, there is the 7th-4th-century B.C. "Tophet" or cemetery at the Phoenician Punic port of Carthage in North Africa. There thousands and thousands of burial urns have been unearthed containing the burned bones of infants. Many burials are accompanied by dedicatory inscrip-tions, indicating that the sacrifice was made to perform a vow, often to "Tanit" or Ba'al Hamon, the former none other than the Phoenician ver-sion of Asherah. The sacrifice itself is usually called a *mulk*.

Some scholars argue that Phoenician *mulk* is equivalent to Hebrew "Molech." But others point out that most of the votive inscriptions make it clear that the sacrifices were usually dedicated to Ba'al Hamon and/or Kronos (above). And it has long been known that Phoenician "Ba'al Hamon" is equivalent to Canaanite "Kronos" and Canaanite-Israelite "El." El was one of the earliest names for the Israelite god. Thus Ackerman con-cludes, after a thorough survey of all the evidence, that there was no god "Molech" who received child sacrifice in Israel. "Rather, the cult of child sacrifice was felt in some circles to be a legitimate expression of Yahwistic faith" (1992:137).

If all this is true, how did women *react* to child sacrifice, common or rare? Did they actually participate? Did men coerce them? It is all unthink-able — or at least it was to previous generations of biblical scholars. Today, however, mainstream scholarship takes seriously the hints in the Hebrew Bible that child sacrifice, like so many other "Canaanite" customs, while rare, could be adopted into the Israelite cult. It may even have had its roots in "orthodox" Yahwistic theology. The biblical writers, in the famous story of Abraham and the sacrifice of Isaac, do not hesitate to suppose that burning Isaac on the altar was Yahweh's original intent, or that Abraham in carrying out the divine command would have been doing anything other than obeying in faith. In the end, Abraham miraculously did not have to do such a desperate deed. But *would he* have done it? Perhaps more pertinent is the question of whether Sarah would have condoned the slaying of her beloved son Isaac, whose name means "(God) makes me happy." How could Yahweh (or Asherah), who wondrously brings children into the world, take them out so capriciously?

Iconographic Evidence of the Goddess

I have examined the textual evidence for the goddess Asherah at some length, both in the Hebrew Bible and in extra-biblical inscriptions. Words are important; but a picture really *is* "worth a thousand words." Do we have any such pictures of the goddess Asherah from biblical times (apart from the female figurines)? Of course, we have images from the preceding Late Bronze Age Canaanite era. But do such representations continue — especially if we take seriously the biblical prohibition of the making of any "graven images" of deities (Exodus 20:4)?

I have discussed the 10th-century B.C. "Cultic Structure" at Taʿanach above (Chapter V), taking it as an example of a high place, a *bāmāh*. And the most extraordinary piece of cult paraphernalia there is a large, square terra cotta offering stand, nearly three feet high (p. 154 above). The top has a low "curb" around it, so as to receive an offering bowl for food or drink, while the column is fenestrated, with openings probably for wafting smoke from incense. The iconographic scenes are in bold relief on four stages that probably represent the four stories of a temple.

The top register depicts on the front a quadruped, probably a bull calf, standing between two stylized trees, bearing a winged sun-disc on his back. On the sides are two lions. The next register down shows the familiar scene of two rampant wild goats nibbling the lower branches of a tree. Again there are two lions on the side. The third register down has two lions on the side facing to the front, this time with wings and human heads wearing the "Hathor" wig (below), so they are clearly cherubs. Between the two cherubs is an empty space that some take to be a doorway.

The bottom register shows what I believe is the most astonishing representation of Israelite iconography that we have ever found. Here again are two lions on the side, staring open-eyed out of the front panel. Between the two lions, holding them firmly by the ears, is a female figure shown frontally nude, again wearing the distinctive Hathor bouffant wig. Who *is* she, this enigmatic smiling "Mona Lisa" of ancient Israel?

Most scholars have not even been willing to speculate, but the answer has been clear to me for thirty years. The stand was excavated by Paul W. Lapp in the 1960s, and for a long time, while I was Director of the American sponsoring institution, the W. F. Albright Institute of Archaeological Research in Jerusalem (1971-1975), the Ta'anach stand was housed in the basement. I saw our "Lady of Ta'anach" every day; to me, she is obviously Asherah. I published this suggestion long ago (Dever 1984), basing myself on several readily documented facts. (1) The wig of Hathor, the cow goddess, is regularly worn by the New Kingdom (1500-1200 B.C.) Egyptian goddess Qudshu, "the Holy One," whom we know to be the Egyptian version of Canaanite Asherah. On the Winchester plaque (above, p. 178), she is shown riding on the back of a lion, and the text gives all three of her names: Qudshu (Asherah), Anat, and Astarte. (2) Dozens of contemporary clay and a few gold and electrum plaques and pendants found in Syria-Palestine not only show the goddess wearing the characteristic Hathor wig, showing that she is indeed Asherah, but they also depict her riding on a lion. (3) Finally, numerous inscriptions, stretching over the third, second, and first millennia B.C., and found throughout the Near East, attest to the fact that "the Lion Lady" was one of the most frequent epithets of the great Mother Goddess, and especially of her Canaanite embodiment Asherah. (See also the lion imagery on the 8th-century B.C. storejar from Kuntillet 'Ajrûd, where the accompanying Hebrew text names her as Yahweh's companion, and undoubtedly his consort; above and Chapter V.)

Despite the *overwhelming* evidence that the nude female on the Ta'anach stand is Asherah, very few scholars have been willing to make that identification. Keel and Uehlinger, usually very perceptive, identify her simply as "mistress of animals," although Asherah specifically is a divine figure generally in the ancient Near East. Pirhiya Beck, an excellent art historian, saw her only as some kind of "fertility goddess" (1990:432). Zevit, always the boldest of biblicists, does identify her as Asherah (2001:323, 324). Most commentators on the Ta'anach stand decline to give an opinion. What more *ex-*

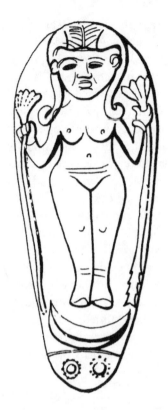

Terra-cotta plaque depicting Asherah with
Hathor wig, holding lotus blossoms;
Syria, 14th-13th cent. B.C.
Negbi 1976, Fig. 117

plicit evidence of the cult of Asherah in monarchic Israel do scholars realistically expect? Here she is, wearing nothing but a great big smile.

Another piece of iconographic evidence comes from a small group of *naoi* (singular *naos*), or terra cotta model temples, dating from the 10th to the 8th century B.C. One from Tell el-Farʿah N., biblical Tirzah, was published years ago, but like the Taʿanach stand it has been overlooked until recently. Standing about a foot high, it has a temple façade that features two fluted, stylized palm-tree columns, complete with curled fronds at the top for capitals. Over the doorway between the columns there appear the moon crescent and the stars of the Pleiades, often associated with Tanit, the Phoenician version of Asherah. Asherah is not "at home" here, that is, standing in the door of her house or temple (Hebrew *bayit* means both). But elsewhere, in other *naoi,* she is at home. On a Phoenician statue (*ca.* 7th century B.C.) from Cyprus, the goddess Asherah, wearing the insignia of her Hathor headdress, carries a *naos* on her head, and there in the doorway stands another representation of Asherah wearing the Hathor wig. From Idalion in Cyprus, comes a roughly contemporary intact *naos,* and the nude goddess is again standing in the doorway. And in case you missed her, she also appears looking out of each side window. Thus there can be no doubt that the *naoi* are model temples associated with Asherah/Tanit. The only question is why the doorway of the Tell el-Far'ah *naos* is empty. Another one, from Transjordan, was found with a female figurine that probably once stood in the doorway, as well as two lions that once may have guarded the entrance — the same combination as on the Ta'anach stand. Perhaps both the "empty doorways" at Tell el-Far'ah and Ta'anach indicate a certain "reticence" in Israelite iconography due to the Second Commandment — what Mettinger (1995) has called "empty space aniconism." On some Phoenician *naoi,* a pair of female deities flanks the open doorway.

Let me turn now to additional iconographic evidence that illuminates Asherah and her cult and has to do specifically with her connection with *trees,* to which I have already alluded. The association with trees in the biblical texts is too consistent to miss, as we have hinted, but let us review it more extensively before looking elsewhere for corroboration.

First, there is the fact already noted that in the majority of the 40 or

Naos, or model temple, from Idalion, Cyprus; 6th cent. B.C., cf. p. 114.
Keel 1997, Fig. 225

Naos; 11th-10th cent. B.C.
Keel 1998, Fig. 74

so occurrences of the word *'ăshērāh*, the term must refer either to a wooden pole, that is, a stylized tree, or to a living tree, both of which are symbols of the goddess Asherah. In a sense, they are "stand-ins" for her in the cult, perhaps because of the second commandment prohibiting any direct representation of the deities themselves. (Note that the First Commandment says that Israel should not have "other gods before me," in the plural, so that was at least a possibility.)

I suggest that the tree-like representations of Asherah were not, in fact, "idols" that people personified and worshipped in place of Yahweh (although the Deuteronomists would have viewed them that way). The ancient Israelites may not have been very sophisticated in our modern sense, but neither were they stupid. The prophets frequently poked fun at handmade idols, and people got the point. In a passage that has to do, in fact, with trees, Jeremiah spins out a wonderfully sarcastic parable:

A tree from the forest is cut down,
    and worked with an ax by the hands of a craftsman.
Men deck it with silver and gold;
    they fasten it with hammer and nails so that it cannot move.
Their idols are like scarecrows in a cucumber field,

and they cannot speak;
They have to be carried,
    for they cannot walk.
Be not afraid of them,
    for they cannot do evil, neither is it in them to do good.

(Jeremiah 10:3-5)

I can hear Jeremiah's listeners laughing, then protesting: "We don't worship trees and wooden poles, but they help us to imagine Yahweh's presence since otherwise we can't see him."

Second, the high places discussed above *(bāmôt)*, often hilltop sanctuaries, typically include *'ăshērîm* and probably also living trees among their features. One phrase describing Israel's "whoring after other gods" occurs again and again: "on every high hill and under every green tree." Of the early-9th-century B.C. reign of the southern Kingdom's first king, Rehoboam, Solomon's son, it is said:

> For they also built for themselves high places, and pillars *(maṣṣēbôt)*, and Asherim on every high hill and under every green tree. (I Kings 14:23)

The same accusation is repeated of Ahaz in the 8th century B.C. (II Kings 16:4) and of Hoshea, his contemporary in the north (II Kings 17:10). The prophets independently use the very same language, "under every green tree": Isaiah (57:5); Jeremiah (2:20; 3:6, 13; 17:2); and Ezekiel (6:13; cf. also Hosea 4:12, 13). And the passage in Deuteronomy 12:2, 3 projects the same language back to Moses' warning before Israel's entry into the Land.

Thus in the biblical writers' view, from Moses to Ezekiel — 600 years, Israel's entire history in Canaan — folk religion is bound up with rites having to do with "green trees," rites prohibited, yet practiced nonetheless. Why the biblical writers' obsession with trees? It seems pretty obvious: a luxuriant green tree represents the goddess Asherah, who gives life in a barren land. (Those of us who have lived in the Arizona desert appreciate why trees seem miraculous.) And on the ridges and hilltops, where one seems closer to the gods and can lift up one's eyes to the heavens, the trees and groups of wooden poles erected to her added to the verdant setting and the ambiance of luxuriousness, of plenty.

Such "hilltop shrines" with groves of trees are well known throughout the Mediterranean world in the Bronze and Iron Ages, and they continued to flourish clear into the Classical era. Why should ancient Israel *not* have participated in this universal oriental culture of "fertility religions," which celebrated the rejuvenation and sustaining powers of Nature? Perhaps Israel's only unique contribution was to see over time that Nature is subsumed *under* Yahweh, "Lord of the Universe," whose power ultimately gives life to humans and beast and field. But that insight was a long time coming, and it was fully realized only in the wisdom gained from the tragedy of the Babylonian captivity (Chapter VIII).

Despite what seems to me the transparency of the "tree" motif in connection with Asherah, ancient commentators seem to have been confused, and so were modern scholars until recently. As I have noted above (Chapter IV), the Greek translators of the Hebrew Bible in the 3rd-2nd century B.C. were already sufficiently removed from the Iron Age reality that they did not understand the real meaning of Hebrew *'ăshērāh*. Thus they rendered the term by the Greek word *'alsos*, "grove," or *dendron*, "tree."

The Latin Vulgate (4th century A.D.) has *lucus*, "copse; sacred grove," or occasionally *nemus*, "forest" (LaRocca-Pitts 2001:255-257; 295). The RSV sometimes translates *'ăshērāh* in the singular as "Asherah or "the Asherah," the latter reflecting the confusion already in the Hebrew text, which sometimes adds the definite article. In other places, however, the RSV has for the plural of *'ăshērāh* "Asherim," where the term refers to the symbol rather than the goddess (one cannot say the "goddesses Asherah"). Thus even the best of modern translations often depend upon context; they are not consistent, and sometimes they simply guess.

Several recent publications may have finally resolved the association of Asherah with trees. The breakthrough came in the mid-1980s. One day Ruth Hestrin, a woman who was not an academic but was one of the devoted curators of the Israel Museum, showed me a manuscript that she was having difficulty getting published. She wanted to know if I thought that she was really on to something, or whether her detractors were right: "too radical." I was struck and excited by the sheer intuition of her work. I encouraged her as enthusiastically as I could; and in 1987 the prestigious *Israel Exploration Journal* published Ruth's article under the innocent-sounding title "The Lachish Ewer and the Asherah." It took a while, but some years later the bombshell dropped. And today Ruth Hestrin's innovative views are widely quoted (and unfortunately taken for granted, as though "we always knew that").

Hestrin began with the fact that in the Late Bronze Age a frequent iconographic scene of Canaanite art depicts two rampant wild goats nibbling at the lower branches of a tree. She then looked at this scene on the famous "ewer" (or dedicatory vase) from the Judean site of Lachish, excavated in the 1930s. It was found in a *favissa* or depository pit near the 13th century B.C. "Fosse Temple III." Painted on the upper shoulder was the familiar scene of two rampant wild goats nibbling at the branches of a tree (looking very much like a menorah, or seven-branched candlestick). Running around the top in Old Canaanite script was a dedicatory formula: "Mattan: An offering for my Lady Elat." "Mattan" is probably the worshipper's name, but it could also be translated "A gift." "Elat" is the feminine form of the name of the Canaanite male deity El, and it is also one of the names of the great Mother Goddess of Canaan, used in *parallel* with "Asherah." Finally, a mutton bone was found in the vase. So here we have an offering for the goddess Elat/Asherah.

Many biblical scholars over the years had commented on the inscription, of course — a *text*. But almost no one had noted the archaeological *context*. Here we have a specific offering, closely dated, presented to a Canaanite goddess. We know her name, and we can see her temple next door. Yet no one except Ruth Hestrin had noticed that from *another* offer-

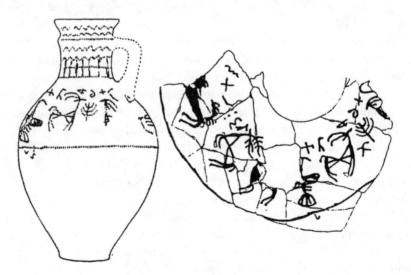

Lachish "ewer," with Canaanite inscription (enlarged)
Keel 1998, Fig. 49

ing pit of the Lachish temple there had come a goblet with a similar scene showing two rampant wild goats. But here the female pubic triangle was *substituted* for the usual tree. So the pubic triangle — symbol from time immemorial of the source of all human conception, birth, and life — and the tree were interchangeable, that is, conceived of as representing the *same thing*. That was what the ancient Canaanites and Israelites had once known instinctively. But in time, the knowledge must have been lost, and only the "mysterious" tree symbol remained.

Hestrin's observation, so obvious in retrospect (like many a stroke of genius), was brilliant. But there was more. She then noticed that on a number of gold or electrum pendants of the Late Bronze Age, the goddess Asherah was depicted in a highly stylized way, as only a torso, yet with

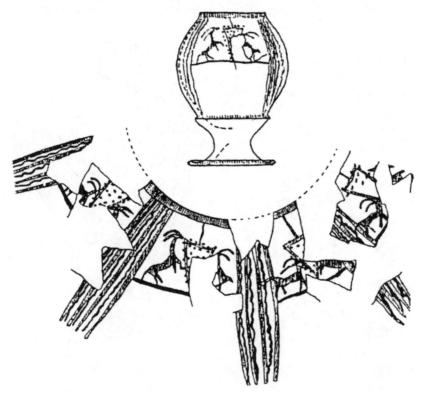

A goblet from a *favissa* of Fosse Temple III at Lachish, showing a pubic triangle flanked by ibexes; below, an enlargement; 13th cent. B.C.
Keel and Uehlinger 1998, Fig. 80

prominent breasts and vulva. It is clear that she is Asherah, because she wears the familiar bouffant wig of the Egyptian cow goddess Hathor, who is pictured and named on plaques as Qudshu, "the Holy One." (See above, on the Winchester plaque.) But what Hestrin saw on the Canaanite pendants was a *tree* growing out of the goddess's vulva. Now it became clearer than ever that Asherah, the symbol of the female pubic triangle, and the tree could all be *interchangeable* in Canaanite cultic iconography.

As though that were not convincing enough, Hestrin went on to cite several Egyptian second millennium B.C. tomb paintings, in which a fully branched tree is shown as a woman, offering a breast with outstretched hand and suckling an infant. One such scene depicts none other than the son of Pharaoh Thutmosis III, complete with inscription. I regard Ruth Hestrin's article (popularized in 1991) as one of the greatest single contributions to our

Electrum pendant of a stylized Asherah, with Hathor wig, and a tree growing from the vulva; 14th-13th cent. B.C.
Keel 1998, Fig. 18

Egyptian 18th Dynasty tomb painting, showing a son of Pharaoh Thutmosis III being nursed by a tree-goddess
Keel 1997, Fig. 253

knowledge of ancient Israelite folk religion. *Now* we understand the whole "tree" business — and why the biblical writers and editors were so adamantly opposed to trees and "groves." It took an unassuming, non-academic woman to see what everyone else failed to see. "Sacred trees" are still revered by Bedouin today, as I have seen in the Syrian Desert near Palmyra.

A number of scholars followed out Hestrin's intuition in a rather cursory fashion. But in 1998, Othmar Keel, the *doyen* of the Freibourg art historical school discussed above (Chapter II), produced a full-scale study, *Goddesses and Trees, New Moon and Yahweh: Ancient Near Eastern Art and the Hebrew Bible.* Curiously, Keel does not list Hestrin in beginning his work with a footnote citing the contribution of previous scholars. His own contribution is first to take the tree-and-goddess iconography back to the early second millennium B.C. He then adds to Hestrin's examples several Canaanite plaques discovered since then, with even more specific connections, as well as a few more Egyptian representations similar to Hestrin's "tree nursing an infant." He further emphasizes of the goddess Asherah that "it is safe to assume that the tree, natural or stylized and named after her, was connected with her" (1998:38, citing also Kletter 1996:76, 77 on the figurines). Finally, Keel adds more than two dozen additional Iron Age figurines, offering stands, model temples, and seals that are based on the identification of Asherah with tree imagery (not all, however, from Pales-

An Egyptian tree-goddess,
the female deity represented
as a tree trunk
Keel 1997, Fig. 254

A "sacred tree" in the desert near Palmyra, festooned with fragments of women's
clothing and Arabic prayers on scraps of paper
Photo: W. G. Dever

tine). The second half of Keel's 1998 book is devoted to "moon cults," to
which I shall return presently.

Let me note here, however, the importance of seals and seal impressions, which have been neglected by many other scholars, but which Keel
and his colleagues have shown to be of great significance for understanding Israelite folk religion. The seal iconography is particularly relevant for
the late 8th–early 6th century B.C., when Israel and Judah came under the
influence of Neo-Assyrian and Neo-Babylonian "astral cults," in which
Asherah (as Ishtar) and Astarte (probably the "Queen of Heaven" of Jeremiah 7:18 and 44:17-25) were venerated. Again, it would be surprising if the
Israelite cults had *not* been influenced by these cults of the wider ancient
Near Eastern world.

Already in 1992 in the German original of *Gods, Goddesses, and Images of God in Ancient Israel* (1998), Keel and Uehlinger had collected a
number of 9th-7th-century B.C. seals, seal impressions, ivories, and other
objects with iconographic motifs. Featured are such things as "the Lord of
animals" and bulls and deities riding on bulls. They argue, however, that

on the seals no goddess is portrayed "anthropomorphically," that is, with human-like anatomical features. Thus they specifically reject my argument that the seated female figure on a Kuntillet ʿAjrûd storejar (above) is Asherah (1998:223, 224). Instead, they think that there is only an "*asherah* atmosphere" on the overall scene; and that perhaps a professional scene of worshippers on the storejar may be more relevant (1998:241, 242). I don't see how the latter can be, since the jar is broken, and the person/object toward which those processing are moving is missing.

Keel and Uehlinger turn instead to seals with solar and astral images (1998:248-277), where they find several 9th-8th-century B.C. scenes involving trees, which they understand as "a cultic symbol assigned to Yahweh, by which his blessing is mediated to the people" (1998:278). That is consistent with their view that Kuntillet ʿAjrûd is not a religious sanctuary of any kind, and that the mention of an *asherah* here and elsewhere does not refer to a female deity, only to a symbol related to Yahweh (above). That seems to me to go against both the evidence and common sense — surprisingly defensive for scholars who are otherwise so innovative. They do document the strong influence of solar and astral symbolism in 8th-7th-century B.C. Israel, but they relate virtually all of this to the male deity Yahweh.

On the other hand, Keel and Uehlinger then argue that *beginning* in the late 8th century B.C., the old Bronze Age connection of trees with Asherah signals the "astralization of the heavenly powers" and the *revival* of the goddess. Here they present a mass of iconographic evidence (1998:283-287), with dozens of examples. But according to them, there are only two goddesses represented, the healing goddess Gula, and Ishtar (Astarte). The latter is easily recognized by her emblems, a shining wreath or a nimbus of stars. In addition, the motifs include other astral symbols, especially the eight-rayed star of Venus, the stars of the Pleiades, and the

Seals depicting quadrupeds and humans
Keel and Uehlinger 1998, Fig. 177; 178

crescent moon. In that sense, the gods and goddesses come to represent deities of the night (1998:292-294; the night demon Lilith will reemerge in later Judaism; below).

Some of these later seals do have trees, so Keel and Uehlinger think that by now (7th century B.C.) Asherah has "reemerged." I don't think that she ever went away. The absence of 12th-8th-century B.C. seals showing her tree emblem means nothing, because we have almost no stamp seals from this period. In archaeology, arguments from silence are meaningless. Nevertheless, Keel and Uehlinger's overall conclusion is worth repeating.

> The predominance of astral symbolism, accompanied by the decline in importance of the mediating, numinous protective powers, is probably connected to a growing need that was in conflict with the concurrent revival of the old, "Canaanite" traditions (1998:318).

Additional iconographic motifs that can be related to Asherah (Keel and Uehlinger say to "the goddess") later in her history in Israel and Judah include doves. Doves appear frequently in connection with the goddess Tanit, the late Phoenician counterpart of Asherah. But they are seen already on 9th-8th-century B.C. objects such as *naoi*, or model temple shrines. Finally, Keel and Uehlinger agree with other scholars that the hundreds and hundreds of pillar-figurines (above), although devoid of obvious symbolism except the breasts, represent the goddess Asherah, as I have argued. To support this supposition, they point out the same representations of the "tree suckling an infant" that Hestrin first noted (1998:331-336). They do not, however, cite a few scholars who early on observed that the plain, columnar lower body of these female figurines closely resembles a tree trunk. (Ruth Hestrin may have been the first.)

A more recent study of seals representing Ishtar/Astarte is that of the Israeli art historian Tallay Ornan (2001). She cites six 8th-7th-century B.C. seals found thus far in Israel, some of which depict the goddess Ishtar characteristically wearing a crown and enclosed with a circle. Similar seals and other artistic representations in art found in Mesopotamia have inscriptions identifying this figure as Ishtar. In many cases the circle appears as a sparkling star with protruding points. A seal found on the surface at the Judean site of Lachish is particularly significant. A tree appears beside her, and her hands are supporting her breasts — both "fertility" symbols. Ishtar can be a "warrior goddess," but she is also the goddess who brings life. The embodiment of such polar opposites, foreign to our modern way of thinking, was common in the ancient world. The Canaanite goddess ʿAnat (below) is a fearsome hunter and warrior who wantonly slaughters her lover Baʿal's enemies. But she is also the great goddess "who conceives but never bears," the goddess of perpetual life-giving power. Ornan concludes that the seals found in Israel were locally made and "strengthen the notion of the Assyrian influence on the image of the Queen of Heaven and the resemblance of her cult to that of Ishtar" (2001:252).

Many previous scholars have identified the "Queen of Heaven" in Jeremiah 7:18 and 44:17-25 as Ishtar, or as she was more commonly known in the West, Astarte, notably Ackerman in her definitive study of late Judean and exilic folk religion (1992). Astarte is the name of one of the three Canaanite female deities in the Ugaritic texts discussed above, alongside Asherah and ʿAnat, and there her fertility roles are clear. She is also named on the Winchester plaque and identified there with Qudshu/ Asherah and ʿAnat. In the Hebrew Bible, however, Astarte plays a minor role compared to Asherah, although several texts prohibit her worship (Judges 2:13; 10:6; I Samuel 7:4; 12:10, all parallel with "Baʿal"; I Kings 11:5; II Kings 23:13, of the "Sidonians," or Phoenicians).

Ackerman has argued persuasively that a mass of linguistic evidence from the second and first millennia B.C. identifies Astarte as a heavenly queen and divine consort. In later Phoenician and Greek sources, she becomes "Aphrodite," goddess of sex and love. Although Ackerman does not cite the seals that Keel and Uehlinger and Ornan note (her work predates their publications), the iconography there strongly supports the roles of

 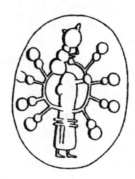 

Seals depicting Astarte, surrounded by stars
Keel and Uehlinger 1998, Fig. 288a-c

Astarte that she describes. The crown that she wears is that of a queen, and the stars reinforce the concept of her heavenly abode.

The most intriguing aspect of all this is the probability that the "Queen of Heaven" in the two passages in Jeremiah discussed above can be identified specifically as Astarte — that is, as *another* "Canaanite" mother goddess venerated in folk religion in late Judean times. One detail is particularly striking. The Hebrew term for the "cakes" baked for her, *kawwānîm*, which occurs only in these two passages, is a loan word from the Mesopotamian term *kamānu*, "cake." Several Mesopotamian texts describe the baking of these cakes for Ishtar (quoted in Ackerman 1992:31):

> O Išhtar, merciful goddess, I have come to visit you,
> I have prepared for you an offering, pure milk,
>> A pure cake baked in ashes *(kamān tumri)*,
> I stood up for you a vessel for libations,
>> Hear me and act favorably toward me!

In the Jeremiah passages, the cakes baked for the "Queen of Heaven" (Ishtar/Astarte) are made "in her image." Several scholars have explained that reference by calling attention to early second millennium clay molds found at Mari on the Euphrates. Some of these show a wide-hipped goddess holding her breasts. They are best explained as molds for making cakes, probably for ritual presentation to a goddess. If accepted, this interpretation would provide a close parallel for the references in Jeremiah to "baking cakes for the Queen of Heaven." And, of course, baking is a "woman's task" *par excellence*. All this has led me to follow the notion of several scholars (although not the majority) in seeing the object held to the breast of the early Iron Age female figurines not as a frame-drum (p. 154 and above), but as a mold-made cake. As far as I know, however, no one has pointed out that the radiating "spokes" on the round object at the breast closely resemble the radiating stars on the depictions of encircled Ishtar on the seals.

The evidence for a second "mother goddess" venerated in ancient Israel alongside Asherah, although circumstantial, may seem confusing, even contradictory. There is, however, evidence of still another goddess who was venerated by the ancient Judeans. The prophet Ezekiel reports that at the gate of the Temple in Jerusalem there sat "women weeping for Tammuz" (Ezekiel 8:14). "Tammuz" was the later name of the 3rd millennium Sumerian god Dumuzi. He was a seasonal "dying and rising" god whose consort was Ishtar (Sumerian Inanna). Like Canaanite Baʿal in the western Semitic world, Dumuzi died annually in the early summer when the rains ceased, and then he descended into the underworld as though dead. Ishtar mourned his passing, but in the fall she helped to bring him back to life, and they re-consummated their sexual union. Thus Nature was fructified in an unending cycle of love, death, and reunion. The Mesopotamian cult of Tammuz was largely the province of women, who naturally empathize with his "widow" Ishtar, and ritually mourn his passing. There seems little doubt that this pan-Mediterranean seasonal myth of Baʿal and ʿAnat, Tammuz and Ishtar, was popular in some circles in Judah, especially after the Assyrian impact in the late 8th century B.C. (Ackerman 1992:79-80).

There is also evidence of other mourning rituals in the Hebrew Bible, for other male deities. In Elijah's famous contest on Mt. Carmel, the prophets of Baʿal attempt to call up the dead vegetation deity Baʿal by ritually gashing their flesh (I Kings 18:28), a typical funerary rite. Baʿal is also known by his other name Hadad, and in Zechariah 12:10, 11 there is a description of "mourning for Hadad-Rimmon in the Valley of Megiddo." Hosea 7:14 may also refer to the same rites, condemning those who "turn to Baʿal" (Hebrew uncertain), who "wail upon their beds" and "gash themselves."

Before leaving what may seem to be a confusing multiplicity of female (and male) deities, and the question of which cultic artifacts may relate to which, let me note one fact that may help. In the eastern Mediterranean world generally, there appear many *local* deities, both male and female, who were probably conceived of as particular manifestations of the more cosmic high gods. Thus in Canaan, we have texts naming Baʿalat (the feminine counterpart of Baʿal) "of Byblos." The male deity Baʿal appears in Canaanite texts as Baʿal Zephon, "Baʿal of the North." Baʿal appears in the Hebrew Bible as "Baʿal (of) Hazor"; "Baʿal (of) Hermon"; "Baʿal (of) Meon"; "Baʿal (of) Peor"; and "Baʿal (of) Tamar." In the Kuntillet ʿAjrûd texts discussed above, we find mention of "Yahweh of Samaria," and "Yahweh of Teman (Yemen)." Thus a number of scholars have called attention to the tendency of the High God or Goddess to appear in the form of the deity of a particular local cult, often with a hyphenated name. This would be a sort of "diffusion" of the deity; but on the other hand, these deities could coalesce again under different conditions into a sort of "conflate" deity. The result is often great confusion of names and identities. For instance, a long chain of textual witnesses over time result in the following equation: Ba'al-Hadad = Ba'al-Shamen ("of the heavens") = Zeus Helio = Heliopolitan Zeus. *All* these names, however, are reflexes of the great West Semitic high god Ba'al, "Lord of the Heavens/Sun" (the Greek equivalent of Ba'al with Zeus and *helios,* "sun," is transparent). Likewise Canaanite 'Anat became Greek Athena, the warlike patron deity of Athens. And Canaanite-Israelite Asherah appears later as Greek Aphrodite and Roman Venus, the latter also goddesses of beauty, love, and sexual pleasure. The similarities are unequivocal: Asherah and Aphrodite are both connected to the sea, and doves are symbols of both. Aphrodite's lover Adonis clearly preserves the earlier Phoenician-Hebrew word *'ādōn,* "Lord."

Of relevance for the female deities worshipped in ancient Israel, we should note the work of my teacher Frank Cross and several of his students. They have argued that the three great goddesses of Ugarit — Asherah, 'Anat, and Astarte — are all in effect "hypostatizations" of the cosmic Great Goddess of Canaan, all playing the same role but each perhaps venerated in a particular local manifestation, tradition, and cult. We could insist on choosing one — but should we? In Roman Catholic piety, especially among ordinary, unsophisticated worshippers we encounter many "Marys" — "Our Lady of Guadalupe"; "Our Lady of Lourdes"; etc. Are these different "Marys," or one in many *guises?*

Often folk religion may be universal and timeless; but it is always the here and now that matters. Thus women in ancient Israel were probably addressing their special concerns to the Great Mother of Canaan who lived on in the Iron Age, whether they knew her as "Asherah," the "Queen of Heaven," or "Ishtar," or "Astarte." I think that most conceived of her as a consort of the male deity Yahweh, but others may have seen her more as simply a personification of Yahweh's more "feminine" attributes.

Asherah and Women's Cults

The emphasis that I have placed thus far upon the role of the female deities in folk religion in ancient Israel — especially the principal goddess Asherah — may give a false impression. It could suggest that it was only the women who were "deviants"; the men were busy writing up the true religion in the Hebrew Bible. Yet the way I have interpreted the stories in

Jeremiah 7:16-20 and 44:15-19 should make it clear that I believe that men also participated in religious practices of which the canonical biblical writers disapproved. In fact, I shall argue that folk religion as practiced by *both* sexes was precisely what is *condemned* in the Hebrew Bible.

A list of proscribed activities would be long and complex, mostly derived from the Deuteronomistic and prophetic writings, but it could be summed up as follows.

1. Frequenting local shrines *(bāmôt)*
2. Setting up standing stones *(maṣṣēbôt)*
3. Making of images of various deities
4. Venerating the goddesses
5. Burning incense
6. Baking cakes for the "Queen of Heaven"
7. Making vows
8. "Weeping for Tammuz"
9. Performing rituals having to do with childbirth and children
10. Holding *marzĕaḥ* feasts
11. Conducting funerary rites; "feeding the dead"
12. Making pilgrimages to holy places and saints' festivals
13. Engaging in various aspects of astral and solar worship
14. Divining and "magic," except by priests
15. Sacrificing children (?)

All these things, mostly discussed above, are condemned by the male writers of the Hebrew Bible as "idolatrous," that is, non-Yahwistic. But their inclusion implies that the *majority* of people, not just an easily-ignored minority, were doing them — and, I would argue, principally doing them in a family context, where women played a highly significant role. (I have also argued that all this was part of "Yahwism," at least until the 7th century B.C. attempts at reform.) After all, half the people in ancient Israel were female; and women reared the other half. While largely marginalized in public (and especially in the perspective of the biblical writers), women nevertheless had a major role in family and household life. There they were the primary custodians of the "religion of hearth and home," the realities of which shaped ancient Israelite belief and practice far more than did the theology of the "official" cult and canonical Scripture.

Several women have written recently on "women's cults" in ancient

Israel. But they are exceptional among biblical scholars, most of whom have been all too typical representatives of the male Establishment (in spite of the feminist movement's inroads; Chapter IX). Phyllis Bird, a Garrett Evangelical Theological Seminary professor, published a thoughtful essay in 1991 entitled "Israelite Religion and the Faith of Israel's Daughters: Reflections on Gender and Religious Definition." Here she drew upon ethnographic parallels of women and religion in other pre-modern societies. She showed how women may seem to be "invisible" in the literary tradition, yet they have their own unique religious practices that were "better suited to the general rhythms and the exigencies of their lives" (1991:115). As Bird concludes:

> The whole question of religious pluralism *within* a national Yahweh cult is just beginning to be explored in relation to evidence for Asherah as a symbol operating within Israelite Yahwism. Women's religion cannot be equated with goddess worship, but there is sufficient evidence to suggest that women's religion did represent a significantly differentiated form of religious expression within Yahwism, which must be studied along with other forms of pluralism in the religion of ancient Israel. To speak of the faith of Israel's daughters means at the very least to reexamine the boundaries of the religion we have reconstructed and to make room for more differentiated forms of piety than we have hitherto imagined — with attention given to hierarchies of power in a gender-differentiated system of roles and office (1991:107, 108).

Carol Meyers of Duke University, both a biblical scholar and an experienced archaeologist, has also written on the roles of women in Israelite religion, especially in family life. In a series of publications (1988; 1991b; 1997; 2000; 2002; 2003a; 2003b), she has laid out a more moderate agenda than some feminists. She argues that women had an unappreciated but significant and honored role in ancient Israelite religion, that "the mother's house" was at least as important as the much-discussed "house of the father" (or patriarch). Meyers thus defends the biblical writers against some current, extreme charges of "male chauvinism," pointing out that the writers were products of their own time and social setting.

Meyers' unique contribution is to illuminate the daily life of Israelite women, especially in their "informal social networks" in non-urban, rural communities, which she (like me here) thinks constituted at least 90 percent of the population. Yet even among feminists, "the varied, and often powerful informal, extra-domestic connections formed by women have gone largely unnoticed" (2003a:187). On the other hand, women and men participated jointly in many *household* tasks, so the rigid "private vs. public" dichotomy of many scholars is unrealistic and unproductive in understanding the real dynamics of ancient family life (here I have some misgivings). And, in spite of the larger framework of a patriarchal society, women were not as powerless as some doctrinaire feminists have argued, not always "victims."

Meyers, like Bird, also uses socio-anthropological theory and ethnographic fieldwork to show that "another significant aspect of informal women's networks in Israelite villages was undoubtedly their role in religious or ritual activities" (2003a:199). Many of these "life-cycle" rituals would have had to do with female biological processes, so "groups of village women probably developed traditions of sacral behaviors for which they, not the men, were experts" (2003a:199). Among women's roles would have been presiding over family shrines and feasts, maintaining tombs of ancestors, making vows, and the like. Meyers does not provide much of the archaeological data that would support her scenario, although she could (as in 2003b).

One of Meyers' latest articles, "From Household to House of Yahweh: Women's Religious Culture in Ancient Israel" (2002), is a mature, philosophical reflection on feminist concerns that balances an appreciation of the biblical texts, modern sociological studies, and archaeology's unique contribution better than any I know (the bibliography is superb). And unlike most other scholars on our subject, male or female, Meyers takes the inquiry into post-biblical Judaism and the continuation of the "magical rituals" that were an essential part of Israelite religion.

I disagree with Meyers on only one major point throughout her work, namely her contention that "the artifacts of Israelites sites are silent about who used them" (2002:297). If they actually were, this book could never have been written.

Archaeological Correlates of Women's Cults

If we look for "archaeological correlates" for the features of the women's (and folk) cults mentioned above, we encounter varying degrees of success. (1) I have already explored the nature, paraphernalia, and rituals of the characteristic *bāmôt,* or local shrines, citing the archaeological evidence. Not much more can be said, except that at these shrines there is no reason to believe that men dominated — or the contrary. The prayer, vows, sacrifices, and rituals had to do not with "correct theology," but rather with the harsh everyday realities of *family* life. Here, women's voices were surely heard and respected. And since these were rural shrines, not official temples, women had unhindered access.

(2) Standing stones *(māṣṣēbôt),* treated above, were usually found at local shrines, and there they must have been familiar, palpable symbols of the presence of the gods and goddesses. Inasmuch as they were rural manifestations of the deities — far removed from the Jerusalem Temple and its oppressive clergy (at least late in the Monarchy) — women would have felt at home with them. And if, as in the Arad sanctuary, these standing stones were paired, and one of them represented Asherah, women would have resonated particularly with that.

(3) The making of images, condemned in the Hebrew Bible, was very much an aspect of rural shrines (see the mold for making them at Ta'anach; above), and even more so of domestic production. Fabrication of the typical female Asherah terra-cotta figurines required no technology, only a mold and clay. And their frequent occurrence in all sorts of household contexts shows that virtually every woman had one (or more). They were probably prominent furnishings at family shrines. Some became family heirlooms and were buried with the deceased, as if to prolong Asherah's blessings into whatever afterlife might have been envisioned.

(4) I have already discussed in some detail the role that Asherah played in family cults and folk religion. The hundreds of female figurines associated with her, and the various iconographic images of the goddesses in general, are proof that women were acutely aware of and responded to the "female aspects of deity," even if they were conceived as somehow associated with Yahweh the male deity.

(5) "Burning incense" poses a problem, because it appears to be an authentic practice of Israelite religion from the beginning (above). Yet again and again, the Deuteronomistic writers and the prophets condemn this practice. Why? The answer is apparently that "burning incense" is usually taken to mean (1) making an incense offering at high places, *bāmôt,* associated with abhorrent "Canaanite" practices; and (2) doing so to gods other than Yahweh. The most recent and most comprehensive study of the

archaeological evidence for burning incense (on the four-horned altars; above) is that of Seymour Gitin (2002). Gitin concludes that it was a part of both official and folk religion, especially by the 7th/6th century B.C. — the period from which most of the biblical texts stem. But if incense offerings were commonly made at home, then women would have presided over them as informal, *ad hoc* "priests."

(6) "Baking cakes for the Queen of Heaven." I have discussed this fully above, including the suggestion that some of the female figurines may provide archaeological evidence of such a practice. I can only add here the fact that in Mesopotamia this custom is confined to women's cults (not surprisingly). In Israel, we have not found the molds for making such cakes; but if they were made of wood, the molds would not have survived in the archaeological record. Nevertheless, the task of baking was gender-specific, and typical only of women.

(7) "Making vows" is essentially verbal, so the only archaeological evidence we might expect to find for it would be the votive objects offered to concretize the vow. I have discussed these above, but admittedly the evidence is scant. Nevertheless, van der Toorn (1994) and Berlinerblau (1996), among others, have pointed out that vows were a characteristic part of women's cults (and, I would add, of men's cults, too).

(8) "Weeping for Tammuz," another verbal expression, would be attested archaeologically only by the iconographic data presented above. But here again, this would have been overwhelmingly a woman's activity, in sympathy with the mourning of dead Tammuz's lover, Ishtar.

(9) We have little direct archaeological evidence for various rituals that we might call "rites of passage." These rites — family rituals, of course, and certainly "religious" — would have celebrated such life-cycle events as conception; birth; lactation; circumcision; passage to adolescence; betrothal; marriage; childbirth; health, welfare, and prosperity; the onset of senescence; death; and burial. The female figurines, however, would almost certainly have had to do with women's prayers to conceive, bear a child safely, and be able to nurse the baby through infancy. They would also have been appealed to in order to secure the deity's general blessings of plenty. For circumcision, however, we have no material evidence (what would the archaeologist look for — flint blades with shreds of dried foreskin?).

(10-11) Since the discovery of the Canaanite mythological texts from Ugarit in Syria in the 1920s, scholars have been able to reconstruct the outlines of a feast known as the *marzēaḥ*. Many scholars believe that this was a banquet for the dead, shared with their lingering spirits. These feasts in Canaan tend to be associated with a particular deity; they involve a meal with cultic rites; and they often feature overeating and drunkenness. They invoke the dead — called in the texts the "Rephaim," those who reside in the underworld — who are summoned to take part, and who must still be provided for.

The textual evidence for the *marzēaḥ* is, however, ambiguous, so to what degree there was an actual "cult of the dead" in Canaanite religion remains uncertain. One other rite, long taken for granted, was "feeding the dead." This was based on the idea of the French excavators at Ugarit that "tubes" led from the surface down into the underground burial chambers at Ugarit though which "libation offerings" could be made. But lately this has been questioned, and these vents may have served some other purpose. Several scholars have thus done an about-face on this subject (cf. Lewis 1989:97, 98).

The term *marzēaḥ* appears only twice in the Hebrew Bible. In Amos 6:7 it has been translated to refer to "those who stretch themselves" (RSV), based on some etymologies of the term that seem to refer to "drunken sprawlers." Here Amos is castigating those sluggards who lie idly about, gorging themselves while Israelite society is going to ruin. These callous revelers will be "the first of those who go into exile." Two points must be made: (1) There is nothing to suggest any connection with funerary cults here; and (2) the scene is not about drunkenness (which was tolerated by the biblical writers at certain feasts), but about the complacency and pride of the upper classes.

The other text that has been discussed in this connection is Jeremiah 16:5-9. This passage does have to do specifically with various rites for the dead, in that Jeremiah is forbidden by Yahweh to perform any of them in mourning for the soon-to-be-destroyed kingdom of Judah. They include going to the "house of mourning"; sitting with those assembled "breaking bread" with the grieving; sharing wine with relatives of the deceased; and even cutting one's flesh and pulling out one's hair. That may sound like the Canaanite *marzēaḥ;* but it also sounds a bit like an Irish wake. The fact is that such mourning rituals *in general* are deeply rooted in human nature and are found in nearly all cultures ancient and modern. The underlying issue is really what such "mourning feasts," which undoubtedly did take place in folk religion in ancient Israel, would have meant.

In the Hebrew Bible there is only a hint of belief in an "afterlife," in the notion of "Sheol" in some late texts, the underground world where departed spirits go (Proverbs 9:18). The dead are sometimes called *'ĕlōhîm*, "the gods," as though the deceased were now with the gods somewhere. But there is no doctrine of a "bodily resurrection," which appears only in some sects of later Judaism (among them the Pharisees of Jesus' day). Even the notion of "the immortality of the soul" (a Greek idea) is very late, seen only vaguely in the reference in Daniel 12:3 to those departed righteous ones who shall shine forever in the heavens "like stars" (probably written in the 2nd century B.C.). For the most part, the dead "sleep"; to quote Daniel again (12:2), we pray for all those "who sleep in the dust of the earth" (although here it is hoped that they will "awake").

Israelite and Judean burial customs in the light of the archaeological evidence have been explored only recently, as in Elizabeth Bloch-Smith's comprehensive *Judahite Burial Practices and Beliefs about the Dead* (1992). She surveys the textual evidence thoroughly, which indicates, as we should expect, that death played a prominent role in life, and thus in the cult. (In the ancient world, the modern notion of the separation of the "sacred" and the "secular," so that one had the option of choosing, was inconceivable.) Bloch-Smith then turns to the archaeological data, which she surveys so well that there is no need to repeat her discussion here.

Everyday religious activities may leave little trace in the archaeological record. But rituals pertaining to death fortunately (for us) may leave considerable evidence, since tombs generally preserve many more intact objects than badly disturbed and frequently destroyed domestic deposits. Some of the items that Bloch-Smith discusses, which we have also treated here, found in underground "bench-tombs," are:

Ceramic vessels (mostly ordinary domestic)
Jewelry
Amulets, "gaming pieces"
"Model" household furnishings
Clay "rattles"
Various personal items, reminiscent of life
Tools
Food remains
Female figurines (although rare)
Zoomorphic figurines (mostly horses)

In addition to these contents, some "royal" rock-cut tombs in Jerusalem have aboveground markers or monumental architectural elements. A very few tombs have produced Hebrew inscriptions. One in Jerusalem appears to be that of one "Shebnah," the 8th-century B.C. royal steward mentioned in Isaiah 22:15-25. The tomb is still visible today. The inscription reads:

> This is the tomb of *(Shebni-)* Yahu,
> who is "over the house." There
> is no silver or gold, only his
> bones and the bones of his slave-wife
> with him. Cursed be the person
> who opens this tomb.   (quoted in Bloch-Smith 1992:210).

My contemporary Kh. el-Qôm tomb inscription discussed above is one of the few clear examples we have of a complete Hebrew tomb inscription, and it is a prayer for blessings upon the deceased.

That various rites pertaining to death and burial were an integral part of *family* religious rituals needs no explanation. And just as women were the primary caregivers in life, so were they in death. "Skilled female mourners" are mentioned in Jeremiah 9:17. Men also mourned; but women needed to *do* something, and their actions are clear in tomb offerings. Overall, the objects found in Israelite and Judean tombs imply that the dead were remembered, honored, seen as still present "spiritually," and (to judge from biblical texts) invoked as diviners. The "shades" or spirits ("Rephaim," healers) lingered on, and the family tombs where they were interred were reused and visited frequently for generations. One of the most conspicuous archaeological proofs for the biblical concept of death as being "gathered unto the fathers" (Genesis 25:8; 35:29; Numbers 20:24; Judges 2:10) is the typical repository found under one of the tomb benches. Here the bones of many previous burials were collected before a new body was placed on the bench.

The "fit" between the textual and artifactual witnesses at this point is so close that only one question remains. Why do the biblical writers seem to *prohibit* such rites as "feeding the dead"? In fact, they do not reject this practice generally, only when food first offered as a sacrifice, a "tithe," is involved (Deuteronomy 26:14); when divination was being practiced (Deuteronomy 18:10, 11; Leviticus 20:6, 27); or when "purity" laws were in danger of being violated (such as that about touching a corpse; Numbers 19:11, 16).

(12) Visiting the graves of those presumed to be "saints," as well as making more extensive trips to "pilgrimage sites," would have been a part of family cults, as in all ancient religions. Tombs in general were venerated (above), the tombs of "holy men" particularly so. That is still true in Muslim folk religion in the Middle East today, where it is almost exclusively village women who visit the *wêlis* or tombs of saints that dot the countryside. In many cases, the "saint" who is said to be buried there is anonymous, unknown, or even fictional; but that doesn't seem to matter. What does matter are the act of piety itself; the prayers and vows solemnized there; and, above all, the "women's networks" that Carol Meyers has described so perceptively (above).

Both Meyers and Phyllis Bird have drawn on ethnographic case studies of women's cults in the modern world in the Middle East, as has my colleague Ann Betteridge at the University of Arizona. All three scholars document the same phenomenon. Non-literate, "non-orthodox," exclusively women's groups and activities give expression to religious concerns that are *unique* to women — especially largely illiterate women, who are the modern counterparts of most women in ancient Israel. Muslim women, shut out of formal worship under the supervision of the gadis and imams, unable to read the Qurân for themselves, have found "alternate" ways to lead what are for them religious, deeply pious lives.

Typically, small groups of village and rural women will get together informally and irregularly, prepare food, take their children, and visit a local *wêli*, a traditional tomb of a holy man or saint (perhaps a woman, real or fictitious). There, far away from the watchful eyes of the men and free from the restrictions of ordinary daily life, women spend the day eating and drinking, enjoying each other's company, playing with the boisterous children, and often performing on drums or flutes, singing, and dancing. These are spontaneous, joyful, liberating occasions. And while they may appear to Westerners to be simply family picnics, for the Muslim women they are authentic expressions of *their* religious needs and aspirations, ignored or denied by the men, especially by the Muslim clerics and by "official" Islam. But who is the "better" Muslim?

I have seen such women's cults myself, among the Sephardic (Oriental) women in Israel. Before the shooting had stopped in Jerusalem in the 1967 war, hordes of pious Jewish women from West Jerusalem were defying

Israeli soldiers in a desperate attempt to get to "Rachel's Tomb" near Bethlehem in the Jordanian sector, off-limits to Jews since 1948. The Muslim *wêli* there does not antedate the medieval period; cannot possibly have anything to do with biblical Rachel's burial place (Genesis 35:19, 20), real or imagined; and in all likelihood is the tomb of a Muslim saint. Nevertheless, orthodox Jewish women wanted to go there to address their prayers for babies to Rachel, who died in childbirth. And it worked! About nine months later, the *Jerusalem Post* reported a sudden rise in the birth rate. Of course, what "really" happened was that the elated women, having risked their lives to pray at Rachel's tomb and having survived, returned home and communicated their excitement to their bemused husbands. And nature took its course, as always. "Superstition," or "real" religion? (See further below.)

Archaeological confirmation of monumental burial shrines would not be expected to survive, as underground tombs do, because they are exposed and vulnerable to many destructive processes. The Muslim *wêlis* discussed above are all very late, despite their "biblical" associations (the "Tomb of Rachel" near Bethlehem; the "Tomb of Joseph" near Nablus; the "Tombs of the Patriarchs" at Hebron; and many other holy places). It can be stated categorically that *none* of these Jewish or Muslim "holy places" is authentic. They are all late.

On the other hand, we do have archaeological evidence for at least one "possible pilgrim site" (excluding Jerusalem and the textual evidence for annual pilgrimages there, since these are presently unattested archaeologically, and will likely remain so). Near the spring of ʾAin el-Qudeirat in the eastern Sinai desert is a small oasis mound that today is identified with biblical Kadesh-barnea. Here the Israelites were said to have been confined for some 40 years as a result of their disobedience in the Sinai wilderness (Numbers 13, 14). The site was excavated in the 1950s and again in 1972-1982 by Israeli archaeologists. The three superimposed forts date from the 10th-6th century B.C. and resemble some other Negev-Sinai forts with their corner towers. Nothing earlier than the 10th century B.C. has been found at the site, however, or indeed anywhere in the general area, despite several intensive surveys. There is no evidence of "domestic" occupation, at the forts, only the presence of a small garrison force. The latest fortress produced among other things an offering stand and fragments of a zoomorphic figurine.

While the absence of any archaeological evidence earlier than the

10th century B.C. poses a problem for the conventional date of an "exodus" in the 13th century B.C., the overall picture of occupation would support the suggestion that Kadesh-barnea *became* a "pilgrim site" much later. Thus Israelites and Judeans may have frequented this outpost on the border of Sinai at a time when the "Sinai-covenant" traditions now enshrined in the Pentateuch were taking shape (8th-7th centuries B.C.).

(13-15) Solar and astral worship, magic, and child sacrifice have been discussed above. The archaeological evidence for the first is principally iconographic, consisting of seals, but offering stands like the one from Ta'anach and the representations on some of the *naoi* are also illuminating. The use of magic is indicated by many amulets, astragali, and the like. Child sacrifice in Israel may have occurred, but if so it has left no archaeological traces (as it has at Phoenician sites like Carthage).

Other Ethnographic Parallels

A recent ethnographic study by the Israeli anthropologist and sociologist Susan Sered, *Women as Ritual Experts: The Religious Lives of Elderly Jewish Women in Jerusalem* (1992), takes the above *ad hoc* observations on women's cults much further. And in so doing I think that Sered provides us with a remarkable window through which to view the religious lives of women and their families in ancient Israel.

The Oriental women (mostly Kurdish and Yemenite immigrants) Sered interviewed extensively come from impoverished lower classes of society. They are largely marginalized in modern Israeli secular society (although they were not in their original homeland), living still in close-knit ethnic communities. They are further isolated by being almost entirely illiterate. Many are widows, or have husbands who are estranged; but they fall back upon a large family made up of children, grandchildren, and other blood relatives. That is their "world."

The women demonstrate allegiance to the State of Israel as they understand the concept, and they are charitable to any individual soldier they may meet. But the larger world of Israeli politics and public life is foreign to them, nor do they show any interest in it. Their "patriotism" consists of seeing themselves as the link between generations of past, present, and yet unborn. They fulfill this role by being the "custodians of traditional values." And it is in their seemingly simple and impoverished daily lives that these women act out the rituals at which they are the experts, and which constitutes *their* piety.

Sered proposes to investigate this community from within, combining the skills of a trained ethnographer with the empathy that I argue here is essential to the study of religious practice. She begins with an indictment of previous male-dominated scholarship in which women were treated more as objects than as subjects. She quotes Judith Bashkin, who observes that "Rabbinic Judaism was produced within a patriarchal society by a group of sages who imagined a man's world, with men at its center" (Sered 1992:138). Sered's aim is rather to let her pious Jewish women speak for themselves, and in so doing "to challenge preconceptions of such concepts as the sacred, the holy, and human spirituality" (1992:3).

I discovered Sered's book through women colleagues (Carol Meyers and Beth Nakhai) after my book was in manuscript. But Sered's agenda for reinvestigating modern religion is astonishingly similar to my own for reconsidering ancient Israelite religion. She focuses on a "domestic piety" (1992:26-33; 90-102) that flourishes in spite of a patriarchal society and a literary tradition that shrines "normative religion." She compares the differing meanings of religiosity and morality in men's and women's conceptual worlds. Men's *mitzvot* (commandments) consist of going to synagogue; study and observance of the Torah; prayer and mystic reflection — all literate exercises. Women's *mitzvot*, on the other hand, consists of keeping a traditional home; preparing food for the Sabbath and all the holidays; maintaining right relations within the nuclear and larger families; prayers and vows for health, healing, and good fortune for one's own; charitable deeds (alms-giving); preserving songs, stories, and miracles; revering the saints and visiting their tombs; remembering the honored dead. This is "domestic religion," routinely ignored or depreciated by the men, in which women nevertheless have become recognized and accepted as "ritual experts."

Sered makes an eloquent case that the largely androcentric academic study of religion previously has been "ethnocentrism at its worst." The tendency has been to regard the motivations and activities of men's piety as "more noble, beautiful, important, true"; those of women as deficient, even debased. But Sered declares that "there is no reason to assume that the experience of the holy is any more immediate to a rabbi in a *yeshiva* than to a woman lighting candles to protect her family" (1992:33). That is precisely the thesis of this book regarding piety in ancient Israel. Biblical scholarship, similarly androcentric, has served to legitimate and "spiritual-ize" the religion of the men who wrote the Hebrew Bible (belief), while ig-noring or trivializing the religion of women (largely practice). I hope to re-dress the balance by restoring ancient folk religion to a position of respect, for the benefit of women *and* men.

Several of the rituals peculiar to Sered's Kurdish Jewish women in-formants are relevant for our inquiry here into ancient Israelite religion, similarly focused as it was on family life, especially in rural areas. These women's rites may seem simple, but they are relatively complex, almost ob-scure to the outsider. (1) First is the elaborate preparation of family meals, especially for Shabbat — "cooking as caring," thus both a moral obligation and a deeply pious act. (2) Next is informal "networking" with other women, their children, and relatives in the extended family, again not merely "socializing," but reaffirming traditional family values of solidarity. (3) Many rituals have to do with belief in miracles, the practical acknowl-edgment that "everything is in God's hands": conception, birth, health and welfare, material blessings. Thus women have their own formulae for warding off the "Evil Eye," based of course, not on Scripture but on folk wisdom, on their own actual daily experiences. Religion as "magic"? Of course; and why not? (4) In addition to many rituals to stay in contact with God (women's "spirituality"), these women constantly utter their own in-tuitive prayers and make frequent vows, not those of the liturgy of Torah and synagogue, which they cannot read or understand. For instance, when they light candles on Friday night, most do not know enough Hebrew even to recite the traditional blessing. Nor do they consult the men or the rab-bis: they typically say "we know what to do." (Note the stress on *doing*; as I have argued, men want to theorize, while women need to do something about religion.) As Sered points out, women's prayers and vows are often expressed more in "body language" than verbally. For example, in syna-gogue (when women go at all, only men are required to do so) the men will be studying the Torah, heads bowed. But when the Torah scroll is held up ceremoniously, the women will kiss it, raise their eyes heavenward, and make a silent wish. (5) Finally, regular pilgrimages to saints' tombs and fes-tivals held there are, just as I noted above, very important, for women of many religious traditions. Again, the men may recite Scripture, but the women (and children) gather separately to kiss the monument, sing tradi-tional songs, and utter their own prayers (mostly for miracles). On other occasions, groups of women and children may go alone, take along elaborate picnics, sit on the ground all day watching the children and exchanging stories from their own lives (often miracles again), and sometimes singing, clapping, and dancing around boisterously, uninhibited by the presence of males and their restrictions.

The above are not "secular" activities at all, nor are they merely "superstitious." They are *deeply religious rituals*, part of a "little tradition" that is as legitimate, truly moral and ethical, as the "great tradition" of Torah Judaism. Sered quotes Clifford Geertz (1969) approvingly:

> It is not necessary to be theologically self-conscious to be religiously sophisticated . . . the disquieting sense that one's moral insight is inadequate to one's moral experience is as alive on the level of so-called "primitive" religion as it is on that of the so-called "civilized" (Geertz 1969:22; quoted in Sered 1992:49).

In short, juxtaposing "morality" and "magic" is a false dichotomy, just as that of "belief" vs. "practice" or "theology vs. cult" is. Ancient Israelite religion, *at its best*, combined both piety and morality, in balance, even through as an archaeologist I have given more emphasis to the latter, where I simply have more evidence.

It may seem that Sered is (and that I am) suggesting that women's piety — their "spirituality" — consists of "warm and fuzzy feelings"; devoid of any *moral* content beyond the concern for the welfare of family. But that is their whole world, and right relations in that sphere is all that these women are responsible for, not the moral dilemmas of public life. Indeed, they see family rituals and charity within their small circle as moral action. *These* are their *mitzvot* (commandments). They even regard themselves as morally superior to the men, who spend too much time with their noses stuck in the Torah and are oblivious to their families' needs. Their cultic implements are kitchen utensils and candles; and their moral imperatives are to use them to bless and safeguard their loved ones.

Note, however, that many of Sered's women's rituals, if typical of ancient Israelite religion, will have left few traces in what we call the archaeological record, as I suggested above. Certainly not body language, vernacular prayers, folk tales, alms-giving, lighting candles (but we do have lamps), or even visits to saints' tombs. Yet I would argue strongly that all these and many other related rites — mostly in the hands of women as "ritual experts" — characterized the largely domestic religion of ancient

Israel. As the artifactual record comes to be read imaginatively and sympathetically alongside the textual record in the Hebrew Bible, our portrait of the *real* religions of ancient Israel will change dramatically. There *is* relevant archaeological information on folk religion; it just hasn't been adequately exploited.

I have taken Sered's modern Jewish women and their distinctive expressions of piety as a "case study" that may powerfully illuminate ancient Israelite women and their piety, equally distinctive, I believe. Certainly the *parallels* between the two communities are indisputable. Both groups of women were poor; illiterate; largely marginalized and disenfranchised; second-class citizens in a patriarchal society. Their religious beliefs and practices are clearly shaped to a great degree by this social context — thus the "little tradition" that they create. The comparison I made above may seem to suggest that women and their religious traditions are not only legitimate but *superior* to those of men and their "great tradition." But one qualification is essential: most *men* in ancient Israel were in the same boat as virtually *all women*. The folk religion, or "popular religion," that we are trying to reconstruct here, despite its major emphasis on women's cults and their role in family rituals, was the religion of nearly all men *as well*. At least it was for all except the fraction of 1 percent of men who happened to have written the Bible. They were "folk," too.

If all of the above aspects of religious activity would tend to be part of *family cults*, where by all counts women played a significant if not dominant role, then Asherah, their patroness, was palpably present. Yahweh, the male deity, was far off in the distant heavens — a warlike god, often angry and vengeful, and even at best not very approachable. Perhaps the men who wrote the Bible could describe Yahweh as "God the Father who will help you," who will give you "blessings of the breasts and of the womb" (Genesis 49:25). But the women who had the breasts and the wombs often found it easier to identify with the Mother. (Perhaps the deities were, after all, a pair, so that a choice wasn't always necessary.)

CHAPTER VIII

From Polytheism to Monotheism

Throughout this survey of folk religion in ancient Israel, I have focused implicitly on polytheism, because that was the reality in the religious lives of most people. This focus may seem to suggest that polytheism was "better," that is, more *realistic,* and that monotheism was somehow inferior, perhaps even artificial. All I have really said, however, is that the development of monotheism came very late in the monarchy, if not later still after ancient Israel's history was over. Yahwistic monotheism was the *ideal* of most of the orthodox, nationalist parties who wrote and edited the Hebrew Bible, but for the majority it had not been the *reality* throughout most of ancient Israel's history. Let us start at the beginning of the process that eventually resulted in monotheism.

"Patriarchal" Religion in Canaan:
El and "the God of the Fathers"

I have faulted the biblical writers for their "revisionist" history of ancient Israel, but I have also credited them with observing and duly recording many aspects of folk religion despite their obvious disapproval and even disgust. They *could* be fairly good historians when they chose to be — at least when judged by the standards of their own day. Thus there is a kind of grudging "matter-of-factness" about many of the biblical stories.

One aspect of this realism is the candid way in which biblical writers talk about the prehistory of Israel in Canaan, their "*Patriarchal* Age." Abraham, Isaac, and Jacob, the "fathers" of later Israel, all lived out their lives in Canaan long before Israelite times. After stories about the creation, the flood, and the genealogies, the Bible's narrative of Yahweh's people and their destiny begins in Genesis 12 with the migration of Abraham "the Hebrew" from Mesopotamia to the Land of Canaan. (The word "Hebrew" comes from the verbal root *'āvar,* "to cross over.") The biblical writers had no fixed chronology, although their "dead reckoning" would place Abraham somewhere around 2100 B.C. and the Exodus about 1450 B.C. (cf. Genesis 47:9; Exodus 12:40; I Kings 11:42; etc.). Today we know that "Israel" appeared in Canaan *ca.* 1200 B.C. and that the "Patriarchal era" (if historical) would have to be dated somewhere in the early-mid 2nd millennium B.C.

Archaeologists have always regarded the Middle-Late Bronze Age in Syria-Palestine, ca. 2000-1200 B.C., as the period when Canaanite culture flourished. When our discipline began in the early 20th century and was conceived of as "biblical archaeology," it naturally took its nomenclature from biblical terminology. Archaeology initially adopted the perspective of the biblical writers, who saw the Canaanites as the predecessors of Israel in the land, and some archaeologists even took up the biblical writers' hostile rhetoric. Thus in the earlier literature biblical scholars and some archaeologists assumed that while the religion of Israel was "morally uplifting," the religions of Canaan were "decadent." Old-fashioned "biblical archaeology" is long since dead, however, and the modern secular discipline has repudiated biblical biases of 25 years ago. Archaeologists now use the ethnic label "Canaanite" in a neutral, purely descriptive sense. And we do so not because of the occurrence of the term in biblical polemics, but because we now have extra-biblical references to "Canaanites" at least as early as 1500 B.C. and possibly even earlier. "Canaan" as a geographical term refers to what some are now calling the "Southern Levant" — approximately the areas of modern Syria, Lebanon, Jordan, the West Bank, Israel, and Gaza. Ethnically, that is, culturally, the term "Canaanite" designates closely related, indigenous West Semitic peoples living in these regions. They would be, in our periods, Canaanites and Amorites; Israelites; Phoenicians; Aramaeans; and various peoples of Transjordan such as Ammonites, Moabites, and Edomites.

In the last decade or so, however, the terms "Canaan" and "Canaanite" have come under concerted attack, not only from radical "revisionists," but also from mainstream biblical and ancient Near Eastern scholars. One of the "revisionists," Niels Peter Lemche of Copenhagen University, in his book *The Canaanites and Their Land: The Tradition of the Canaanites*

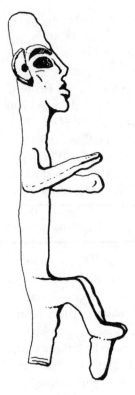

Bronze seated figure of El;
Megiddo Str. IX-VII,
ca. 13 cent. B.C.
Negbi 1976, Fig. 132

(1991), argues that the biblical writers "invented" the Canaanites. As he puts it: "The Canaanites of the ancient Near East did not know that they were themselves Canaanites" (1991:152). But *Lemche* knows that they were not! Deliberately excluding "mute archaeological remains" (1991:172), Lemche concludes that "The Canaanites of the Old Testament are not historical persons but actors in a 'play' in which the Israelites got the better, or the hero's part" (1991:155). Furthermore, of the Canaanite deities, "no such 'gods of Canaan' ever existed" (1991:171).

Lemche is the most extreme of recent scholars, many of whom in "revisionist" circles are really nihilists, as I have shown at some length (Dever 2001). Many others, however, while more mainstream, like Mark Smith whose *Early History of God* I discuss here, nevertheless recommend abandoning the term "Canaanite," since it is a modern "scholarly construct." In particular, it is problematic as a description of the West Semitic *languages* of the area (such as at Ugarit; Smith 2002b:21, 22). Smith and others do note that the term can be and has been used instead as a description of *culture*. But they do not seem to be aware that this archaeological usage is well documented and easily defended. The perplexity of philologians and linguists about how to classify languages is their problem. We archaeologists deal with cultures.

Lemche's views are nothing but currently faddish "political correctness" ("race" is bad). The objections of many other biblical scholars are worth considering, but they tend to be myopic. Distinguished ancient Near Eastern linguists and historians such as Anson Rainey, Nadav Na'aman, and Dennis Pardee favor retaining the term "Canaanite." So do I, especially since labels are necessary for any kind of classification and comparative discussions. And for the second millennium B.C. we have none that is better attested geographically, historically, and culturally.

Whatever the linguistic limitations of the term "Canaanite," the culture of the region of Canaan itself in the mid-late 2nd millennium B.C. is best illuminated textually by the hundreds of alphabetic cuneiform tablets excavated at Ugarit on the north coast of Syria since the late 1920s. Many of them are mythological texts that tell stories of the gods and goddesses, their loves and wars. The interpretation of these texts has revolutionized biblical studies because, while several hundred years earlier, they dramatically illuminate the common West Semitic Bronze Age world from which Israel evolved in the Iron Age. Fortunately, the bulk of these texts have been made available in English translations with excellent commentaries (see Bibliography).

A recent work by one of the foremost Ugaritic scholars is Dennis Pardee's *Ritual and Cult at Ugarit* (2002), which deals specifically with religion, although the author cautions that the texts here are nearly all concerned with the royal cults, not folk religion. In that sense, they are the "canonical" texts of official religion, very much as the later Hebrew Bible is. Nevertheless, they are instructive. The list of Canaanite deities in Pardee's *corpus*, fleshed out with other texts, runs to more than 150. Some of their deities are familiar from their reappearance in the Hebrew Bible and in other later texts:

El (the "god")
Ba'al ("Lord" of the heavens; also "Hadad")
Dagan (a grain deity)
Yamm (Sea)
Mot (Death)

Shapsh (Sun; feminine)
Yarih (Moon, feminine)
Resheph (underworld deity)
Asherah ("Lady" of the sea)
Astarte (androgynous deity)
Anat ("virgin," warrior)

As Pardee notes, it becomes clear in the texts that reflect the daily religious practice of the court, where the king himself was the principal actor, that "bloody sacrifice, that is, the slaying of a sacrificial animal, is at the very heart of the Ugaritic cult" (2002:3). The principal animals sacrificed are bulls and cows; sheep; goats; and birds. The sacrificial rituals described in the texts pertain to many concerns, among them:

Marking the days, months, and seasons
Propitiation
General petitions for healing, well-being
The interpretations of dreams
Divination
Incantations for good luck
Incantations against the "evil eye"
Rituals for malformed animal fetuses
Mortuary rituals

There is even a sacrifice and a ritual to ward off male impotency (the forerunner of Viagra).

Another recent major study of religion at Ugarit is J. David Schloen's Harvard dissertation, published as *The House of the Father as Fact and Symbol: Patrimonialism in Ugarit and the Ancient Near East* (2001). Schloen stresses how important families and clans were in Ugaritic society at all levels, including the royal bureaucracy. Thus he proposes a "patrimonial household model" for the cult, understanding the structure of the pantheon in the mythological texts as a "divine family" of many hierarchically ordered gods, often functioning through a "divine council" (cf. also Handy 1994).

The point of departure for Mark Smith, whose works (2002a; 2002b) are prominent in our discussions here, is also the *corpus* of Ugaritic texts, of which he is a leading interpreter, especially with regard to parallels with the Hebrew Bible and Israelite religion. In a recent state-of-the-art essay (2002b) Smith surveys much of the literature and notes future trends that he thinks will prove significant. In general, he follows Schloen and concludes that such studies will reinforce the notion that "polytheism at Ugarit expressed a sense of divine singleness or cohesion through a series of familial relationships" (2002b:24). Since much of this statement has to do with the character of Israelite monotheism and the reasons for its rise late in the monarchy, I will defer further discussion.

One classic work of the older school that tended to compare "Canaanite-Israelite" is still relevant, Frank Cross's epochal work *Canaanite Myth and Hebrew Epic: Essays in the History of the Religion of Israel* (1973). It was Cross, followed by many of his Harvard students, who first made a conclusive case for the fact that "patriarchal religion" was deeply indebted to much older Canaanite religious traditions, especially as revealed in the mythological texts from Ugarit. Cross began by noting, as several German scholars had, that in the *oldest* literary strands of the traditions in the Pentateuch, it is the Canaanite deity El who regularly appears, not Yahweh. Furthermore, the epithets, or "titles," of El are especially revealing. They are, like the divine name itself, antique.

Here are some examples of these early epithets.

(1) *"El-Shadday."*
Genesis 17:1. When Abraham is 99 years old and has long been resident in Canaan, God appears to him as "El-Shadday" to renew the covenant. The RSV translates the divine name as "God Almighty," but that is misleading. The Hebrew "Shadday" means "mountain," here possibly in the dual, so the divine name is really "El, the One of the mountains." Many deities in the ancient Near East are associated quite naturally with mountains. And in the Ugaritic texts, El in particular sits on his throne at the base of the cosmic Mt. Saphon ("north") at the sources of the two waters, sweet and salt. Cross points out that the Hebrew term *shad,* "mountain," derives from earlier West Semitic *thad,* "breast." Thus the twin mountain peaks "Shadday" are likened to two breasts (think of the name "Grand Tetons" for the high-peaked Wyoming ranges). It may be significant that God, although clearly male here, is associated with female imagery (as in the reference to "breasts and womb" in Genesis 49:25). "El-Shadday," "the one of the mountains," was thus probably conceived

of in pre-Israelite religion as the old Amorite-Canaanite storm god, associated with the awesome (and procreative) powers of nature.

Genesis 35:11. At the old shrine of Bethel, God introduces himself to Jacob as "El-Shadday," and again he renews the covenant with "the fathers."

Genesis 43:14; 48:3. In the first passage, grandson Jacob ("Israel") blesses his sons who have sold Joseph into slavery, but are about to go to Egypt themselves in the name of "El-Shadday." In the second passage, Jacob in Egypt tells Joseph that "El-Shadday" had appeared to him at Bethel (as also to Abraham), and again the context is one of renewing the divine covenant with "the fathers."

Genesis 49:25. This passage is part of the "Song of Jacob," Jacob's death-bed recitation, thought by many scholars to be among the oldest texts preserved in the Hebrew Bible (11th century B.C.). It is perhaps our most revealing story. Here we have *three* epithets of the patriarchal deity, all very ancient: "Bull of Jacob" (Canaanite El's principal epithet is "Bull"); "Shepherd, Rock of Israel"; and "El-Shadday." (Again, the RSV and other translations obscure the original meaning.) Furthermore, the text specifies, regarding the patriarch's blessing, "by El of your father," so these are all epithets of *one* god, ancestral El. Finally, the blessings are associated: (1) "blessings of the eternal mountains"; and (2) "blessings of the breasts and of the womb." Here again, the conjoined imagery of male "storm god" and female "breasts and womb" is suggestive of primitive conceptions of the deity who would later become the Israelite god.

Exodus 6:3. Here, much later, God introduces himself to Moses, explaining that formerly he was known to Abraham, Isaac, and Jacob as "El-Shadday," and under that name he had covenanted with the fathers. But henceforth, he wishes to be known to the soon-to-be Israelites as "Yahweh" (below).

(2) *"El-Elyon."*
Genesis 14:18-24. Here Melchizedek, king and priest of Salem (Jerusalem), blesses "Abram the Hebrew" by "El-Elyon," "God Most High."

In the Ugaritic texts the storm god Ba'al's principal epithet is *'aliyan Ba'al,* or "Puissant *Ba'al,*" *'aliyan* being cognate with Hebrew *'elyōn,* "high, uppermost."

Deuteronomy 32:8, 9. This passage is another archaic Hebrew poem, the "Song of Moses" (11th century B.C.?). On his deathbed Moses exhorts the people of Israel that they are to remember "the days of old" (Hebrew *'ōlām;* below), when "El-Elyon" made a covenant with "your fathers." But then the poem goes on to specify that now *"Yahweh"* will preserve and bless his people. The "evolution" from "El-Elyon" to "Yahweh" is significant (below).

(3) *"El-Olam."*
Genesis 21:33. Here Abraham goes to Beersheba, an old tribal center and shrine, where he worships at a *tree,* swears an oath with Abimelech, and "calls on the name of 'El-Olam.'" Hebrew *'ōlām* means "eternal," so the divine name here is "El the Everlasting." It is worth recalling that one of Canaanite El's epithets in the Ugaritic texts is "Father of Years."

(4) *"El-Bethel."*
Genesis 31:13. God appears to Jacob at Paddan-aram and identifies himself with past appearances, the famous story of Jacob and the angel, saying "I am El-Bethel." There is a play on words here, since the place-name "Bethel" means "House/temple of El." Thus God may be pictured as saying "I am the God of the shrine of Bethel"; or "I am the God whose name is (also) 'Bethel.'" Either way, this is a very old epithet, attached to a particular place.

Genesis 35:7. Again, the story is about Jacob and Bethel. Jacob builds an altar there and calls the altar "El-Bethel."

(5) *"El Elohay-Israel."*
Genesis 33:20. Here Jacob is at another old shrine, Shechem, where he also builds an altar, this time naming it "El, Elohay-Israel." This phrase clearly refers to the deity El as the God of the patriarch Israel (Jacob's alternate name).

(6) *"El-Roi."*

Genesis 16:13. El epithets appear not only in stories about the patriarchs, but also in stories about their wives and concubines (the matriarchs). In this passage, Hagar, Abraham's pregnant maid, who
would soon bear him a son named Ishmael, has fled to the wilderness
to escape Sarah's wrath. There God appears to her to comfort her
and makes a covenant with her. Having miraculously "seen" God and
lived, Hagar calls his name "El-Roi," "El who sees" — again a word
play, but very revealing.

Cross is careful to point out that *grammatically* these El epithets are
somewhat ambiguous. Thus "El-Olam" could mean either "El, the Eternal
One" (Cross: "the god of eternity"), or "El, who is (the god) Olam." Double divine names are known in ancient Near Eastern pantheons, identifying two deities with each other. But in the light of the overall evidence,
Cross prefers taking all these names as referring to the single, preeminent
deity El. The epithets, then, assign to him somewhat differing attributes or
manifestations, or perhaps (less likely) local spheres of influence (such as
at Bethel). As Cross says:

> To be sure, we can speak no longer of the *'ēlīm* [that is, "gods"] of Ca-
> naan as 'local *numina*.' The great gods of the Canaanite pantheon were
> cosmic deities (1973:49).

I have followed Cross's arguments in seeing Asherah, too, as a "cosmic deity" in Canaan and Israel, albeit with various local manifestations (and
perhaps names; above).

From this brief review of the biblical texts *themselves,* without re-
course to any external evidence except the earlier Ugaritic texts, two things
are clear. (1) The biblical writers had some authentic knowledge of earlier
"evolutionary stages" in Israelite religion, whether based on oral tradition
and "historical memory," written sources, or simply intuition. (2) While
they themselves were orthodox monotheists, looking back at much earlier
times from that perspective, they candidly acknowledge that the "god of
the fathers" was Canaanite El, not their own deity Yahweh. This datum is
noteworthy, and it shows how much "reading between the lines" in the Hebrew Bible can tell us — especially when supplemented by extra-biblical
evidence, both textual and archaeological.

It is also noteworthy that the Hebrew Bible, despite its monotheistic biases, *preserves* the old Canaanite name El for the Israelite deity, and even uses it in the plural. Examples of "El" in the singular are too numerous to cite even briefly (more than 230), but some references are of special interest, because they still carry transparent Canaanite imagery. Isaiah's taunt to the King of Babylon (14:12-14) includes the warning:

How you are fallen from heaven,
O Day Star, son of Dawn!
How you are cut down to the ground,
you who laid the nations low!
You said in your heart,
"I will ascend to heaven;
above the stars of God
I will set my throne on high,
I will sit on the mount of assembly
in the far north;
I will ascend above the heights of the clouds.
I will make myself like the Most High."

The "stars of El"; the "throne on high"; "the mount of assembly in the far north"; and "the heights of the clouds" are all transparent allusions to Canaanite mythology — right out of the pages of the Ugaritic texts.

Several texts speak of *'ēlîm,* "the gods," not using the term here as the name of a god or gods of Israel, but as a reference to other gods. Thus the very archaic "Canaanite" Psalm 29 declares in verse 1: "Ascribe to Yahweh, O heavenly beings (*běnê-'ēlîm,* 'sons of gods') . . . glory and strength."

Psalm 29 is so similar to some of the Ugaritic poems that many phrases are borrowed almost word for word:

Ascribe to the Lord, O heavenly beings,
ascribe to the Lord glory and strength.
Ascribe to the Lord the glory of his name;
worship the Lord in holy array.
The voice of the Lord is upon the waters;
the God of glory thunders,
the Lord, upon many waters. . . .

> The Lord sits enthroned over the flood;
> the Lord sits enthroned as king forever.
>
> (Psalm 29:1-3, 10; cf. Psalms 82:1; 89:5-7)

The "heavenly beings" here (*'ēlîm*, "gods," in "holy array") are the subservient members of the Divine Council, precisely as with El and his council at Ugarit. The references in Psalm 29 to the "waters" and the "flood" on which Yahweh is "enthroned" mirror exactly El, who sits at the "sources of the floods, in the midst of the headwaters of the Two Oceans." Even the word for "flood" (Hebrew *mabbûl*) is the same in both languages (see also Psalms 93:3; 98:7, 8).

Several Psalms, such as Psalm 65 (below), invoke the "storm god" imagery of Canaanite Baʿal, who brings back the rain upon his return from the underworld, and they transfer this imagery to Yahweh. When Baʿal revives,

> The heavens fat did rain,
> The wadis flow with honey.

Several specific epithets are shared by Canaanite Baʿal and Israelite Yahweh. In the Ugaritic texts, one of the lesser gods addresses Baʿal the storm god:

> Hearken, transcendent Baʿal,
> Give heed, O Rider of the Clouds.

Psalm 68 says of Yahweh:

> Sing to God, O kingdoms of the earth;
> Sing praises to the Lord,
> to him who rides in the heavens,
> the ancient heavens;
> lo, he sends forth his voice, his mighty voice.
> Ascribe power to God,
> whose majesty is over Israel,
> and his power is in the skies.
> Terrible is God in his sanctuary,
> the God of Israel,
> he gives power and strength to his people. (Psalm 68:32-35)

Both texts use the imagery of God "riding the clouds."

Thus the notion of a multiplicity of deities sitting together in council — so typical of the Canaanite pantheon and its functions — is taken for granted in the Hebrew Bible, even *after* Yahweh is said to have come into his ascendancy. Indeed, the very first words of the Hebrew Bible are "When God began to create the heavens and the earth." The Hebrew does not say "Yahweh," but rather *'ĕlōhîm*, "the gods" (plural). Even a rather thick reader is bound to ask, "Why does the text say 'the gods'?" Then in verse 26, the text says: "Then God said, 'Let us make man (NRSV: "humankind") in our image.'" But a literal translation would read, "Then the gods *('ĕlōhîm)* said." Again, the reader may ask, "Who is 'us'?" Who *else* is there with "the gods" at creation? The fact is that the biblical writers, even in their most doctrinaire espousal of Yahweh as sole deity, are fully aware of the polytheistic setting of most of their world — even in Israelite folk religion. That is why the First Commandment is phrased the way it is: "You shall have no other gods before [or 'besides'] me" (Exodus 20:3). One *could* have other gods; and many, if not most, ancient Israelites did have. For that reason, most scholars today regard Israel's faith not as monotheism, but rather as "monolatry." This is the acknowledgment of other gods, but the worship of only one of them, in this case, Yahweh, the supreme deity (further below).

But how does Yahweh *become* the supreme deity — that is, how does he finally supplant Canaanite El? Here again, the biblical texts are remarkably candid, and I would say *knowledgeable* about the real evolution of Israelite religion. Exodus 3 is the story of how Moses, long after the age of the patriarchs, was *reintroduced* to their god by another name. God appears in the burning bush and identifies himself to Moses specifically as the God of Abraham, Isaac, and Jacob. God then tells Moses how he is going to free the people from Egyptian bondage, and how he is going to dispatch Moses as his agent. Moses protests that when he declares "God has sent me," people will say "Who? What's his name?" And *now* the text gives God's personal name: "Yahweh." The RSV translates the first part of verse 14 "I AM WHO I AM" or "I WILL BE WHAT I WILL BE." That is because the name "Yahweh" comes from a verb meaning "to be"; but the exact meaning here is ambiguous. The later text, however, when God repeats his name and the command, is clear (verse 16): "Yahweh, the God of your fathers, the God of Abraham, of Isaac, and of Jacob." The implication of the passage in Exodus 3 is of enormous importance. The god of Israel about-to-be is the same god of the patriarchs centuries earlier, the "El" of that era in Canaan. But now "in the fullness of time" he deigns to reveal his personal name "Yahweh," and by that name he wishes to be known and worshipped henceforth.

Any doubts about this reading would be removed by turning to Exodus 6:1-9. Here God appears again to Moses, after he has begun his mission to Pharaoh. He refers not only to "Abraham, Isaac, and Jacob" again, but he explains that he revealed himself to them then only as "El-Shadday" (above) and deliberately did not reveal his name "Yahweh." And again he specifies to Moses that he is really "Yahweh," and under this name he will covenant with the people of Israel and will deliver them.

"Holy Places" in Pre-Israelite Times

Considering the fact that the biblical patriarchs seem at home with the older Canaanite deities (at least with El in various guises), we are not surprised to find them visiting traditional Canaanite shrines and holy places. In Chapter IV I discussed such sites, typically called in later proscriptive texts "high places" *(bāmôt)*. Often associated with these public, open-air sanctuaries are (1) trees, groves of trees, or wooden poles (the *'ăshērāh*) symbolizing the Canaanite Mother Goddess Asherah, consort of El; (2) altars *(mizbĕḥôt)* for sacrifice; and (3) standing stones (*maṣṣēbôt;* RSV = "pillars") symbolizing the presence of deities.

Similar high places seem to be referred to in connection with several patriarchal narratives, but interestingly enough they are not designated specifically as *bāmôt,* except in Leviticus 26:30, where God promises to destroy them. The reason for the general silence is not clear, but it is probably because by the time the biblical authors were writing, in the late monarchy, reform movements were under way, and these *bāmôt* were now anathema (below). Nevertheless, Abraham (or "Abram the Hebrew") is said matter-of-factly to have frequented several holy sites, some of which appear to have been ancient Canaanite places of worship.

(1) *Shechem; Genesis 12:6-8.* Shechem is the first place Abram *(sic)* heads to when he migrates from Mesopotamia to Canaan, the clear implication being that he had already heard of the famous shrine there (called "the" *māqôm,* the "holy place" of Shechem). The brief account mentions several significant features of this visit, which the authors specifically state

belongs to an era when "the Canaanites were in the land": (1) a central place called "*the* sanctuary"; (2) the "oak of Moreh," a terebinth tree that was sacred and was renowned for giving oracles (Hebrew *mōreh*, "instruction"); (3) altars for sacrifice, another of which Abram erected on his visit; (4) a theophany, or appearance of the deity (Yahweh); and (5) subsequently, near Bethel, the act of "calling on the name" of God, that is, acknowledging him in a covenant relationship.

(2) *Bethel; Genesis 13:2-4.* The Hebrew name and its early West Semitic ancestor mean "house/temple of El" (above), so this was also an old, well-known Canaanite sanctuary. Already mentioned in the story of Abram at Shechem, this shrine is another holy place where Jacob builds an altar and calls on the name of God.

(3) *Beersheba; Genesis 21:31-34.* Beersheba represents the southernmost area of settled occupation in the monarchy, on the border of the Negev desert, but it is also portrayed as an ancient gathering place of pastoral nomads. There again, Abraham knows of the famous wells ("Beersheba" may mean "seven wells," but it can also mean "well of the oath"). Here, too, we have the making of a covenant (with Abimelech), which is sealed by planting a tree (a tamarisk), and then "calling on the name of God." Significantly, God is identified here with the old Canaanite deity "El-Olam," "El the Eternal One" (above).

(4) *Mamre (Hebron); Genesis 13:18; 14:13; 18:1.* Hebron is closely associated with patriarchal migrations, no doubt because of its ancient sacred character. Abraham and Sarah were buried there, as were the bones of Joseph, brought back from Egypt (the "tombs of the patriarchs" reputedly under the Herodian temple are still revered by both Muslims and Jews). At nearby Mamre, Abraham finds another sacred oak (several of them) and there again he builds an altar.

The patriarch Jacob, Abraham's grandson, is said to have frequented some of these same ancient holy places, especially Bethel (Genesis 31:13; 35:7) and Shechem (Genesis 33:20). The detailed account of a new (?) shrine at Mizpah (Genesis 31:45-54) is especially revealing. Here there are numerous elements: (1) a deity named "Fear of his father Isaac" (Jacob's father); (2) a sacrifice offered on a mountain; (3) communal feasting lasting all night; (4) the making of a covenant between Jacob and Laban; (5) a "stone-heap" piled up and ceremonially named "Galeed" (the "heap of witness"); (6) a stone pillar set up, also as a witness, and named "Mizpah" ("watch-post"); and (7) an oath sworn by "the God of the Fathers."

The Israelite Sacrificial System as "Canaanite"

I have already discussed the Canaanite sacrificial system, especially as revealed in the Late Bronze Age Ugaritic texts. What we now need to look for are continuities, if any, into Israelite times. There, too, we have already treated in some detail the biblical conception of "sacrifices" and the regulations governing them. Here I need only to point out the extraordinarily strong similarities.

The primacy of animal sacrifice — the shedding of *blood*, as the symbol of life — is obvious in both the Canaanite and the Israelite cult. The biblical writers, despite their universal polemics against the "Canaanites," did not have much direct knowledge of them in their original Bronze Age context, centuries earlier. So they assume that the Israelite sacrificial system was "unique," revealed to Moses at Sinai, and overseen from the beginning by the Levitical priests. In fact, there was little new in the *practice* of animal sacrifice; it was nearly all inherited from the local, centuries-old Canaanite culture. It may be, of course, that the accompanying Yahwistic theology of the Pentateuchal and Deuteronomistic writers was different, even innovative in some aspects. But we do not know that from comparisons themselves, since the earlier Ugaritic texts present us only with the practice of animal sacrifice, not the theory behind it. And, as we have noted, these texts deal almost exclusively with the royal or "official" cult, not folk religion. (That is true also of the biblical texts.) So at least the external features are the same.

There were other forms of sacrifice in ancient Israel, notably food offerings other than the flesh of animals; drink and various forms of libation offerings; and incense offerings. These are not well attested in the Ugaritic or other Canaanite texts that we happen to have. But they are well known where we have more copious documentation, as in Mesopotamia from the 3rd millennium onward, and also in Egypt from early times. For instance, in the well-known second millennium B.C. Gilgamesh Epic — containing the "Babylonian Flood Story" — after the ark comes to rest the grateful survivors make an offering of burnt incense to the gods. At that, "the gods smelled the sweet savor, the gods crowded around like flies about the sacrificer." The same concept of the gods relishing the smell of burning animal flesh appears in the Hebrew Bible (Leviticus 1:9, 17). The only difference here is what one might call a "loftier" notion of deity in the Bible — one god only, not buzzing around in an undignified manner, only enjoying the odor. But *both* pictures are clearly anthropomorphic, embodying the conception of the gods as having human-like features and functions.

One aspect of the biblical system of sacrifice may be innovative, the references to clean or "kosher" animals. Yet one must note first that *all* animals deemed fit for sacrifice to the gods in the ancient Near East had to be unblemished. Second, the laws of *kashrut* are notoriously difficult to rationalize, so comparing them with any other customs is difficult, even if we had the necessary comparative textual documentation. What *makes* one animal unclean, another acceptable? Why do the "holiness laws" in Leviticus specify that animals that "chew the cud or part the hoof" (11:4) are unclean? Some prohibitions do seem to make sense (who would want to eat a mouse, or a vulture?), but others do not. Why are pigs non-kosher? The common answer that insufficiently cooked pork can cause trichinosis is irrelevant, since the ancient could not possibly have known that. The best solution to the phenomenon of "unique" Israelite laws of *kashrut* may simply be to suppose that these are what anthropologists call "ethnic markers." In other words, "We do not do those things, because the Canaanites do them."

The Calendar

As I have noted in Chapter IV, the liturgical calendar of ancient Israel was based not on our arbitrary Julian calendar, but upon the more natural agricultural year and the unending rhythm of the changing season. Thus each festival has its forerunner in Canaanite lore customs.

(1) *Rosh ha-shanah*, the "new year's" festival, marked the onset of the annual fall rains, triggering the renewal of nature's dormant, life-giving powers for another year. In the Ugaritic texts from Canaan, the new year is heralded by the resurrection of the storm god Baʿal, who triumphs over Mot, "death," and brings back the rain to fructify the earth once more. Then Anat, his lover, rejoices, declaring exultantly:

> The heavens fat did rain,
> The wadis flow with honey.
> So I knew
> That alive was Baʿal Most
> Existent the Prince, Lord of Earth.

Compare this Canaanite poem with the song of praise in Psalm 65:9-13.

> Thou visitest the earth and waterest it,
> > thou greatly enrichest it;
> The river of God is full of water;
> > thou providest their grain,
> > for so thou hast prepared it.
> Thou waterest its furrows abundantly,
> > settling its ridges,
> softening it with showers,
> > and blessing its growth.
> Thou crownest the year with thy bounty;
> > The tracks of thy chariot drip with fatness.
> The pastures of the wilderness drip,
> > the hills gird themselves with joy,
> the meadows clothe themselves with flocks,
> > the valleys deck themselves with grain,
> > they shout and sing together for joy.

(2) *Sukkôt* ("huts or booths"), the fall harvest festival, when various fruits are in season, comes next. In time it was "historicized" in ancient Israel so as to commemorate the Sinai covenant and the wilderness wanderings, when the Israelites dwelt in tents. But originally it continued the tradition of the old Canaanite fall harvest festival, so pregnant (as it were) with meaning: would it be a good year?

(3) *Pesach,* which fell in early spring, commemorated primarily the exodus from Egypt, but it also remembered the hardships in the Sinai wilderness. It was originally a Canaanite pastoral feast, when young lambs (born in the late fall and winter) were sacrificed. In Israelite tradition, the feast was easily assimilated with the "liberation from bondage" theme, because of the common motif of blood: the blood of lambs, in this case smeared over the doorways of the Israelites so that the Angel of Death would "pass over" them and spare their firstborn sons.

(4) *Shāvu'ôt,* the feast of "weeks" that comes 50 days after Pesach, was a late spring harvest festival, at the time when wheat and barley were ripe. It marked the culmination of the agricultural year, just as the winter and spring rains were ceasing. Such a grain harvest festival would certainly have been celebrated in Canaan in pre-Israelite times. In Israel, it became a

pilgrimage festival, but it may have been of lesser importance until later Judaism.

(5) *Yom Kippur,* the "day of atonement," came in the early fall, just after the new year began. It was a solemn day of repentance and renewal, especially prominent in the later priestly traditions (Leviticus). How early it began and whether it had a Canaanite origin are uncertain. But it does have parallels in the Akitu festival in ancient Babylon.

The Question of "Syncretism"

Older, partisan portraits of Canaanite and Israelite religions saw almost everything through the lens of the Deuteronomistic historians, whose programmatic ideal was "Mosaic monotheism." Assuming that such monotheism was "unique" and had been the religious reality from the very beginning (although both the biblical writers and modern biblicists knew better), any lingering "Canaanite" features in the Israelite cult had to be rejected as "syncretistic."

Recent scholarship, however, with its more realistic understanding and appreciation of Canaanite religion and its more critical approach to Israelite religion, has questioned the very notion of "syncretism." It is now being argued that most of the supposedly "pagan" practices of Israelite folk religion were not borrowed from Canaanite culture, but should be regarded rather as "native" aspects of Israelite culture, since it had so readily assimilated them. Rejection of ideas of "syncretism" are so common that they appear to be part of current "political correctness" (Olyan 1988:5, 8; Ackerman 1992:213-217; Miller, 2000:57-62; Smith 2002b:3-9). The more extreme view simply declares that Israelite religion *was* "Canaanite religion" (thus Coogan 1987). Part of the confusion, it seems to me, is semantic: What do we really *mean* by "syncretism"? The essential meaning is to incorporate various beliefs, some of which may once have been contradictory, into a fusion on the basis of other beliefs held in common. In that sense, nearly all religions are syncretistic, since none is wholly unique.

The thrust of the current rejection of "syncretism" certainly does not intend to deny the point that I am making here, only to stress how much Canaanite and Israelite religion had in common, and that from the earliest phases of the latter's development. Thus Israelite religion, however distinctive it finally became (as in later Judaism), *grew out of* Canaanite religion, not, as biblical propagandists claimed, in *opposition* to it. That is surely correct. (I have discussed Israel's Canaanite origins in detail in *Who Were the Early Israelites and Where Did They Come From?*; 2003.)

This clarification may also apply to another term now deemed politically incorrect: "pagan." The word comes from the Latin *pagus,* "countryside." When many Romans converted to Christianity in the 4th century A.D., unsophisticated folk in rural areas were slow to accept the new beliefs and thus were called "pagans" (and in later Roman Catholic theology they became "heathens"). In an early treatment of folk religion, I myself had used the term "pagan," for which I was subsequently criticized (cf. Keel and Uehlinger 1998:9). But I was simply paraphrasing the biblical writers, for whom folk religion, largely Canaanite, *was* "pagan." I was also being a bit ironic, since folk religion was predominantly "rural."

This exercise in political correctness brings me to another, less amusing case, the questioning of the Canaanite and Israelite cults as "fertility religions." Denying the existence of ancient "fertility cults" has almost become a mantra. One can easily see why, given the caricatures common in early scholarship, which regarded Canaanite religion as obscene but were obscenities themselves, professing to be repulsed but in fact being transparently prurient (Chapter II). These views were, of course, those of the commentators at the time, all males. But the reaction has gone too far in the other direction in my opinion, and it is more driven by currently fashionable ideologies than by genuine advances in scholarship.

One victim of the purging of the language is the goddess Anat. She appears often in the Ugaritic texts as the consort of Baʿal, this pair being the younger West Semitic rival deities of El and Asherah, now somewhat in their dotage (above). But the character and roles of Anat are difficult to rationalize. Her regular title is "Maiden Anat"; yet she is portrayed as Baʿal's lover, copulating with him endlessly. She has been understood as a "Fertility Goddess," a giver of life, because of her sexuality; yet she is a warrior goddess who rounds up Baʿal's enemies and slaughters them, wading up to her vulva in blood and gore, laughing triumphantly. Anat is also a huntress. So who is she *really?*

Several scholars have recently sought to "rehabilitate" Anat, arguing that she is not a "fertility goddess" at all (Day 1991; Smith 2002b:22; but see the better balanced treatment of John Day, 2000:132-144). Thus Peggy Day complains that seeing Anat as Baʿal's consort reduces her to the status of a "hooker" and is part of a male strategy to blame the female goddesses for the alleged "moral depravity" of Canaanite religion (1991:141, 142). Day's own view is a caricature. I don't know of any male scholar who actually did place the blame for what he considered "depraved" only on the female deities. As for "warrior vs. sexual" goddess, why can't Anat be both? Finally, what's wrong with a little bawdiness? (Or, for that matter, with being a consort, if that status is not necessarily subservient?)

Much of the recent critique of Anat as a "fertility goddess" I regard as simply another form of political correctness, and the rest is what I call the "new prudery." There is very little of modern prudery in the Hebrew Bible, which is surprisingly earthy. There was even less prudery in ancient Israelite folk religion, which celebrated the union of male and female and venerated sexuality as a life-giving force. To be sure, it was a force to be regulated because it was potent, but nevertheless one to be enjoyed since it renewed life and validated humans as part of creation. "God saw everything that he had made, and behold, it was very good" (Genesis 1:31). As I argued in Chapter I, if religion is about "ultimate concern," nothing in ancient Israel was more fundamental, more urgent, than the continued fertility of humans and beasts and the fields. Modern religions may be all about moral and theological niceties, but ancient religion was largely about brute survival, only after which might one indulge in reflection on what it all meant. And in early Israel (the "period of the Judges"), folk religion was still very close to its roots, sunk deep in the soil of traditional Bronze Age Canaan.

Changes With the Monarchy: Religion in Crisis

By the 10th century B.C., after some two centuries of experience during a formative era, when Israelite society was largely rural and egalitarian and "every man did what was right in his own eyes" (Judges 17:6), a major change took place. There occurred what anthropologists have called in past a cultural and socio-economic evolution from "tribe," to "chiefdom," to "state." In biblical terms, the "period of the judges" was supplanted by the "United Monarchy" — the reigns of Saul, David, and Solomon, which we now know date to *ca.* 1020-930 B.C.. The historicity of the United Monarchy, however, has become one of the most hotly contested issues in both recent biblical studies and archaeology.

The biblical "revisionists" reject the notion altogether, declaring that this is just another "myth" concocted by the biblical writers, who wrote in the Persian or Hellenistic period and knew next to nothing about the Iron Age centuries earlier. A few idiosyncratic archaeologists (among them, notably, Israel Finkelstein) lend support to the "minimalist" view by downdating the monumental "Solomonic" architecture traditionally dated to the 10th century B.C. at Hazor, Megiddo, and Gezer (I Kings 9:15-17) to the 9th century B.C., thereby robbing us of crucial archaeological data. The minimalists would date the rise of the state in the north (Israel) to the 9th century B.C. and comparable development in the south (Judah) to after the Neo-Assyrian campaigns in 701 B.C. (but then, "campaigns" against what?).

I have reviewed the whole controversy about the "United Monarchy," with full references, in *What Did The Biblical Writers Know and When Did They Know It? What Archaeology Can Tell Us about the Reality of Ancient Israel* (2001). The issues need not concern us in detail here, however, because it is the *fact* of statehood and its consequences, not exact chronology, that is relevant for our look at ancient Israelite religions.

It is noteworthy that the writers of the Hebrew Bible themselves are ambivalent about kingship. In one strand of the literary tradition the tribal elders, concerned about the Philistine military threat, come to the judge and prophet Samuel, a charismatic folk hero. They demand that he appoint for Israel a king "like all the nations" (I Samuel 8:1-5). But Samuel refuses, warning them that a king will tax them mercilessly, will conscript their sons for military service, and will oppress them. Furthermore, it is Yahweh — the old "Divine Warrior" like the Canaanite gods — who is Israel's king, their only Sovereign (I Samuel 8:6-22). But in another passage (I Samuel 9), Samuel is said to accede to popular demand, and he appoints Saul as Israel's first king, with Yahweh's tacit approval (I Samuel 8:9-10). Saul then reigned some 20 years, followed by his son-in-law David (40 years) and David's son Solomon (40 years). Thus there was established the Davidic dynasty, which ruled over Israel (mostly Judah) for the entire 400 years of the monarchy, until the fall of Jerusalem in 587 B.C.

Turning from the literary and theological version of "what really happened," about which many scholars are somewhat skeptical, the archaeological evidence and the historical implications are clear. I have already referred to the clear 10th-century B.C. archaeological evidence for the origins of the state. But even if one regards this as merely a "chiefdom" and places the full-blown state later, the results were the same. I would summarize then, in accord with known state formation-processes elsewhere, as the development of: (1) urbanism; (2) economic specialization; (3) social complexity ("stratification"); (4) political centralization; (5) religious conformity; and (6) the beginnings of the literary tradition and the composition of the great national epic that culminate in the Hebrew Bible as we now have it. Let us look at the archaeological evidence for each development, then assess the consequences for popular religion and its evolution (see further Dever 2003).

(1) *Urbanism.* Early Israel was exclusively rural: village, hamlets, and a few isolated homesteads. Of the 300 or so 12th-11th-century B.C. Israelite sites that are currently known, none had a population of more than 300, and most had fewer than 100. None was a town, much less a city, by any criteria (below). A total population of about 50,000 (12th century B.C.) to 75,000 (11th century B.C.) was widely dispersed over the countryside, concentrated mostly in the central hills, stretching from Galilee, through Samaria and Judea and into the northern Negev.

Between the late 11th and the early 10th century B.C. the picture changed. The majority of the "proto-Israelite" villages characterized above were abandoned, new towns were established in a few more centralized locations, and an urban society began to develop. By the mid-late 10th century B.C. in the "Age of Solomon," when the population may have reached some 100,000, there were about 20 "towns" by suitable local criteria, that is, centers with a population of 500-1,000. There may have been a few real cities, with up to 2,000 people. The latter might have totaled some 5,000 people in all, or roughly the five percent urban population that I suggested above. It is clear that the bulk of the population remained rural, as recent studies have shown. The significant fact, however, is that with the beginnings of statehood there now emerges a small nucleus of urban elites that had not existed before. It is this new urban, privileged class that will soon come to clash with traditional, rural-based folk religion as they begin to focus on their own vested interests (Dever 2001:124-44).

(2) *Economic specialization.* In villages and farm families in early Israel, everyone was a farmer; there were really no other options. Each family made and produced everything that it needed, perhaps now and then in cooperation with other families. But there were no professional or mercantile classes, no specialized artisans — and no priests. These villages may have been relatively poor, depending as they did upon subsistence farming. But they possessed a strong sense of solidarity, and they were able to maintain and enforce traditional values. And folk religion was the glue that held

everything together — simple, but adequate for the needs of a simple agrarian society. As the Hebrew Bible puts the vision of the "good life":

> They shall all sit under their own vines
> and under their own fig trees,
> and none shall make them afraid. (Micah 4:4; NRSV)

(3) *Social stratification.* Rural lifestyles tend to be "egalitarian," as we have seen, especially in marginal, small-scale societies where farms are family enterprises, plots of land are limited, and primitive technology produces poor yields. Families may be self-sustaining, but no one gets rich, and few if any amass enough land to build up a large estate. The typical agrarian society and economy have been characterized by some anthropologists as based on the "domestic mode of production," as opposed for instance to Marx's "Asiatic despotism." Here the independent, self-contained *family* is the basic unit in "cottage industry" rather than "industrial production." As Marshall Sahlins notes, "the domestic economy is in effect the tribal economy in miniature, so politically it underwrites the condition of primitive society — society without a Sovereign" (1972:95). In rural early Israel, before the founding of the state, *Yahweh* was sole Sovereign (at least in the biblical ideal).

All that changed beginning with the growth of urbanism and the monarchy. Kin-based villages, in which all were roughly equal (equally poor, that is) and were closely related to each other, gave way to new towns and cities where entrepreneurs moved to seek their fortune, becoming anonymous in the process. Fewer and fewer uprooted people were blood relations, or even knew each other. Some clever opportunists got rich, but many more became trapped in a cycle of urban poverty. A once homogeneous people gradually became "stratified," differentiated into economic and social classes that were often in conflict.

In particular, there arose around the court of the newly formed capital in Jerusalem a circle of officials, bureaucrats, priestly functionaries, and wealthy aristocrats who were dependent upon crown subsidies, as well as literati, all of whom constituted a powerful "lobby." They represented, however, a small elite class, not the majority of Jerusalemites. And they had scarcely any contact with the majority of people in the countryside. Yet these elites would soon dominate life in the capital. Now Israel's early egalitarian ideals were severely tested, and traditional cultural and religious values were threatened. Religion would have to meet these new and increasingly sophisticated challenges.

(4) *Political centralization.* Much of the skepticism noted above about statehood ignores the principal criteria for defining "states." Statehood is not about size, wealth, or even power. It is about *centralization* — the concentration of decision-making and the distribution of goods and services in the hands of some central authority. Early Israel was small and still not very powerful or prosperous in comparison with its neighbors in Syria, Mesopotamia, and Egypt. But it was nevertheless a true "state" by accepted standards in current anthropological literature on state-formation processes (Dever 1997:247-251). Centralization, however, resulted in just what the prophet Samuel had warned about — the gradual usurpation of power by king and court and the consequent loss of independence and freedom that once belonged to ordinary people. This must have been especially onerous for those in the rural areas, which increasingly became dependent upon a managed economy that drained off the few surpluses there were. Free enterprise was soon no longer free.

(5) *Religious conformity.* Religion was an integral part of all life in ancient Israel, as we have seen, so all the changes we have discussed affected religious beliefs and practices. Accompanying the growth of socio-economic complexity and political centralization, there were inevitable developments that resulted in religion becoming as "official" as everything else. The need to manage the cult fostered a priestly class, soon a large bureaucracy, aligned with the state and utilizing religion to legitimate both.

In theory, the priesthood went back to Israel's origins in the Sinai, but the texts are largely late royal propaganda. There is no evidence in premonarchical Israel of *any* organized religious leadership, especially of an established priesthood. We know only of *ad hoc* family "priests," such as Micah's sons whom he appointed to minister at his family shrine (Judges 17:1-6; cf. also the Shiloh shrine). But now the supposed "sons of Aaron," Moses' brother, are set up to regulate religion under crown supervision, as part of the new state apparatus. Thus the state or "official" religion that we have sometimes contrasted with folk religion comes into being — for the first time, 200 years or more into Israelite history. It is not so much a development of tradition as it is a departure from tradition, a momentous change that will set the stage for all subsequent changes in Israelite religion.

(6) *The growth of a literary tradition.* The changes described above were all interrelated, and they combined to bring into existence for the first

time a small class of reasonably well-educated people who had the leisure, the opportunity, and the motivation to pursue intellectual and aesthetic interests. We may call them "literati." They were at least functionally literate, and as the state grew they became interested in writing its history. They collected old oral traditions and the few written sources that may have existed, such as archaic Hebrew poems like the "Blessing of Jacob" (Genesis 49); the "Song of Moses" (Exodus 15) and the "Song of Deborah" (Judges 5; above). They began to keep archives and eyewitness accounts, mostly of important public events. At first these were probably little more than king-lists, but soon the *corpus* came to incorporate much more anecdotal material, like the detailed information that eventually formed the composition known as the "Court History of David" (I Samuel 16–II Samuel 24).

Some of the first attempts at writing a "national history" have not survived, but they are mentioned in the Hebrew Bible. These include the "Book of the Chronicles of the Kings of Judah" and the "Book of Jasher." Until recently, many biblical scholars held that the "J" or Yahwist document that forms part of Genesis-Numbers (above) was first put into writing in the 10th century, during the reigns of David and Solomon. But current opinion leans to an 8th- or (more likely) a 7th-century date for the literary composition, because the archaeological evidence for widespread literacy is no earlier than that. In any case at least the notion of a great, sweeping "national epic" was undoubtedly born early in the monarchy. And that becomes the basis for both the later Tetrateuch/Pentateuch and the Deuteronomistic traditions that we have taken here as our major textual sources for Israelite religion. Note, however, two qualifications: (1) most of this literature arises relatively late in Israelite history, by any estimate; and (2) it is the product of a very few intellectuals and literati and reflects almost exclusively their concerns and vested interests.

Let us assume that only five percent of the population lived in cities, and only a small percentage of them lived in Jerusalem (perhaps 2,000 in the 10th century B.C.; more later). If we subtract half of that number as women, who certainly were not among the biblical authors, and then select out a very small percentage of the remaining group as elites, we arrive at the following statistic. The urban elites who wrote and edited the Hebrew Bible cannot *possibly* have constituted more than a tiny fraction of one percent, isolated from and largely alienated from the vast majority. How "representative" *were* they when they spoke of religion?

The significant fact for us here is the emergence now of what van der Toorn aptly characterizes as "Book religion," a force that would define orthodoxy for the remainder of Israel's history. While "Book religion" did incorporate aspects of folk religion and always overlapped with it to some degree, clashes were inevitable, and by the 8th century B.C. they had provoked a painful crisis. But there were even earlier flashpoints.

By far the most significant yet most controversial departure accompanying the rise of an "official" state-sponsored cult was the construction of a national shrine, the Solomonic Temple in Jerusalem. According to tradition, David had hoped to build such a shrine early on, but only Solomon with his unprecedented wealth and a stable kingdom at peace could accomplish such a monumental task. Only recently has the detailed description of the Temple and its elaborate furnishings in I Kings 5–8 been adequately understood. "Minimalists," of course, dismiss the Temple, along with every other aspect of Solomon's "Golden Age" in the Bible, as pious fiction. But the archaeological evidence now in hand removes any doubt that such a building once existed. Perhaps it was not quite as grandiose as the Bible makes it seem, but it was nonetheless a royal sanctuary like other Phoenician and Aramaean temples of the day (Dever 2001:144-157).

What is more significant than the technical details and furnishings of the Solomonic temple is the very fact of its existence. More than any other single thing, it marked a radical departure from earlier religious traditions, for many reasons. (1) The Temple was not a piece of vernacular architecture, erected by a voluntary association of villagers. It was the result of a monumental, *royal* building project, carried out in part no doubt with conscript labor (I Kings 5:13; 9:15), and financed by huge levies of taxes. Once free men, Israelites now labored for the king, on his projects, for his benefit. Only the monarchy could have found the men and material to complete such a huge project, or for that matter needed such men and material.

(2) The biblical text itself acknowledges that the "Israelite" tripartite temple was really *Phoenician* in design, designed by Phoenician architects and built by Phoenician craftsmen and artisans (I Kings 5:1-12; 7:13, 14), and the archaeological data confirm this overwhelmingly. The Phoenicians were not only the contemporary Iron Age descendants of the Canaanites and heirs of their long civilization, but they were now despised foreigners who worshipped Ba'al, not Israelite Yahweh. So the building of the Temple must have been an insult to many traditionalists, despite the Deuteronomists' sycophantic adulation of Solomon "in all his glory" ("his," not the

peoples'). A very similar Canaanite-Phoenician style temple of the 9th century B.C. has now been found in north Syria, at ʿAin-Derʿa, sharing more than fifty traits with the Solomonic Temple as described in the Hebrew Bible.

(3) The Temple was, and was meant to be, a conspicuous symbol that projected the new state's prosperity, power, prestige among the nations, and national unity centering in Israel's national god Yahweh. The Temple eclipsed all other religious institutions, and it now attempted to transfer the locus of primary religious life from family and clan to the *royal* cultus in Jerusalem, under priestly supervision.

(4) The Temple served principally not to house public religious rituals, but to legitimate the authority of the king as Yahweh's designated representative. The Temple was, in effect, a "royal chapel," where few but the king and his high priest officiated. It disenfranchised the people who paid for it, most of whom never saw the inside of the building, much less worshipped there.

(5) Despite its failure to represent the people at large, the Temple became henceforth the center and exclusive province of the "state cult," with its focus on the Davidic dynasty, the divine covenant with Israel's (really Judah's) kings forever, and the Deuteronomistic "royal theology" according to which Yahweh's "name" (his effective presence) dwelt only in the Je-

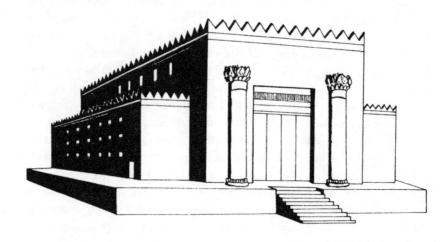

Reconstruction of the Solomonic Temple, after G. E. Wright and W. F. Albright
Keel 1997, Fig. 213

rusalem Temple. The implications of the latter were implicit from the beginning, although it took several centuries for the royalists actually to suppress local cults (below).

The Solomonic Temple was no doubt a potent symbol. But how *real* was it to most Israelites, especially the majority who lived outside Jerusalem and rarely even visited the city? The answer must be, I think, scarcely real at all. It represented an *ideal* forced upon the public, many of whom probably resented its overpowering image. And I would argue that as the "Temple theology" was elaborated it became less and less relevant to the religious beliefs and practices of most people's lives. Even the canonical Scripture that developed in Temple circles over time had little impact on most people's everyday lives. That is why the Deuteronomists — the party that promoted state and "Book religion" — found themselves so much at odds with the populace by the 8th-7th centuries B.C. and attempted reforms, most largely unsuccessful (below).

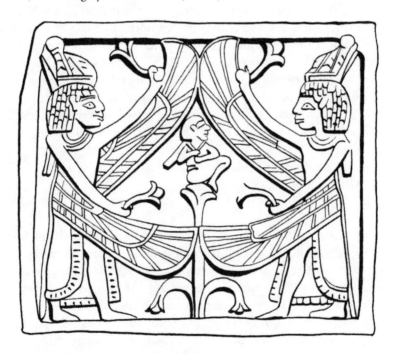

Ivory panel showing two cherubs flanking a seated Horus on a lotus blossom; Syria, 9th-8th cent. B.C. The cherubs symbolize the divine presence.
Keel 1997, Fig. 261

279

Rebellion: "To Your Tents, O Israel"

The first rebellion against the monarchy came from within, when Absalom, David's son, deserted his father and fled to the Land of Geshur in Transjordan. There he lived for three years, no doubt nursing his ambitions to be king. Upon his return, Absalom first fomented rebellion against David, then raised his own army of insurgents. In the end, Absalom was killed, almost certainly by David's own command to his general Joab, although the Hebrew Bible portrays David as mourning inconsolably. This long, involved story (II Samuel 14–19) is somewhat ambiguous as to who supported Absalom in the rebellion. But his open attempt to incite the populace must have met with widespread enthusiasm, for he "stole the hearts of the men of Israel" (II Samuel 15:6). And when Absalom appropriated David's concubines (II Samuel 16:20-23), it signaled to all that he meant to depose the king and seize the throne in his stead. Only his assassination by David's men prevented him from doing so. An undercurrent of this first revolt was also the old, still smoldering rivalry between the ten northern tribes of Israel and the two southern tribes of Judah, David's home territory (II Samuel 19:41-43), which would eventuate in civil war after Solomon's death. The issues were tribal and territorial to be sure, but differing religious traditions may also have been at stake in the anti-royalist sympathies of the north.

Even before that, factionalism triggered a second rebellion, led this time by another Judean, one Sheba. His battle cry is revealing:

> We have no portion in David,
> no share in the son of Jesse!
> Everyone to your tents, O Israel! (II Samuel 20:1; NRSV)

Here is a clarion call to throw off kingship and return to the "rural ideal" of early, pre-monarchic Israel. It is rhetoric, of course (no one really lived in tents anymore, or wished to), but it met with a powerful, almost visceral response. It appealed to more than the nostalgia of some for a simpler lifestyle. It recalled the days when religion was unfettered, when "every man did what was right in his own eyes." The old family cults were so strong that not even David — "a man after God's own heart" — could succeed in establishing himself as sole religious authority. Thus Sheba's uprising, although he is dismissed contemptuously by the biblical writers as "a worthless fellow" (II Samuel 20:1), commanded enough support from the populace that "all the men of Israel withdrew from David" (II Samuel 20:2), even before the split between Israel and Judah.

Civil War: The "State Cult" in the North

With the end of the united monarchy and the schism between northern Israel and southern Judah toward the end of the 10th century B.C., the two "Israels" launched off on a disastrous collision course that lasted nearly 300 years. The issues were as much about religion as politics.

The northern kingdom seceded and attempted to continue the Davidic line of kings following Jeroboam, one of Solomon's retainers, but the effort was short-lived. For nearly fifty years, the north could not even settle on a capital, until Omri, a usurper, seized power in 876 B.C. and established the capital at Samaria. His son Ahab succeeded him but ruled only 19 years before he was overthrown by Jehu, an army officer incited to violence by the prophet Elijah. There followed sheer chaos, several kings murdered, some lasting less than a year. Every single king in the north is condemned by the biblical writers. Prophets like Amos and Hosea are scathing in their denunciation (below).

One of the difficulties we face in characterizing the state cult in the north is the obvious bias of the biblical texts, all written by Judean authors. It might be very different if we had a "northern Bible," but we do not (except possibly for the E source). Even allowing for the bias of the southern writers, however (especially the Deuteronomists), religion in the north *was* unorthodox.

Nothing in Samaria except local shrines ever replaced the Temple in Jerusalem; the Davidic line was exterminated and the Covenant abrogated; and there were no reformist kings like Hezekiah and Josiah (below). It was more, however, than a lack of a temple and temple leadership. The north bordered on Phoenicia and was open to Phoenician influence from the beginning. Ahab married a Phoenician princess, Jezebel, and installed her cohort of 450 prophets of Baʿal in Samaria, the capital, where he built a temple to Baʿal. The contempt of the biblical authors was due largely to the perception that the north was utterly "pagan." In the north the state cult readily embraced not only Canaanite religious customs that had long since come to be regarded as native Israelite in folk religion. It went further in adopting Phoenician elements that really were foreign. Albertz calls this "official syncretism" (1994:146-156), the sanctioning of precisely what the southern writers condemned.

As Albertz shows, however, Jeroboam, the first king in the north, did try to reconnect with older Yahwistic traditions in two ways. First he restored the old pre-monarchic shrine at Bethel, now on his southern border. There and at Dan in the far north, he set up two "golden calves" (I Kings 12:28ff.), clearly reminiscent of the golden calves in the wilderness in the time of Moses (although these had been condemned; Exodus 32). If we interpret these calves as "bull" symbols, Jeroboam was also hearkening back to the old El cult with its patriarchal associations (Canaanite "Bull El" and "El, the god of the Fathers"; above). Second, Jeroboam, according to Albertz, may have likened his own "liberation" of the people from forced labor under Solomon to the liberation of the Exodus. If so, that would have given this old, central tradition a new "home" in the north — another link with the past, one that might have helped to legitimate the secession.

In any case, the attempt of Jeroboam and his successors in the north to make "official syncretism" and the Ba'al cult palatable failed, at least according to the biblical writers, who blame Israel's destruction by the Neo-Assyrians in the late 8th century B.C. on apostasy. In the short run, however, Ba'al and Asherah remained popular in folk religion, as we have seen in looking at the Dan "high place," the Tell el-Far'ah evidence, and the "Cultic Structure" at Ta'anach, all from the 10th-9th century B.C. (Chapter V).

It was the prevalence of this kind of folk religion in the north that sparked the first prophetic protests, under Elijah and Elisha in the 9th century B.C. Such early, non-literary prophets (they have left no books bearing their names) were at first itinerant charismatics, diviners, and healers, traveling about in bands, often employing dreams and trances (I Samuel 9:15-20; 10:1-9). They operated largely in rural areas, where they were popular figures, and they were probably seen as informal leaders in various folk religion movements. Gradually these prophets became involved in public affairs — in politics. First, they protested against usurpers like Omri and Ahab (whose dynasty Elijah overthrew), and then in defense of "the poor of the Land" against abuses by royalty and the elite classes. In the end, however, they became spokesmen for "Yahweh alone" and thus opposed to much of folk religion.

Two "classical" prophets followed in the 8th century B.C., Amos and

Hosea. Amos, born in the south, emerged in the north briefly around 760 B.C. It is significant that he came by his "populism" naturally, as a farm boy (Amos 1:1: 7:14). He resisted being lumped together with the "official" prophetic guilds and spoke out of his own religious vision. His was a message of almost relentless doom. But Israel had incurred Yahweh's wrath not so much by the abuses of folk religion as by the abuses of the official cult and its functionaries.

> Woe to those who are at ease in Zion,
> And to those who feel secure on the mountain of Samaria,
> The notable men of the first of the nations,
> > to whom the house of Israel come! . . .
> Woe to those who lie upon beds of ivory,
> and stretch themselves upon their couches,
> and eat lambs from the flock,
> > and calves from the midst of the stall;
> who sing idle songs to the sound of the harp,
> and like David invent for themselves instruments of music;
> who drink wine in bowls,
> > and anoint themselves with the finest oils,
> but are not grieved over the ruin of Joseph!
> Therefore they shall now be the first
> > of those to go into exile. (Amos 6:1, 4-7)

It is not only the abuses, but the official cult itself that offends Amos. It has become a sham, an empty cover-up for the cynical exploitation of the poor. Thus Yahweh says:

> I hate, I despise your feasts,
> and I take no delight in your solemn assemblies.
> Even though you offer me your burnt offerings and cereal offerings,
> > I will not accept them,
> and the peace offerings of your fatted beasts
> > I will not look upon.
> Take away from me the noise of your songs;
> to the melody of your harps I will not listen.
> But let justice roll down like waters,
> > and righteousness like an everflowing stream. (Amos 5:21-24)

Now, while defending the common man and the rights of ordinary folk, Amos insists that *ethical behavior* is the true essence of religion, not cultic acts, not the attempt to propitiate the gods for selfish ends.

The prophet Hosea is unique — a tortured, fascinating individual whose life with a prostitute he took for a wife mirrored Yahweh's life with his people Israel, who had "gone whoring." Yahweh declares his intention:

> Now I will uncover her lewdness
> in the sight of her lovers,
> and no one shall rescue her out of my hand.
> And I will put an end to all her mirth,
> her feasts, her new moons, her sabbaths,
> and all her appointed feasts.
> And I will lay waste her vines and her fig trees,
> of which she said,
> "These are my hire,
> which my lovers have given me."
> I will make them a forest,
> and the beasts of the field shall devour them.
> And I will punish her for the feast days of the Baʿals
> when she burned incense to them
> And decked herself with her ring and jewelry,
> and went after her lovers,
> and forgot me, says the Lord.   (Hosea 2:10-13)

Here Hosea, like Amos, rejects the official cult because it has become utterly corrupt. Therefore, Yahweh will punish Israel, his unfaithful lover.

> They love sacrifice;
> they sacrifice flesh and eat it;
> but the Lord has no delight in them.
> Now he will remember their iniquity,
> and punish their sins;
> they shall return to Egypt.
> For Israel has forgotten his Maker,
> and built palaces;
> and Judah has multiplied fortified cities;

but I will send a fire upon his cities,
and it shall devour his strongholds.   (Hosea 8:13, 14)

The deliberate sexual imagery throughout the book of Hosea reflects
the language of the Deuteronomists, of Jeremiah and Ezekiel, who de-
nounce Israel for prostituting herself with strange gods "on every high hill
and under every green tree." Now the "fertility" motifs associated with the
veneration of the tree-goddess Asherah, long accepted in folk religion,
come under prophetic attack and are no longer a legitimate expression of
religion. Yahweh has no lover, not even Israel. He laments:

My people are bent on turning away from me;
so they are appointed to the yoke,
and none shall remove it.   (Hosea 11:7).

Judah and the "Yahweh Alone" Movement

We have already characterized the "state cult" in the north, the opposition
to it there, and the way that all these developments impinged on traditional folk religion. In the south, things were different from the beginning
of the divided monarchy in the early 9th century B.C. There the Davidic
line of kings continued upon the throne; Jerusalem, where Yahweh's
"name" dwelt exclusively in his Temple, remained as the political and religious capital, and the Sinai Covenant with Israel and its obligations became the central focus of religion. Much of this, however, was *theoretical*
— more part of the Deuteronomistic propaganda of the "state cult" in the
south than it was the reality. The fact is that virtually all the "Davidic"
kings were corrupt; the Jerusalem Temple was never the center of religious
life; and "covenant theology" developed only late and probably never affected the religious practices of the majority. Furthermore, the ascendancy
of the Deuteronomistic school reflects the growth of a normative *theology*
that gradually came into conflict with traditional folk practice. Thus by the
8th century B.C., *monotheism* is presented as the only acceptable ideal, and
according to the biblical writers it had in fact been so from the days in the
wilderness. Then, by the 7th century B.C., "Mosaic monotheism" was enshrined permanently in the literary tradition as this was now taking shape.
It is this *final*, yet still theological, stage of Israelite religion that has been

taken by scholars until recently as "normative." But it is largely a late liter-ary construct — "Book religion," as I have argued here.

The Deuteronomistic parties and their orthodox theological agenda were buttressed powerfully by the 8th-7th-century B.C. prophetic move-ment in the south (on their counterparts in the north, see above). An ear-lier generation of scholars described the prophetic message as "ethical monotheism," that is, as superior to the supposedly sterile legislation and obsession with "ritual purity" of the priests (this was typically a Protestant characterization). But Bernhard Lang regarded this perhaps more appro-priately as part of the "Yahweh alone" movement in his *Monotheism and the Prophetic Minority* (1983). Note the last word; the prophets, in their outspoken opposition to polytheistic folk religion, were indeed a minority. They burst on the scene relatively late, but dramatically, and they spoke with religious fervor. But their message was too extreme — too diametri-cally opposed to traditional religious beliefs and practices — to have been widely accepted, at least at first. Today we read the prophets with admira-tion as representing the highest spiritual achievement of Israelite religion. But their eloquent calls for social justice were either unheard or ignored in their own day. Had it not been for a small circle of fiercely faithful disciples who collected their works later, the prophetic works would likely never have been preserved. They certainly would not have found their way into the canonical literature. There, together with the works of their visionary partners the Deuteronomists, the prophetic writings form what some have called "the Bible, a minority report."

The greatest prophet of the 8th century B.C. (perhaps the greatest of all) was Isaiah, whose career overlapped with that of the first Judean reformer-king, Hezekiah (715-687/6 B.C.). But only chapters 1–39 of the book now bearing his name are to be attributed to the historical Isaiah. And even this portion has probably been added to and edited later, in the light of the bitter experience of the exile and aftermath. Thus Isaiah's "foretelling the future" is a retrojection from a later era, when monotheism actually *was* the reality, and Isaiah's "predictions" seemed to have been ful-filled. Yet the original historical Isaiah (about whom we know almost nothing personally) is portrayed in II Kings 19–20 as Hezekiah's mentor and principal advisor in his efforts at reform.

Assuming that it was Isaiah and prophetic sympathizers who sup-plied the theological rationale for Hezekiah's attempted reforms, the spe-cifics are significant. Among these are (1) removing the high places (*bāmôt*); (2) tearing down the standing stones (*maṣṣēbôt*); (3) cutting down the "Asherah" trees or poles, and (4) breaking up a bronze serpent that was called "Nehushtan" and was used for burning incense (II Kings 18:3, 4). *All* these acts are aimed at polytheism in general, and the worship of Asherah in particular. And even though Lang states that "Isaiah was no Yahweh-aloneist" (1983:36), these iconoclastic acts would seem to be the logical extension of such passages as the prophecy in Isaiah 27:9 (although this passage is a later insertion). Yahweh will make "all the stones of the altars like chalk stones crushed to pieces, no Asherim or incense altars will remain standing." Furthermore, in Isaiah cultic reform is the primary focus, and the impetus for this, although not often explicitly stated, is certainly monotheistic Yahwism. Isaiah foresees a day when all

> will look to the Holy One of Israel; they will not have regard for the altars, for the work of their hands, and they will not look to what their own fingers have made, either the Asherim or the altars of incense (Isaiah 17:7, 8).

And it is in character for later disciples of this Isaiah to mock those who make idols of ordinary materials with their own hands, then fall down to worship them (Isaiah 44:9-20).

The other 8th-century B.C. prophet in the south who castigated folk religion was Micah. He also overlapped with Hezekiah (Micah 1:1), and his message was also consonant with purging the state cult of its "official syncretism" (to use Albertz's phrase again):

> All this is for the transgression of Jacob
> and for the sins of the house of Israel.
> What is the transgression of Jacob?
>   Is it not Samaria?
> And what is the sin of the house of Judah?
>   Is it not Jerusalem?
> Therefore I will make Samaria a heap in the open country,
>   a place for planting vineyards;
> and I will pour down her stones into the valley,
> and uncover her foundations.
> All her images shall be beaten to pieces,
> all her hires shall be burned with fire,

and all her idols I will lay waste;
for from the hire of a harlot she gathered them,
and to the hire of a harlot they shall return.   (Micah 1:5-7)

But like Isaiah, Micah not only requires exclusive loyalty to Yahweh, he also calls for the rightful expression of this belief in terms of *social justice* (the "ethical monotheism" of earlier scholars). He thunders:

Woe to those who devise wickedness
And work evil upon their beds!
When the morning dawns, they perform it,
because it is in the power of their hand.
They covet fields, and seize them;
    and houses, and take them away;
they oppress a man and his house,
    a man and his inheritance.   (Micah 2:1, 2)

The message of Micah may seem somewhat contradictory. On the one hand, he attacks the polytheism that must have been the stock-in-trade of folk religion. On the other hand, he is a passionate defender of the economic rights of ordinary folk, attacking the nobility "who eat the flesh of my people, and flay their skin from off them" (Micah 3:3). And in the end, Micah's vision of "the good life" is a populist one.

He shall judge between many peoples,
and shall decide for strong nations afar off;
and they shall beat their swords into plowshares,
and their spears into pruning hooks;
nation shall not lift up sword against nation,
neither shall they learn war any more;
but they shall sit every man under his vine and under his fig tree,
and none shall make them afraid;
for the mouth of the Lord of hosts has spoken.   (Micah 4:3, 4)

Roughly a century after Hezekiah and his prophetic collaborators mounted their attack on both the "state cult" and folk religion, the "Yahweh alone" parties gained momentum. Part of the apparent success was due to their client Hezekiah, who with Isaiah's support and reassurance was able to fend off the attempt of the Neo-Assyrian king Sennacherib to seize Jerusalem in 701 B.C. (II Kings 18:13–19:37 and Isaiah 36, 37). Then in the late 7th century B.C., Josiah attempts an even more far-reaching reform, described in detail in II Kings 23. And the encouragement and support of the prophet Jeremiah is strongly implied (cf. II Kings 23:2 and Jeremiah 1:1-2.

Josiah's reawakening religious conscience was apparently inspired by the "discovery" of the long lost "book of the law" (that is, "of Moses") hidden away in the Temple archives (II Kings 22:3–23:3). When the scroll was brought to Josiah and read to him, he was extremely distraught and fearful: "Great is the wrath of the Lord that is kindled against us, because our fathers have not obeyed the words of this book" (II Kings 22:13). As I noted above, the scroll that then becomes the *Constitution* of Josiah's reforms was almost certainly planted in the Temple by members of the Deuteronomistic parties, whose orthodox monotheistic agenda they attributed to Moses. What better way to start a revolution than by rediscovering a lost work of the founder, Moses? If this seems deceptive, we might remember that, as Lang puts it, "Yahweh-aloneists stop at nothing to achieve their objectives," and that "religious zeal shrinks at no methods" (1983:39).

The specific measures that Josiah took are outlined in II Kings 23 and have been discussed above. Again, as with Hezekiah's reforms, these acts are aimed at folk religion — here not out in the boondocks where people may be expected to be "pagan," but rather in the Jerusalem Temple and the "official" cult. Of particular interest are the numerous references to the cult of Asherah (II Kings 23:4-14 and above).

There have been so many scholarly analyses of II Kings 23 that such studies almost amount to a cottage industry. But most authorities regard the whole story of "Josiah's reforms" as simply a piece of Deuteronomistic propaganda. That may be, and it would seem reasonable given the "Mosaic bias" of the reform parties. And perhaps the attempted reforms were unsuccessful, which would also be reasonable. Certainly folk religion persisted well into the exile and beyond, as Ackerman has shown (1992). However that may be, I have recently written an "archaeological commentary" on II Kings 23 (1994a), looking at the Josianic reforms in the light of what we actually *know* of the religious situation in 7th-century Judah. Despite the biblical biases, and quite apart from the question of Josiah's "success," the portrait of folk religion in II Kings 23 is accurate in every detail.

There are two intriguing bits of archaeological evidence that are relevant to the account of the Josianic reform. First, the date of the Judean pillar-base figurines, which I discussed extensively in Chapter V and related to the cult of Asherah, can now be narrowed to the late 8th and particularly the 7th century B.C. (Kletter 1996; 2001). That means that the "Asherah" figurines were flourishing *precisely* during the attempted reforms of Hezekiah and Josiah, one of whose principal objectives was eliminating the cult of Asherah. Again, the biblical writers, despite (or because of) their polemics knew what they were talking about. Folk religion was not only *perceived* as a threat to their agenda, it *was* a threat to their agenda. The continued use — even the growing popularity — of the Asherah figurines in the late 7th century B.C. proves just how popular and persistent her cult was, right to the end of the monarchy.

The second piece of archaeological evidence comes from the temple at Arad, near Beersheba, discussed above (Chapter V). It may be recalled that this three-room temple, constructed it now seems in the early-mid 8th century B.C. (Str. 10), was deliberately put out of use somewhat later in that century (the end of Str. 9). The building itself was clearly not destroyed, but the large standing stone *(māṣṣēbāh)* in the back of the holy of holies and the two squarish stone incense altars flanking the entrance to this inner chamber were found carefully laid on their sides. They had then been covered over completely by an earthen floor and new walls (in Str. 8). The large altar in the open courtyard was similarly buried.

Thus the Arad temple underwent *deliberate alterations* in the late 8th century B.C. that put it out of use as a sacred structure. Many biblical scholars have been reluctant to follow Aharoni in attributing the dismantling of the Arad temple to the reforms of Hezekiah, who is said to have "removed the high places" (II Kings 18:4) in accordance with the Deuteronomists' program of centering all worship in the Jerusalem Temple. It may be that Aharoni's original hasty interpretation was an example of bad "biblical archaeology." But Herzog's detailed, dispassionate reexamination of all the evidence (2001), while rejecting Aharoni's flawed field methods, reaches essentially the same conclusions. And as an archaeologist who had been highly critical of the Arad excavations in the 1960s, I concur with Herzog. Here we do have dramatic external confirmation that Hezekiah did attempt to remove local shrines and sanctuaries. And unlike the case with the attempt to prohibit the female figurines, here he was apparently successful.

In conclusion, it is clear as I have argued frequently here that the *real* religions of ancient Judah consisted largely of everything that the biblical writers *condemned.* The inevitable clash of "Book" religion with folk religion had been nearly 600 years in the making, and now that the Book was taking shape the denouement had come. What would be the result? When and how — and *why* — would monotheism triumph over polytheism? Would this be the religion of "Israel" any longer, or would it become the religion of Judaism?

The Fall of Judah and Religious Crisis

The end of the southern kingdom of Judah and the fall of Jerusalem at the hands of Nebuchadnezzar in 586 B.C. were as predictable as the end of the northern kingdom a century and a half earlier. And indeed the prophets had predicted both — and had blamed both national tragedies on the people's wanton betrayal of Yahweh. Their punishment was deserved, precisely because Yahweh was just: "just deserts."

The southern kingdom of Judah was the sole survivor of the larger catastrophe, hanging on until the early 6th century B.C., after the disappearance of the northern kingdom (the "ten lost Tribes of Israel"). So let us deal only with Judah and how the Neo-Babylonian victory and the exile of the leadership affected the situation, religious life in particular. (1) First, the Temple — locus of Yahweh's effective presence among his people and sign of his covenant forever — was destroyed. Nothing could have been more devastating, for even though the Temple had been largely rather distant from the everyday lives of most people, it was nevertheless a powerful symbol of national identity. (2) Second, the priesthood was now diminished, the only official religious leadership that existed, even though this, too, had been somewhat remote. (3) Third, although it was mostly the elite classes that had been deported, and only the "poor of the land" were left (II Kings 25:12), *family life* for the survivors was severely disrupted. And the family life of ordinary people had been the place where folk religion had flourished. Now, with the loss of the state and "Israelite" identity, there was little economic or social context for folk religion. Individuals were on their own — impoverished, isolated, and confused. If folk religion had been the counterfoil of "Book religion," Book religion and the people who wrote the Book seemed now to be gone forever. Inexplicably, however, the Book would prevail. In the meanwhile, Yahweh, the "omnipotent" God of Israel, had been routed by the Babylonian god Marduk. But even in defeat, his vow of vengeance upon Israel had been fulfilled:

> Thus says the Lord, the God of Israel, Behold, I am bringing upon Jerusalem and Judah such evil that the ears of every one who hears of it will tingle. And I will stretch over Jerusalem the measuring line of Samaria, and the plummet of the house of Ahab; and I will wipe Jerusalem as one wipes a dish, wiping it and turning it upside down. And I will cast off the remnant of my heritage, and give them into the hand of their enemies, and they shall become a prey and a spoil to all their enemies, because they have done what is evil in my sight and have provoked me to anger, since the day their fathers came out of Egypt, even to this day (II Kings 21:12-15).

The prophet Ezekiel lived through this horror. He accompanied some of the earlier captives to Babylon and continued his prophetic ministry there. And Ezekiel, the most morbid of all the prophets of doom, survived to experience his famous vision of the "Valley of the Dry Bones" (Ezekiel 37). So Yahweh was *not* dead, *not* powerless, after all. And out of his great mercy he says to his people:

> Behold, I will open your graves, and raise you from your graves; and I will bring you home into the land of Israel. And you shall know that I am the Lord (Ezekiel 37:12, 13).

Yet Ezekiel is, above all, a realist. No prophet, no biblical writer, is as scathing as he in describing the continuing apostasy of Israel, even *after* the conflagration and exile that should have taught them the folly of their ways. In some oracles he complains again and again about the high places; the pagan altars; the standing stones; the idols; the incense burning; the child sacrifice; the harlotry (Ezekiel 6:4-13; 16:15-44). For Ezekiel, these are all "Canaanite" abominations; yet he recognizes how completely Israel had *assimilated* them. His protest is poignant, but it reveals the true measure of Israelite accommodation:

> Your origin and your birth are of the land of the Canaanites;
> your father was an Amorite, and your mother a Hittite.
>
> (Ezekiel 16:2)

In any case, Yahweh's judgment is certain, and the punishment of his faithless people is deserved.

> Behold, I, I will destroy your high places. Your altars shall become desolate, and your incense altars shall be broken; and I will cast down your slain before your idols. And I will lay the dead bodies of the people of Israel before their idols; and I will scatter your bones round about your altars. Wherever you dwell your cities shall be waste and your high places ruined, so that your altars will be waste and ruined, your idols broken and destroyed, your incense altars cut down, and your works wiped out. And the slain shall fall in the midst of you, and you shall know that I am the Lord (Ezekiel 6:3-7).

The Empty Land

The book of Kings, which was supplemented and reworked during the exile, recounts the fall of Judah in its last two chapters (24, 25). According to this account, 10,000 people had already been deported under Jehoiachin, the next-to-last king, including virtually all the leadership (the "men of valor") and the professional classes. Only the "poor of the land" remained (II Kings 24:14). That would have been in 597 B.C. When Jerusalem finally fell in 586 B.C., the biblical writers state that Nebuchadnezzar "broke down the walls around Jerusalem" and carried off into exile the remainder, noting again that there were left only "some of the poorest of the land to be vine dressers and plowmen" (II Kings 25:10-12).

These accounts, together with the story of Cyrus the Persian king's freeing of many captives to allow them to return to Judah after 538 B.C. (Ezra 1–2), have given rise to what some recent scholars have called "the myth of the empty land" (Barstad 1996). Biblical revisionists have seized upon this notion (which the biblical writers never actually claim) to argue that here we have the second of two "foundation myths" concocted by later Judaism (the first being, of course, the "exodus and conquest"). The archaeology of the Persian period in Palestine is said to support the idea that the biblical "exile" is fiction (a convenient argument, since the Persian period is so poorly known that almost any kind of claim can be made).

For our purposes here, the numbers don't really matter much, since despite skeptics Jerusalem did fall; the Temple was destroyed; and parts of

Judah were depopulated. And these events precipitated a religious as well as a political crisis that brought the religions of ancient Israel to an end over the next half-century or so. Thus were laid the foundations for what we must call Judaism, beginning under Ezra and the returnees (below). That such changes did take place over time is beyond reasonable doubt. It only remains to speculate how and why — in particular, with respect to the ways in which traditional Israelite polytheism evolved into monotheism.

Out of the Ashes

What possible good could come out of the fall of Judah, the destruction of the Temple, the exile of so many to Babylon? By all reasonable expectations, nothing should have survived such a catastrophe. This ought to have been the end of the story. In fact, it was only the beginning of a new chapter. The wretched survivors, straggling their way on foot to Babylon hundreds of miles away, to a foreign land, took with them in their knapsacks all they had: a few scrolls. These precious possessions were the collected writings that would soon form the core of the Hebrew Bible — the Pentateuch; the great historical epic contained in the books of Joshua through Kings; and the classical Hebrew prophetic works.

The supreme irony of Israelite and Jewish history is that the first edited version of the Hebrew Bible was not a product of the Jerusalem Temple and court in their heyday, but of the experience of slavery, destitution, and despair in a foreign land. There the faith that we think of as "biblical" was born, after Israel's history was over. Thus "Book religion" triumphed over life — and over death as well. Yet herein lies a mystery: *why* did tragedy issue in what many regard as the sublime achievement of ancient Israel and the biblical tradition, monotheism? Shouldn't this tragedy have meant not only the death of all the other gods, but also of *Yahweh*, who seemed to have deserted his people?

Toward One God

A generation ago, when I was a graduate student, biblical scholars were nearly unanimous in thinking that monotheism had been predominant in ancient Israelite religion from the beginning — not just as an "ideal," but as the reality. Today all that has changed. Virtually all mainstream scholars (and even a few conservatives) acknowledge that true monotheism emerged only in the period of the exile in Babylon in the 6th century B.C., as the canon of the Hebrew Bible was taking shape. That is why van der Toorn's term, which I have used here — "Book religion" — is so appropriate. Monotheism did not arise out of folk religion, out of common *practice,* but rather out of theological reflection *after* the fact. This reflection on experience, including disaster, is what informs the Hebrew Bible.

The Bible is thus "revisionist history," revised on the basis of the lessons that the authors presumed to have drawn from their own stormy history. The fundamental lesson for them was that Yahweh was indeed a "jealous god," punishing those who flirted with other gods. The conclusion? Don't do this again! And many of the exiles in Babylon, as well as the remnant left back in Judah, learned that lesson. Nothing teaches us like pain. If some readers find my explanation for the rise of monotheism simplistic (that is, "functional"), I sympathize. But I can do no better, nor can any other historian. Some things remain mysteries, and we can only speculate.

The *context* of the new emphasis on exclusive Yahwism is clear, however. Ezra, a "scribe skilled in the law of Moses" (Ezra 7:6, 12, 21), is usually credited with leading the restoration and reforms (his career begins either in 458 B.C. or 398 B.C.). He based himself apparently on the Pentateuch, which had already been edited into very much its present form. Ezra and his disciples would also have possessed what we have called here the completed "Deuteronomistic history" (Joshua through Kings) and most of the canonical prophetic works. Thus *Scripture* ("holy writings") — the "Law" and its interpretation by professional clerics — became normative for religious life, replacing the Temple and the old priesthood. And needless to say, the *new* source of authority completely abrogated the traditional independence of the family and clan where folk religion had flourished during the settlement period and the monarchy. These profound changes in the very foundations of religious beliefs and practices were what occasioned the ascendancy of "Book religion."

As an instructive example of the coercive power of the Book and of the "new orthodoxy," we may look at one of Ezra's first actions upon assuming leadership back in Jerusalem (Ezra 9-10). He gathered a large assembly, including community leaders, and presented himself to them, "weeping and casting himself down before the house of God." Ezra is distraught because "from the days of our fathers to this day we have been in great guilt." For the people's iniquities they had been delivered into the hands of conquerors, "to the sword, to captivity, to plundering, and to utter shame." Now, however, Ezra declares that there is a "brief moment" of opportunity, of hope. The people are deeply moved and respond by admitting that they had "broken faith with God," especially in marrying foreign women among the non-Israelites brought into the land by the Babylonians. They resolve to divorce their wives and put away their children because they "tremble at the commandment of God" and vow to do everything "according to the law" (Ezra 10:1-6).

It is difficult to imagine a more radical departure from traditional folk religion, which centered upon the family. Now, conformity with the written law *supersedes* the old family values; theology trumps real life. There is only one God, rigidly male; and he is a jealous god, demanding, vengeful. Perhaps it is not too much to say that the men who wrote the Bible and henceforth will dominate the cult now have "their" god firmly in control at last. Asherah has finally been driven underground, and with her disappearance what little voice women had was silenced.

But what *is* the "monotheism" that was finally achieved? And depending on how we define monotheism, did it perhaps have some precedents? Monotheism is usually defined as "belief in only one god" (from the Greek etymology). But that is theological (or philosophical) monotheism. It does not preclude acknowledging the *existence* of other deities, even if they are regarded as lesser gods, and not actually worshipped. And the theoretical "belief" in one god may not affect practice all that much.

Some would argue that we are dealing not with monotheism, but with "monolatry," the pragmatic preference for one god among the many who are presumed to exist. Others call it "henotheism," the elevation of one's own national god to a preeminent position, while tacitly admitting that other nations have their own gods (although they may be dismissed as impotent). I have already suggested above that ancient Israelite religion from the beginning looked at matters in this very practical way. Folk religion — always the dominant expression — was grounded in real-life experiences, not in esoteric intellectual exercises. And if one had a variety of needs, then a variety of deities "made sense." Why *not*? All the other nations had multiple deities.

Yet in the end, in the "twilight of the gods," these deities all failed — even Asherah. To the Babylonian exiles, as well as those left behind in Judah, it must have seemed that the whole world created by their gods had ended; and for them, it had. Henceforth the very notion of divinity would have to be radically rethought, if *any* of the gods were to be resurrected. That rethinking began, against all odds, during the exile, and it was codified in the systematic theological formulations of Ezra and his followers during the return in the late 6th and 5th centuries B.C.

Why Monotheism? and Whither?

I have suggested, along with most scholars, that the emergence of monotheism — of exclusive Yahwism — was largely a response to the tragic experience of the exile. It was, in effect, a "rationalization" of defeat, an attempt to forge a *new* identity and destiny for a people who otherwise would have been left without hope. Thus there came into being the "New Israel" envisioned by the later prophets, Jeremiah, Ezekiel, and especially Second Isaiah (chapters 40–66, by later hands).

Jeremiah foresees Yahweh's promise of restoration:

> Now therefore thus says the Lord, the God of Israel, concerning this city of which you say, "It is given into the hand of the king of Babylon by sword, by famine, and by pestilence": Behold, I will gather them from all the countries to which I drove them in my anger and my wrath and in great indignation; I will bring them back to this place, and I will make them dwell in safety. And they shall be my people, and I will be their God. (Jeremiah 32:36-38)

It is Isaiah, however, who is most eloquent and universal in his vision of the New Israel:

> Arise, shine; for your light has come,
> And the glory of the Lord has risen upon you.
> For behold, darkness shall cover the earth,
> and thick darkness the peoples;
> but the Lord will arise upon you,
>   and his glory will be seen upon you.
> And nations shall come to your light,
>   and kings to the brightness of your rising.   (Isaiah 60:1-3)

Break forth together into singing,
    you waste places of Jerusalem;
for the Lord has comforted his people,
he has redeemed Jerusalem.
The Lord has bared his holy arm
    before the eyes of all the nations;
and all the ends of the earth shall see
    the salvation of our God.   (Isaiah 52:9, 10)

It is in such late prophets, who lived through the fall of Judah and into the exile, that we find two new religious concepts. (1) First, Israel is "elected" not to special privilege, but to service on behalf of all peoples — in short, a move from parochialism to *universalism*. (2) Second, we find a heightened *moral sensibility* accompanying this new vision of Yahweh as the God of all nations — the "ethical monotheism" of which a former generation of scholars spoke. It continues and expands the ethical imperatives of Isaiah's and Jeremiah's predecessors Amos, Hosea, and Micah: justice and mercy are more important than sacrifice and other cultic performances. (One may suggest that folk religion had *always* felt that way.)

Having looked at both the negative aspect of monotheism and the Law (legalism and exclusivity), as well as at their better prospects (universal justice), we still have not satisfactorily explained *why* monotheism developed at all. In the history of religions, monotheism is a late, very restricted, and even somewhat arbitrary development. From a secular perspective, it could even be argued that monotheism does not necessarily represent "progress," because it is in some ways *less* sophisticated — that is, less comprehensive, less flexible, less natural. In any case, it is not polytheism that needs to be explained, but rather monotheism. (Of course, for many believers all this was simply another stage in the unfolding of God's mysterious plans.)

Some attempts to explain the transformation of polytheism during the exile invoke a changed "social context." During the monarchy, Israel had been relatively isolated, and its worldview was correspondingly restricted. But during the exile, Israel's surviving leaders were suddenly exposed to the larger outside world, where there were now *other* national gods who had to be taken seriously. If Yahweh's reputation was to be salvaged, the picture of him must somehow be enlarged to *embrace* "the nations." Ironically, as Judah's political fortunes were reduced, its religious vision expanded. Correspondingly, the rethinking resulting from the collapse of the monarchy and the destruction of the Temple meant that the "monarchic" metaphor for earthly and heavenly kings was less convincing. As Smith puts it, "the original inspiration for so much religious discourse of Temple prayer and sacrifice, of divinity and cosmos, would lie largely dormant in the meantime" (2002b:26).

I would go even further. I don't think that the Deuteronomists' "Temple theology" *ever* had much to do with the realities of local and family folk religion. And I doubt whether the written version of official religion — "literary piety," as in the Psalms — was widespread in a largely illiterate society. Even the "Ten Commandments" in their present form were probably peripheral to most people's lives, along with the "Sinai" and "Mosaic covenant" themes. There probably was a historical Moses, who introduced the desert deity Yahweh to tribal groups in the Sinai. And "Mosaic" traditions may have lingered, at least orally, throughout the monarchy, even in folk religion. But the promotion of Moses to the position of "founder of Israelite religion," the elevation of "law" to a preeminent position, is almost certainly the product of the 7th-6th century B.C. Deuteronomistic theological agenda.

These are all late theological and literary *constructs* propagated by extremists toward the very end of the monarchy — right-wing, orthodox, nationalist parties. These concepts became normative *only* when "Book religion" came to the fore, as the new "Jewish" community began the process that would lead eventually to the formation of canonical Scripture.

Archaeological Evidence for Reforms

Thus far the evidence we have surveyed for the emergence of monotheism has been textual, and the biblical texts are always somewhat suspect as being biased, especially on this subject. Is there any external, corroborating evidence from archaeology? Here, for a change, an "argument from silence" is helpful. What is conspicuous in the archaeology of the province of "Yehud" in the Persian era in the late 6th-4th century B.C. — the biblical period of "the return from exile" — is the *complete absence* of all the evidence of polytheism that we have surveyed above. That includes high places *(bāmôt);* local shrines and sanctuaries of all kinds; Hebrew cultic inscriptions; and especially the female figurines. All these things end with the end of the Iron Age, sometime in the mid-6th century B.C.

To be sure, Ackerman (1992) and others have shown that polytheistic folk religion persisted well into the exile, as we know from such texts as Jeremiah 7 and 44, Ezekiel 8, and Isaiah 57 and 65. So the abandonment of old ways did not occur overnight. And for the biblical writers, beginning with the "Yahweh alone" movement of the Deuteronomists and the prophets of the 7th century B.C., this was their vindication. The test of "true" versus "false" prophecy was always whether the prophecy was fulfilled, and Yahweh's promised triumph in the "New Israel" seemed now to have happened.

The Afterglow

Archaeological evidence shows that polytheistic practices died out at the end of the Iron Age and monotheism prevailed in the Persian period and later. But some vestiges of folk religion did survive in later Judaism. Most of these have to do with magic and mysticism.

Magic Bowls and the Goddess Lilith

The clearest evidence comes from a series of small "incantation bowls" with a text written around the inside in Aramaic (now the language of the Jewish community). Dozens of them were found in a 6th-7th-century A.D. context at Nippur in southern Iraq, where there had been a Jewish population for centuries. And there are examples elsewhere in Jewish contexts. The texts make it clear that these bowls were used by Jews to protect them against the night goddess "Lilith," who was a ghostly demon, sometimes a consort of the male gods, who steals children at night (Patai 1990:221-254). Lilith is known as early as the 3rd millennium B.C. in Mesopotamia, but she becomes especially feared in the eastern Mediterranean world in late antiquity. Some of the incantation bowls picture her on the bottom, naked, with long loose hair, pointed breasts, exaggerated pubic triangle, and chained ankles. The texts are very explicit about her. One reads in part:

> Hag and Snatcher, I adjure you by the Strong One of Abraham, by the Rock of Isaac, by the Shaddai of Jacob, by Yah (is) his name. . . . I adjure you to turn away from this Rashnoi, the daughter of Marath (Patai 1990:226).

Here the epithets of Yahweh are striking: they mirror precisely the old "patriarchal" names discussed above. It is also worth pointing out that Lilith is a consort of male deities, as Asherah was.

"Asherah Abscondita" and Jewish Mysticism

In later Jewish traditions, Lilith does in fact have a counterpart in another female divine figure, the "Shekinah" (Patai 1999:96-220). Here we come to one of the most fascinating bodies of Jewish lore: the medieval mystical tradition known as the Kabbala, in which a feminine figure, the "Shekinah," comes to represent God's earthly presence (below). The notion, although late in the evolution of Judaism, clearly goes back to the biblical idea of Yahweh's "name" — his effective cultic presence — which dwells in the tabernacle tent in the wilderness (*mishkān,* from the same verbal root as Shekinah, "to dwell"). In later biblical texts such as Job and Proverbs, there is a tendency toward "hypostatizing" particular divine attributes, that is, personifying individual traits and elevating them almost to the status of independent deities. Thus "Lady Wisdom" (Hebrew *hokmâ;* later Greek Sophia) appears in several texts (Job 28:12-28; Proverbs 1:20-33; 3:7-19; 8:1-36; 9:1-18). It is significant that Lady Wisdom is portrayed in these biblical texts as a partner with Yahweh in creation; that she goes about on her own, speaking publicly for Yahweh; that she brings specific blessings and long life; and, above all, that "she is a *tree of life* to them that lay hold upon her" (Proverbs 3:18). All these traits and activities sound like Yahweh; but they also sound like Asherah, do they not?

In somewhat later Jewish sources, like the Apocryphal books (3rd century B.C.–1st century A.D.), Philo of Alexandria (1st century A.D.), the targums (Aramaic translations, Roman times), and the Talmud (commentaries, late Roman-Byzantine), the Shekinah appears regularly. By the 3rd century A.D. she is already thought of in some circles as a separate divine entity, ever referred to as God's "Holy Spirit." But a real "doctrine" of the Shekinah does not develop until the late 13th century A.D. in Spain, when Moses de Leon wrote a mystical work called the *Zohar* ("Book of Splendor"), crystallizing no doubt earlier Kabbalistic thought. The *Zohar* became extremely popular throughout European Jewry, and by the 17th century it had spawned an influential "school" at Safad in upper Galilee in what was then Ottoman Palestine. Kabbalistic writings and sects proliferated, in spite of some Rabbinical opposition, until the Jewish Enlightenment *(haskala)* in the 18th century A.D. drove the movement underground. In recent years, however, Kabbalistic thought has enjoyed a resurgence of popularity, due in part to the magisterial works of the Israeli scholar Gershom Scholem.

The literature is too divergent and Kabbalistc thinking is too fluid to permit a summary here (see Scholem 1974; Silberman 1998). But several aspects of Kabbala are noteworthy for our purposes, especially the names and the role of the feminine figure as opposed to the male figure. He, obviously God, is called the "Father" (or "Y," for "Yahweh"); she is the "Mother," "Supernal Mother," the "Matronit," the "Shekinah" (even "Bride" in some texts). The sexual imagery in this esoteric mystical literature, little known to moderns, even Jews, is striking. The pair are lovers, so close that they are inseparable, indeed almost a composite androgynous deity. Some descriptions of love-making are graphic.

> When the seed of the Righteous is about to be ejaculated, he does not have to seek the Female, for she abides with him, never leaves him, and is always in readiness for him. His seed flows not save when the Female is ready; and when they both as one desire each other; and they unite in a single embrace, and never separate. . . . Thus the Righteous is never forsaken. (Patai 1990:124)

It is not surprising that humans are encouraged to emulate the gods. Kabbalism, no doubt building on older traditions of the proper observance of the Sabbath, came to endow the performance of sexual intercourse on Friday evening with cosmic significance. As Patai puts it, they "turned the Sabbath itself into a veritable divine queen, the bride of God himself" (Patai 1990:257). Thus the Kabbalists celebrated the divine, as well as their own, sexual union on the Sabbath.

> When is a man called complete in his resemblance to the Supernal? When he couples with his spouse in oneness, joy, and pleasure, and a son and a daughter issue from him and his female. This is the complete man resembling the Above: he is complete below after the pattern of the Supernal Holy Name, and the Supernal Holy Name is applied to him. (Patai 1990:130)

In Kabbalistic piety the Sabbath itself took on a special, earthy, even sexual significance. On Friday evening, the Sabbath was identified with the Shekinah returning to earth from heaven, and she/it was hailed as "Queen Sabbath," as the "Bride." A wedding song was sung to welcome her, *lekha dodi*, "Come, my Beloved" — not surprisingly, based on the biblical Song of Songs (or Solomon), an old erotic oriental love-song. In Jewish congregations still today, the congregation turns to face the back door and sings this song to greet the Sabbath. The old mythology is forgotten, but the Sabbath is really Yahweh's *bride, come to reunite both with* him and with the people of Israel. As Patai describes the Friday night family ritual:

> With the Sabbath, a queenly visitor entered even the humblest abode, which, due to her presence, was transformed into a royal palace, with the table set, the candles burning, and the wine waiting. The mistress was also identical with the Shekhina, the divine Matronit, God's own consort. As for the master of the house, he felt his chest swell and his consciousness expand due to the "additional soul" which came down from on high to inhabit his body for the duration of the Sabbath. (Patai 1990:275)

The Rabbis were aware, of course, that the veneration of the Shekinah as a divine entity raised the old specter of polytheism. They themselves were sophisticated enough to know that the Kabbala was "myth," not Scripture. But ordinary, untutored folk could not and did not need to make such a distinction. In the enormous popularity of the Shekinah, later Jewish folk religion found its real needs met once again, as Asherah had met them long ago. Scholem was reluctant to make that direct connection, arguing that there was too long a gap between the biblical world and the *Zohar* — a "missing link," he said. Nearly 20 years ago I read a paper at national professional meetings entitled "Asherah Abscondita: The Changing Fortunes of the Mother Goddess in Judaism and Christianity," arguing that *archaeology* had now supplied Scholem's "missing link." My colleagues seemed a bit embarrassed and dissuaded me from publishing it. But now Patai agrees fully (1990:276; elsewhere citing my publications). He also compares the "invention" of a Jewish female deity to "Mary, Mother of God" in Roman Catholic piety, as I had done earlier.

My point has always been that in time orthodoxy drove the Great Mother underground, where she was almost forgotten for centuries, until popular piety *and* archaeology rediscovered and revived her. Asherah, in whatever guise, appears to be alive and well.

303

CHAPTER IX

What Does the Goddess Do to Help?

Throughout this extended dialogue with ancient Israelite religions (attempting to speak with the dead), I have simply assumed that the portrait I am painting of Israelite folk religion will be relevant to readers. But *is* it? And if so, *why?* Does any of this *really matter?* Perhaps this is simply an antiquarian pursuit (mine). Let me try to address these questions with respect to several potential "audiences" in turn.

(1) What does our new appreciation of ancient Israelite folk religion imply for archaeologists? For one thing, archaeologists should pay much more attention to "cult" and to cultic remains. The all-too-typical antipathy toward religion is indefensible, whatever one's personal predilections. We don't have to approve of any particular religious beliefs and practices to accept the fact that religion was absolutely *fundamental* to all ancient societies. If we want to understand these cultures, we need to be more empathetic, to participate intellectually even if not emotionally. But the problem is more than neglect. It is a fact that many cultic sites and installations have been very carelessly excavated, and badly published (if at all). That needs to change.

(2) What does all this have to do with biblical and theological studies? Throughout this book I have been highly critical of many biblical scholars and theologians, because I believe that they are mostly elitists, that their attitude toward the *real* religions of ancient Israel is cavalier, if not condescending (it's all about *texts* — theirs). But as historians, if indeed they purport to be such, they should put aside their own notions of what is "genuine religion" — that is, sophisticated by *their* standards —

304

and seek to find out what it was really like in the past. Theology and one's own faith-judgments should be strictly segregated from the historical inquiry, if the latter is to be honest. In my view, virtually *all* histories of Israelite religion are deficient, because they are biased against what I have called here "real-life" religion, both ancient and modern. Radically new histories are needed, and in future the rapidly expanding archaeological data base should be considered as primary evidence. It can help to revitalize biblical and theological studies.

Already in Europe there is a growing movement in liberal Protestantism and Roman Catholicism that combines "revisionist" biblical scholarship of the best kind with feminist theology. Several of these scholars, both men and women, are aligned partly with the "Freibourg school" discussed above. My eyes were opened to their work when I participated in a marvelous colloquium in Bern, Switzerland in 1993 entitled "One God Alone?" Since their works are not published in English, I have not cited them here. One of the participants, however, Erhard Gerstenberger, a staunch Lutheran, has since then published a work on Christian theology (2002; above) that includes a passionate appeal for a more universal view of God. It is based *precisely* on how understandings arising from feminist scholarship aid in the appreciation of the "feminine characteristics" of God. Among Gerstenberger's last words in an Appendix on "God in Our Time" are these:

> The question of God is a problem for mankind [*sic*]. Like all religious action and contemplation it is a question of being or non-being. If we want to preserve civilization on this planet, we shall have to change the way we think about God. (Gerstenberger 2002:331)

Another European "school" of biblical scholars with a strong interest in the theological implications of the archaeological and pictorial evidence for polytheism in ancient Israel has its center at Utrecht University in the Netherlands. I have discussed a recent work of theirs above, *Only One God? Monotheism in Ancient Israel and the Veneration of the Goddess Asherah* (2001). Most of the authors start out from the position that I outlined in the mid-1980s, arguing for Asherah as the consort of Yahweh — a heretical view then. Vriezen's chapter on the archaeological evidence is excellent, as is Dijkstra's on the epigraphic evidence. Dijkstra also has a fine chapter on "Women and Religion in the Old Testament."

Perhaps the most provocative chapter is by the well-known biblical scholar Bob Becking, entitled "Only One God: On Possible Implications for Biblical Theology." Having acknowledged both the fact that Jewish and Christian faith must somehow be grounded in biblical traditions, but that "we are confronted in the biblical traditions with a pluriformity of views," Becking cuts right to the heart of the issue.

> How does the archaeological and epigraphic evidence on Asherah and its interpretation influence the theology of today? Does it imply the end of the faith in only one God? To put it boldly: Should a Jewish or a Christian community start venerating Asherah? (Becking 2001:200)

At the very least, Becking hopes that "unreflective" talk about monotheism will gradually disappear. So do I.

(3) The relevance of new understandings of Israelite folk religion for modern feminism is perhaps the most obvious, although knowledge of the Goddess does a great deal to help us all, not only women. Throughout this book I have underscored the fact that women's voices are scarcely heard in the Hebrew Bible. They may play a role here and there in the stories, to the extent that they are "real life" stories. But women's needs, their viewpoints — their experiences — are scarcely reflected at all. Yet many modern feminist scholars (and even a few men) have argued that women's actual contributions to Israelite society and life were no doubt substantial — and especially in religious rituals, where women have been shown to be "folk experts" (above). Unfortunately, almost no evidence of women's contributions at any level has found its way into the Hebrew Bible.

There is no point today in either attacking the Hebrew Bible or trying to "save" it: it is what it is, a very androcentric document. But what the *archaeological rediscovery* of the long-lost Goddess can do is to give back to the women of ancient Israel their distinctive long-lost voice, allowing them to speak to us today of *their* religious lives, the "unwritten Bible."

Women today (not just feminists) ought to find all this encouraging in their long battle to be heard and to be taken seriously, not least of all in religious and theological circles. Some doctrinaire feminists have gone to extremes, of course, arguing without any evidence that originally there was only one Great Mother, who prevailed until she was dethroned by upstart male deities in later historical times and was thereafter suppressed. This was most forcibly argued by the European archaeologist Marija Gimbutas in books like *Language of the Goddess* (1989). Such pseudo-scholarship has been embraced by various New Age Goddess cults and "Neopagan" religions that selectively resuscitate the beliefs, images, deities, and practices of ancient religions. Some of these groups want to adopt me when I give public lectures, but the portrait of the ancient goddesses that I am painting here should give them no comfort. I do not want to revive the Goddess as a living deity whom we should venerate, only to listen through her to women's voices in the past. As Phyllis Bird comments: "Women's religion cannot be equated with goddess worship" (1991:107).

An excellent antidote to the foolishness perpetuated by the "Goddess movement" is a collection of scholarly essays edited by Lucy Goodison and Christine Morris, *Ancient Goddesses: The Myths and the Evidence* (1998). The authors offer a critical review of literature going back a century or more, in the light of the archaeological data from many areas of the world (the chapter on ancient Israel is by Karel van der Toorn). They also include a critique of some extremist Christian feminist theologians and their substitution of female chauvinism for male chauvinism, simply another "mystique." Above all, they show that there was never a single ancient "Goddess," but that each culture must be appreciated for its diversity. The "monolithic Goddess," whose biology and that of all women is their destiny, is an illusion, created by modern psychological needs. The editors conclude:

> The caricature which pictures the feminist on an ancient earthwork communing with the 'Goddess' while the academic sits crouched over books in the library does justice to no-one. Glamorizing 'female' intuition, while demonizing archaeologists as 'grubby schoolboys' seeking shelter in the 'hutch of reason' reinforces the very gender stereotypes we could be questioning. Subjectivity without self-awareness can lead to a colonization of the past whereby the remains of ancient peoples' lives get sucked into a self-centered image of modern desires. In the rush to reclaim female history Goddess writers have not addressed the complexity and diversity of the archaeological record; in the search for eternal verities they have failed to engage with its fluidity. By plucking out only those ancient artifacts whose faces fit their theory, they have not engaged with the primary evidence in a way which respects its context. (Goodison and Morris 1998:14)

In addition, the highly respected archaeologists (and avowed feminists) Ruth Tringham and Margaret Conkey also repudiate Gimbutas and the "Goddess movement" so often indebted to her. They observe:

> The story that has been presented by the Goddess literature is neither the only story nor 'the' story, despite its power and seduction for those who actively seek to re-imagine the past and to create a 'usable' past for contemporary contexts. . . . It may seem more satisfying to be given the 'facts' of temples, of shrines, and reverence for a deity, but as feminists we are sure that longer-term interpretative satisfaction is more complicated than that (in Goodison and Morris 1998:45).

Another useful, sensible collection of essays is the volume *Women and Goddess Traditions in Antiquity and Today,* edited by Karen King (1997). Several writers examine Egyptian and ancient Near Eastern traditions, as well as Buddhist, Hindu, and other non-Jewish and non-Christian religious traditions, and the experiences of women within them (Susan Ackerman on ancient Israel). All these writers are feminists, but none are doctrinaire "Goddess devotees" (except Emily Erwin Culpepper, a self-styled "Amazon"). They acknowledge that most previous studies have been androcentric and patriarchal. But they do not think that men are always the enemy; that women's spirituality is necessarily superior; that the Goddess reigns supreme. They document in detail both the historical and the psychological fallacies of the "Goddess movement" — especially when the Goddess *redivivus* looks stereotypically Jewish or Christian.

The essay by Judith Ochshorn (author of *The Female Experience and the Nature of the Divine,* 1981) is one of the best. She points out that patriarchal religion is hardly to be blamed exclusively on the ancient Israelite men who wrote the Bible; that their single "male deity" does not necessarily justify male domination on earth. With other more moderate feminists (and me), she believes that Judaism's and Christianity's vision of God can be expanded considerably and reformed to embrace women's experiences. That includes the belief in monotheism in particular, which must be broadened. Finally, Ochshorn objects to focusing too narrowly on the "fertility" aspects of the Goddess, since women have many concerns and needs beyond biological urges to motherhood. In short, the "Goddess movement," while it may have comforted some women superficially, has left them still in need of the *truth,* not a naïve Utopia where all is women's supposedly unique "strength, beauty, fertility, love, harmony, and peace" (1997:390).

Appreciation of the Goddess in the history of religions should bring warmth, caring, and healing to religion, as well as joy in the sexual union ordained and celebrated by the gods. That would be a sufficient contribution in itself. It is not enough to treat feminism generally, however, in asking what the Goddess can do to help. There are many "schools" within the feminist movement (Foreword). (1) For instance, many current feminist scholars sprang directly out of the religious community, mostly in Christian biblical studies, but occasionally in Jewish biblical scholarship. The former would include leading figures like Phyllis Chester, Adela Yarbro Collins, Mary Daly (in her early works), Rosemary Radford Ruether, Elisabeth Schussler Fiorenza, and Phyllis Trible; the latter, Athalya Brenner, Naomi Goldberg, and Judith Plaskow, among others. Representative works would include Collins' edited volume *Feminist Perspectives on Biblical Scholarship* (1985); and Trible's *God and the Rhetoric of Sexuality* (1978) and *Texts of Terror* (1984). Jewish works are fewer in number, but one could cite Plaskow's *Standing Again at Sinai: Judaism from a Feminist Perspective* (1990); *Changing of the Gods: Feminism and the End of Traditional Religion* (1979); and Brenner and Carole Fontaine's edited volume *A Feminist Companion to Reading the Bible: Approaches, Methods and Strategies* (1997). (One might add Susan Ackerman, Phyllis Bird, and Carol Meyers — treated above — although it is not clear, as noted in the Foreword, that they would care to be characterized principally as "feminists.") While "radical" in some senses, most feminists do not necessarily seek to dethrone the male deity, only to dismantle patriarchal religion. Such feminists do not ordinarily buy into the "Goddess movement," since in their work they are critical scholars first, women second.

There is another, secular "school" of feminists, much more radical. Many of these are simply "post-Christian" (or post-Jewish) scholars. They are quite willing to abandon religion altogether in their quest for equality for women; there are no "goddesses," male or female. Alternatively, they espouse a sort of "generic religion" which sometimes appeals to a sort of Goddess mystique to inspire female spirituality. A representative work might be that co-edited by Carol Christ and Judith Plaskow, *Womanspirit Rising: A Feminist Reader in Religion* (1979). Sometimes in this discourse, "theology" becomes "thealogy"; "history" becomes "herstory."

Finally, still more radical secular feminists may style themselves

"Neopagans," or "Wiccans" (witches). Many were inspired by Gimbutas' early works (above), celebrating a supposedly universal Earth Mother whom traditional and official religions have sought to suppress. These occult works, which romanticize "primitive women's religion," are represented by Mary Daly's later work *Beyond God the Father* (1973); Christine Downing's *The Goddess* (1984); Merlin Stone's *When God Was a Woman* (1978); and Starhawk's *(sic)* *The Spiral Dance: A Rebirth of the Ancient Religion of the Great Goddess* (1979). (Some of the Wiccan magazines and journals are fascinating, too, but beyond our purview here.)

Whatever ideological agendas various feminist groups may have, and quite apart from their identification with any goddesses, there is one development that has received little notice: the growth of anti-Semitism among some feminists. The German Protestant scholar Katharina von Kellenbach has called attention to this phenomenon in her *Anti-Judaism in Feminist Religious Writings* (1994). The "rationale" escaped me at first, but then I realized that these feminists blame all patriarchal religions and their obvious oppression of women on the ancient Israelite ("Jewish") writers of the Hebrew Bible. They argue that monotheism *itself*, as enshrined in the Hebrew Bible — an almost exclusively male deity — is inevitably oppressive, cannot be mitigated by any sort of theological dualism. These accusations are so mindless that they do not deserve a response. But the rhetoric is alarming — especially since most of it is European, where the phenomenon of the revival of anti-Semitism is becoming all too apparent. The Goddess would surely not approve, whoever she may be.

In trying to seek a balance, I would observe that while some in the feminist movement have found support in the rediscovery of the Goddess, many men who are sympathetic to women's special concerns resonate with her as well. We all know instinctively that gender-specific terminology describing the deity may be built into human language, but it is nonetheless inadequate. The biblical language about God speaks about the deity in terms of predominantly male attributes simply because it was men who wrote the Bible. I have argued above that if women had written their own Bible, God would have appeared very differently — and perhaps more humanely. That is not reverse sexism, but simply the recognition of biological facts. Men and women are not of differing worth or achievements, just different. My stepdaughter Hannah explained this to me one day when she was five and we were talking about theology. She asked me: "Do you know that God is both a man and a *woman*"? I replied that I did, and that her mother and I often spoke and wrote about the Goddess. Then I asked her why it should be that God was also a woman. She gave me a withering look such as only a child can to a thick adult, and she said: "Silly! Half the people in the world are women, and God has to be for everybody." That says it all.

The rediscovery of the Goddess and of women's popular cults in ancient Israel redresses the balance. It helps to correct the androcentric bias of the biblical writers. It "fleshes out" that concept of God, brings the divine mystery closer to the heart of human experience, and yes, to the mystery of human sexual love. We humans are engendered; if we are to think and speak about God at all, it must be in a way that combines all that is best in males and all that is best in females. Even the androcentric biblical writers sometimes employ female imagery. Yahweh "gave birth" to Israel (Deut. 32:18); he has a "womb" (Job 38:29).

Such a single "composite deity" may be the logical outgrowth of polytheism, may even retain some of its advantages in a plurality of divine rules. But it can also be confusing. How can one God embrace such apparently contradictory qualities? A god of vengeance and also a god of mercy? Yet the Canaanite goddesses sometimes combine these polar opposites, as we have seen. Raphael Patai speaks of the "conflated image of the virgin-wanton-mother." And here the paradox of God confronts the paradox of human nature. We, too, are a bundle of contradictions — in God's own image?

(4) Do the Hebrew Goddess and her veiled presence in later Judaism and Christianity offer anything of value to the non-Western world, or is this just another example of the "cultural imperialism" of the West? Certainly one of the impediments in our reaching out to the rest of the world has been the Judeo-Christian notion that the religion of ancient Israel (ironically an "eastern" religion) is "unique" and therefore superior. In particular, the resultant monotheism, which became the foundation of the Western cultural tradition, has been held to be superior to all "primitive" animism, polytheism, and even to other unenlightened forms of monotheism.

While I have little respect for "postmodernism" and have written elsewhere to expose it as simply another form of nihilism (Dever 2001), its critics of the Western cultural tradition are right about the dominant influence of "dead, white, Europeanized males." Perhaps we need to listen now to the voices of living females, many of color, and no longer so outspokenly Euro-centric. We now know that the religions of ancient Israel were *not* unique; that they were not what the male Establishment wanted us to believe they were; that they gladly embraced many universal human beliefs and values; and that they evolved dramatically over time. Such knowledge ought to result in a certain humility about "our" religious traditions.

Already biblical studies are being challenged by Third World theologies. In the last words of Keel and Uehlinger's ground-breaking work *Gods, Goddesses, and Images of God* (1998) the authors address the challenge of creating a better world for all people, of all races and both sexes, which they believe can be created only by a "revolutionary restructuring of our symbol world." Such work

> will not only expose the buried feminine aspects of the Judeo-Christian image of god with their salvific power, it can also open our eyes to the theological dignity of many images and concepts that can nourish us from the thriving Christian groups and from the encultured theologies of Asia, Africa, and Latin America (Keel and Uehlinger 1998:409).

(5) Finally, what does our new understanding of the reality of ancient Israelite folk religion say, if anything, to the "ordinary" people whom I addressed in beginning this book? For Jewish or Christian believers, for whom the Bible is still authoritative in some sense, the answer may vary.

Some of orthodox or even conservative persuasion will tend to reject out of hand everything that I have said here. It cannot be true, because "biblical religion" *has* to be monotheistic: the Bible says so. (This is simply the typical fundamentalist protest: "My mind is made up, don't confuse me with facts.") Other believers, however, may be secretly relieved. The biblical writers maintain that polytheism was evil and had to be overcome. This did in fact happen over time, so the Bible was right after all. Asherah may have existed; but she is gone now — and good riddance.

Those who are more liberal by temperament, training, and experience (and the latter is really what counts), even if believers, may not be too surprised. After all, they always knew instinctively that all our conceptions of God are too small. If rediscovering the "feminine qualities" of God is new for some of us, it is not really revolutionary — just a sign of progress on our universal human odyssey. Those on the radical left, virulent secularists, will dismiss all this as piffle: the Bible is nonsense, and so is religion.

I can only speak for men, and for myself in particular. Knowledge of the Goddess has introduced me to the other half of myself. As Patai puts it:

> The goddess thus speaks to man with four tongues: keep away from me because I am a Virgin; enjoy me because I am available to all; come shelter in my motherly bosom; and die in me because I thirst for your blood. Whichever of her aspects momentarily gains the upper hand, there is a deep chord in the male psyche which powerfully responds to it. Her voices enter man and stir him; they bend man to pay homage to her and they lure man to lose himself in her, whether in love or in death. (Patai 1990:154)

Afterword (and Foreword Again)

I began this book with a concern for ordinary people and their religious beliefs and practices, ancient and modern. Now we come full circle, having surveyed the archaeological evidence for religion in ancient Israel. I have argued that it is this material evidence that constitutes our primary data, at least for illuminating folk religion, obviously the religion of the masses. The assumption throughout this work is that a contrast can be drawn between "Book religion" and "folk religion," neither of which alone can be regarded as "normative," but that the latter has been neglected.

In "book religion" (1) belief is primarily intellectual (theology); (2) piety consists mostly of liturgy (institutional religion); and (3) morality focuses largely on overarching theoretical principles. We can call this the "Great tradition" — that is, the *literary* tradition, deriving its authority from writings that are considered canonical Scripture. This is the characteristic religion of elites, the few who can appreciate great literature and its lofty ideals. This dimension of religion we may characterize as predominantly *verbal.*

On the other hand, we have folk religion, in which (1) belief is mostly intuitive; (2) piety consists of private and family rituals to insure well-being ("magic"); and (3) morality is defined by right relations and charitable acts within the immediate circle. This we can call the "little tradition," characterizing the masses as more *visceral* than verbal. It is the religion, for example, of the poor, illiterate Jewish women in Jerusalem that Susan Sered studied.

I have argued that it was also the religion of both the majority of

314

women *and* men in ancient Israel. I have tried not to regard either expression of religion as "better" than the other, only different — piety in different dimensions. But as an archaeologist, I have privileged folk religion because it more readily illuminates *practice* than theory, and that is what I am interested in here. I am convinced that in the final analysis religion is not what institutions and clerics legislate, but what the majority of people *do*.

Because they represented the Great tradition, most previous scholars, men and women, have concentrated almost exclusively on the biblical texts, as though these alone reflected the "true" religion of ancient Israel. I regard most traditional works, however, not only as obsolete, but also as dangerously misleading. Think of what the Great tradition in many religions has wrought historically: the Roman Catholic hierarchy and its Canon Law; Protestantism and its scholastic *sola Scriptura;* Orthodox Judaism and its exclusionist Torah; and militant Islam and its Qurân. Of course, one may object that this is judging those religions by their worst excesses, overlooking their great contributions to both the Western and Eastern civilizations in their heyday. I simply say that the price may have been very high.

Monotheistic, patriarchal *literary* religions have had a long and often bloody history, largely because their concept of God seemed to require them to force their Book on others, even marginalized groups (especially women) within their own communities. As a historian, I cannot avoid the conclusion that triumphant monotheism tends to foster cultural imperialism. Monotheism defined exclusively by a male clergy in terms of *their* male deity almost inevitably results in a hierarchical and patriarchal system. But all such systems are now facing momentous challenges as the modern world struggles with the defining issue of our time: the sacred versus the secular. Where do we go from here? Is there a better way? And are there more pluralistic, kinder and gentler expressions of religion?

I have argued as forcefully as I can for broadening our concept of deity by envisioning divine qualities that are more "feminine" alongside the traditional masculine qualities — and enshrining these attributes in appropriate language. (After all, why should all our imagery and language be male?) Rediscovering the Great Mother in ancient Israelite folk religion, as illuminated recently by archaeology, may help us to redress the balance.

Is mine, then, a "feminist manifesto"? And by a *man?* I am not so presumptuous. I do not pretend to speak for women, ancient or modern, only with them; not to give them a voice, but only through archaeology to help them to find their own long-lost voice, and thus to speak for themselves, out of their own experience. I do presume, however, that women's demand for an equal voice in defining religious belief and practice is entirely legitimate and has been denied for far too long. It is their turn.

Mine is finally a *humanist* manifesto, a plea to restore religion to its original and proper place. It is a vision of religion seen not from the institutional perspective, "from the top down," but from the perspective of the individual, "from the bottom up." What this vision hopes to do, while not ignoring its transcendent dimensions, is to "humanize" religion — to put a face on it, often a woman's face. This is the first face that we all see upon coming into this world, and in that face, the face of a mother, we glimpse the unconditional love that is the essence of all true religion. The hand that rocks the cradle *will* rule the world, and it will ultimately make the world more humane.

Meanwhile, we are burdened with "Book religion," the creation of men in order to enshrine their concerns. And until very recently, women have been systematically *excluded* from the study, interpretation, and proclamation of the Book, that is, from the clergy and institutional religion. That has been true historically of such great monotheistic religions as Judaism and Christianity; and it is still true of Islam. But that is changing finally, if only slowly. Women's new access to the Book and to its claims to authority — to the scholarly and clerical worlds of academy and cloister — is revolutionizing religion. And this change is coming just in time to keep the religious Establishment from becoming irrelevant to the modern world.

Women are writing their own "bibles," and thus for the first time in history moving beyond the "religion of hearth and home" into the *public* arena. And much of the impetus has come as mothers and women everywhere are rediscovering the Great Mother. Now we are beginning to speak less of the "Fatherhood of God" and "the brotherhood of Man"; and more of "God the Father and Mother" and "the *whole* family of humankind."

This is not as radical as it may sound. It is simply a recognition that Nature has engendered all species and made us humans uniquely aware of the fact that all our experiences *and* language are engendered. Thus it is difficult to speak of the deity except in reference exclusively to one gender, traditionally as "Father." Yet we instinctively know that this conception of God is too small. If God has indeed created us — male and female — "in his own image" (Genesis 1:27), then it must be in his and *her* images (Genesis 1:27; remember, the Hebrew text has "God" in the plural).

To focus as I have here on the human rather than the divine aspects of deity is not to trivialize religion, to reduce it to New Age theobabble and superficial "pop spirituality." It is to give back to religion its depth and immediacy in human nature and in universal human experience, that of women as well as men. It is not to marginalize religion, but to move it toward the real center.

With the full recognition of women — the other half of humanity — in religion and society, the spirit of the Great Mother will at last be freed. Here I have tried simply to anticipate her emancipation by showing that in the world of ancient Israel, among other places and times, she was once alive and well, at least until she was driven underground by the men who wrote the Bible. Archaeology brings her back to life.

Some Basic Sources

The following does not pretend to be a comprehensive bibliography, only a listing of works quoted in the text, together with a few suggestions for further reading. It gives preference to recent publications and to works with extensive bibliography. Works in languages other than English, while consulted, are omitted, since this is a book for general readers and this bibliography is meant to be an aid to them.

General Reference Works

1. Geography and Topography

Aharoni, Y. *The Land of the Bible: A Historical Geography.* Philadelphia: Westminster Press, 1979.

2. Archaeological Sites

Meyers, E. M., ed. *The Oxford Encyclopedia of Archaeology in the Near East.* New York: Oxford University Press, 1997.

Stern, E., ed. *The New Encyclopedia of Archaeological Excavations in the Holy Land.* New York: Simon & Schuster, 1993.

3. Archaeological Handbooks

Ben-Tor, A., ed. *The Archaeology of Ancient Israel.* New Haven: Yale University Press, 1992.

Levy, T. E., ed. *The Archaeology of Society in the Holy Land.* New York: Facts on File, 1995.

Mazar, A. *Archaeology of the Land of the Bible, 10,000-586 B.C.E.* New York: Doubleday, 1990.

Richards, S., ed. *Near Eastern Archaeology: A Reader.* Winona Lake, Ind.: Eisenbrauns, 2003.

4. *"Biblical" and Syro-Palestinian Archaeology*

Dever, W. G. "Syro-Palestinian and Biblical Archaeology." In *The Hebrew Bible and Its Modern Interpreters,* edited by D. A. Knight and G. M. Tucker. Philadelphia: Fortress Press, 1985.

————. "Palestine, Archaeology of Bronze and Iron Ages." In *The Anchor Bible Dictionary,* 3.545-58, edited by D. N. Freedman. New York: Doubleday, 1992.

————. "On Listening to the Texts — and the Artifacts." In *The Echoes of Many Texts: Reflections on Jewish and Christian Traditions. Essays in Honor of Lou H. Silberman,* edited by W. G. Dever and J. E. Wright. Atlanta: Scholars Press, 1997 (=1997a).

Drinkard, J. E.; G. L. Mattingly; and J. M. Miller, eds. *Benchmarks in Time and Culture: An Introduction to Palestinian Archaeology.* Atlanta: Scholars Press, 1988.

Fritz, V. *An Introduction to Biblical Archaeology.* Sheffield: JSOT Press, 1994.

Moorey, P. R. S. *A Century of Biblical Archaeology.* Louisville, Ky.: Westminster/John Knox Press, 1991.

5. *Handbooks on Method in Biblical Scholarship,* Particularly on Historiography

Baker, D. W.; and B. T. Arnold, eds. *The Face of Old Testament Studies: A Survey of Contemporary Approaches.* Grand Rapids, Mich.: Baker Book House, 1999.

Barr, J. *History and Ideology in the Old Testament: Biblical Studies of the End of a Millennium.* New York: Oxford University Press, 2000.

Barton, J. *Reading the Old Testament: Method in Biblical Study.* Philadelphia: Westminster Press, 1984.

Brettler, M. Z. *The Creation of History in Ancient Israel.* London: Routledge, 1995.

Dever, W. G. "Philology, Theology, and Archaeology: What Kind of History Do We Want, and What Is Possible?" In *The Archaeology of Israel: Constructing the Past, Interpreting the Present,* edited by N. A. Silberman and D. Small. Sheffield: Sheffield Academic Press, 1997 (= 1997c).

Grabbe, L. L., ed. *Can a "History of Israel" Be Written?* Sheffield: Sheffield Academic Press, 1997.

Halpern, B. *The First Historians: The Hebrew Bible and History.* San Francisco: Harper & Row, 1988.

Knight, D. A.; and G. M. Tucker, eds. *The Hebrew Bible and Its Modern Interpreters.* Chico, Calif.: Scholars Press, 1977.

Knoppers, G. N.; and J. G. McConville, eds. *Reconsidering Israel and Judah: Recent*

Studies on the Deuteronomistic History. Winona Lake, Ind.: Eisenbrauns, 2000.

Long, V. P., ed. *Israel's Past in Present Research.* Winona Lake, Ind.: Eisenbrauns, 1999.

Long, V. P.; D. W. Baker; and G. J. Wenham, eds. *Windows into Old Testament History: Evidence, Argument, and the Crisis of "Biblical Israel."* Grand Rapids, Mich.: Eerdmans Publishing Company, 2002.

McKenzie, S. L. *The Trouble with Kings: The Composition of the Book of Kings in the Deuteronomistic History.* Leiden: E. J. Brill, 1991.

McKenzie, S. L.; and S. R. Haynes, eds. *To Each Its Own Meaning: An Introduction to Biblical Criticisms and Their Application* (revised edition). Louisville, Ky.: Westminster John Knox Press, 1999.

Millard, A. R.; J. S. Hoffmeier; and D. W. Baker, eds. *Faith, Tradition, and History: Old Testament Historiography in Its Near Eastern Context.* Winona Lake, Ind.: Eisenbrauns, 1994.

Provan, I. W. *2 Kings.* Peabody, Mass.: Hendrickson Publishers, 1997.

Pury, A. de; T. Römer; and J.-D. Macchi, eds. *Israel Constructs Its History: Deuteronomistic Historiography in Recent Research.* Sheffield: Sheffield Academic, 2000.

6. Handbooks and Histories of Ancient Israel

Bright, J. A. *History of Israel.* Philadelphia: Westminster Press, 1959 (revised 1965).

Coogan, M. D., ed. *The Oxford History of the Biblical World.* New York: Oxford University Press, 1995.

Hayes, J. H.; and J. M. Miller, eds. *Israelite and Judean History.* Philadelphia: Westminster Press, 1977.

McNutt, P. *Reconstructing the Society of Ancient Israel.* Louisville, Ky.: Westminster John Knox Press, 1999.

Miller, J. M.; and J. H. Hayes. *A History of Ancient Israel and Judah.* Philadelphia: Westminster Press, 1986.

Noll, K. L. *Canaan and Israel in Antiquity: An Introduction.* Sheffield: Continuum, 2001.

Noth, M. *The History of Israel.* London: A. & C. Black, 1958 (revised 1965).

Provan, I.; V. P. Long; and T. A. Longman. *Biblical History of Israel.* Louisville, Ky.: Westminster John Knox Press, 2003.

Rendtorff, R. *The Old Testament: An Introduction.* Philadelphia: Westminster Press, 1983.

Shanks, H., ed. *Ancient Israel from Abraham to the Roman Destruction of the Temple.* Washington, D.C.: Biblical Archaeology Society, 1999.

Soggin, J. A. *A History of Ancient Israel from the Beginnings to the Bar Kochba Revolt, A.D. 135.* Philadelphia: Westminster Press, 1985.

————. *Israel in the Biblical Period: Institutions, Festivals, Ceremonials, Rituals.* New York: T&T Clark, 2001.

7. Salvaging the Biblical Tradition: History or Myth?

a. Revisionist Works, to the Left

Davies, P. R. *In Search of "Ancient Israel."* Sheffield: Sheffield Academic Press, 1992.

Lemche, N. P. *The Israelites in History and Tradition.* Louisville, Ky.: Westminster John Knox Press, 1998.

Thompson, T. L. *The Mythic Past: Biblical Archaeology and the Myth of Israel.* London: Basic Books, 1999.

Whitelam, K. W. *The Invention of Ancient Israel: The Silencing of Palestinian History.* New York: Routledge, 1996.

b. Conservative Works, to the Right

Baker, D. W.; and B. T. Arnold, eds. *The Face of Old Testament Studies: A Survey of Contemporary Approaches.* Grand Rapids, Mich.: Baker Book House, 1999.

Harrisville, R. A.; W. Sundberg. *The Bible in Modern Culture: Theology and Historical Critical Method from Spinoza to Käsemann.* Grand Rapids, Mich.: Eerdmans Publishing Company, 1995.

Kitchen, K. A. *On the Reliability of the Old Testament.* Grand Rapids, Mich.: Eerdmans Publishing Company, 2003.

Millard, A. R.; J. K. Hoffmeier; and D. W. Baker, eds. *Faith, Tradition, and History: Old Testament Historiography in Its Near Eastern Context.* Winona Lake, Ind.: Eisenbrauns, 1994.

See also "Handbooks and Histories of Ancient Israel"

c. Mainstream or Centrist Works

Barr, J. *The Bible in the Modern World.* New York: Harper & Row, 1973.

————. *Fundamentalism.* Philadelphia: Westminster Press, 1977.

Barton, J. *What Is the Bible?* London: SPCK, 1991.

————. *Reading the Old Testament: Method in Biblical Study.* Louisville, Ky.: Westminster John Knox Press, 1996.

Dever, W. G. *What Did the Biblical Writers Know and When Did They Know It? What Archaeology Can Tell Us about the Reality of Ancient Israel.* Grand Rapids, Mich.: Eerdmans Publishing Company, 2001.

Spong, J. S. *Rescuing the Bible from Fundamentalism: A Bishop Rethinks the Meaning of Scripture.* San Francisco: HarperSanFrancisco, 1991.

Recent Works on Israelite Religion

Albertz, R. *A History of Israelite Religion in the Old Testament Period.* Louisville: Westminster John Knox Press, 1994.

Dever, W. G. "Material Remains of the Cult in Ancient Israel: An Essay in Archaeological Systematics." In *The Word of the Lord Shall Go Forth: Essays in Honor of David Noel Freedman in Celebration of His Sixtieth Birthday,* edited by C. L. Meyers and M. O'Connor. Philadelphia: American Schools of Oriental Research, 1983.

————. "Will the Real Israel Please Stand Up? Part II: Archaeology and the Religions of Ancient Israel." *Bulletin of the American Schools of Oriental Research* 298 (1995): 37-58.

————. "Archaeology and the Israelite Cult: How the Kh. el-Qôm and Kuntillet 'Ajrûd 'Asherah' Texts Have Changed the Picture." *Eretz-Israel* 26 (1999): 8*-15.*

Miller, P. D. *The Religion of Ancient Israel.* Louisville, Ky.: Westminster John Knox Press, 2000.

Miller, P. D.; P. D. Hanson; and S. D. McBride, eds. *Ancient Israelite Religion: Essays in Honor of Frank Moore Cross.* Philadelphia: Fortress Press, 1987.

Nakhai, B. A. *Archaeology and the Religions of Canaan and Israel.* Boston: American Schools of Oriental Research, 2001.

Niditch, S. *Ancient Israelite Religion.* New York: Oxford University Press, 1997.

Zevit, Z. *The Religions of Ancient Israel: A Synthesis of Parallactic Approaches.* New York: Continuum, 2001.

See also "Deities, Canaanite and Israelite"; "Monotheism"; "Folk Religion"

Old Testament Theology

Brueggemann, W. *Theology of the Old Testament: Testimony, Dispute, Advocacy.* Minneapolis: Fortress Press, 1997.

Collins, J. J. "Is a Critical Biblical Theology Possible?" In *The Hebrew Bible and Its Interpreters,* edited by W. H. Propp, B. Halpern, and D. H. Freedman. Winona Lake, Ind.: Eisenbrauns, 1990.

Dever, W. G. "Theology, Philology, and Archaeology: In the Pursuit of Ancient Israelite Religion." In *Sacred Time, Sacred Place: Archaeology and the Religion of Israel,* edited by B. M. Gittlen. Winona Lake, Ind.: Eisenbrauns, 2002.

Gerstenberger, E. S. *Theologies in the Old Testament.* New York: T & T Clark, 2002.

Goshen-Gottestein, M. H. "Tanakh Theology: The Religion of the Old Testament and the Place of Jewish Biblical Theology." In *Ancient Israelite Religion: Essays in Honor of Frank Moore Cross,* edited by P. D. Miller, P. D. Hanson, and S. D. McBride, 617-44. Philadelphia: Fortress Press, 1987.

Hafemann, S. J., ed. *Biblical Theology: Retrospect and Prospect*. Downers Grove, Ill.: InterVarsity, 2002.

Hayes, J. H.; and F. Prussner. *Old Testament Theology: Its History and Development*. Atlanta: John Knox Press, 1985.

Levenson, J. D. "Why Jews Are Not Interested in Biblical Theology." In *The Hebrew Bible, The Old Testament, and Historical Criticism*. Louisville, Ky.: Westminster John Knox Press, 1993.

Moberly, R. W. L. "Theology of the Old Testament." In *The Face of Old Testament Studies: A Survey of Contemporary Approaches*, edited by D. W. Baker and B. T. Arnold. Grand Rapids, Mich.: Baker Book House, 1999.

Ollenburger, B.C.; E. A. Martens; and G. F. Hasel. *The Flowering of Old Testament Theology: A Reader in Twentieth-Century Old Testament Theology*. Winona Lake, Ind.: Eisenbrauns, 1992.

Monotheism

Becking, B.; M. Dijkstra; C. A. Korpel; and K. J. H. Vriezen. *Only One God? Monotheism in Ancient Israel and the Veneration of the Goddess Asherah*. New York: Sheffield Academic Press, 2001.

de Moor, J. C. *The Rise of Yahwism: The Roots of Israelite Monotheism*. Louvain: Leuven University Press, 1990.

Dever, W. G. "Folk Religion in Ancient Israel: Did Yahweh Have a Consort?" In *Aspects of Monotheism: How God is One*, edited by H. Shanks and J. Meinhardt. Washington: Biblical Archaeology Society, 1997 (= 1997b).

Gnuse, R. *No Other Gods: Emergent Monotheism in Israel*. Sheffield: JSOT Press, 1992.

Lang, B. *Monotheism and the Prophetic Minority*. Sheffield: Almond Press, 1983.

Shanks, H.; and J. Meinhardt, eds. *Aspects of Monotheism: How God Is One*. Washington: Biblical Archaeology Society, 1997.

Smith, M. S. *The Origins of Biblical Monotheism: Israel's Polytheistic Background and the Ugaritic Texts*. New York: Oxford University Press, 2001.

Tigay, J. H. *You Shall Have No Other Gods: Israelite Religion in the Light of Hebrew Inscriptions*. Atlanta: Scholars Press, 1986.

See also "Deities, Canaanite and Israelite"; "Canaanite Religion"

Deities, Canaanite and Israelite

Day, J. *Yahweh and the Gods and Goddesses of Canaan*. Sheffield: Sheffield Academic Press, 2000.

Handy, L. K. *Among the Host of Heaven: The Syro-Palestinian Pantheon as Bureaucracy*. Winona Lake, Ind.: Eisenbrauns, 1994.

Keel, O.; and C. Uehlinger. *Gods, Goddesses, and Images of God in Ancient Israel.* Minneapolis: Fortress Press, 1998.

Smith, M. S. *The Early History of God: Yahweh and the Other Deities in Ancient Israel* (revised edition). Grand Rapids, Mich.: Eerdmans Publishing Company, 2002 (=2002a).

van der Toorn, K.; B. Becking; and P. W. van der Horst, eds. *Dictionary of Deities and Demons in the Bible.* Leiden: E. J. Brill, 1999.

See also "Recent Works on Israelite Religion"; "Monotheism"; "Folk Religion"; "Canaanite Religion"; "Asherah, as Goddess"

Canaanite Religion

Coogan, M. D. *Stories from Ancient Canaan.* Louisville, Ky.: Westminster Press, 1978.

Cross, F. M. *Canaanite Myth and Hebrew Epic: Essays in the History of the Religion of Israel.* Cambridge, Mass.: Harvard University Press, 1973.

Day, P. L. "Why Is Anat a Warrior and Hunter?" In *The Bible and the Politics of Exegesis: Essays in Honor of Norman K. Gottwald on His Sixty-Fifth Birthday,* edited by D. Jobling, P. L. Day, and G. T. Sheppard. Cleveland: Pilgrim Press, 1991.

Dever, W. G. "The Contribution of Archaeology to the Study of Canaanite and Early Israelite Religion." In *Ancient Israelite Religion: Essays in Honor of Frank Moore Cross,* edited by P. D. Miller, P. D. Hanson, and S. D. McBride. Philadelphia: Fortress Press, 1987.

Mullen, T. E. *The Assembly of the Gods: The Divine Council in Canaanite and Early Hebrew Literature.* Cambridge: Harvard University Press, 1980.

Pardee, D. *Ritual and Cult at Ugarit.* Atlanta: Society of Biblical Literature, 2002.

Smith, M. S. "Ugaritic Studies and Israelite Religion: A View." *Near Eastern Archaeology* 65/1 (2002): 17-29 (=2002b).

See also "Deities, Canaanite and Israelite"

Biblical Terminology

Larocca-Pitts, E. C. *"Of Wood and Stone": The Significance of Israelite Cultic Items in the Bible and Its Early Interpreters.* Winona Lake, Ind.: Eisenbrauns, 2001.

"Folk Religion"

Ackerman, S. *Under Every Green Tree: Popular Religion in Sixth-Century Judah.* Atlanta: Scholars Press, 1992

————. "At Home with the Goddess." In *Symbiosis, Symbolism, and the Power of* the Past: Canaan, Ancient Israel, and Their Neighbors from the Late Bronze Age through Roman Palaestina, edited by W. G. Dever and S. Gitin. Winona Lake, Ind.: Eisenbrauns, 2003.

Berlinerblau, J. *The Vow and the "Popular Religious Groups" of Ancient Israel.* Sheffield: Sheffield Academic Press, 1996.

Bird, P. A. "The Place of Women in the Israelite Cultus." In *Ancient Israelite Religion: Essays in Honor of Frank Moore Cross,* edited by P. D. Miller, P. D. Hanson, and S. D. McBride. Philadelphia: Fortress Press, 1987.

———. "Israelite Religion and the Faith of Israel's Daughters: Reflection on Gender and Religious Definition." In *The Bible and the Politics of Exegesis: Essays in Honor of Norman K. Gottwald on His Sixty-Fifth Birthday,* edited by D. Jobling, P. L. Day, and G. T. Sheppard. Cleveland: Pilgrim Press, 1991.

Holladay, J. S. "Religion in Israel and Judah under the Monarchy." In *Ancient Israelite Religion: Essays in Honor of Frank Moore Cross,* edited by P. D. Miller, P. D. Hanson, and S. D. McBride, 249-99. Philadelphia: Fortress Press, 1987.

Marsman, H. *Women in Ugarit and Israel: Their Social and Religious Position in the Context of the Ancient Near East.* Leiden: E. J. Brill, 2003.

Meyers, C. "'To Her Mother's House': Considering a Counterpart to the Israelite Bêt 'āb." In *The Bible and the Politics of Exegesis: Essays in Honor of Norman K. Gottwald on His Sixty-Fifth Birthday,* edited by D. Jobling, P. L. Day, and G. T. Sheppard. Cleveland: Pilgrim Press, 1991 (= 1991b).

———. "From Household to House of Yahweh: Women's Religious Culture in Ancient Israel." In *Congress Volume, Basel 2001: Supplements to Vetus Testamentum* 92, edited by A. Lemaire. Leiden: E. J. Brill, 2002.

———. "Everyday Life in Biblical Israel: Women's Social Networks." In *Life and Culture in the Ancient Near East,* edited by R. Averbeck, M. Charalas, and D. Weinberg. Bethesda, Md.: CDC Press, 2003 (= 2003a).

Sered, S. S. *Women as Ritual Experts: The Religious Lives of Elderly Jewish Women in Jerusalem.* New York: Oxford University Press, 1992.

van der Toorn, K. *From Her Cradle to Her Grave: The Role of Religion in the Life of the Israelite and the Babylonian Woman.* Sheffield: Sheffield Academic Press, 1994.

———. *The Image and the Book: Iconic Cults, Aniconism, and the Rise of Book Religion in Israel and the Ancient Near East.* Leuven: Peeters Press, 1997.

———. "Nine Months among the Peasants in the Palestinian Highlands: An Anthropological Perspective on Local Religion in the Early Iron Age." In *Symbiosis, Symbolism, and the Power of the Past: Canaan, Ancient Israel, and Their Neighbors from the Late Bronze Age through Roman Palaestina,* edited by W. G. Dever and S. Gitin. Winona Lake, Ind.: Eisenbrauns, 2003.

See also "Recent Works on Israelite Religion"; "Deities, Canaanite and Israelite"; "Family and Daily Life"; "Feminist Scholarship"; "Iconography"

Daily Life; Family; Society

Bender, S. *The Social Structure of Ancient Israel: The Institution of the Family* (Beit 'ab) *from the Settlement to the End of the Monarchy.* Winona Lake, Ind.: Eisenbrauns, 1996.

Borowski, O. *Agriculture in Iron Age Israel.* Winona Lake, Ind.: Eisenbrauns, 1987.

————. *Every Living Thing: Daily Use of Animals in Ancient Israel.* London: Altamira Press, 1998.

————. *Daily Life in Biblical Times.* Atlanta: Society of Biblical Literature, 2003.

Fritz, V. *The City in Ancient Israel.* Sheffield: Sheffield Academic Press, 1995.

de Geus, C. H. J. *Towns in Ancient Israel and in the Southern Levant.* Louvain: Peeters Press, 2003

Hopkins, D. C. *The Highlands of Canaan: Agricultural Life in the Early Iron Age.* Sheffield: Almond Press, 1985.

King, P. J.; and L. E. Stager. *Life in Biblical Israel.* Louisville, Ky.: Westminster John Knox, 2001.

Matthews, V. H. *Manners and Customs in the Bible: An Illustrated Guide to Daily Life in Biblical Times.* Peabody, Mass.: Hendrickson, 1991.

McNutt, P. *Reconstructing the Society of Ancient Israel.* Louisville, Ky.: Westminster John Knox Press, 1999.

Meyers, C. "Material Remains and Social Relations: Women's Culture in Agrarian Households of the Iron Age." In *Symbiosis, Symbolism, and the Power of the Past: Canaan, Ancient Israel, and Their Neighbors from the Late Bronze Age through Roman Palaestina,* edited by W. G. Dever and S. Gitin. Winona Lake, Ind.: Eisenbrauns, 2003 (= 2003b).

Perdue, L. G.; J. Blenkinsopp; J. J. Collins; and C. Meyers. *Families in Ancient Israel.* Louisville, Ky.: Westminster John Knox Press, 1997.

Stager, L. E. "The Archaeology of the Family in Early Israel." *Bulletin of the American Schools of Oriental Research* 260 (1985): 1-35.

See also "Folk Religion"

Anthropology; Philosophy of Religion; Comparative Religion

Blanton, M., ed. *Anthropological Approaches to the Study of Religion.* London: Tavistock Press, 1966.

Eilberg-Schwartz, H. *The Savage in Judaism: An Anthropology of Israelite Religion and Ancient Judaism.* Bloomington, Ind.: Indiana University Press, 1990.

Eliade, M. *The Quest: History and Meaning in Religion.* Chicago: University of Chicago Press, 1969.

Geertz, C. "Religion as a Cultural System." In *Anthropological Approaches to the Study of Religion,* edited by M. Blanton. London: Tavistock Press, 1969.

Hall, T. W., ed. *Introduction to the Study of Religion.* San Francisco: Harper & Row, 1978.

Jensen, J. S "Is a Phenomenology of Religion Possible? On the Ideas of a Human Social Science of Religion." *Method and Theory in the Study of Religion* 5/2 (1993): 109-33.

Layton, R. *An Introduction to Theory in Anthropology.* Cambridge: Cambridge University Press, 1997.

Penner, H. H. *Impasse and Resolution: A Critique of the Study of Religion.* New York: Peter Lang, 1989.

Smart, N. *The Science of Religion and the Sociology of Knowledge: Some Methodological Observations.* Princeton: Princeton University Press, 1973.

See also many issues of the journal *Method and Theory in the Study of Religion*

Asherah, as Goddess

Binger, T. *Asherah: Goddesses in Ugarit, Israel and the Old Testament.* Sheffield: Sheffield Academic Press, 1997.

Coogan, M. D. "Canaanite Origins and Lineage: Reflections on the Religions of Ancient Israel." In *Ancient Israelite Religion: Essays in Honor of Frank Moore Cross,* edited by P. D. Miller, P. D. Hanson, and S. D. McBride. Philadelphia: Fortress Press, 1987.

Dever, W. G. "Asherah, Consort of Yahweh? New Archaeological Evidence from Kuntillet Ajrud." *Bulletin of the American Schools of Oriental Research* 255 (1984): 29-37.

Hadley, J. M. *The Cult of Asherah in Ancient Israel and Judah: Evidence for a Hebrew Goddess.* Cambridge: Cambridge University Press, 2000.

Hestrin, R. "The Lachish Ewer and the Asherah." *Israel Exploration Journal* 37 (1987): 212-23.

————. "Understanding Asherah — Exploring Semitic Iconography." *Biblical Archaeology Review* 17/5 (1991): 50-59.

McCarter, P. K. "Aspects of the Religion of the Israelite Monarchy: Biblical and Epigraphic Data." In *Ancient Israelite Religion: Essays in Honor of Frank Moore Cross,* edited by P. D. Miller, P. D. Hanson, and S. D. McBride. Philadelphia: Fortress Press, 1987.

Olyan, S. M. *Asherah and the Cult of Yahweh in Israel.* Atlanta: Scholars Press, 1988.

Patai, R. *The Hebrew Goddess.* Third enlarged edition. Detroit: Wayne State University Press, 1990.

Figurines

Kletter, R. *The Judean Pillar Figurines and the Archaeology of Asherah*. Oxford: BAR International Series, 1996.

———. "Between Archaeology and Theology: The Pillar Figurines from Judah and the Asherah." In *Studies in the Archaeology of the Iron Age in Israel and Jordan*, edited by A. Mazar. Sheffield: Sheffield Academic Press, 2001.

See also "Asherah, as Goddess"; "Folk Religion"; "Iconography; Art History"

Iconography; Art History

Hendel, R. S. "Aniconism and Anthropomorphism in Ancient Israel." In *The Image and the Book: Iconic Cults, Aniconism, and the Rise of Book Religion in Israel and the Ancient Near East*, edited by K. van der Toorn. Leuven: Peeters, 1997.

Keel, O. *The Symbolism of the Biblical World: Ancient Near Eastern Iconography and the Book of Psalms*. Winona Lake, Ind.: Eisenbrauns, 1997.

Keel, O. *Goddesses and Trees, New Moon and Yahweh: Ancient Near Eastern Art and the Hebrew Bible*. Sheffield: Sheffield Academic Press, 1998.

Keel, O.; and C. Uehlinger. *Gods, Goddesses and Images of God in Ancient Israel*. Minneapolis: Fortress Press, 1998.

Mettinger, T. N. D. *No Graven Image? Israelite Aniconism in Its Ancient Near Eastern Context*. Stockholm: Almquist and Wiksell International, 1995.

Ornan, T. "Ishtar as Depicted on Finds from Israel." In *Studies in the Archaeology of the Iron Age in Israel and Jordan*, edited by A. Mazar. Sheffield: Sheffield Academic Press, 2001.

See also "Asherah, as Goddess"; "Figurines"; "Folk Religion"

Women in Antiquity; Feminist Models; "Goddess Movements"

Ackerman, S. *Warrior, Dancer, Seductress: Queen: Women in Judges and Biblical Israel*. New York: Doubleday, 1998.

Brenner, A.; and C. Fontaine, eds. *A Feminist Companion to Reading the Bible: Approaches, Methods and Strategies*. Sheffield: Sheffield Academic Press, 1997.

Christ, C. P.; and J. Plaskow, eds. *Womanspirit Rising: A Feminist Reader in Religion*. San Francisco: Harper & Row, 1979.

Gaden, E. W. *The Once and Future Goddess: A Symbol of Our Time*. San Francisco: Harper & Row, 1989.

Gerstenberger, E. S. *Yahweh the Patriarch: Ancient Images of God and Feminist Theology*. Minneapolis: Fortress Press, 1996.

Gimbutas, M. *The Language of the Goddess*. San Francisco: Harper & Row, 1989.

Goodison, L.; and C. Morris, eds. *Ancient Goddesses: The Myths and the Evidence.* London: British Museum Press, 1998.

Hewitt, M. A. "Cyborgs, Drag Queens, and Goddesses: Emancipatory-Regressive Paths in Feminist Theory." *Method and Theory on the Study of Religion* 5/2 (1993): 135-54.

King, K. L., ed. *Women and Goddess Traditions in Antiquity and Today.* Minneapolis: Fortress Press, 1997.

Kraemer, R. S. *Her Share of the Blessings: Women's Religions among Pagans, Jews and Christians in the Greco-Roman World.* New York: Oxford University Press, 1992.

Meyers, C. *Discovering Eve: Ancient Israelite Women in Context.* New York: Oxford University Press, 1988.

————. "Gender and God in the Hebrew Bible — Some Reflections." In *Ihr Völker alle, Klatscht in die Hände! Festschrift für Erhard S. Gerstenberger zum 65. Geburtstag,* edited by R. Kessler, K. Ulrich, M. Schwantes, and G. Stansell. Berlin: LIT, 1997.

————. "Recovering Objects, Re-Visioning Subjects: Archaeology and Feminist Biblical Study." In *Magic. A Feminist Companion to Reading the Bible: Approaches, Methods, and Strategies,* edited by A. Brenner and C. Fontaine, Sheffield: Sheffield Academic Press, 1997.

Schutroff, L.; S. Schroer; and M.-T. Wacker. *Feminist Interpretation: The Bible in Women's Perspective.* Minneapolis: Fortress Press, 1998.

Watson, N. K. *Feminist Theology.* Grand Rapids, Mich.: Eerdmans Publishing Company, 2003.

See also "Figurines"; "Folk Religion"; "Asherah, as Goddess"

Magic

Jeffers, A. *Magic and Divination in Ancient Palestine and Syria.* Leiden: E. J. Brill, 1996.

See also "Folk Religion"; "Iconography; Art History"

Mortuary Practices

Bloch-Smith, E. *Judahite Burial Practices and Beliefs about the Dead.* Sheffield: Sheffield Academic Press, 1992.

Lewis T. J. *Cults of the Dead in Ancient Israel and Ugarit.* Atlanta: Scholars Press, 1989.

Tappy, R. "Did the Dead Ever Die in Biblical Judah?" *Bulletin of the American Schools of Oriental Research* 298 (1995): 59-68.

Literacy; Ancient Texts

Davies, G. I. *Ancient Hebrew Inscriptions: Corpus and Concordance.* Cambridge: Cambridge University Press, 1991.

Hess, R. S. "Literacy in Iron Age Israel." In *Windows into Old Testament History: Evidence, Argument, and the Crisis of "Biblical Israel,"* edited by V. P. Long, D. W. Baker, and G. J. Wenham. Grand Rapids, Mich.: Eerdmans Publishing Company, 2002.

McCarter, P. K. *Ancient Inscriptions: Voices from the Biblical World.* Washington: Biblical Archaeological Society, 1996.

Niditch, S. *Oral Word and Written Word.* Louisville, Ky.: Westminster John Knox Press, 1998.

Smelik, K. A. D. *Writings from Ancient Israel: A Handbook of Historical and Religious Documents.* Louisville, Ky.: Westminster John Knox Press, 1991.

The Kabbalistic Movement

Scholem, G. *Kabbalah: A Definitive History of the Existence, Ideas, Leading Figures and Extensive Influence of Jewish Mysticism.* New York: Penguin Books, 1974.

Silberman, N. A. *Heavenly Powers: Unraveling the Secret History of the Kabbalah.* New York: Grossett/Putnam, 1998.

Additional Works Cited

Ahlström, G. *Royal Administration and National Religion in Ancient Palestine.* Leiden: E. J. Brill, 1982.

Barkay, G. "Mounds of Mystery." *Biblical Archaeology Review* 29/3 (2003): 32-39, 66-68.

Barr, J. *The Concept of Biblical Theology.* London: SCM Press, 1999.

Barstad, H. M. *The Myth of the Empty Land: A Study in the History and Archaeology of Judah during the "Exilic Period."* Oslo: Scandinavia University Press, 1996.

Beck, P. "The Ta'anach Cult Stands: Iconographic Traditions in Iron I Cult Vessels." In *From Nomadism to Monarchy: Archaeological and Historical Aspects of Early Israel,* edited by I. Finkelstein and N. Na'aman. Jerusalem: Israel Exploration Society, 1994.

Biran, A. *Biblical Dan.* Jerusalem: Israel Exploration Society, 1994.

Bloch-Smith, E. "Solomon's Temple: The Politics of Ritual Space." In *Sacred Time, Sacred Place: Archaeology and the Religion of Israel,* edited by B. M. Gittlen. Winona Lake: Eisenbrauns, 2002.

Brueggemann, W. *Theology of the Old Testament: Testimony, Dispute, Advocacy.* Minneapolis: Fortress Press, 1997.

Carroll, R. P. "Madonna of Silences: Clio and the Bible." In *Can a "History of Israel" Be Written?* edited by L. L. Grabbe. Sheffield: Sheffield Academic Press, 1997.

Cavanagh, R. R. "The Term Religion." In *Introduction to the Study of Religion*, edited by T. W. Hall. San Francisco: Harper and Row, 1978.

Collins A. Y., ed. *Feminist Perspectives on Biblical Scholarship.* Chico, CA: Scholars Press, 1985.

Carter, C. E.; and C. L. Meyers, eds. *Community, Identity, and Ideology: Social Science Approaches to the Hebrew Bible.* Winona Lake: Eisenbrauns, 1996.

Dever, W. G., *Recent Archaeological Discoveries and Biblical Research.* Seattle: University of Washington, 1990.

———. "The Silence of the Text: An Archaeological Commentary on 2 Kings 23." In *Scripture and Other Artifacts: Essays on the Bible and Archaeology in Honor of Philip J. King,* edited by M. D. Coogan, J. C. Exum, and L. E. Stager. Louisville: Westminster John Knox, 1994 (= 1994a).

———. "Ancient Israelite Religion: How to Reconcile the Differing Textual and Artifactual Portraits." In *Ein Gott allein? YHWH-Verehrung und biblischer Monotheismus im Kontext der israelitischen und altorientalischen Religionsgeschichte,* edited by W. Dietrich and M. A. Klopfenstein. Freibourg: University of Freibourg, 1994 (= 1994b).

———. "Biblical and Syro-Palestinian Archaeology: A State-of-the-Art Assessment at the Turn of the Millennium." *Currents in Research: Biblical Studies* 8 (2000): 91-116.

———. "Philology, Theology, and Archaeology: What Kind of History Do We Want and What Is Possible?" In *The Archaeology of Israel: Constructing the Past, Interpreting the Present,* edited by N. A. Silberman and D. Small. Sheffield: Sheffield Academic Press, 1997 (= 1997c).

———. *Who Were the Early Israelites and Where Did They Come From?* Grand Rapids: Wm. B. Eerdmans Publishing Company, 2003.

Douglas, M. *Purity and Danger: An Analysis of Concepts of Pollution and Taboo.* London: Routledge and Kegan Paul, 1969.

———. *Implicit Meanings: Essays in Anthropology.* London: Routledge and Kegan Paul, 1975.

Durkheim, E. *The Elementary Forms of the Religious Life.* London: Oliver Unwin, 1915.

Eliade, M. *The Sacred and the Profane.* Chicago: University of Chicago, 1979.

Evan-Pritchard, E. E. *Kinship and Marriage among the Nuer.* Oxford: Clarendon Press, 1951.

Exum, J. C. and D. J. A. Clines, eds. *The New Literary Criticism and the Hebrew Bible.* Sheffield: Sheffield Academic Press, 1993.

Frazer, J. G. *The Golden Bough: A Study in Magic and Religion.* New York, Macmillan, 1925.

Freedman, D. N., ed. *The Anchor Bible Dictionary.* New York: Doubleday, 1992.

Frymer-Kensky, T. *In the Wake of the Goddess: Women, Culture, and the Biblical Transformation of Pagan Myth.* New York: Free Press, 1992.

Geertz, C. *The Interpretation of Cultures.* New York: Basic Books, 1973.

Gitin, S. "The Four-Horned Altar and Sacred Space: An Archaeological Perspective." In *Sacred Time, Sacred Space: Archaeology and the Religion of Israel,* edited by B. M. Gittlen. Winona Lake: Eisenbrauns, 2002.

Gottwald, N. K. *The Tribes of Yahweh: A Sociology of the Religion of Liberated Israel 1250-1050 B.C.E.* New York: Orbis Books, 1979.

Halpern, B. "Text and Artifact: Two Monologues?" In *The Archaeology of Israel: Constructing the Past, Interpreting the Present,* edited by N. A. Silberman and D. Small. Sheffield: Sheffield Academic Press, 1997.

Hens-Paizza, G. *The New Historicism.* Minneapolis: Fortress, 2002.

Herzog, Z. The Fortress Mound at Tel Arad: An Interim Report. *Tel Aviv* 29/1 (2002): 3-109.

Kellerbach, K. von. *Anti-Judaism in Feminist Religious Writing.* Atlanta: Scholars Press, 1994.

Knauf, E. A. "From History to Interpretation." In *The Fabric of History: Text, Artifact and Israel's Past,* edited by D. V. Edelman. Sheffield: Sheffield Academic Press, 1991.

Knoppers, G. N. "The Historical Study of the Monarchy: Developments and Detours." In *The Face of Old Testament Studies: A Survey of Contemporary Approaches,* edited by D. W. Baker and B. T. Arnold. Grand Rapids: Baker Book House, 1999.

Lemche, N. P. *The Canaanites and Their Land: The Tradition of the Canaanites.* Sheffield: Sheffield Academic Press, 1991.

Levy, S.; and G. Edelstein. "Cinq années de fouilles a Tel ʿAmal (Nir David)." *Revue biblique* 79 (1972): 325-67.

Marx, K.; and F. Engels. *The Communist Manifesto.* Harmondsworth: Penguin, 1967.

Mazar, A., "The 1997-1998 Excavations at Tel Reḥor: Preliminary Report." *Israel Exploration Journal* 49 (1999): 9-42.

Mazar, A.; and J. Camp. "Will Tel Reḥor Save the United Monarchy?" *Biblical Archaeological Review* 26:2 (2000): 38-51, 75.

Meshel, Z. *Kuntillet ʿAjrud: A Religious Centre from the Time of the Judean Monarchy on the Border of Sinai.* Jerusalem: Israel Museum, 1978.

Meyers, C. L. "Of Drums and Damsels." *Biblical Archaeologist* 54 (1991): 16-27 (= 1991a).

Meyers, C. L. "Informal Female Networks in Ancient Israel." In *Ruth and Esther,* edited by A. Brenner. Sheffield: Sheffield Academic Press, 2000.

Miller, P. "Israelite Religion." In *The Hebrew Bible and Its Modern Interpreters,* edited by D. A. Knight and G. M. Tucker. Atlanta: Fortress Press, 1985.

Niehr, H. "Some Aspects of Working with the Biblical Texts." In *Can a "History of Israel" Be Written?,* edited by L. L. Grabbe. Sheffield: Sheffield Academic Press, 1997.

Plaskow, J. *Standing Again at Sinai: Judaism from a Feminist Perspective.* New York: Harper & Row, 1990.

Rosenau, P. *Post-Modernism and the Social Sciences: Insights, Inroads, and Intrusions.* Princeton: Princeton University Press, 1992.

Sahlins, M. *Stone Age Economics.* Chicago: Aldine, 1972.

Sass, B.; and C. Uehlinger, eds., *Studies in the Iconography of Northwest Semitic Seals.* Fribourg: Vandenhoeck and Ruprecht, 1993.

Sasson, J. M., ed. *Civilizations of the Ancient Near East.* New York: Simon and Schuster/Macmillan, 1995.

Schroer, S. *In Israel Gab es Bilder: Nachrichten von darstellender Kunst im Alten Testament.* Fribourg: Vandenhoeck and Ruprecht, 1987.

Smith, J. Z. *To Take Place: Toward Theory in Ritual.* Chicago: University of Chicago Press, 1987.

———. *Drudgery Divine: On the Comparison of Early Christianities and the Religions of Late Antiquity.* Chicago: University of Chicago Press, 1990.

Smith, W. R. *Lectures on the Religion of the Semites.* Edinburgh: A. & C. Black, 1894.

Stager, L. E. "The Shechem Temple: Where Abimelech Massacred a Thousand." *Biblical Archaeology Review* 29/4 (2003): 26-35, 66-69.

Stendahl, K. "Biblical Theology, Contemporary." In *The Interpreter's Dictionary of the Bible,* edited by G. A. Buttrick. New York: Abingdon Press, 1962.

Tylor, E. B. *Primitive Culture.* London: J. Murray, 1871.

Trible, P. *God and the Rhetoric of Sexuality.* Philadelphia: Fortress, 1978.

———. *Texts of Terror: Literary-Feminist Readings of Biblical Narrative.* Philadelphia: Fortress Press, 1984.

Vaux, R. de, *Ancient Israel: Its Life and Institutions.* London: Darton, Longman and Todd, 1962.

Weippert, H., *Palästina in Vorhellenistischer Zeit.* Munich: C. H. Beck, 1988.

Winter, U., *Frau und Göttin: Exegetische und ikonographische Studien zum weiblichen Gottesbild im Alten Israel in dessen Umwelt.* Fribourg: Vandenhoeck & Ruprecht, 1983.

Wright, G. E., *Biblical Archaeology.* Philadelphia: Westminster, 1957.

Younger, K. L., "Early Israel in Recent Biblical Scholarship." In *The Face of Old Testament Studies: A Survey of Contemporary Approaches,* edited by D. W. Baker and B. T. Arnold. Grand Rapids: Baker Book House, 1999.

Index of Authors

Ackerman, Susan, 6, 47-48, 51, 55, 88, 179, 201-2, 203, 214, 216, 218, 233-35, 269, 289, 300, 308-9
Aharoni, Yohanan, 158-59, 170-71, 173, 290
Ahlström, G. W., 175
Albertz, Rainer, 6, 41, 77, 103, 126, 175, 202, 281-82, 287
Albright, W. F., 76, 179, 187, 197
Arnold, Bill T., 207

Barkay, Gabriel, 158
Baron, Salo, 39
Barr, James, 35, 83
Barstad, H., 293
Bashkin, Judith, 248
Beck, Pirhiya, 220
Becking, B., 78, 205, 206, 306
Ben-Tor, A., 42, 62
Berlinerblau, Jacques, 6, 50-51, 78, 88, 106, 189, 195-96, 241
Betteridge, Ann, 245
Binger, T., 198
Biran, A., 139
Bird, Phyllis, 42, 57-59, 78, 216, 238-39, 245, 307, 309
Blenkinsopp, J., 56

Bloch-Smith, Elizabeth, 97, 133, 243-44
Bloom, Harold, 61
Brenner, Athalya, 61, 309
Brettler, M. Z., 85
Brueggemann, Walter, 35-37, 59

Camp, J., 115
Carroll, R. P., 77
Cavanagh, R. R., 1
Chester, Phyllis, 309
Childs, Brevard, 35
Christ, Carol, 309
Clines, David J. A., 73
Collingwood, R. G., 84
Collins, Adela Y., 61, 309
Collins, John, 36, 56
Conkey, Margaret, 308
Coogan, M., 106, 186, 200-201, 269
Cross, Frank M., 43, 47, 197, 236, 257, 260
Culpepper, Emily Erwin, 308

Daly, Mary, 309-10
Davies, G. I., 73
Davies, P. R., 78
Day, John, 41-42, 203-4, 270
Day, P., 270-71
Dever, W. G., 5, 9, 40-41, 43, 46, 50-52,

Index of Subjects and Places

Index of Scripture References

341